STATE OF
THE ARK

Red Colobus monkey

STATE OF THE ARK

LEE DURRELL

Researched by IUCN

DOUBLEDAY

A GAIA ORIGINAL

From an idea by Joss Pearson

This book was researched by **Robert Burton**
with the IUCN Conservation Monitoring Centre
in Cambridge, and written by **Lee Durrell**
with John May, Chris Madsen, and Gaia.

Project editor	Michele Staple
Art editors	Bridget Morley
	Patrick Nugent
Picture research	Terry Gross
with	Maureen Rusted
Copy preparation	Leslie Gilbert
Artists	Wendy Bramall
	Bill Donohoe
	Hayward Art Group
	Elizabeth Riches
	Ann Savage
	Alan Suttee
	Gill Tomblin
Production	David Pearson
Direction	Patrick Nugent
	Joss Pearson

First US Edition

Published by Doubleday & Company Inc
Garden City, New York

First published by
The Bodley Head Ltd, London

Library of Congress Cataloging-in-Publication Data
Durrell, Lee
    State of the ark
    Includes index
    1. Nature conservation. 2. Conservation of natural
    resources. 3. Environmental policy. I. Title
    QH75.D87 1986   333.95'16   86-11500

ISDN 0-385-23667-0
ISBN 0-385-23668-9 Pbk

Filmset by Marlin Graphics Ltd,
Orpington, Kent

Reproduction by F.E. Burman Ltd,
London

Printed in Italy
by Arnoldo Mondadori Company Ltd,
Verona

To GMD
for his contribution to conservation,
which is greater than most
because he shares his delight in the natural world so well

The Jersey Wildlife Preservation Trust

Some of our exciting new projects at the Wildlife Preservation Trust are the rehabilitation of the habitat of Round Island, the reintroduction of the pink pigeon to its original home in Mauritius and the reintroduction of the hutia, a guinea-pig-like creature, to Jamaica. We are also intitiating a variety of conservation and educational programmes in Madagascar and Brazil. Back at Jersey, we are developing a sophisticated research unit on nutrition and diseases of endangered animal species, and expanding our school – for people from all over the world – in the management of endangered species in captivity and in the wild. If you would like to find out more about what we at The Wildlife Preservation Trust do in conservation and education, please write to us.

In the United States, write to Bill Konstant, Wildlife Preservation Trust International, 34th Street and Girard Ave, Philadelphia, Pa. 19104.

In Canada, write to Jenny Ferns, Wildlife Preservation Trust Canada, 219 Front Street East, Toronto, Ontario, M5A 1E8.

From anywhere else in the world, write to Gerry and Lee Durrell, Jersey Wildlife Preservation Trust, Jersey, Channel Islands, via UK.

The Conservation Monitoring Centre

This book was rersearched by the Conservation Monitoring Centre, the division of IUCN (The International Union for Conservation of Nature and Natural Resources) that provides a data service to IUCN and to the whole conservation and development community. CMC is building an integrated and cross-referenced data base on species, areas and ecosystems of conservation concern, and can produce a wide variety of specialist outputs and analyses as well as major publications such as the *Red Data Books* and *Protected Area Directories*. Their computer-based information system is also available to many national environmental agencies, international development banks and aid agencies, as well as to the business, commercial and educational communities. CMC is based at Cambridge and Kew, UK, and is supported by the World Wildlife Fund and UNEP (the United Nations Environment Program), and is a contribution to the UNEP Global Environmental Monitoring System (GEMS).

If you wish to find out more about the the work of the Conservation Monitoring Centre write to: The Director, Conservation Monitoring Centre, 219(c) Huntingdon Road, Cambridge CB3 0DL, England.

Mangroves. Monajo Island, Amazon mouth

CONTENTS

Yellow butterfly fish (Chaetodon semilarvatus)

"Nobody made a greater mistake than he who did nothing because he could only do a little."
Edmund Burke

"If every person in the world planted and nurtured one tree, Gaia would be eternally grateful."
Lee Durrell

FOREWORD

In the last thirty years, conservation work of many different kinds has proliferated around the world and even people intimately connected with these problems are hard pressed to keep themselves abreast of every new development in the overwhelming task of preserving everything from savannahs to rainforests and the creatures that live in them, from insects to elephants. That is where this book will be invaluable, for it gives in its pages a picture of what is being done – sometimes successfully, sometimes unsuccessfully – to save the living world. It is, in fact, a compendium of conservation which gives one a clear and concise guide to the progress we are making in the all-important work of saving the planet from the ravages of our own greed and stupidity. It is a book that should certainly be on every sabre-rattling politician's desk, for it shows clearly the urgent need for still greater efforts in conservation and the wise utilization of the world's resources. Otherwise, the politicians are in danger of waking up one day and finding that there is nothing left to fight over and that we have destroyed the world as successfully as any nuclear holocaust would do. What this book underlines is that if our resources are used wisely and human growth limited, there would be no need for pop groups to take up the cause of famine relief, generous and altruistic as such gestures are.

Finally, may I say that I am delighted to see that my wife has managed to expunge that awful phrase "Third World" from her text. The person who invented this should be ashamed of him/herself – it is one of those glib, dangerous, journalistic phrases that is as misleading and damaging as such descriptions as "the working classes". It promotes the "them" and "us" syndrome of which there is far too much in the world. Anyone who is literate and in possession of their right senses knows that there is no "Third World". There is only one world, and that belongs to all of us, and it is the only one we have.

Gerald Durrell.

Introduction

How the billions of organisms that live on this planet with us interact with each other is a constant source of amazement. Most striking are the unusual eating-and-being-eaten relationships, from giant whales that feed only on tiny sea-creatures, to plants that ward off animals by their bad-tasting leaves - and animals which eat them anyway, to make themselves unpalatable to their predators. But there are other, more subtle connections. Some big fish float quietly, mouths agape, to let little fish inside to clean them of parasites, and some tropical birds lay their eggs in the nests of other species, where their chicks are tolerated because they eat the flies that plague their weaker nest-mates. There are even relationships so close that one organism cannot exist without the other. Ants and acacia trees are remarkable examples of this. The ants live in the swollen thorns of the acacia, deriving shelter and a proper diet for every stage of their life cycle. If an animal, like a hungry plant-eater, so much as nudges the tree, the ants rush out of their thorn houses and attack it until it goes away. The tree offers shelter and food to the ants and the ants protect it from being eaten; one species is never found without the other. Another case is the slow-moving sloth that needs the algae living on its fur to give it a green camouflage; the algae in return need the sloth because they live between the ridged hair cells found only on sloth fur. This sort of dependence is called "mutualism" - which simply means that the organisms rely on each other to stay alive, and is fairly common in the natural world.

As well as being amazed by it, we need to understand how nature works, if only for our immediate benefit. Farmers and foresters must know which insects pollinate their crops and trees, and which devour them; herders must know which plants can be grazed by their stock, and which ones are poisonous. We must know the physical requirements of the plants and animals we cultivate and depend on: how much warmth or shade they need, which side of a hill plants grow on, how big a pasture animals roam in and under what regimes of water and other nutrients, like nitrogen or calcium, they all do best.

The assurance of people's future well-being, called "development" in modern terms, is also reliant on an understanding of the natural world. We need to know which plants and animals could be domesticated, what and where are the best soils for agriculture; how a dam should be designed, and where placed on a river, to benefit from power production but not damage the edible fish stock or interfere with the water requirements of croplands downstream.

Development that misunderstands the natural world is like climbing up one rung of a ladder and then falling down one, or maybe two. Profits from cutting too many trees in a watershed forest, for instance, go to pay for controlling the resultant floods in the lowlands. High crop yields maintained by the use of pesticides will be followed by low yields if new, more resistant pests then take over, or the tiny soil organisms that ensure the field's fertility are killed off by the sprays. Further such misunderstandings can lead to the permanent removal of the natural resources that development requires, and to the release of wastes that are harmful, directly or indirectly, to the development's intended beneficiaries.

Understanding nature and acting accordingly safeguards a certain set of physical human needs. But there are other needs, less tangible and often less articulatable, yet long characteristic of our species. These involve the exercise of sentiment and the stimulation of our sense of order and purpose, our appreciation of beauty and freedom. These no

Opposite *Mutual interdependence is evidenced in many animal relationships. Cleaner fish (top left) swim unharmed into the open mouths of larger fish to feed on, and cleanse them of parasites. Ants (top right) nest in the gall at the base of the whistling thorn,* Acacia drepandobium, *and protect the tree from browsers. The two-toed sloth,* Choloepus hoffmanni *(bottom), is camouflaged by the green colouring which resident algae give to its fur.*

10

less pressing needs are served admirably by our knowing that mother gorillas somewhere cuddle their babies, that a distant forest still produces the clouds that bring rain, that multi-coloured butterflies fill the mountain meadows, that great birds soar high in the sky and that all these things happen with or without our presence.

Human needs, immediate and future, of the flesh and of the spirit, are being severely compromised by our lack of understanding of how nature works and where we fit into its patterns. At present, the fabric of the natural world that supports us is rotting away thread by thread because of the way *we* work and intend to develop.

This book is about that fabric, the threads, and human actions and intentions. I will take a very utilitarian approach to the matter, reluctantly leaving consideration of our more profound feelings about nature to other writers. My reason is that today's attitudes towards the environment and the issues uppermost in people's minds are largely self-seeking and self-interested, regardless of their validity. But if the "me first" energies can be infused with some understanding of the natural world, then there is hope for the development of our own species and for the future of other species - the plants and animals - that share the planet with us.

Actually, people's attitudes and concerns are not so surprising. Any wild animal works hard to obtain the necessities of life and also tries to make itself as comfortable as possible. Human beings are simply more demanding than other animals in terms of their perceived comforts. They like fast cars and smooth roads, diamonds, transistor radios, cigarettes, cognac, palm wine, full tummies and frequent sex. Any animal avoids pain and suffering, but usually it dies if badly hurt. Here again, humans surpass the animals; modern medicine has generally reduced pain, suffering and early death, for both people and their livestock.

Within a number of animal species, however, demand coupled with rising population results in tragedy. These are the species whose individual members have equal access to a vital, but limited resource, and who compete with each other for it by "scrambling". Initial success results in an increase in population, but as the resource dwindles, each individual obtains less and less and finally dies. This fatal outcome of scramble competition is not often seen in nature because of other factors, such as predators and disease, regulating the sizes of wild populations.

The values of modern human society seem to encourage a form of scramble competition, and it has even been given a name: the "tragedy of the commons". Say, for example, that a big lake is considered common property and anybody from the shoreline communities is allowed to fish in it. Good fishing attracts more people, their children are encouraged to go into the business and some of the fishermen acquire extra boats to increase their catches. The number of fish taken begins to exceed the natural rate of increase of the fish population. However, although the number caught per boat must decline, the fisherman with several boats still catches more than the one with a single boat. So everyone aspires to having several boats. The trends continue until the fishing industry (and with it perhaps the well-being of the communities) collapses because there are no more fish.

This tragic scenario assumes, of course, that people have unlimited access to a limited resource and are basically selfish, and that there are no regulations on the manner and degree of exploitation. Unfortunately these assumptions are fairly accurate descriptions of almost all modern nations who – metaphorically speaking – are the fishermen. The whole planet, with its resources of land, water and living organisms, is their big lake. Even the air that surrounds the planet should be considered a resource, for if it is overutilized as a waste receptacle, it is no longer good for carrying clean rain, much less for breathing.

What about the old times? Early human societies developed with little contact between each other and depended on what their local environment had to offer - fish and shellfish, rich soils and large plains, animals or forest trees and delectable fruits. Many of them evolved traditions that regulated resource utilization, both in terms of access and of total amount taken - though probably not for reasons of biological conservation *per se*, but more for the sake of the continuing well-being of the human community, a sort of collective selfishness. The argument that this so-called "wise" use of natural resources was not wise at all but simply constrained by the primitive technologies of the times is strong, but does not always hold true. Resource depletion has occurred among people using simple tools, as with the extinctions of the large animals of the Pleistocene, caused or hastened by people with fire and stone weapons. A more recent example is the depletion of salmon stocks off the west coast of Canada by the commercial canneries that employed traditional fishing technology - the Amerindian fishtrap.

Traditional systems of sustainable resource management are not entirely things of the past; they are still going strong in the few quiet corners of the earth that are left. Some native fisheries in Micronesia and North America, for example, work on such systems, which is not unexpected, but so do some Cornish oystermen, Maine lobstermen and Japanese fishermen. Parallel patterns in pastoralism and agriculture are followed by a few communities in the tropical continents.

Traditional systems of sustainable resource management cannot suddenly be reintroduced and substituted for modern systems. Their success depends on regulations accepted by people within communities, who *know* each other - they can laugh at, chide, praise or ostracize each other to keep the system working. But any social pressures applied to outsiders would be like water rolling off a duck's back, and equally, a system not accepted by a whole community would be bound to fail. Furthermore, traditional trade was usually in kind, and operated in a more or less closed economy, not, as today, an open one using a universal currency and subject to the whims of a global market. Finally, since the new technologies that make resource gathering less tiresome *do* exist, people, looking to their comforts as usual, will try to obtain them. The point about the existence of rational management systems in human history, and even in the present, is that it shows that human beings are *capable* of using living resources wisely - of taking merely enough for their needs and leaving enough so that the resource renews itself in time for the next harvest.

One of the sad turns that modern development has taken, however, is to ignore the lessons to be learned from the old traditions, and even worse, to try to squelch them deliberately, dismissing them as outmoded, primitive, repressive or ungodly. The infiltrators, from nineteenth-century missionaries to twentieth-century revolutionaries and development planners, have brought with them ideas, methods and materials that they thought would benefit the people. But they insisted that these supplant the traditional ones, without seeing first if the traditions could be built on or modified which is surely a more sensible way for development to proceed, if only to help preserve social harmony. But as it's only just being widely realized that modern development usually entails overuse and abuse of resources, the past disruption of so many traditional human societies is not really all that surprising.

Modern life has its good points. It offers material comfort, time to relax and enjoy music or play games and greater freedom from pain and suffering. Although these are still beyond the grasp of some people for a variety of reasons, everyone aspires to them. But humanity and the rest of the planet are paying for the manner in which we've achieved or are trying to achieve those points, and the price is too dear. We will be forced to forfeit our pleasures and long lives, and our hopes for them, unless we mend our ways. The root of the problem is human selfishness, individual or collective, coupled with a gross misunderstanding of nature on the part of those societies that were in the forefront of the technological advances of this and the last century. Collapse of civilizations because they misunderstood the natural world they depended on is not new - it happened to the Mesopotamians and the Mayans. The difference today is that modern misunderstanding has affected *nearly every part of the whole planet*, and will reach the few remote parts still left very soon. And there is only one planet capable of supporting life as we know it - this one.

Some of the inventors, investors and users of the modern technologies were callous and greedy people, ruining or killing others for personal gain; some were kind and philanthropic, trying their best to relieve others of the poverty and misery so created. But virtually none of them thought out the long term consequences of the applications of technology, be it the internal combustion engine or the ability to explode an atom, the power-driven saw or penicillin, in the context of the natural world and its needs.

The heaven-sent miracles of modern medicine and nutrition, for example, should never be withheld from anyone. But as, with their aid, the world human population has grown healthier, it has also grown to an extraordinary number, and is still growing. Today there are four and a half billion people on the planet, and at the projected rates of growth, every year during the next three to four decades will add, on average, a number of people equivalent to the present populations of Mexico, Hong Kong and Belgium. And there are population "hotspots", like Nigeria, whose present population of 85 million is expected to grow to nearly the present population size of all of Africa - which is almost half a billion - before levelling off. Even if every human being suddenly decided to have children at "replacement rate" only, that is, two surviving children for every pair of adults, the world population would still expand over the next sixty years, because of the number of children there are now who will grow up to become parents.

This burden of numbers that one species has imposed on the planet is sapping natural resources at an astonishing rate, as we shall see in the following chapters. Every government everywhere has the responsibility to see to it that its people are now, and will be in the future, able to feed and care for themselves. Indeed many have implemented at least some rational resource utilization measures within their countries. However, in view of the inexorable rise in human population, these are not yet enough. Meanwhile, outside of their own national boundaries (in the oceans, for example) and within other peoples' countries, scramble competition among nations is still the order of the day.

The point I'm trying to make here about the growth in human population subsequent to the advances in medicine and nutrition should not be taken as "reactionary", "red", "antireligious" or "fascist", the diverse epithets often hurled at us conservationists by equally diverse sectors of society. It's just that if enough people and governments had had the foresight to offer, along with the medicine and nutrition, a method that would have slowed the rate at which people began to have healthy babies, and to explain why population control was so vitally important, the planet (and many people on it) wouldn't be in the sorry state we see today. Of course, such an offer would have faced (and, incredibly, still faces) major objections from certain cultural, social and religious points of view. But these pale into insignificance beside ecological considerations - the "point of view" that encompasses all people and the natural resources they depend on, limited by the one planet available.

In any case, there were not enough strong voices raised against the rampant growth of human population. Although the growth could be eased by the decision of people to reproduce at replacement rate, which

Misunderstanding of nature is often at the root of destructive human actions.
Above *The ancient eucalyptus forests of Australia, seen here at the "Camelback", Jidbinbilla Reserve, serve to protect the environment and provide home for much wildlife. Yet their clearance and plantation with introduced species is undertaken as an "improvement" (see following page).*
Opposite *Natural desert can be dramatically beautiful, as the Namib Desert of S.W. Africa shows; the dunes of Sossusulei pictured here are some of the highest in the world. Though often regarded as a hostile, barren environment, the natural desert has its own communities of wildlife, well adapted to its conditions. But human over-use of the fragile, arid lands that lie on its margins is leading to the appearance of truly barren lands - newly desertified and eroded areas where nothing thrives.*

would help matters enormously (and I will gladly take issue with any world religious leader who cares to dispute that statement as ungodly), it's already here to stay for well over the next half a century. What do we do now? How can our species develop so that everyone is healthy and happy despite this huge increase in population and at the same time bring down the use of resources to a sustainable level?

The answer is simple. Think of the relationship between human development and the conservation of natural resources as a sort of mutualism, a relationship like that of the ant and the acacia or the sloth and the algae, in which one cannot exist without the other. The way we are using resources now - overfishing and overhunting, felling forests, exhausting soil, polluting air and water - means that they will soon disappear, or become useless or inimical to health, which will prevent our ever achieving the goals of development because development relies on these very resources. Conservation of resources relies on *sustainable* development.

The methods needed to achieve sustainable development are known. The accompanying technology has been and is being invented, and the willing work force required to carry it forward is growing. But conservation and development have for so long been viewed as antagonistic forces, it is difficult for some people to believe that they actually can and must work in concert. Too many leaders of nations, although aware of the urgency of the environmental situation and, indeed, the solutions, are conspicuous in the conservation movement only by their absence, or their rhetoric that makes a mock of its efforts. The notion of a mutualistic relationship between conservation and development is open to misinterpretation, accidental or deliberate. My husband tells the story of his visit to Australia to see the ancient eucalyptus forests (illustrated on the previous page). On the great dunes of the east coast, they protect the inland regions from high sea winds and are home to lovely, lively Australian birds, like fairy bluebirds and pink cockatoos, and a number of unusual marsupials. He drove along the coast until suddenly, as if a knife had sliced through the dunes, the landscape changed to flat sands planted in row after dreary row of the foreign Norfolk pine. Never one to be silent about such things, my husband commented on the "development" to the press, and eventually received a tear-stained letter from a spokesman for the titanium company that had levelled the dunes and planted the pines. The man said he wished he could have shown Mr. Durrell round the site to explain how the company was "replacing nature".

The simple answer to the planet's woes - that conservation and development go hand in hand - is described in more detail in the *World Conservation Strategy*, an amazing document published a few years ago, and in this book. But it will not be very easy to put into practice, for the Ark that we're travelling on is like Noah's in one sense, and very unlike it in another. Noah, at God's insistence, took his family and a few each of all the animals (he was not asked to take any live plants) aboard a boat to save them from the great flood by which the earth would be rid of wicked and violent people. When the flood came it covered mountains, and the only thing around was the Ark "upon the face of the waters", which must have looked rather like the modern photographs of our bright planet spinning alone in the dark blue of space. But the waters finally receded, and Noah and all disembarked, finding not only plants, but clean air and water and rich land - all the requisites for the "development" that God then asked Noah and his sons to oversee. The difference between our Ark and Noah's is that we cannot "disembark". Our Ark *is* the air, water and land, and all the species of plants and animals, including ourselves, are the crew. How can we be so blind as to continue our acts of sabotage?

Opposite   *"The State the Ark" by the noted wildlife artist Jonathan Kingdon. "The World and Ark are one," wrote the artist "and the phyla of life are depicted over it. Man is a central but ambiguous figure, simultaneously unleashing cascades of destruction, symbolized by waves of bright colour, and trying to halt it; he is also a Noah figure. The negative past is symbolized by the quagga and dodo (both now extinct) falling away, the positive future by the phoenix-like néné goose, rising from the flames of human destructiveness. The black falling figure of the gorilla, and the white rhino, warn of the imminence of more extinctions. The Arabian oryx is a symbol of practical conservation in action. The texture of the painting suggests a fabric or tapestry, symbolizing a holistic view of the living world."*

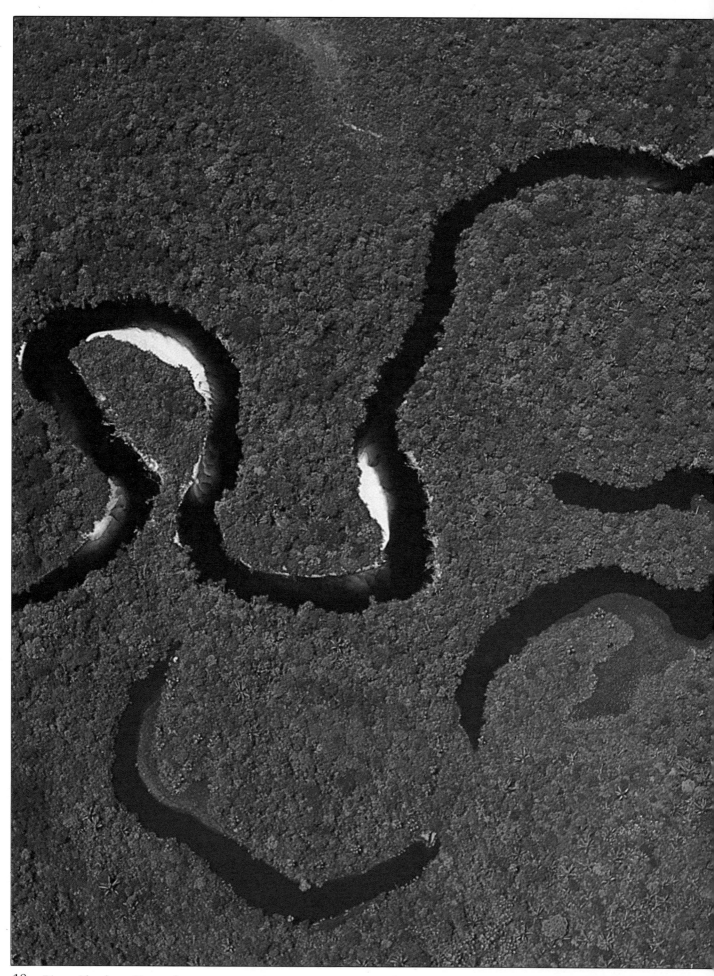

18   *River with oxbows, Venezuela.*

CHAPTER ONE

The State of the Ark

Persistent but renewable, elegantly organized but dynamic, and as thin as the bloom on a plum, is the biosphere, the zone of life on Earth. Using energy from the sun, it takes particles from the rocky crust of the planet that supports it, the air that surrounds it and the water that runs through it, to assemble living matter. Death's disassembly is just one part of the self-regenerating, vibrant cycle.

Rather than speculate on the origins of life or why this planet and not another is its home, it is more important today to understand how the biosphere works. In the polished and precise terms of the physicist, the biosphere is a collection of interdependent, working parts, receiving inputs of energy from the sun and materials from the physical environment, and maintaining internal stability by recycling some of its own outputs. A naturalist would say that, thanks to the sun's light and heat and the planet's supply of water, carbon dioxide and vital elements, plants grow, animals eat them and each other, and microbes break down both into their constituent chemicals, which then let more plants grow in the sunshine. However the biosphere is described, it's obvious that life cannot exist apart from its physical environment. What is perhaps less obvious is how the "outputs", the chemical building blocks of life, get back into the biosphere once they've left it and how then, as inputs, they keep the biosphere stable.

It is helpful to picture the biosphere, within its physical environment, as one section in a whole collection of working parts, called Gaia or Mother Earth by the ancient Greeks, and now called the Ark by the poets and the ecosphere by the scientists. Rocks and soil, rivers, oceans, clouds and air contain the materials that go to feed living beings and then are returned by living beings. The time-frame for the exchanges between living and non-living can be as quick as a breath or as slow as the progress of a carbon atom, from air to leaf to coal to hearth to air again.

The pathways and rates of progress of energy and materials within the ecosphere have evolved over time with the organisms that carry them. Natural perturbations, even dramatic ones, like plagues of leaf-eating insects in a forest or fires sweeping through a grassland, are soon dissipated by the checks and balances inherent in that local branch of the ecosphere, although many organisms may die in the meantime. Aside from global events such as the advance of glaciers or showers of comets, the only natural cataclysms that could quickly and for a long time overturn such local balances are volcanic eruptions and unusually powerful typhoons. But now there is a new, unnatural type of disturbance, capable of causing rapid and sometimes near-permanent damage, not only locally and regionally, but globally, too. This new disturbance is caused by the creature that any god might once have been proud of, the species erroneously named *Homo sapiens*, which means Wise Man.

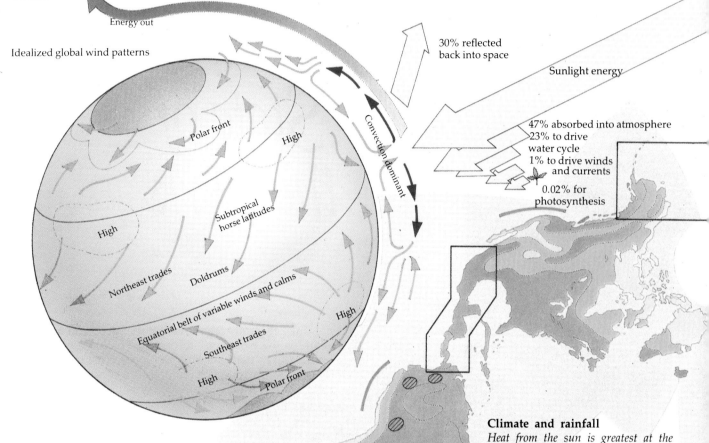

Energy out

Idealized global wind patterns

30% reflected back into space

Sunlight energy

Convection dominant

47% absorbed into atmosphere
23% to drive water cycle
1% to drive winds and currents
0.02% for photosynthesis

Polar front

High

High

Subtropical horse latitudes

Northeast trades

Doldrums

Equatorial belt of variable winds and calms

High

Southeast trades

High

Polar front

Climate and rainfall

Heat from the sun is greatest at the equator and least at the poles. This difference creates the tropical and temperate zones, and also sets air and water in motion. The movement, modified by the Earth's spin and interrupted by landmasses, results in varying rainfall patterns as moisture from the oceans is dropped over land. Rainfall and warmth determine the quality of terrestrial life, from tundra to forest.

The ark in motion

Seen from space, our planet glows with colour, motion, and swirling patterns that mark it as the home of life.

Nothing on its surface is still. There are the streaming masses of clouds and the great currents and gyres of the oceans, travelling faster than any express train. These currents influence climate thousands of miles away, and where they meet the continents are lifted up in great upwellings teeming with life.

There are slower motions too - waves of green spreading over the landmasses in spring, ice-caps that shrink and grow again - and longer patterns still of climate change. Slowest of all is the movement of the continents, drifting across the face of the Earth over a vast timescale, and carrying their inhabitants with them. About 250 million years ago, there was one supercontinent, called Pangaea. 60 million years ago the Alantic began to divide Old and New worlds; Australia and Antarctica separated from S. America about 45 million years ago. Life has evolved and spread in an environment of motion and change.

Surface currents of the oceans

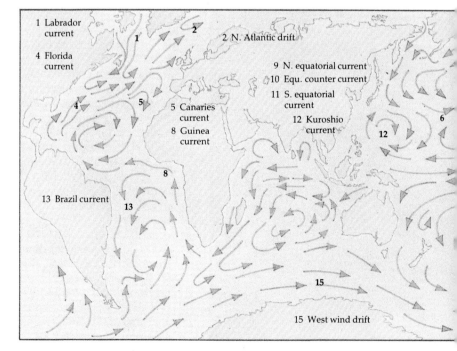

1 Labrador current

4 Florida current

2 N. Atlantic drift

9 N. equatorial current
10 Equ. counter current
11 S. equatorial current

5 Canaries current

12 Kuroshio current

8 Guinea current

13 Brazil current

15 West wind drift

The solar powerhouse

Energy from the sun is the force that drives the ecosphere of Earth. Vast amounts of solar energy bathe the planet in a continual flux of radiation. Almost a third is immediately reflected back into space, nearly half goes to warm the atmosphere, sea and land, and one per cent drives the winds and ocean currents. A mere 0.02 per cent is captured by plants for photosynthesis - this tiny proportion powers life on Earth.

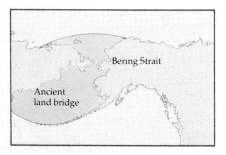

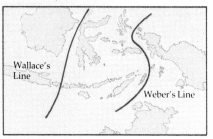

Continental drift

Continental drift helps to explain present day species distribution. The southern beech (see map) evolved when Australia and South America, now thousands of miles apart, were joined. The wildlife of North America and Eurasia once had free passage over the land bridge which crossed the Bering Straits; squirrels, parrots and deer spread between the continents before the Straits opened about 13,000 years ago. Wallace's Line and Weber's Line divide the Indomalayan and Australasian regions. The islands between emerged fairly recently, and have a mixture of species from both. When South America finally become joined to North America 2.5 million years ago, an influx of northern mammals wiped out many original species.

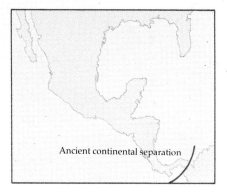

✳   Range of southern beech genus *Nothofagus*

▨   Refugia

〰   Upwelling zones

Over 3000 mm
1000-3000 mm ⎫
250-1000 mm ⎬ Rainfall
Less than 250 mm ⎭

Refugia

The history of global climate has left its mark on species distribution. The advancing Ice Ages killed susceptible species, or isolated small populations in refugia - "islands" amid harsher habitat. As the climate improved, these relict populations could spread out from the refugia, whose sites are recognized today by the richness of their speciation.

El Nino and climate change

A change to the normal circulation patterns of sea and atmosphere can have immediate and drastic impact. When the usual cool current that sweeps up the west coast of South America fails, and the normal westerly winds falter and shift to the east, warm water flows out eastward across the equatorial Pacific. This is el Nino (see left). In the arid Galapagos Islands, torrential rain falls, plant life burgeons and birds breed well. But then the rains cease, and fires set in. In 1982-3, el Nino was especially severe, bringing floods to America and drought to Africa, Asia and Australia.

3 Alaska current
6 N. Pacific current
7 California current

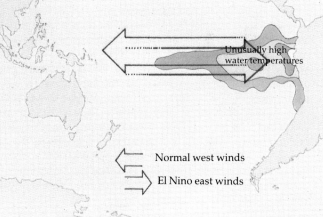

Unusually high water temperatures

Normal west winds

El Nino east winds

14 Peru (Humboldt) current

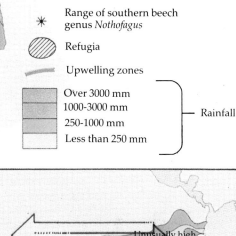

How the biosphere works

The sun is the external driving force of the biosphere. Its heat energy makes most biochemical reactions possible, and its light energy permits photosynthesis, the particular reaction that green plants use to make simple sugars and oxygen out of carbon dioxide and water. The sun is also responsible for shifting non-living matter about from place to place. As the planet spins and tilts and moves around the sun, winds and ocean currents are created by variations in the heat received from it. These in turn move air and moisture, and whatever they carry, around the planet, ready to re-enter the biosphere at points far from the places they left it.

The "points and places" lie within the natural units of the ecosphere, the ecosystems. These various assemblies - ocean, forest, marsh, desert - are made up of plants, animals and non-living materials that interact intimately and frequently with each other. But ecosystems are not "closed", for they rely on inputs from other ecosystems. Forests generate some of their own precipitation but are watered as well by storms that gather moisture and air over oceans; a coral reef is fertilized by the droppings of fish that return to rest from feeding out in the distant beds of sea grass. Nor are ecosystems static. They persist because their organisms have adapted to conditions set by the physical environment, like temperature and rainfall, and by each other, like competition and predation. But the persistence is a vigorous, rough-and-tumble affair, with the checks and balances continuously in operation.

The operation of an ecosystem is most simply described in terms of the rôles of its basic components - non-living matter and living beings -within the context of prevailing light, temperature, fire and force of wind. Living beings are conveniently labelled producers or consumers. The primary producers are the plants. Sometimes called autotrophs, which means self-feeding, they are sustained by the energy-rich sugars they make by photosynthesis. What is left over after a plant meets its own energy requirements is stored as plant tissue, and called the net primary production of an ecosystem. It will eventually be consumed, directly or indirectly, by the other organisms, the heterotrophs, to meet their own energy requirements. And again, whatever is left over will be stored as their tissues.

Energy is stored as tissues of organisms in the sense that it builds them up, and is released when they are broken down. But the actual building blocks, the nutrients, like carbon, hydrogen, oxygen, nitrogen, phosphorous, sulphur and about 40 more trace elements, are scattered about in the physical environment until they are gathered up, usually by plants, which in turn feed the animals (although animals can obtain some of them directly just by drinking and breathing).

The various routes by which sun-derived energy flows and nutrients are recycled through an ecosystem are called food chains. There are usually many cross-links between the chains: a single species of plant can be eaten by a number of different herbivorous animals, and each one of these can be eaten by a number of different carnivorous animals. All the interconnecting chains together form the food web. The top carnivores in an ecosystem, like lions and tigers, are not usually preyed upon by other animals, and are thought of as the last links in a food chain, but the decomposers, the bacteria and fungi, are just as voracious as the rest of the consumers, and, most importantly, they close the nutrient cycle. They enter the web at all points, whenever any plant or animal dies, of course, but also when a leaf falls or an animal deposits its droppings, to dismantle the material put together in the first place by a plant and the sun. The decomposers obtain their own energy and nutrients this way, but leave behind most of the building blocks of life in such a form that only a plant and the sun can reassemble them.

There is more to the interactions within an ecosystem than just the food web, although it is the most vital in maintaining the checks and

CASE STUDY
The ruination of Terschelling Island

The Netherlands island of Terschelling, part of the shifting dune system off the northwest European coast, was once a "wreckers' paradise". Ships often came to grief on the moving sandbanks, and many a rich cargo washed ashore on the island.

Besides the proceeds of wrecks, the islanders enjoyed an abundance of seafood, natural fruits such as wild cranberries, and prosperous farming on the fertile land. The coast facing the North Sea was virtually a natural barrier and thus a refuge for seabirds and marine life.

The island was so attractive that, when the whaling industry declined, tourism brought a new source of income. What has happened to Terschelling since then encapsulates what the pressure of people is doing to the whole world.

The island's dunes, stripped of their vegetation by acid rain and trampling by human feet, have become unstable. In an attempt to remedy this, trees were planted. Drainage canals for the trees, dug to lower the water table, destroyed even more of the natural vegetation. Rabbits and water voles became pests. Stoats and weasels, imported to control water voles, succeeded, but are now the poultry-farmer's nightmare.

Chemicals used on the farmlands have polluted the polder water. The beaches where wrecks were once washed up are covered with modern garbage, and the wealth of seabirds that nest on the dunes have to contend with over 140,000 tourists a year. The islanders' profit from tourism has been nature's loss - the very wealth of natural beauty that attracted people therein.

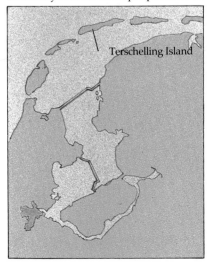
Terschelling Island

CASE STUDY
The Gaia hypothesis

Our unique planetary home, as photographed from space. The view stretches from the Mediterranean Sea to Antarctica.

In a process known as photosynthesis, plants make sugars from water and carbon dioxide, drawing on the sun's energy. They also utilize elements in the soil to build their tissues. Perhaps an extremely simple plant could live alone on Earth, but few of the higher plants would survive for long without microbes in the soil to produce nutrients from the remains of other plants and animals, the shade or drainage or other special conditions provided by neighbouring plants, or animals to pollinate them and disperse their seeds.

Very little that lives on this planet could do so in isolation. Each species depends on a host of others for its livelihood, and all organisms are a part of the biosphere, giving and taking from one another in every phase of their life and death. Remove any one of them, and the pattern must alter. Remove too many, and it falls into chaos.

Three billion years of evolution have gone into building this complex system. The earliest organisms on Earth that were able to photosynthesize their own hydrocarbons for food - the blue-green algae - lived in the shallow oceans, protected from the intense ultraviolet radiation that bathed the land. But, by their own chemistry (chiefly to do with the oxygen that was produced as a by-product of photosynthesis), an oxygen-rich atmosphere and a thin ozone layer that blocked much of the ultraviolet radiation were created. Eventually life emerged from the oceans on to the land and into the full light and warmth of the sun, safe from the damaging ultraviolet solar rays. Thus, from the earliest times, life was dependent upon life.

The modern scientific hypothesis that life itself controls the physical and chemical condition of the Earth's surface, the atmosphere and the oceans, to make and keep them fit for living, is called the Gaia hypothesis. This hypothesis has led to the development of a new systems-science, which studies all the interrelations of the ecosphere. The name "Gaia" was chosen after the ancient Greek concept of Mother Earth, or Gaia as the deity was known.

During the tenure of life on Earth, many changes have occurred and the system has had to reorganize itself many times. There have been periods of rapid evolution, and times of mass extinctions. Small balancing actions take place constantly, from day to day. Many species have come and gone but, through it all, life has protected itself, rearranged itself, and carried on.

Whatever we do to this planet, it is unlikely that all life will be extinguished. We are but a single species, however, and our own survival is by no means secure. If our extinction would remove a threat to life on Earth, then one sobering interpretation of the Gaia hypothesis might suggest that this is inevitable.

Life support systems

In terms of essential nutrients planetary life is a "closed system".

The carbon, oxygen, nitrogen, water and other elements on which life depends are neither added to, nor lost, but cycled and recycled through the life-support system – from nitrogen in the air, to nitrates in fertilizer, or from carbon in oil, to carbon dioxide released when it burns.

Organisms draw materials from the environment to build the chemicals of life. And in doing so they also shape the environment. The air we breathe, the climate and soil and elemental cycles are all sustained continuously by living organisms - from nitrogen-fixing bacteria to photosynthesizing plants.

Carbon, oxygen, and CO$_2$

The interlocking cycles of carbon, oxygen and hydrogen - as CO$_2$, water and free oxygen especially - lie at the heart of the life-support system. Plants use carbon dioxide and water for photosynthesis, storing the carbon (as carbohydrates) and releasing free oxygen. Animals eat the plants, breathe the oxygen, and release carbon dioxide. The stored carbon is passed up food chains, and eventually "fixed" in buried organic matter in the soil. Photosynthesis by blue-green algae in the oceans first released oxygen into the atmosphere, to provide the air we breathe, and form the atmospheric ozone layer which protects life on earth from ultra-violet radiation.

The water cycle

Of all water on the planet, 97% is salt, and of the freshwater most is locked up in the ice caps. Under 1% is circulated in the water cycle, powered by the sun. Its heat lifts water vapour from the sea, and drives about winds to carry 10% of this over land to fall as rain. Plants transpire some water again; some goes to groundwater stores; the rest runs back to the ocean, its flow regulated by vegetation cover. If this is removed, a cycle of floods, erosion and droughts may set in.

Eutrophication

Nitrogen and phosphorus help plants to grow, as farmers know. However, if they get into the wrong places, problems can be severe. Human output of fertilizer, vehicle exhausts, and sewage effluents are adding these fertile elements to water run-off at a considerable rate, with most obvious effects on lakes, rivers, and coastal waters. Algae blooms, discolouring the water, and odours and disease risks result. Ultimately, oxygenation of the water is reduced to a point where the whole aquatic system dies.

- Carbon cycle
- Oxygen cycle
- Water cycle
- Nitrogen cycle
- Sunlight energy

The sun and living energy

All life on Earth depends on energy from the sun. Yet only plants can tap it directly to manufacture and store their own energy foods, the carbohydrates. This store is the basic energy supply of all food chains. It also provides all our fossil fuels, oil, coal, and gas, as well as the living fuels of wood, peat, or dung.

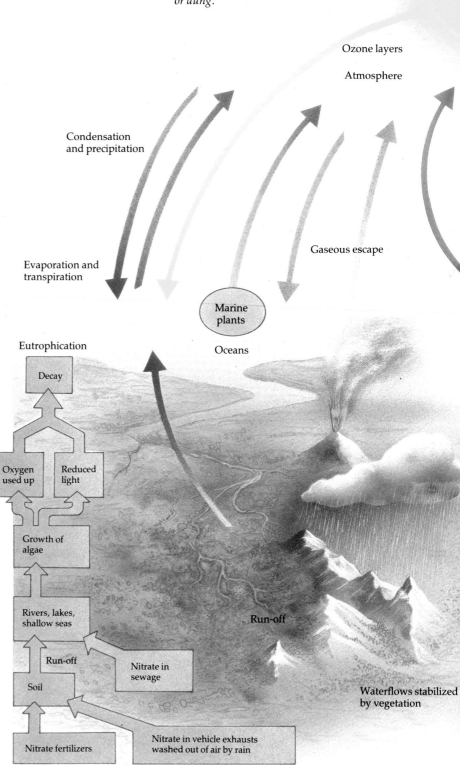

Ozone layers

Atmosphere

Condensation and precipitation

Gaseous escape

Evaporation and transpiration

Marine plants

Oceans

Eutrophication

Decay

Oxygen used up

Reduced light

Growth of algae

Rivers, lakes, shallow seas

Run-off

Nitrate in sewage

Soil

Run-off

Nitrate fertilizers

Nitrate in vehicle exhausts washed out of air by rain

Waterflows stabilized by vegetation

The nitrogen cycle

Nitrogen is essential to living matter. There is a huge store of this vital element in the atmosphere, but most organisms can only use it in specific chemical forms. Continuation of life on Earth depends absolutely on the tiny bacteria and algae that can "fix" atmospheric nitrogen, and convert it to ammonia. Animals and plants use the ammonia, and nitrates yielded from it (by other bacteria), to build amino acids, and from them, proteins. Decomposers of dead and waste matter break these down again, and denitrifying bacteria release free nitrogen.

The web of life

All life on this planet is linked in an intricate web of exchange of energy and services - between the eaters and the eaten, the living and the dead, the producers (plants) and the consumers (animals), the habitat and its populations of species. At the simplest level, these relationships are demonstrated by food chains. In the soil, litter feeders eat dead parts of organisms, decomposers break them down to nutrients, and bacteria fix and release nitrogen. Plants use sunlight to combine gases, soil nutrients and water into stored energy. Animals eat the plants, predators prey on the plant eaters, and other predators still prey on them. Energy and nutrients are transferred up the chain, with populations (or "biomass") at each level determined by their supply.

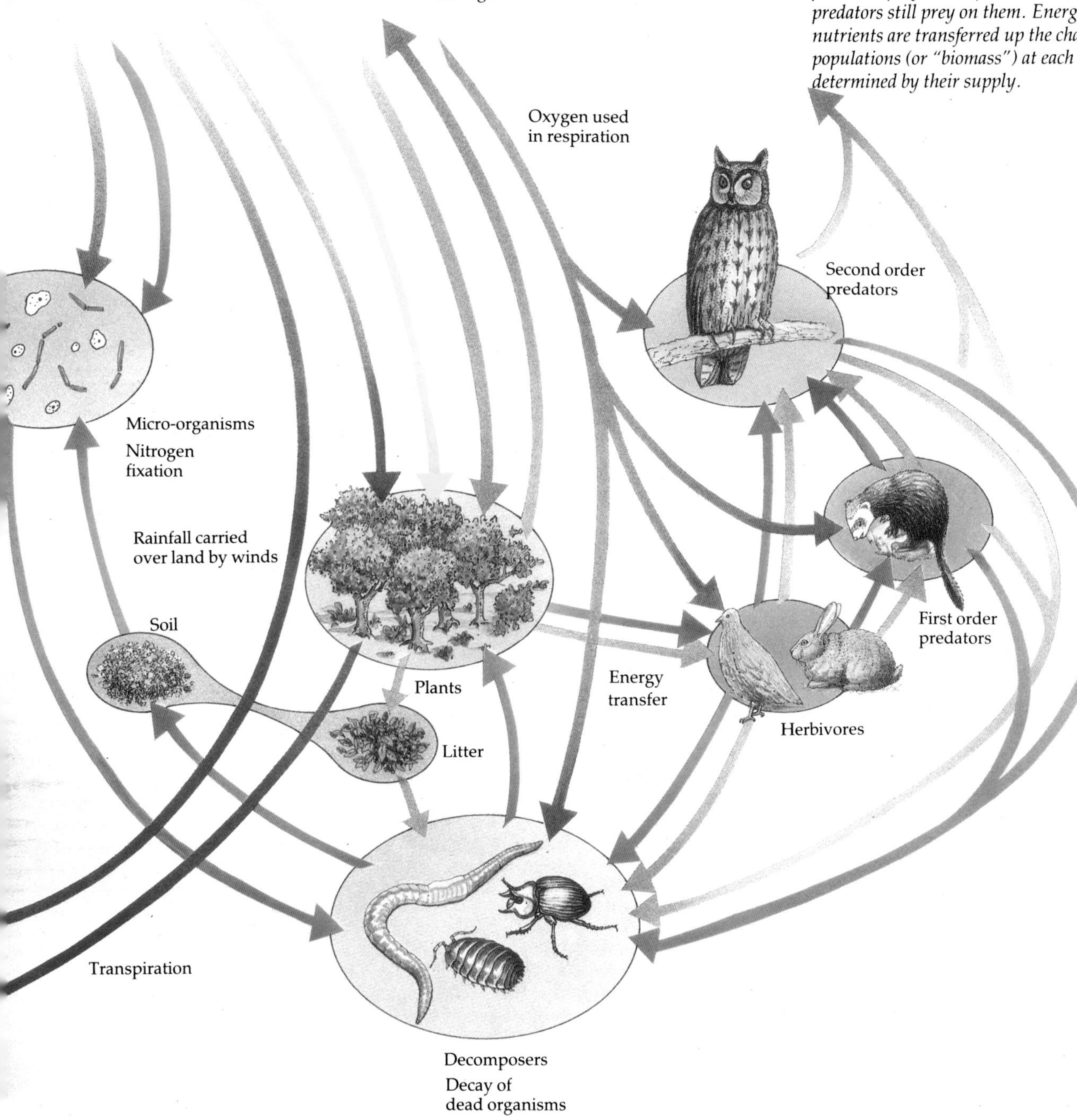

Oxygen used in respiration

Second order predators

Micro-organisms

Nitrogen fixation

Rainfall carried over land by winds

First order predators

Soil

Plants

Litter

Energy transfer

Herbivores

Transpiration

Decomposers

Decay of dead organisms

The events in Etosha National Park, in southern Africa, illustrate how a seemingly minimal disturbance to the ecosystem can have major ramifications. The gravel pits in the park, dug out for road construction, filled with rainwater which became stagnant and alkaline, providing perfect conditions for anthrax bacteria. Wildebeest and zebra began to sicken and die, becoming easy prey to lions and spotted hyenas, which increased in number. The anthrax-resistant eland began to suffer from higher lion numbers, yet the springbok, also anthrax-resistant, increased because of lack of grazing competition with wildebeest… These are only a few of the ramifications. But once the disease has run its course, the ecosystem will probably settle down.

balances. The more links there are in the feeding relationships, the less likely will disturbance to one affect the whole, because organisms can take up the "slack", like foxes that concentrate on mice and voles during a cold spring because there are fewer insects and, therefore, fewer baby birds to eat that year. But plants and animals have evolved other "threads" within ecosystems to take advantage of each other in finding food and shelter and in reproducing. Geckoes, for example, ride tortoises to eat the mosquitoes attracted to their hosts' soft necks and to hide under their carapaces when alarmed; plants produce nectar-filled flowers to attract the animals that will cross-pollinate them. The strength of these threads also helps to maintain the stability of an ecosystem.

How much can an ecosystem take?

The "fragility" of an ecosystem depends on its response to interference with its checks and balances. Does it offer strong resistance to disturbance, as does a forest when new leaves are killed by a late frost but which can replace them because of the energy reserves of the trees? Or is it resilient in the face of disturbance, like the desert which is parched and lifeless during prolonged drought, but greens and blossoms at the first rains because of the seeds and roots that lay dormant through the bad times? Resistant or resilient, how much disturbance can an ecosystem take before it disintegrates forever?

The answer is that ecosystems are surprisingly forgiving if the threads of life-relationships within it are merely tugged. The danger of deliberately tinkering with ecosystems lies more in actually cutting the threads. The loss of species may be buffed by other species taking over their rôles or by artifical means, but the substitutes are rarely as good as the originals, and the ecosystem becomes degraded, with consequences unforeseen by the tinkerers.

The tinkerers are ourselves, once of such small numbers and benign habits that our impact on the ecosphere was no greater than that of any other large omnivorous mammal. When we began using fire and hunting with efficient weapons our impact was certainly felt, but this behaviour developed over a period of time sufficient to allow the local ecosystems to adjust (even to the Pleistocene megafauna extinctions). The early methods of farming and herding, like shifting cultivation and nomadic pastoralism, were practised by so few people in such a vast expanse of land that the affected areas always recovered in the fallow periods, when the threads of the ecosystem had time to reconnect themselves. Hunting and fishing were also carried out in a sustainable manner, although perhaps not consciously. Certain cultural taboos regulated the use of obviously limited resources, especially on small islands, and on the larger islands and continents there were simply not enough humans to prevent animal populations from recovering after being cropped.

Human intelligence eventually gave rise to "civilizations". A useful definition of civilization is the invention and wide application of artificial techniques to increase the ability of the local ecosystem, by many orders of magnitude, to support human beings and the plants and animals associated with them (the numbers supportable are termed the "carrying capacity"). But the elevation of the carrying capacity, if developed without a thorough understanding of how the ecosystem works, is illusory. The fall of some past civilizations was connected to the environmental consequences of their very achievements.

A usual corollary of civilization is that human numbers readily overshoot the artificially increased carrying capacity of the ecosystem, and so either new techniques must be invented to care for them, or they die, bringing their numbers and environment back into balance. What has happened over the last few hundred years is that the tempting, sometimes forced, offerings of civilization have been so widespread that there is no human population untouched by them, and therefore, no check on the growth of human numbers. We are now engaged in a technological race to

Mesopotamia: second time around

The River Euphrates has always been subject to floods at an inconvenient time. It floods between April and June, too late for summer crops and too early for winter ones. Irrigation takes some water on to the plain, but the ground there is badly drained and prone to waterlogging, with a consequent build-up of salt year by year.

Ancient management of this difficult situation made use of wild plants, allowing the land to lie fallow in alternate years. The wild legumes of the region helped to dry the land as well as put some nitrogen back into the soil. After some years, though, the salt would have built up to such a degree that the land would have to be left to recover for a hundred years or more.

This system probably began about 5000 BC. It seems to have worked well until, some time in the third millennium BC, irrigation was greatly increased. Salinization of the land then became a much more serious problem. By 2500 BC, salt-sensitive wheat only made up one-sixth of the grain grown; none at all was produced by 1700 BC. At the same time fertility was falling: the yield of barley in 1700 BC was barely a quarter of the yield in 2400 BC.

Increased irrigation had brought the whole of the Euphrates plain under cultivation. This caused a population explosion and great urban growth, with centralization of financial and other controls. Demand for water increased, yet shortage followed, because the improved water supply was unable to cope with the growing human numbers. As the soil became infertile the agricultural system collapsed, and with it the urbanized society it supported; cities were abandoned, and the old system of agriculture was reborn from the ruins.

The demise of Mesopotamian civilization is history. But what is happening on the banks of the Euphrates now is history being helped to repeat itself through almost the same sequence as before.

Centralization and urbanization were, and are, the beginning of the end. Taxes, rents and debts put pressure on farmers to use land that ought to be fallow. Eventually, when they can no longer make ends meet, they sell to an absentee landlord, who imports tenants who do not understand the special local farming system.

Added to this, there has again been mismanagement of water. New dams have burst and faulty canals, as in ancient times, have aggravated salinization. Nearly one-half of the land is now ruined by waterlogging - and salt, again.

The development of a water supply for more intensive agriculture is an investment that expects, and exacts, a return. On land as difficult as this, however, the system that works is one which sets no targets and accepts whatever comes; in other words, the traditional tribal system. Productivity may not be high, but it is as much as the land will bear. The way technology is being applied at present, it cannot save the situation - indeed, it is hastening a second, seemingly inevitable, collapse.

Irrigation channel near Zavâre in Dasht-i Kavir.

THE STATE OF THE ARK
No room for our friends

Few parts of the world can still be considered true wilderness today. Yet in the next hundred years, human numbers will rise two or threefold. Where then will the wild find space?

Our dependence on wild species and ecosystems for survival often goes unrecognized. Yet from the insect pollinators of our crops to the algae that supply the oxygen we breathe, all life is linked into our own survival system. Wild areas hold reserves of species and genetic characters essential both to the progress of evolution and to the ability of nature - and human cultivation - to respond to changed conditions.

Yet the pressure of human need for fuel, housing, food, more land, mines, industry, and leisure - is driving the co-passengers and life-boat crew on our ark into ever faster retreat. It is not just the dramatic extinctions of tigers or rhinos we need fear, but the eradication of tens and hundreds of thousands of the unnoticed, obscure species that do the work of the biosphere. The map shows the present division of humanized and (largely) wild territories. The diagrams portray the likely future.

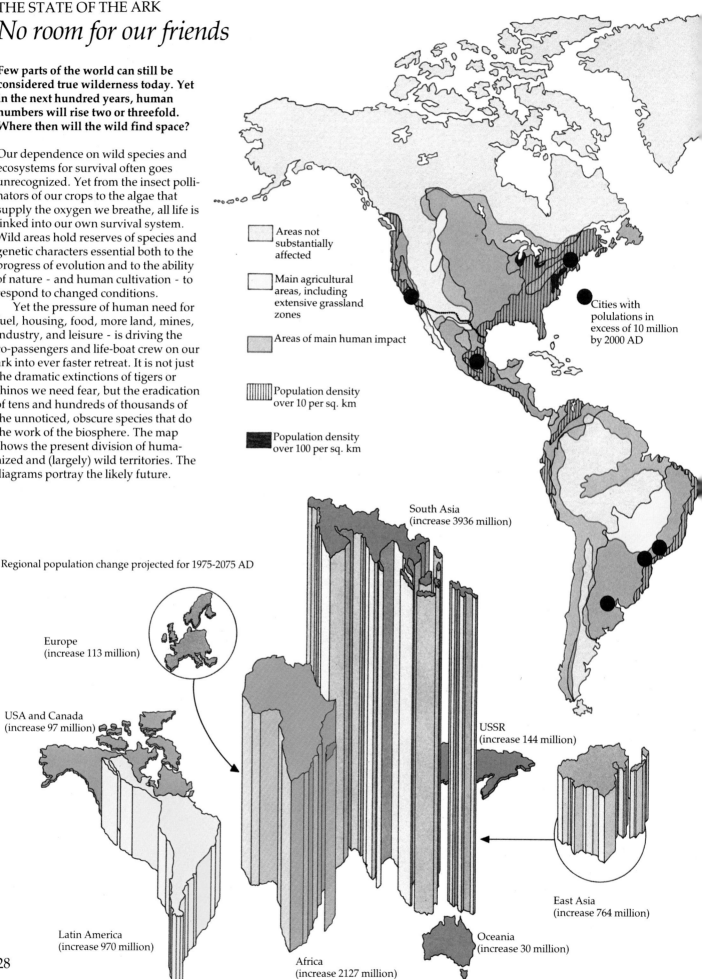

Areas not substantially affected

Main agricultural areas, including extensive grassland zones

Areas of main human impact

Population density over 10 per sq. km

Population density over 100 per sq. km

Cities with polulations in excess of 10 million by 2000 AD

Regional population change projected for 1975-2075 AD

Europe (increase 113 million)

USA and Canada (increase 97 million)

USSR (increase 144 million)

South Asia (increase 3936 million)

East Asia (increase 764 million)

Oceania (increase 30 million)

Latin America (increase 970 million)

Africa (increase 2127 million)

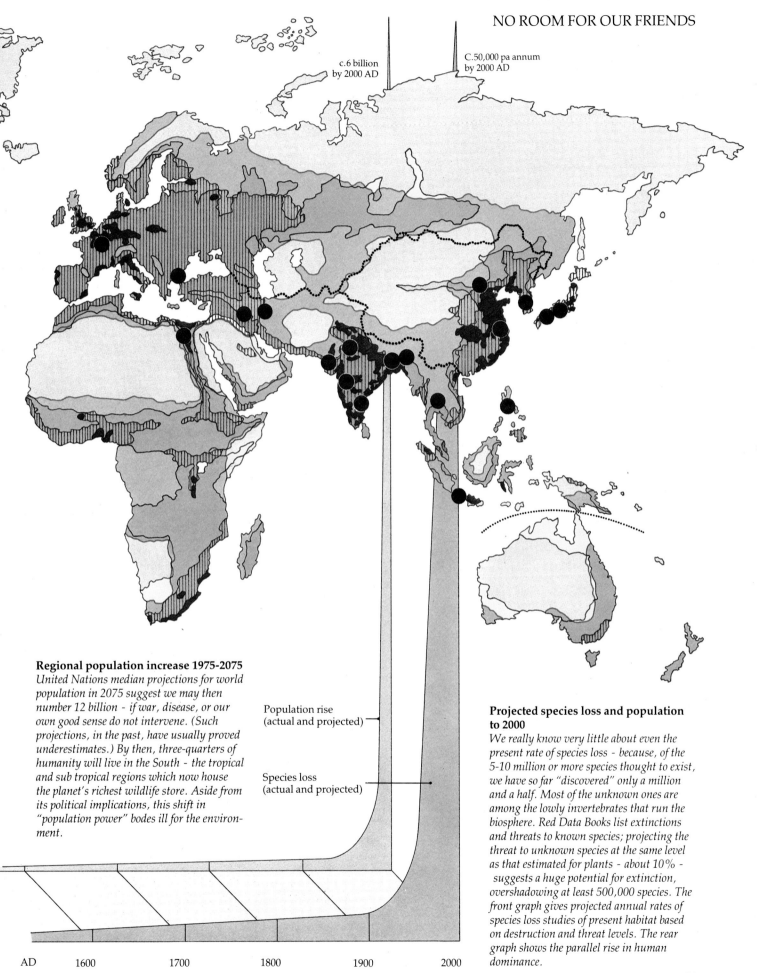

c.6 billion
by 2000 AD

C.50,000 pa annum
by 2000 AD

Regional population increase 1975-2075

*United Nations median projections for world
population in 2075 suggest we may then
number 12 billion - if war, disease, or our
own good sense do not intervene. (Such
projections, in the past, have usually proved
underestimates.) By then, three-quarters of
humanity will live in the South - the tropical
and sub tropical regions which now house
the planet's richest wildlife store. Aside from
its political implications, this shift in
"population power" bodes ill for the environment.*

Population rise
(actual and projected)

Species loss
(actual and projected)

Projected species loss and population
to 2000

*We really know very little about even the
present rate of species loss - because, of the
5-10 million or more species thought to exist,
we have so far "discovered" only a million
and a half. Most of the unknown ones are
among the lowly invertebrates that run the
biosphere. Red Data Books list extinctions
and threats to known species; projecting the
threat to unknown species at the same level
as that estimated for plants - about 10% -
 suggests a huge potential for extinction,
overshadowing at least 500,000 species. The
front graph gives projected annual rates of
species loss studies of present habitat based
on destruction and threat levels. The rear
graph shows the parallel rise in human
dominance.*

AD   1600   1700   1800   1900   2000

bail out the Ark, leaking badly under its human burden, and, in spite of our intelligence, we are amazingly oblivious to the fact that *how* technology has been applied is one cause of the problem, and not the solution.

Mismanagement of the planet

Our growing ability to manage nature has resulted in mismanagement, the scale of which ranges from local degradation and outright destruction of habitats to global interference with nutrient cycles. Human activities that alter ecosystems can be grouped into two categories: how we use them for our own ends and what we put into them.

The first involves the total or partial manipulation of habitats: totally, by intensive farming or grazing of livestock on arable or "reclaimed" land (drained marshes, irrigated desert margins and cleared forests) and by urbanization; and partially, by the forms of cultivation and pasturage practised by poor people. Total or partial, the manipulation is usually carelessly done in the context of the modern world, and results not only in the loss of the "wild" living components of ecosystems, the native plants and animals, but also in erosion and, depending on the region, salinization and waterlogging of soils and desertification.

The second way in which humans alter ecosystems is covered by the broad term "pollution". It means the introduction to the environment of unnatural substances (like plastics or DDT) or natural substances (like phosphorus or soil) at unnatural levels or the creation of physical conditions (like the industrial discharge of hot water) that alter the usual circulation of nutrients. The direct effects of pollution are sudden and dramatic. Many organisms suffer or are killed outright by the use of toxic chemicals or their unintentional release, as happened in Bhopal, India. Animals and plants are also killed by the spread of oil, silt and hot water, and animals die by eating or getting trapped by "junk", like plastic bags and old fishing nets (*see p.73*).

The indirect effects of pollution are more subtle, but no less harmful. Sometimes the pollutant is selectively lethal, as for insects especially sensitive to pesticides, or selectively promotional, as for lake algae that flourish on sewage and other organic matter (*see p.64*). Then the species composition of an ecosystem changes, and previously innocuous species, ones with small roles to play in the ecosystem, can themselves get out of control. New agricultural pests appear; and lakes and their inhabitants suffocate under the blanket of algae in a process called "cultural eutrophication". (Eutrophic simply means rich in nutrients, and over a long period of time, most lakes undergo eutrophication naturally.)

Certain chemicals are taken up by organisms at non-toxic levels, but because they are not degradable, they are stored in the tissues. The animals higher up a food chain accumulate them until they become directly toxic or interfere with growth and reproduction. The case of Minamata disease in Japan is a horrifying example. The methyl mercury dumped into a bay by a chemical company was taken up by the fish. The birds, cats and people who ate them suffered gruesome neurological disorders, and many died. Other chemicals react with substances in the environment to produce deadly compounds, like the controversial "acid rain", or unusually heavy concentrations of the original chemicals. DDT is highly soluble in oil, and so exposure to it is magnified wherever oil is spilled and spread.

Natural organic pollutants, like sewage, silt and even oil, are eventually decomposed, and if the source of pollution is removed and the damage has not been too great, ecosystems can repair themselves. However, natural inorganic pollutants, like heavy metals and elements made radioactive by the various uses of nuclear energy, and many of the synthetic organic compounds, like DDT, are so persistent that they ride through the ecosphere long after and far from the place they entered it.

In December 1984 an invisible cloud of poisonous methyl isocyanate gas leaked rapidly out of a manufacturing plant in Bhopal, India. Many hundreds of people died, thousands were blinded and suffered other injuries, and much valuable livestock was lost. Even more insidious were the events in 1978 around Love Canal, in New York. A thousand families (and field mice) living around the canal experienced severe health problems when the chemical wastes long buried in the canal began to seep through the soil.

Bhopal, India. This woman is suffering from the typical effects of MIC gas poisoning.

CASE STUDY
Losing our ancient soils

Soil is not easily come by. Millions of years of baking sun, cracking frosts, wind and weather, of living things - dying, decomposing, and leaving their remains in sand and silt - are gone to make the soil we have today. It can take 500 years to create one centimetre of soil. With the current urgency to produce food, we cannot spare even a pinch of it. Yet each year 13 million hectares of arable land are lost through erosion.

Farmland is caught up in a deteriorating cycle of growing, harvesting, ploughing and tilling. Every year, the farmlands of Europe are stripped and left naked under the sun. Two natural agencies cause erosion: wind and water. Bare soil on hillsides can be washed off by rain, and bare soil anywhere can be blown away by a drying wind. Europe loses a billion tons of good soil every year in this way - and this is one of the least-affected regions on the globe. Grain-growing areas are effectively being reduced by 300,000 hectares per year. Annual losses averaging 18 tons of soil per hectare occur in East Anglia, where sowing winter crops on the flat lands present a fine tilth to winter winds. Intensively farmed like this, the soil will last less than a hundred years.

Huge prairie-style fields in France baking in the sun.

CASE STUDY
The greenhouse effect

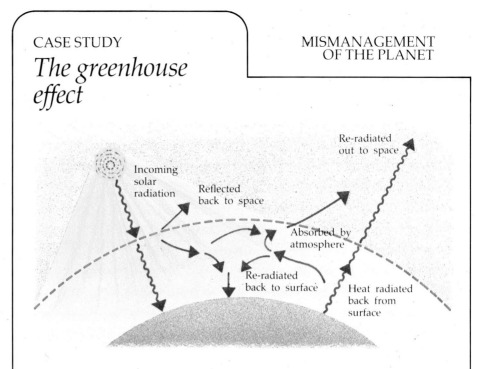

The Earth's atmosphere is all that lies between us and space. It protects us from the life-damaging rays of the sun during the day and retains warmth at night. Without its atmosphere, the Earth's surface would be alternately roasted and frozen.

Much of the short-wave radiation from the sun, around the wavelengths of visible light, passes through the atmosphere. Some is absorbed by land and sea, which warm up. These warmed surfaces re-radiate energy outwards, but at the much longer infrared wavelengths. These infrared rays are absorbed by water vapour and carbon dioxide in the atmosphere, and some of this heat is then radiated back to the surface. It is as though the atmospheric carbon dioxide traps heat, like glass in a greenhouse.

For the most part this process has been in a steady state. Theoretically, however, if there were more carbon dioxide in the atmosphere, it might trap more heat. This could raise the temperature on Earth, causing major climatic upheavals.

This so-called "greenhouse effect" was first postulated in 1861. Since then, the quantity of carbon dioxide in the atmosphere has indeed risen from around 270 ppm (parts per million) to a present concentration of about 350 ppm.

Carbon dioxide is generated by burning fossil fuels - coal and oil - and living fuels such as wood. A rise in carbon dioxide has also been produced by cutting down forests, thereby reducing the amount of plant tissues using it up in photosynthesis. It has been calculated that, by the year 2065, the concentration will have reached 600 ppm.

Carbon dioxide in the atmosphere helps to retain much of the heat radiated out from the Earth's surface.

Theoretically, doubling the carbon dioxide in the atmosphere would cause a global temperature rise of the order of 3°C. It is also likely that the polar regions would warm up faster than the rest of the Earth, so that melting ice would flood large areas of land (especially major coastal cities) as sea levels rose.

Measurements of global temperature have so far shown no real evidence of the predicted warming. There was an upward trend from 1860 to 1945, but it fell away towards the mid-1960s. Since then there has been another rise, but the meaning of these small changes is hard to interpret.

There could be advantages, too, in a rise in carbon dioxide. More carbon dioxide would also enable plants to make more efficient use of water, and thus to grow better, giving another level of significance to the term "greenhouse effect". Since 1850, plant productivity has measurably improved. Tree rings indicate an increase in growth rate of 90% in this time.

It is too early to draw conclusions about the ultimate effects of the load of carbon dioxide released into the Earth's atmosphere by our combustions. A possible greenhouse effect may be suppressed by other atmospheric interactions we do not yet understand. It may only be delayed, however, or could cause quite different results that we cannot predict. The fact that we have "got away with it" so far ought not to lead to complacency, when the Earth's atmosphere is at risk.

Damaging the ark

The World Conservation Strategy has three fundamental objectives: to maintain essential life-support systems, to preserve genetic diversity, and to ensure sustainable use of species and ecosystems.

In setting these targets, the WCS pinpoints some of the major threats to our planetary ark, now growing day by day from human activities. In our agriculture, we are polluting ecosystems, increasing the nitrogen cycle, and replacing genetic diversity with monoculture. In our cities and industries, we are polluting air and water, and over-consuming resources not well managed at their point of origin. In our hunger for land, we are destroying forests, essential guardians of species and environments, and their burning threatens global climate stability. In our great numbers, and in our failure to help the landless poor and the migrant pastoralists, we are creating deserts. And in our ignorance, we are altering stable natural ecosystems everywhere to gain increased - yet short term - production, before each system fails. Sustainable management means perceiving the future within the present.

Burning cerrado forest, Brazil.

Major climatic change

One grave consequence of deforestation and industrialization is the possibility of global climate change. The planetary mechanisms that maintain surface temperature and rainfall patterns within stable patterns are still little understood. But we do know that two factors - planetary "albedo" (reflectivity) and the mix of "greenhouse" gases (CO_2 and water) in the air, are significant. In additon, plant cover, by transpiring water, keeps rainfall stable.

Albedo depends on the darkness or lightness of the Earth's surface - cloud cover and oceans and ice caps (high albedo) reflect back heat; forests and vegetation (low albedo) absorb it. Clearance of forests may alter Earth's albedo rating. More immediate is the measurable rise of CO_2 in the atmosphere, due to forest burning and industry. Global warming is predicted as a result, with dramatic changes in ocean levels and rainfall patterns.

Pollution over Mexico City.

Pollution

Succinctly described as "materials in the wrong place", pollution takes two forms. Quantitative pollution is the introduction of unnaturally high levels of a naturally occurring substance. The eutrophication of water by agricultural nitrate fertilizers is a good example. Qualitative pollution is the introduction of substances not normally occurring in the environment at all. Species have no natural defences against such chemicals as DDT, Dieldrin, and other insecticides, and the PCB's (polychlorinated biphenyls) used in plastics. Once in the food chain, they are biologically amplified - concentrated at each step up the chain, to hit hardest at the top predators (including, of course, ourselves). So too are some heavy metal pollutants such as mercury, which damage, vital organs. Our rate of noxious waste output is huge - the USA alone generates 250 million tonnes per year.

Total land area of planet
13.5 billion ha

Salination in Pakistan.

Risk of desertification

Moderate
High
Very high
Permanent hyper-arid
desert zones

Desertification

In many thousands of years of agriculture and pastoralism, humanity has not yet learned how to avoid land failure. Climates do change, of course. But we now understand that some apparent "acts of nature" are in fact triggered by human activity. Desertification is an ugly process. Fertile lands are overworked, or salinated by poor irrigation; forests are cleared, causing the water cycle to alter; arid lands are overgrazed and picked clean of every bush and leaf by pastoralists with nowhere else to go. Then the irreversible process of soil loss, drought, famine, and desertification begins. Today this process threatens a huge belt of lands across the tropical and subtropical zones totalling some 28% of the ice free land.

Hedgerow-cleared farmland, UK.

Genetic erosion

Three billion years have gone to create the diversity of life on this planet - not just the millions of species, but all the different races and strains and populations of each. This is the evolutionary capital on which life - and human civilization with it - draws to meet every new eventuality or opportunity. We need this store to find new medicines, foods, and products, or cross-breed our crops. We also need it as an insurance for all our futures.

Nature is complex, with mixed populations of much variety. But modern development prefers to simplify, planting monocultures of "improved" crops or trees across vast acres (see left) - easy to keep tidy and farm, but empty of diversity, and greatly vulnerable to disease or pests. Hundreds of traditional domestic crop and livestock strains are being lost, and wild populations everywhere reduced in number and range. The "gene-rich" areas, especially, need immediate protection.

33

Some animals and plants are more sensitive to overexploitation than others. These are usually species that have a long life span and breed more slowly - that is, have a low "reproductive potential". Whales and large tropical hardwood trees come into this category. They cannot recover their numbers at the rates needed to make their harvesting both sustainable and economical - yet it is these very species that are most desirable and so stimulate human greed.

Destruction and extinctions

Not only did the advances of civilization ignore how new wastes would be recycled within a local ecosystem and how the inputs and outputs would be handled, but also how an ecosystem (and those down the line) would respond when its "wild" living components were removed and whether it would work with substitutes. Loss of some species permits explosive population growth of others which then damage the environment; loss of pollinators and seed dispersers means loss of plants, including those harvested by humans. Substituting maize, say, for a patch of forest in the tropics reduces the quality of the soil and, if cultivation continues, it leads to permanent infertility and erosion. Excessive grazing by cattle and goats in regions that once supported numerous wild herbivores results in soil compaction and the proliferation of unpalatable vegetation.

There are possibly as many as ten million species of plants and animals making up the biosphere today, and it is estimated that if present trends in planet mismanagement continue, up to 20% of these could become extinct by the year 2000. As most of these species have not even been scientifically described, and those that have are still little studied, we do not even know what rôles they play in their ecosystems.

Regardless of whether species are of greater or lesser importance to the fabric of the ecosphere, each of them may hold a secret we would greatly benefit from knowing. Ironically, so much that is good in civilization (when used wisely) - our domestic crops and animals, medicines, textiles, technology, art and poetry - has been derived from or modelled on wild things, and new discoveries are constantly being made. The grave consequences of the erratic and rapid depletion of what is sometimes called the "genetic resource", the wild plants and animals that not only share the biosphere with us but also keep the Ark on its steady course, are only just now beginning to be realized.

And yet the depletion continues at an ever-increasing pace. Degradation and destruction of species' habitats are the primary cause, but, in addition, certain species are singled out for abuse. Overexploitation means that a local population or an entire species will be driven to extinction by a harvest that removes more individuals than can be replaced by natural processes. Many slow-breeding organisms such as whales have been reduced to numbers so low that it is doubtful whether they will ever recover. Even the species with great recuperative powers are not safe, like the passenger pigeon, now extinct, whose numbers once darkened the skies of North America and was an early casualty of "modern" harvesting methods. Nearly 400 species and subspecies of birds and mammals have died by our hand in the last 400 years.

How is it that we, supposedly the most intelligent creatures, have come to foul our own nest and kill the golden goose? Such maladaptive behaviour is not new, as the artefacts from Mesopotamia and the even older bones of the Pleistocene megafauna silently acknowledge from their corners in museums. Perhaps the people of those times can, like children, be forgiven for thinking that the resources of their surroundings were infinite and there for the taking. Today, there is little excuse.

What gives cause for hope is that ways and means actually do exist for human beings to meet all their needs and many of their comforts from a healthy, self-perpetuating biosphere. What is frustrating is that they are known by relatively few people on this planet of four and a half billion, understood by fewer and willingly employed by even less.

Stemming the tide

The carrying capacity of the planet for plants, animals and people is being steadily reduced by the current activities of one species, ourselves. Improvements to the human lot in life, both in countries where such development is well advanced and in those where it is at an early stage,

CASE STUDY
Spare the bat, enjoy the fruit

Tube-nose bat feeding.

Not all bats feed on insects or fruit. About 5% of the bat species of Africa, America and Asia do not hunt insects, but join them in a midnight feast of pollen and nectar. Nectar-eating bats have a long snout and a protrusible tongue with a brushy tip. Bat-pollinated flowers are large and strong, wide-mouthed and deep, and cannot be pollinated by insects.

Among the flowers pollinated by bats are bananas, breadfruit and guava. Another fruit that has recently entered the Western luxury market is the durian, whose strange flavour has acquired a gourmet following worth about $120 million a year to the region of Malaysia where it grows.

The bats that pollinate durian are small relatives of the fruit-eating bats called flying foxes. During the day vast numbers of them roost in caves near Kuala Lumpur, within flying distance of the coastal mangrove swamps. When not feeding on durian nectar, they rely on flowers in the mangrove swamps for food.

These durian-pollinating bats are under attack on two fronts. Drainage, reclamation and building are destroying the coastal swamplands, and with them the bats' major supplementary food source. Also, the bats' caves are being destroyed as the limestone is blasted for concrete works, although this aspect is now under a measure of control. However, the bats are already becoming scarce, and durian flowers are losing their pollinators. When the bats are finally destroyed, the durian will soon follow, and with it a sizeable local income.

CASE STUDY
Whales - on the brink of extinction

Nature is not inexhaustible. When the hunting or harvesting of an animal or plant species outstrips its rate of reproduction, that species begins to slide towards extinction. Some of the cases of extinction caused by humans' reckless predations are well known. The dodo, only plentiful in a small area, was easily wiped out. Even abundant species, like the passenger pigeon, can be exterminated by determined slaughter.

Among the species brought to the limits of survival by humans are the great whales. When whaling began there seemed to be no end to the numbers of these large mammals cruising the oceans of the world. Slow, easily caught "right" whales, hunted from small boats with hand lances, were the first to show signs of overhunting. As they became scarce, the old whaling industries of Iceland and New England foundered. The whalers had to act: so they developed faster boats and explosive harpoons, allowing them to catch the faster blue, fin and sei whales. Again, stocks were overhunted and the new industries that had grown up off the traditional hunting grounds of Norway, Iceland, the Shetlands and Ireland dwindled and died.

Whalers began to travel further afield in search of blue and fin whales, and soon the Antarctic populations were on the decline. The whaling industry, having changed its methods to overcome the consequences of its own greed, is again running short of quarry. Now there is hardly a whale species that is safe from extinction.

It is plain that extinction of whales will mean the end of whaling. But economics dictates that a kill today is money in the bank tomorrow. To the financiers, a whale tomorrow is merely a whale.

Only a few thousand blue whales now exist, out of a population that once exceeded 100,000. It is possible that these numbers might be too few now ever to recover. Even sperm whales, once caught at a rate of 30,000 a year, are now seen only in groups of ten or less. We know too little about many other species to predict their future.

Whales could have been exploited rationally, within their biological limits. Even without detailed knowledge of an animal's habits, the signs of decline are a clear-enough signal that overhunting is occurring. The world's living resources are too important to be left to the machinery of finance and commerce. Maintenance of future stocks can only be regulated by informed and disinterested bodies.

Whaling ship and whale kill on deck.

have been undertaken with one species as the sole reference point, while the proponents of "nature conservation" were at best allowed a desk in an underfunded weak governmental department, but usually regarded as crackpots and cranks with nothing of real value to contribute.

Occasionally, rulers or leaders of societies set aside pockets of wild lands and managed them well, but they were few and far between and did little to match the needs of people to the needs of nature. More often, priests, poets and thinkers reminded people of the realities of the ecosphere - from the Vedic scribes of India, who urged the planting of trees, and Plato, so worried about what was happening to the vegetation of the Mediterranean, to St Francis of Assisi, who ministered to the animals, and the 19th-century American writer, Henry David Thoreau, who asked, "What is the use of a house if you haven't got a tolerable planet to put it on?" On balance, their words were not heeded, but by the middle of the 20th century, such views were being listened to by an increasing number of people, who began to gather in local, national and international groups to press their governments to take action on environmental concerns. Certain successes have been achieved, like partial control over emissions of pollutants in the industrialized countries, the birth of networks of nature reserves in developing countries, and the slowing of international trade in endangered species. The word "conservation" no longer has an eccentric, reactionary ring to it, but is associated instead with safeguarding the natural resources of the planet. However, the rate of achievement of the new conservationists is far below the speed with which the carrying capacity of the planet is dropping.

Because environmental matters have always been "pigeonholed" in the minds of most people, there has never developed an infrastructure within any government capable of addressing the multiple abuses to the ecosphere - much less devising a rational strategy for working along with it rather than against it. Although it has become certain that each thread of the ecosphere is attached, tightly or loosely, directly or indirectly, to every one of their citizens, governments have lumbered along like old dinosaurs, with one brain for the head and another for the tail. Weak laws or no laws, poorly trained personnel or no personnel, bad planning or no planning, little information on priorities and management options, lack of coordination, and overall emphasis on short-term gain, while ignoring long-term loss, have stood in the way of integrating the operating principles of the ecosphere with the development of their people.

What is needed is a comprehensive, global strategy, and the will of people, from the subsistence farmer to the head of state, to implement it. The World Conservation Strategy was prepared by the International Union for the Conservation of Nature and Natural Resources (IUCN) and proposed to world governments in 1980. Its strategic aspect is embodied in the concept of "sustainable utilization of species and ecosystems" and in its concrete suggestions as to how people and governments can put the concept into practice. Its conservation aspect automatically follows the strategic one: the "maintenance of essential ecological processes and life-support systems", such as water cycles and soil vitality, and the "preservation of genetic diversity" - that is, the organisms that service the processes and systems, like native trees in a forest, those that provide goods directly, like wild animals of a savannah, and those that may one day do so, like the myriad denizens of coral reefs, just now being studied for their potential in medicine.

The Strategy has been discussed and accepted in principle by many countries, and a number of them have prepared National Conservation Strategies, modelled on the global one, but tailored to their particular ecosystems and development goals. Quite a few countries have begun to implement their Strategies, some with foreign assistance. In these early days of the new way of thinking about being a member of crew on the Ark, it has already become clear that the single most important key to success is the willing participation of the ordinary citizen.

CASE STUDY
Sebungwe, working for wildlife

The government of Zimbabwe is developing a wildlife management policy different from many others in the world today. Instead of rules from above, via laws and enforcement agencies, their system depends on fostering a responsible sense of good husbandry among the people who both carry it out and benefit from it.

The history of some regions in Zimbabwe is somewhat chequered. For example, the Sebungwe region is infested with tsetse fly. During attempts to control tsetse there in the first half of this century, 805,000 head of 36 mammal species were shot. Then an important breakthrough in tsetse control was made in 1963, when the four main hosts of tsetse were identified. These animals - warthog, bushpig, kudu and bushbuck - continued to be killed, together with elephant and buffalo, as agriculture struggled to survive.

Lack of success in agriculture, however, led to alternative land usage. In 1964 a game reserve was established at Charisa in the Sebungwe region. A study was set up to look into tsetse-vertebrate relationships. When this

became a hunting safari area in 1975, the income was allocated to neighbouring rural communities, and this has formed the basis for the present management plans.

The scheme is based on dividing the safari area into territories, each to be managed by a separate community. Farming in the territory will be encouraged by providing grants for gameproof fencing, which will free the game from being classed as "pests" and enable the community to manage game and farms separately. It is hoped that, by giving each community a "private" territory, with the chance to manage the wildlife there for profit, a sense of responsible management will develop.

One of the most powerful influences against sensible management of wild resources is the knowledge that, if one chooses to spare a particular animal or tree, someone else will probably come along and take it. In Charisa's allotted territories, however, the game is safe from all except the community to which it "belongs".

The Charisa Safari Area covers 170,000 square kilometres. It contains a

great deal of game, as well as a current elephant stock of about 9000. The elephants have been culled to protect the plant communities of the wildlife research area, and this has provided finance for the district council as well as some employment for local people. Safari hunting earned nearly $87,000 in 1981, and the sale of elephant products made over $400,000.

Setting up the scheme will be expensive, particularly establishing the gameproof farmlands which are crucial to the project's success. Each community will need about 50 kilometres of game fencing. When established, however, the enterprise should be self-financing and, most importantly, self-sustaining. The growing safari industry will benefit from increased game, and tourists will stimulate the economy by providing a market for hospitality, local artefacts and curios.

The people of forest regions used to live in harmony with wild animals. It is hoped that, in spite of increasing populations, schemes such as Sebungwe's will re-establish the creative and self-sustaining use of the wild.

Impala cull at Chiredzi, Zimbabwe.

38   *Tramserku, Himalayas, Nepal*

CHAPTER TWO

The State of the Wild

The pieces in the mosaic of wilderness that graces our planet today were shuffled around by the advance and retreat of the northern glaciers during the last two million years. Whenever the ice loomed large in Eurasia, the landscape became covered with tundra and steppe, and when the ice retreated, mixed forest grew instead. Vegetation of the equatorial continents reflected the fact that atmospheric moisture was locked up in vast ice-fields - the borders of deserts, savannahs and jungles expanded and contracted according to the whim of the glaciers.

Early humans, too, had a hand in rearranging the mosaic. Although they didn't produce their own food until the last glacial retreat, they hunted wild animals and gathered wild plants. They set extensive fires to drive game and to encourage the growth of certain plants, and their stone weapons and hunting skills were formidable.

The dates of the well-known extinctions of giant mammals in Africa, Europe, Australia and the Americas suspiciously coincide with the presence of these advanced hunters and gatherers, the wielders of fire and stone. The opponents of the "prehistoric overkill" theory say that climatic changes hastened the demise of the mammals and, anyway, humans at this stage in their history lived more or less in balance with nature. Whatever the answer, it's clear that the people of the Ice Age could profoundly affect their environment, both by altering habitats and overexploiting wildlife.

Still, the most devastating extinctions, those in North America, took over a millennium to complete, and 10,000 years ago there were no more than a few million people on Earth. Taken as a whole, the human species held stable at such numbers for quite a long time, limited by the way that available resources were used, wisely or unwisely. The planet was an untouched wilderness.

But by 500 years ago, human activities had made certain regions virtually unrecognizable - the forests of the Mediterranean were almost gone, with those of other parts of Europe heading the same way. Even in places like Madagascar and New Zealand, natural habitats had been drastically reduced. World human population had risen to 350 million. People had found a way to "create" resources by growing crops and keeping livestock - and so were able to elevate the carrying capacity of their environment. From their point of view, of course.

Quite expectedly, many plant and animal species suffered during this period, from the contraction of ranges in the larger regions, like wolves in Britain and Europe, to extinctions on the islands, like the giant lemurs of Madagascar and the moas of New Zealand.

The Age of Exploration again raised the human carrying capacity of the global environment. Timber, furs, new croplands and pasturage were found outside of Europe, and, correspondingly, human numbers

Life communities

Before we can effectively protect the living heritage of our planet, we must first map and understand its diverse communities, and assess their unique value in different regions.

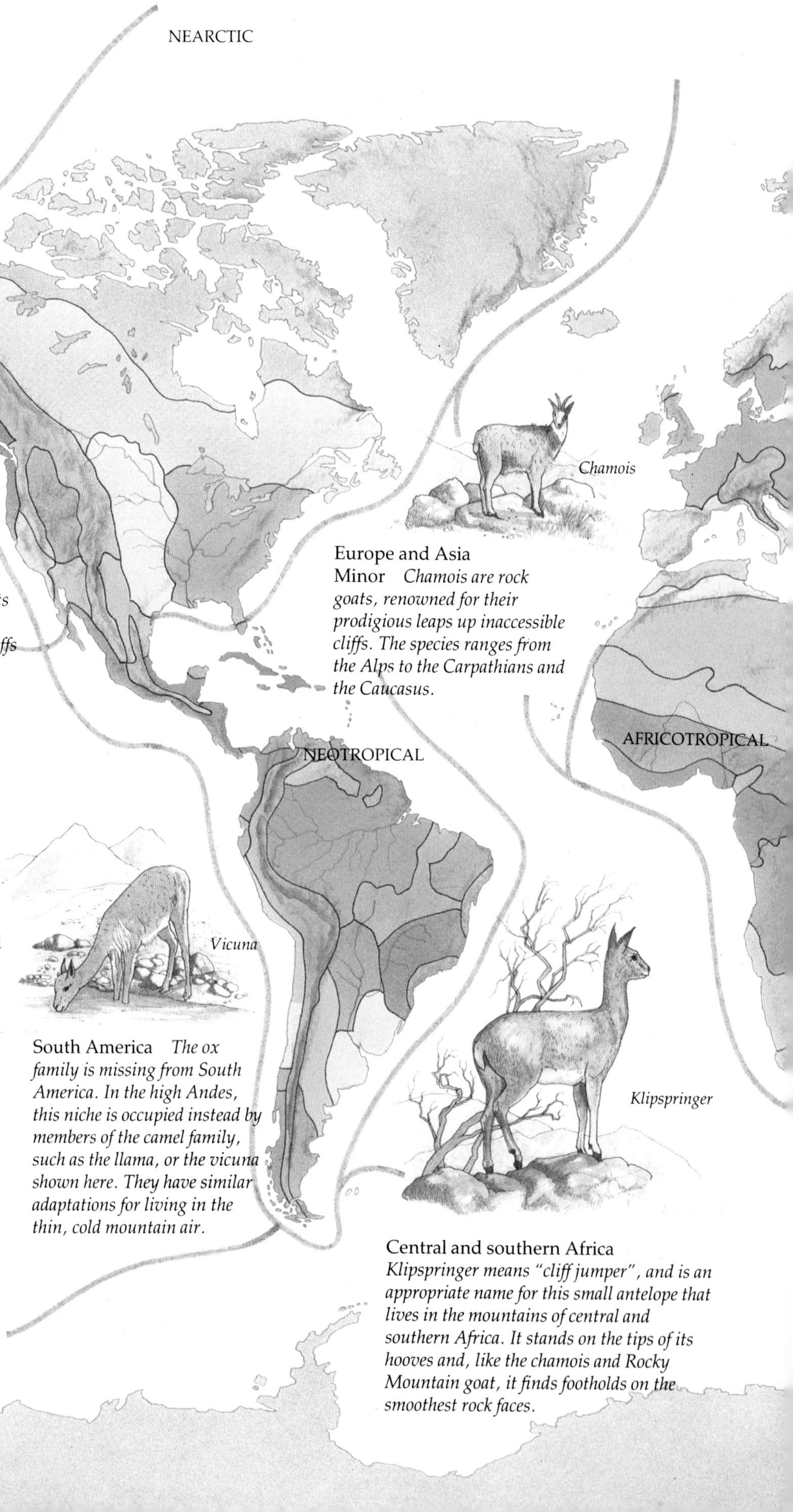

NEARCTIC

Rocky Mountain goat

North America *Rocky Mountain goats are not true goats but are related to the chamois. They live on steep slopes and cliffs and their hooves have hard sharp rims to give a good grip on rock and ice.*

Just as politics classifies the human world into states and cultures, so natural history divides the biosphere – the Earth's layer of living matter – into *biogeographic realms* (the map zones) and *biomes* (the map colours). The eight biogeographic realms – Nearctic, Palaearctic, Neotropical, Africotropical, Indomalayan, Oceanian, Australian and Antarctic – reflect the Earth's evolutionary history. In each realm, the plants and animals share a common history. A biome, on the other hand, is a major *type* of living community – a desert, say, or a rainforest. It may occur in various realms, wherever climate and terrain are similar. In different realms, the animals and plants of a biome will have different evolutionary histories, although they will broadly resemble each other because they will have adapted to similar conditions. The map illustrates this relationship by featuring the range of even-toed hoofed mammals (Artiodactyla) and their habitats from one biome in various parts of the world. All fill a similar niche in the mixed mountain biome.

Vicuna

South America *The ox family is missing from South America. In the high Andes, this niche is occupied instead by members of the camel family, such as the llama, or the vicuna shown here. They have similar adaptations for living in the thin, cold mountain air.*

Chamois

Europe and Asia Minor *Chamois are rock goats, renowned for their prodigious leaps up inaccessible cliffs. The species ranges from the Alps to the Carpathians and the Caucasus.*

NEOTROPICAL

AFRICOTROPICAL

Klipspringer

Central and southern Africa *Klipspringer means "cliff jumper", and is an appropriate name for this small antelope that lives in the mountains of central and southern Africa. It stands on the tips of its hooves and, like the chamois and Rocky Mountain goat, it finds footholds on the smoothest rock faces.*

Biomes are variously categorized by different systems. This map shows 14 biome types, distributed over the realms (after Udvardy). Conservationists are now trying to assess the unique value of each biome, in each realm, and the extent to which it is protected. The percentages given here are an approximate indication of that protection.

Key to biomes (plus percentage area protected)

Tropical humid forests (5%)

Temperate needleleaf forests or woodlands (3%)

Subtropical and temperate rainforests or woodlands (4%)

Tropical dry or deciduous forests (including monsoon forests) or woodlands (4%)

Temperate broadleaf forests or woodlands, and subpolar deciduous thickets (2%)

Evergreen sclerophyllous forests, scrubs or woodlands (3%)

Warm deserts and semi-deserts (2%)

Cold-winter deserts and semi-deserts (8%)

Tundra communities and barren arctic desert (11%)

Tropical grasslands and savannahs (1.5%)

Temperate grasslands (0.3%)

Mixed mountain and highland systems with complex zonation

Mixed island systems

Lake systems (0.2%)

PALAEARCTIC

INDOMALAYAN

OCEANIAN

Yak

Central Asia   *Although ungainly in appearance, the yak (a true ox) is surefooted and an expert climber. It is also very sturdy and is an invaluable beast of burden on the high plateaux of central Asia.*

Walia ibex

AUSTRALIAN

ANTARCTIC

Markhor

Northeastern Africa   *The Abyssinian or walia ibex lives at high altitudes, feeding on grass or lichens. One of the eight closely related forms of ibex distributed across the mountains of Europe, Asia and northeastern Africa, this species is critically endangered.*

Himalayas   *The markhor, a true goat of the northwestern end of the Himalayan chain, ranges up to 4000 metres in summer. Its habitat must include steep cliffs where it takes refuge when danger threatens, and it also avoids deep snow.*

The Alamo Hueco Mountains, located in one of the wildest parts of New Mexico and home to the desert bighorn sheep, is currently being recommended for oil and gas development by the Bureau of Land Management (BLM). To fight against this, and other proposals to open up large areas of New Mexico's remaining wild lands, the citizens of New Mexico have joined together as the New Mexico Wilderness Coalition. The coalition, which includes the New Mexico Wilderness Study Committee, Friends of the Earth, the Sierra Club and the Wilderness Society, is advocating the protection of 500,000 hectares of BLM wilderness – bringing the total protected area up to a mere 3.3% of the state.

rose to over 900 million by the 19th century. North America and Australia began to lose their natural habitats.

Finally, there came the ability to use vast amounts of energy to extract vital resources, but this was not energy of human origin, as before. The buried remains of ancient forests, compacted with the bodies of creatures dead for hundreds of millions of years to form coal and oil, began to fire the multitude of machinery we use today in the modern production, marketing and distribution of food - all of which should enable us to sustain our present population of over four and a half billion people.

Perhaps all this sounds like an extraordinary success story for *Homo sapiens*, who can now lay claim to having altered 35% of the land and affected even the remotest parts of the oceans. It isn't. Although we may think that our reliance on wild places is a thing of the past, it is not.

How much wild is left?

Even in the most recently published atlases, the vegetation maps are wrong. During the year such a book takes from being written to being sold in the shops, forest cover the size of England will have disappeared and a further area larger than Portugal will have become degraded. Natural grasslands and steppe, again the size of England, will have turned into artificial desert, millions of hectares of wetlands will have been drained or filled in, and more and more of our rivers, lakes and oceans will have been used as dustbins. Human beings are solely responsible for these depredations to the planet, and the long-term losses far outweigh the short-term gains.

The causes of loss of natural habitat are multifold. There are the big-time, hi-tech operations, like the clearance of Central American forests for pasturing "hamburger" cattle, and the almost overnight conversion of wetlands in the industrialized countries. There are small-scale activities, like the peasant who cuts and fires tropical forests only one hectare at a time (but along with 250 million other peasants) to grow food, and the herders who graze their few goats or cattle on marginal lands (along with millions of others), thereby promoting desertification. There are the insidious effects of certain industrial practices, such as the release of factory wastes high in the air where they acidify the rain that falls on the forests and into thousands of far-away lakes. And plain old urban sprawl puts nearly 500,000 hectares of land under buildings and tarmac every year in the developed countries.

Even so-called wilderness areas are not left alone. Millions more tourists a year pour through the national parks in North America and Europe than ever before, and disturbance to plant and animal life from trampling, litter and simple human presence is reaching alarming proportions in some places. Most parks and reserves in the developing countries are protected on paper only; financial priorities mean that their actual supervision is non-existent, and the activities of the small-scale cultivators, wood-cutters and poachers are taking their toll.

Throughout history, we have talked about "taming" the wild. Can we think we've been successful when we see the degradation, erosion, desertification, pollution - and human misery - our efforts have wrought?

Guardians of the planet

Given today's patterns in the Earth's climate, natural forest could be growing on about 40% of the land's surface. It is the most widespread and diverse kind of vegetation to have evolved on the planet, from the vast tracts of northern coniferous woods to lush equatorial jungles, from chaparral to "wildwoods" to cloud forests. More species of plants and animals live in forests than in all other ecosystems combined. Because forests are "tall", they offer many options for living quarters and feeding

CASE STUDY
Land use in the UK

Left to itself, most of Britain would become a vast forest as it was in King Arthur's day. But because farming has been the norm for so long in Britain, most people tend to think of Britain's "wild" in terms of the flora and fauna of field, pasture, hedgerow and covert.

Farming began to change the face of Britain thousands of years ago. As the population has grown, so has the area of land under cultivation. The Industrial Revolution meant more townspeople to feed; with fewer country people to grow the food, machines were needed to help. Since then, technology has become more sophisticated and the land has been dominated to a greater degree.

Up to about a hundred years ago, the changes brought about by farming were largely a matter of quantity. As more land was steadily cleared, the farmland habitats increased while woodlands decreased. More recently, however, the effect has become qualitative. Methods have changed drastically, reducing the land to little more than a sterile piece of blotting paper, sprinkled with seeds and chemicals.

There is no chance for wildlife in this "new agriculture". Not even the long-settled species of traditional farmland can cope with ever-larger fields smothered with herbicides and pesticides. The land itself is altered to suit the machines. Ponds and ditches are filled, drains are laid, hedgerows removed, to enable the huge machines to move easily. Technology is a powerful force. Used indiscriminately, it can utterly destroy the wild.

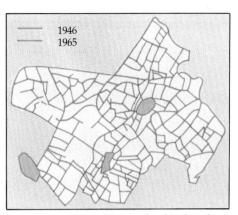

Three parishes in Huntingdonshire have lost 60% of their hedgerows between 1946 and 1965. Hedges are the last retreat of many woodland species. About ten million birds nest in Britain's hedgerows, still disappearing at a rate of 3000 km a year.

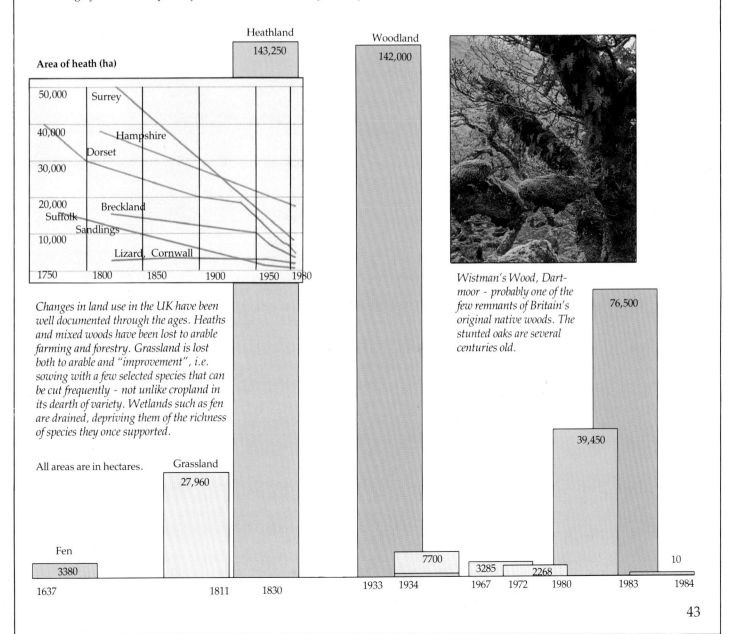

Changes in land use in the UK have been well documented through the ages. Heaths and mixed woods have been lost to arable farming and forestry. Grassland is lost both to arable and "improvement", i.e. sowing with a few selected species that can be cut frequently - not unlike cropland in its dearth of variety. Wetlands such as fen are drained, depriving them of the richness of species they once supported.

All areas are in hectares.

Wistman's Wood, Dartmoor - probably one of the few remnants of Britain's original native woods. The stunted oaks are several centuries old.

grounds, each differing in light, moisture, warmth and air flow according to height above ground, and a vast array of organisms have adapted to them. Tropical forests alone harbour over half the world's species, and during its lifetime, a single old English oak may have supported 300 different species.

Forests are also the greatest living producers of energy, the energy taken from sunlight which enables plants to grow. But the expectation that clearing a forest to get at the soil beneath will allow us to sustain equally productive crops on a long-term basis is a false hope, especially in tropical forests, for most of the nutrients are locked up in the bodies of the trees themselves and not in the soil.

In the long run, we stand to gain more in keeping the forests than in cutting them down. By retaining moisture, absorbing sunshine and clinging to the earth, they guard our climate and our supplies of water and fertile soil. When forests are cleared, water is lost by evaporation and run-off, which can alter regional patterns of rainfall and cause massive floods that wrench loose the soil, leading to erosion and sedimentation. More sunlight is reflected from land bared of its trees and from a "dusty" atmosphere (caused, among other things, by wind erosion after deforestation), which means less warmth for the planet. On the other hand, an increase in carbon dioxide in the atmosphere from the burning of forests and fossil fuels traps warmth. The interaction of these two phenomena is complex, and one does not simply cancel the other. In any case, major temperature changes could disrupt precipitation on a worldwide scale. The global effects of forest removal are still being disputed, but even small alterations in world temperature and moisture would have phenomenal impact on the current agricultural situation, and the economic and social consequences are almost unimaginable.

Also unimaginable is the steady loss of the denizens of the forests, for they are the source of so much of the materials, foods and medicines we rely on today, that we count on them being the source of more goods and services yet to be discovered. What is taken from forests each year is worth over a hundred billion dollars, but, unhappily, many forest products are not being extracted on a sustainable basis, and the loss of unknown species during this wasteful process is a certainty.

Better management and more reafforestation programmes are possible, but in today's economic mood, perhaps not probable. Saving forests by using them sustainably requires the re-education of massive numbers of people, from the stubborn controllers of the timber industry to the poor peasants who are, understandably, incapable of looking further than their own immediate hunger. The process is long and expensive. Is it being done and what is happening in the meantime?

Tropical moist forest has received a lot of "hype" from the media recently, as well it should, being the most diverse and threatened ecosystem on the planet. But had the press been around in Plato's time, it may have been just as vociferous about the loss of temperate forests.

Temperate forests

Outside the tropics, the type of forest depends on the seasonal interplay of temperature and moisture. The most northerly forest - the wide boreal belt of spruce, fir, pine and larch that encircles the globe like a tonsure - thrives on a long season of cold and snow. Much of this belt is still intact, but timbering for construction materials and pulp has severely depleted the most accessible parts in Western countries, and in Siberia Soviet scientists are worried about the effects of ill-considered cutting and flooding, and of acid rain.

To the south, where winters are warmer and shorter and rain falls more evenly throughout the year, grow the deciduous forests. But the variegated blanket of beech, maple, oak, poplar or hickory that covered the eastern parts of Asia and North America has become tattered and torn,

Top *Amazon rainforest.*
Bottom left *Wet sclerophyllous forest on the eastern slopes of the Great Dividing Range, New South Wales, Australia. Eucalypts and tree ferns predominate.*
Bottom right *Autumn mists in a beech wood in Ashridge, Hertfordshire, UK.*

Forests under threat

Human progress has been built on the ashes of forests since prehistory. Only when we suffer the effects of this destruction will we learn, too late, to protect the forests, the source of much of our wealth.

Before the development of agriculture, large areas of the planet were covered by forests of six major biome types. In the temperate north, thousands of years of human exploitation have taken their toll of the forests, although further major loss is now prevented by afforestation.

In many tropical countries, however, large-scale forest loss is accelerating, with some ten million hectares each year toppling to the ground. Rising human numbers consume wood faster than it can be grown, and create pressure to clear the forests for farming – a situation that is worsened by the resulting loss in soil fertility, with erosion, flooding and drought to follow. As the forests fall, so too do the indigenous cultures of thousands of forest peoples, along with countless species of plants and animals, many of which will become extinct and remain unknown to science.

Those countries giving cause for most concern are outlined in red on the map – at present rates of destruction, they will exhaust their forests by 2035.

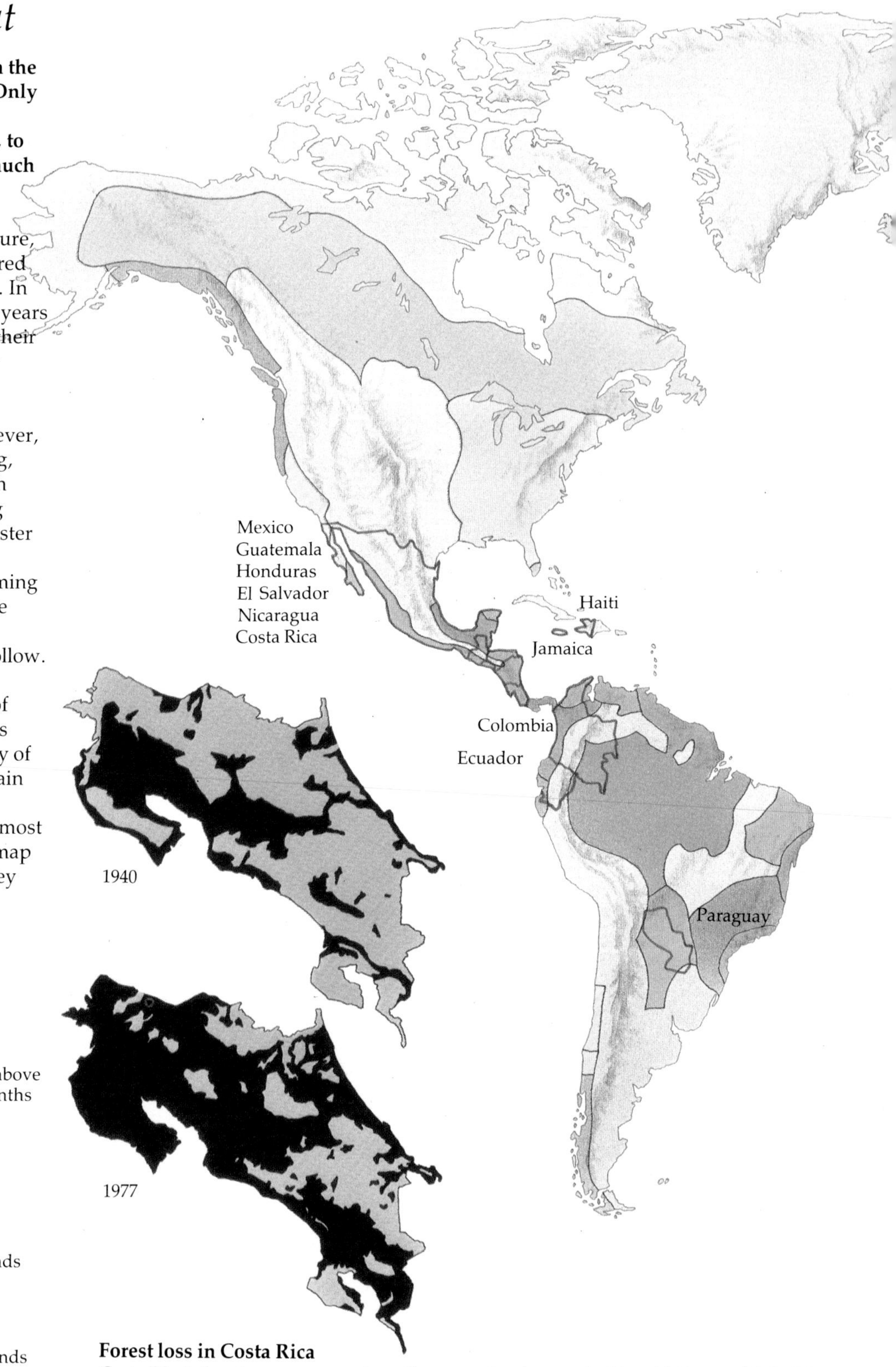

Mexico
Guatemala
Honduras
El Salvador
Nicaragua
Costa Rica

Haiti

Jamaica

Colombia

Ecuador

Paraguay

1940

1977

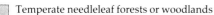 Tropical humid forest – annual rainfall above 2000 mm, dry season shorter than 2 months

Subtropical and temperate rainforests

Temperate broadleaf forests or woodlands

Temperate needleleaf forests or woodlands

Evergreen sclerophyllous forests, scrubs or woodlands

Tropical dry or deciduous forests or woodlands – annual rainfall above 1500 mm, dry season 2-3 months

Forest loss in Costa Rica

Costa Rica's forests possess an extraordinary diversity of life – in a single hectare, as many as 269 bird species have been recorded, and insects, amphibians and other animals may be equally abundant. Yet these forests are under threat – approximately 65,000 hectares are being cleared each year, many by cattle ranchers who are, according to Dr Gerardo Budowski, "turning forests into hamburgers". Since 1960, one-third of Costa Rica's forests have been felled to provide grazing land for cheap beef. Ranches have doubled in size, and beef exports have risen sevenfold.

The two maps, one by aircraft and the other by Landsat orbiting satellite, show forest loss in Costa Rica over 37 years.

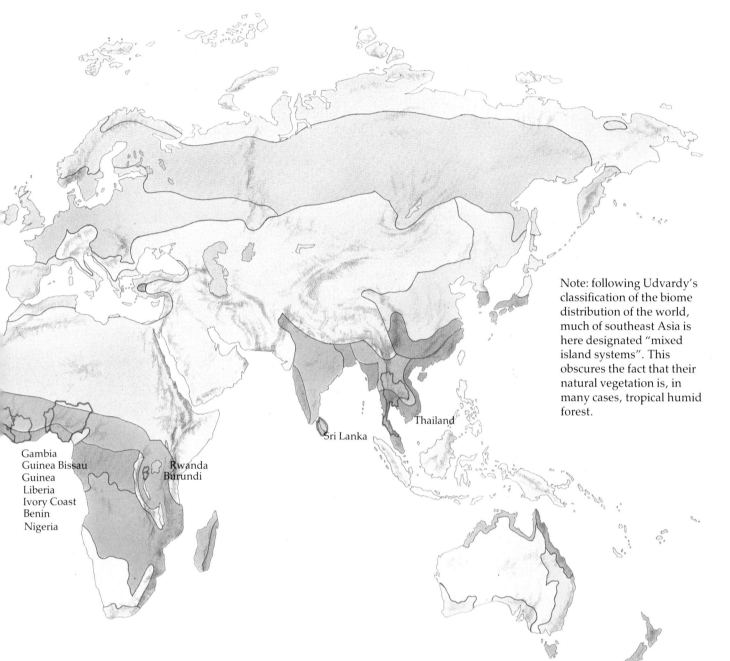

Note: following Udvardy's classification of the biome distribution of the world, much of southeast Asia is here designated "mixed island systems". This obscures the fact that their natural vegetation is, in many cases, tropical humid forest.

Thailand

Sri Lanka

Gambia
Guinea Bissau
Guinea   Rwanda
Liberia   Burundi
Ivory Coast
Benin
 Nigeria

Brazil (land area 846 million ha)

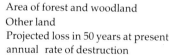
Area of forest and woodland
Other land
Projected loss in 50 years at present annual rate of destruction

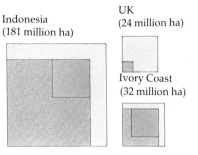

Indonesia
(181 million ha)

UK
(24 million ha)

Ivory Coast
(32 million ha)

A finite resource

Since World War II, we have witnessed the destruction of over half the world's rainforests. Forests which once blanketed almost entire countries have been reduced to a fraction of their former extent.

Forest loss is by no means uniform around the world. Countries such as Brazil and Indonesia, while undergoing heavy annual losses, will still have huge areas of forest in 50 years' time. It is the smaller countries such as the Ivory Coast and Costa Rica (see left) which will feel the effects of deforestation most keenly.

The UK, with only 8% of its land covered by forest, is shown as an example of the fate that has already befallen much of the temperate forests.

and the great beech and oak forests that stretched in a broad wedge from western Europe to the Urals lie in fragments, although there remain large segments towards the east.

In temperate regions where the winters are mild and wet and summers are hot and dry, a peculiar sort of dwarf forest known as chaparral can be found. Southern California, the South African Cape, parts of Chile and southwestern Australia still feature this forest, but the most extensive tract, around the Mediterranean basin, was destroyed long ago by ancient civilizations - indeed, Plato compared the landscape he knew to the skeleton of a body wasted by disease.

A total lack of disturbance in a forest ecosystem is unnatural. In the boreal forests, periodic fires stimulate new growth, while treefalls in deciduous forests open the way for light-loving herbs and shrubs and the creatures associated with them. Even some human interference is not necessarily counterproductive in terms of species richness. A large tract of maple forest in eastern Canada that had not been disturbed for 200 years was found to have less species diversity than other maple forests subjected to a certain amount of cutting, burning, grazing and fragmentation, and surprisingly, no rarities were discovered hiding there. Moderate fragmentation of an extensive forest simply allows one set of species to replace another at the forest edges, enhancing the species richness of the region.

Rapid, wholesale destruction of any forested region means environmental disaster and the irrevocable loss of species, but the relatively protracted clearance of temperate forests at least yielded a robust soil capable of supporting crops for longer than tropical soils and reverting to natural vegetation more quickly. Also, at least under feudalism in Europe some "conservation" was practised, in that certain tracts of forest were preserved for the hunting rights of the privileged few. Later, while even more land was cleared and more timber taken for ship-building and smelting of ore, certain forests were managed communally as self-renewing resource bases.

Inevitably local timber became scarce, and Europeans turned elsewhere for supplies, as later did the North Americans and then the Japanese. This gave them the time to develop and implement good forestry practices and reafforestation programmes. Although most of the primeval deciduous forests of temperate zones are lost forever, it is likely that by the year 2000 North America will be only marginally less wooded than it is today and Europe and Japan will gain slightly.

These happy figures do not, however, reflect the quality of the forests in terms of the numbers of native species. Reafforestation usually means the planting of quick-growing single-species stands of exotic trees, and such uniformity severely reduces the diversity of native plants and animals. Also single-species stands are inherently vulnerable to sudden, catastrophic loss by a single disease or pest, and the long-term effects of some exotics on soil quality are detrimental.

Still, any forest cover steadies the climate and prevents erosion, so the countries in the temperate zones are not faring too badly. It's tragic, though, that their fortune, which was having enough time to learn proper forest management while not running out of agricultural land and timber, has now turned out to be the misfortune of the countries of another region, the tropics.

Tropical forests

Since the beginning of the century, the forest cover in temperate zones has remained the same, whereas in the tropics it has been reduced by half. Most of the environmental tragedies in tropical countries - flood, drought, famine, fire and desertification - can be linked directly or indirectly to the loss of forests.

Lessons learned from the abuse of temperate forests are misleading when applied to the tropics, because the forests are so different.

CASE STUDY
Forestry threatens wildlife

White-backed woodpecker

The wild reindeer of Finland and North America (where they are known as woodland caribou) are being threatened by modern forestry. Reduced to herds of some 600 and 20 individuals respectively, their mixed forest habitat is being severely reduced by logging.

In Finland, a programme of help is now under way, which entails leaving some old forest areas alone and allowing others to make new sapling growth as a diet supplement for the reindeer. Where their numbers are too low, the woods are being restocked with corral-bred reindeer. In North America, the species has been listed as endangered in an emergency ruling, and efforts are being made to preserve its habitat and reduce poaching.

In Sweden, loss of highland deciduous forests has already caused the extinction of the middle-spotted woodpecker, and another species, the white-backed woodpecker, is down to 50 pairs. New legislation to protect the wooded pastureland favoured by this and other species will hopefully reverse the decline. Hollow trees, too, are to be given special protection for the sake of the birds that nest in them.

The plight of the reindeer, caribou and woodpeckers has been noticed, but the status of many species is unknown. It is inevitable that more will be lost before forestry management is based on a sound understanding of ecological principles.

CASE STUDY
Poland's primeval forest

Hard by the Soviet border, the Bialowieza National Park was once an ancient hunting ground for Polish royalty. It has been a protected area since 1921 (not counting an interruption during World War II), which is why so much of its original fauna has survived.

The central "core" of the forest reserve, an area of 47.4 square kilometres, is protected by a buffer zone, 10-20 kilometres wide, of managed forest. It is thus isolated from the activities of people, including farmers. A few rides are kept clear, to permit limited access by scientists, but otherwise the forest is left to manage itself as it has done since the Ice Age.

The forest even has its own climate. The tall, dense trees cut down the effects of wind. Humidity is high and temperature fluctuates only slowly so that snow lies longer here than in the surrounding countryside.

The richness of the wildlife is a vivid reminder of what has been lost from the rest of Europe. Although most of the forest's 81 species of trees and shrubs still exist elsewhere, their size and shape are striking. Pine, oak and ash grow to heights of 45 metres, and their huge trunks, supported by buttress-like structures, are often more reminiscent of tropical than temperate forests. As the trees fall, the earthen discs created

European bison or wisent survived in the Bialowieza Forest until the disturbances of World War I destroyed all the remaining wild populations of these beasts. A few animals still existed in a number of European zoos, and six of them were gathered into a reserve in the Bialowieza Forest in 1929. The herd now roaming the forest contains over 200 individuals.

by the huge root plates are utilized as nest-sites by many of the forest's 228 species of birds - a behavioural phenomenon not observed in the same species in "modern" woods.

Among the mammals there are lynx, wolf, wild boar, elk, red deer and roe deer. Some animals, such as the wild cat, brown bear, flying squirrel and European mink, have disappeared during the last 300 years, as they have in many other places. But the greatest triumph of all has been the reintroduction of the European bison.

The unique value of this ancient tract of woodland has not gone unnoticed in Poland. Since the early 1920s, the forest has been used for research, and three permanent scientific institutions are now established there. The forest has also achieved international acclaim as a habitat which so far seems to have escaped human intervention.

"Rainforests", the ever-moist, ever-growing jungles, wealthier in species than any other ecosystem and crowned by an unbroken canopy of leaves, are many millions of years older than temperate forests. But they are cushioned by less soil, for the nutrients released by decomposition of forest "litter" are absorbed immediately by the trees' roots to sustain growth in the perpetual summertime. The forests act like sponges, too, soaking up rain and "breathing" it out gradually through their leaves. Clouds form and the rain falls again.

Paradoxically, this powerhouse of an ecosystem is difficult to start up again, once it's been shut down. When a patch of temperate deciduous forest is cleared, it will regrow to maturity in 200 years, but when an equal area of rainforest is destroyed, it will take 400 years for its myriad components to reassemble themselves. This is because the rainforest comprises a multitude of species, whose individuals are very sparsely distributed. In the tiny state of Brunei, for example, grow 2000 species of trees, whereas in Holland, seven times larger, there are only 30, and yet in Brunei one may have to search through a whole hectare of forest to find one specimen of a particular species. Furthermore, rainforest trees are not very good "travellers". The pollen and seeds of many temperate species are dispersed by the wind, but rainforest trees depend on animals as carriers. Therefore, unless the cleared patch of land is small and surrounded by intact forest, it will wait a very long time for the arrival of the kinds of seeds and animals needed to bring it up to maturity.

The diversity of life that is the essence of rainforest is both its strength and its weakness. The forest copes marvellously with the "little deaths" wrought by a single tree falling, or even by a small family clearing a half hectare of land to farm for a season or two and then moving on, leaving a "forest fallow". The pioneer plants rush in and hold the soil, and the secondary-stage species and their associated animals are there ready to follow. If one species is absent, there is always another to take its place. Given time, the surrounding forest slowly closes over its wound.

Some people in temperate countries claim that their forests have been saved by their own cleverness and hard work, and that lack of such in the tropics is to blame for the present situation there. What arrogance! All people need food, fuel and building material, and this century's attack on tropical forests to procure them is no more than the attack on temperate forests in earlier centuries. The difference is that, for economic and political reasons, methods of sustainable use of tropical forest resources at the high levels required by the now millions of people (not just those living in the tropical regions, but in temperate countries as well) are not yet widely applied.

Of the two billion inhabitants of the tropical countries, only a tiny fraction (including the governments) own most of the land. The hemmed-in poor practise shifting cultivation in such staggering numbers that they are responsible for nearly half of the forest destruction, be it of undisturbed, logged-over or secondary forest. The opening of vast, virgin areas for resettlement is not a solution: the millions of small farmers moved under the Brazilian and Indonesian programmes have mostly failed because of the poverty of forest soils. Furthermore, the only fuel available to the poor is wood, and they burn eight times as much as is taken for industrial purposes. Damage by collecting fuelwood is particularly acute in the drier, open forests of the tropics, as is grazing and the seasonal fires set deliberately to stimulate growth of fodder.

And who is responsible for the rest of the destruction and degradation? Developers and timber and cattle barons, both foreign and local, are always smiling at the elbows of governments of developing countries, often by invitation. They clear the forests to build roads and settlements, extract wood or create pasture. Between 1950 and 1980 the importation of tropical timber by Japan, Europe and the USA increased sixteen-fold; since 1950 two-thirds of the forests of Central America have been cleared, much of it to pasture cattle destined to become North American hamburgers.

True rainforest covers about half of the still-intact forested regions of the tropics. The rest, like the wooded savannahs of Africa and the "cerrado" of Brazil (above), is subject to a periodic dry season. The longer the season, the more scattered the trees and the grassier the ground cover. Tropical woodlands are no less fragile than rainforest but they experience an added burden of excessive burning, grazing and cutting for firewood. Soil exhaustion, erosion and, eventually, desertification, follow.

CASE STUDY
Sinharaja - Sri Lanka's last wet-zone forest

The unique Sinharaja Forest of Sri Lanka is under siege. When it was originally classified as a wet-zone forest reserve, it was about 10,000 hectares in extent. No special protection measures were introduced then, and the forest's existence was noted but not assured of any future.

By 1959, nearly 2750 hectares had been nibbled away around the forest fringes by the normal processes of traditional agriculture. In the interior, cane cutting, illegal mining for gemstones, tapping palm tree flowers for the sap to make a sweet liquor called jaggery, and collection of oils and resins from living trees were causing great damage. This depredation was joined by frank government exploitation when logging concessions were granted in 1972. Thirty-two kilometres of roadway were cut to provide access for mechanized logging operations, and nearly 1400 hectares of forest were felled. Incidentally, many forest animals were killed to feed the work force.

Policies changed, however, and the felling ceased in 1977. Only 5600 hectares of forest remained undisturbed by then. In 1978 about 2000 hectares of this untouched forest was declared a Man and Biosphere reserve (see p.84), and is now managed for protection with emphasis on scientific research.

As well as being the only extensive wet lowland forest left in Sri Lanka, the

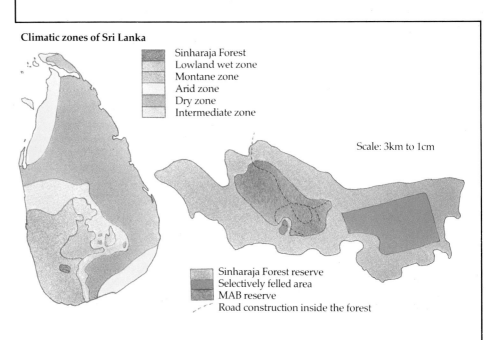

Climatic zones of Sri Lanka

Sinharaja Forest
Lowland wet zone
Montane zone
Arid zone
Dry zone
Intermediate zone

Scale: 3km to 1cm

Sinharaja Forest reserve
Selectively felled area
MAB reserve
Road construction inside the forest

Sinharaja Forest may prove to be a living relic of the ancient forests of Gondwanaland. Sri Lanka became an island millions of years ago, and its forests have been cut off from the mainland of India ever since. Evolution on islands tends to follow its own course, and over 25% of the Sri Lankan flora is unique to the island. Of 143 different tree species that have been identified in the forest, well over half are endemic. Furthermore, these endemics comprise a large proportion of the dominant trees in the forest, thus representing an important gene pool.

So far only the trees have been systematically studied, but it is almost certain that there will be a high proportion of endemics among the shrubs and herbs. Many locally cultivated plants are related to wild species found in the Sinharaja; hence these wild plants could be used to improve the disease resistance and yield of the cultivated strains. As for the potential medicinal value of the endemic plants, investigation hasn't even started.

The fauna of the forest should not be overlooked. Out of 103 species of birds there, 18 are endemic and at least three of these are in danger of extinction. Of the 15 mammals endemic to Sri Lanka, more than half live in the Sinharaja Forest. The forest is also home for the increasingly rare leopard, as well as elephants.

The Sinharaja Forest is also an important watershed. Two main rivers are fed by streams arising within it, and when logging was in progress the inevitable soil erosion was plainly visible in the muddied waters of these rivers.

There is great interest in conserving the forest among the people of Sri Lanka. Its importance as an economic resource and as a natural phenomenon is appreciated by the eight "amateur" environmental organizations there as well as an equal number of government establishments more or less concerned with conservation. It was partly due to pressure from these bodies that the tree-felling was stopped in 1977. Increasing understanding of the forest and its inhabitants will be of enormous benefit to the people and the economy of Sri Lanka.

Two residents of the Sinharaja, the purple-faced langur (right) and the Ceylon jungle fowl (below), are both endemic to Sri Lanka. The purple-faced langur has been classified as vulnerable.

The governments of the debt-beleaguered countries, where most of the tropical forests are found, seem to view their forest resources as a "licence to print money". But selling off the forests is the governments' short-term gain and the countries' long-term woe, for virtually none of the money is put to renewal or replacement - for every ten trees felled, only one is replanted - nor into compensating the people for the environmental disasters that always follow.

Figures for the overall rate of destruction of tropical forests have been much in dispute recently, not least because of the many ways to define "destruction" and even "tropical forests". They range from six million to an astounding 29 million hectares a year. At the latter rate, not a scrap of natural forest would be left in the tropics by 2050. Whatever the real figure, it's clear that the rates and causes of forest destruction are extremely variable in the tropics, and that some places are indisputable "hotspots", certain to lose all their forests within 15 years unless something is done.

Saving the tropical forests

Probably land reform would save the tropical forests, but this is not an option, for the forests are disappearing faster than present economic and political policies regarding land ownership can constructively change. Improvements in agriculture to obtain higher yields from land already under cultivation would take some pressure off the forests, but people, both in developing and developed countries, still need what these forests can provide.

The issue is not saving the forests untouched, but ensuring that they are utilized as a self-renewing resource, with all that this means for the future: a steady supply of forest products, and the stabilization of climate, soil and water. The technology for such self-sustainable use exists.

One branch of this technology, agroforestry *(see left)*, is centuries old and can be applied with great long-term productivity on land deemed marginal for intensive agriculture. Another branch, that of commercial logging, from which the income is crucial to many tropical countries, need not be destructive nor wasteful. Of course, the wood-pulpers and clearfellers must go, but light, selective logging, if done properly, seems to have much less adverse effect on the environment and diversity of species than previously thought, especially if the usual corollaries of logging - the influx of cultivators and hunters - can be controlled. Furthermore, revenues from processing the timber in the country that's selling it rather than sending it raw to the buyer are potentially enormous. In the long term, the costs of ousting the pulpers and clearfellers will be more than offset by lessening environmental damage and increasing direct revenue and jobs. Finally, modern plantation forestry offers hope for reducing pressure on virgin forest while meeting the world's ever-increasing demand for tropical wood products.

The horrifying devastation of the tropical forests has already been shown to be unnecessary by the sensitive applicaton of the techniques outlined above. Surely governments can insist that they be more widely applied for the sake of the future?

Grasslands

Like forests, natural grasslands once flourished on 40% of the Earth's land surface, but today only half of them remain, reduced by hoof and by plough. Prairie, pampas, savannah and steppe used to lie in the zone where rainfall is too little to support the growth of big trees and too much to give way to desert, but where the climate is just right for starting fires. Curiously, of all the world's ecosystems, the climate associated with grasslands is the most variable, but the integrity of grasslands is maintained by two factors - the prevalence of fire and the presence of a

The Lua tribe of Thailand, the Chagga of Tanzania and many others have long prac-tised "agroforestry" – a land-use system which involves growing trees and food crops alongside each other. The variety of plants meets all their needs for food, fuel, fodder and building, and the manure from their animals is used for fertilizer. They also grow nitrogen-fixing plants to enrich the soil and commercial plants, like coffee, to bring in some cash. Meanwhile, the natural forest is left to do its job of keeping the soil moist and in place, buffering the spread of pests and disease and providing traditional medicines. Native animals abound, protected by local custom.

CASE STUDY

New forestry practices in the tropical regions

The human race is ever increasing, and the areas left for exploitation are ever decreasing. If the world's rainforests are not going to be totally destroyed in this race for resources, some way must be found to use them on a sustainable and rational basis.

Selective cropping of forest resources seems, in theory, to be a sensible, sensitive and intelligent use of resources compared to the total destruction of clearfelling. Whether it will serve the interests of both conservation and industry still remains to be proved, however. The main damage caused by such methods has often been accidental. During the felling and removal of chosen timber, a great deal of damage is caused to the trees left standing. Wide paths also have to be cleared for the passage of machinery and felled timber. Thus, even taking a few trees will cause widespread damage to the surrounding forest.

Another massive effect is the reduction of the forest canopy. A field study in Malaysia showed that taking 18 timber trees per hectare actually caused a loss of 50% of total tree cover, with serious consequences for many tree-dwelling primates. Not only was their food supply drastically reduced, but their travelling arrangements were also badly disrupted. With time, however, certain species were able to recover their populations, although these creatures tended to be more flexible in their dietary habits that other, more specialist feeders.

Regarding the survival of the forest itself, selective logging is still a potentially destructive operation. The introduction of light and air is bound to change the nature of the forest, and whether it can regenerate depends very greatly on how carefully the assault is planned and carried out in the first place. In Queensland, Australia, experiments have shown a number of procedures that can help to lessen the long-term effects of selective logging. The use of vehicles with large rubber tyres helps to prevent soil compaction; but even these can only be used in the dry season, as any vehicle will crush the soil structure if it is wet. Passage through the forest is limited to a few marked paths, and the rate of logging is matched precisely to the rate at which new growth can follow.

Forests can also be helped to regenerate after felling damage by replanting some important species. In

Plantation of obeche trees in the Ivory Coast. Plantations of this fast-growing indigenous hardwood can help take the pressure off virgin forests in West Africa.

fact, in some places where the forest cover has already been irreparably damaged, replanting can be a source of new timber that could take the pressure away from virgin forest land. If a new plantation is carefully mixed it will grow into a forest of sorts - not as rich a habitat as the true forest, but by no means useless to wildlife and a great deal more useful than a single-species plantation.

Softwoods have been grown in tropical areas for a long time. These serve to provide pulp and firewood, and take some pressure off the virgin forests. But much of the commercial value in the tropical forest is found in the exotic hardwoods. These slow-growing species have proved more difficult to replace, but

now new techniques using rooted cuttings are bringing hope for future plantations.

Given the high rate of degradation and destruction of tropical forest, these measures are urgently needed. Plantations are so far only established at a rate of one hectare for every four lost in Asia (the best) or one hectare for every 35 lost in West Africa (not the worst). This must be very greatly improved if we are to have any hope of preserving our tropical forests.

Open lands

Open lands range from the tundras of the Arctic to the deserts of the tropics.

Between these two extremes lie the grasslands which sustain the world's human population by providing agricultural land. But they are in danger of destruction by overexploitation. As human numbers increase, the area of arable land per capita decreases.

Tundra *During the short Arctic summer, the tundra blossoms and many birds and mammals breed. But it is too cold, dry and infertile to be exploited except by nomadic reindeer herders.*

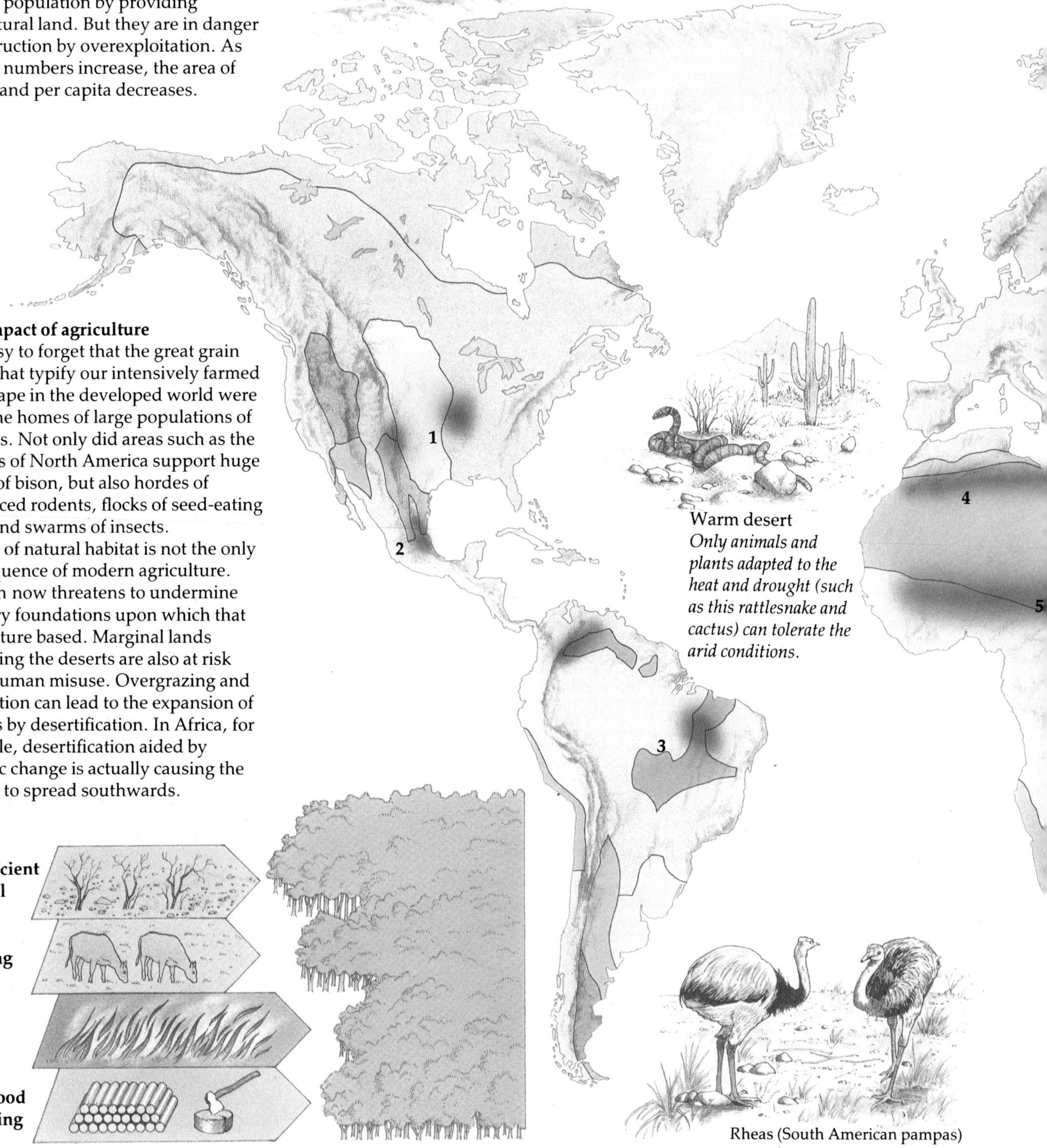

The impact of agriculture

It is easy to forget that the great grain lands that typify our intensively farmed landscape in the developed world were once the homes of large populations of animals. Not only did areas such as the prairies of North America support huge herds of bison, but also hordes of unnoticed rodents, flocks of seed-eating birds and swarms of insects.

Loss of natural habitat is not the only consequence of modern agriculture. Erosion now threatens to undermine the very foundations upon which that agriculture based. Marginal lands bordering the deserts are also at risk from human misuse. Overgrazing and cultivation can lead to the expansion of deserts by desertification. In Africa, for example, desertification aided by climatic change is actually causing the Sahara to spread southwards.

Warm desert
Only animals and plants adapted to the heat and drought (such as this rattlesnake and cactus) can tolerate the arid conditions.

Insufficient rainfall

Grazing

Fire

Fuelwood gathering

Rheas (South American pampas)

Why do open lands occur?

Natural open lands are mainly the result of low rainfall preventing the growth of trees, but they can also occur where the existing woodland has been destroyed by fire or grazed by animals. These are natural processes. However, people can and do increase open land by excessive burning, overgrazing and cutting for fuel.

Temperate grassland *These grasslands are found in the interior of continents. They include the prairies, steppes, pampas, veld and Australian downlands, which are now the world's great grain lands.*

Musk ox (Arctic tundra)

Tropical grasslands and savannahs

Temperate grasslands

Warm deserts and semi-deserts

Cold winter (continental); deserts and semi-deserts

Tundra communities and barren arctic desert

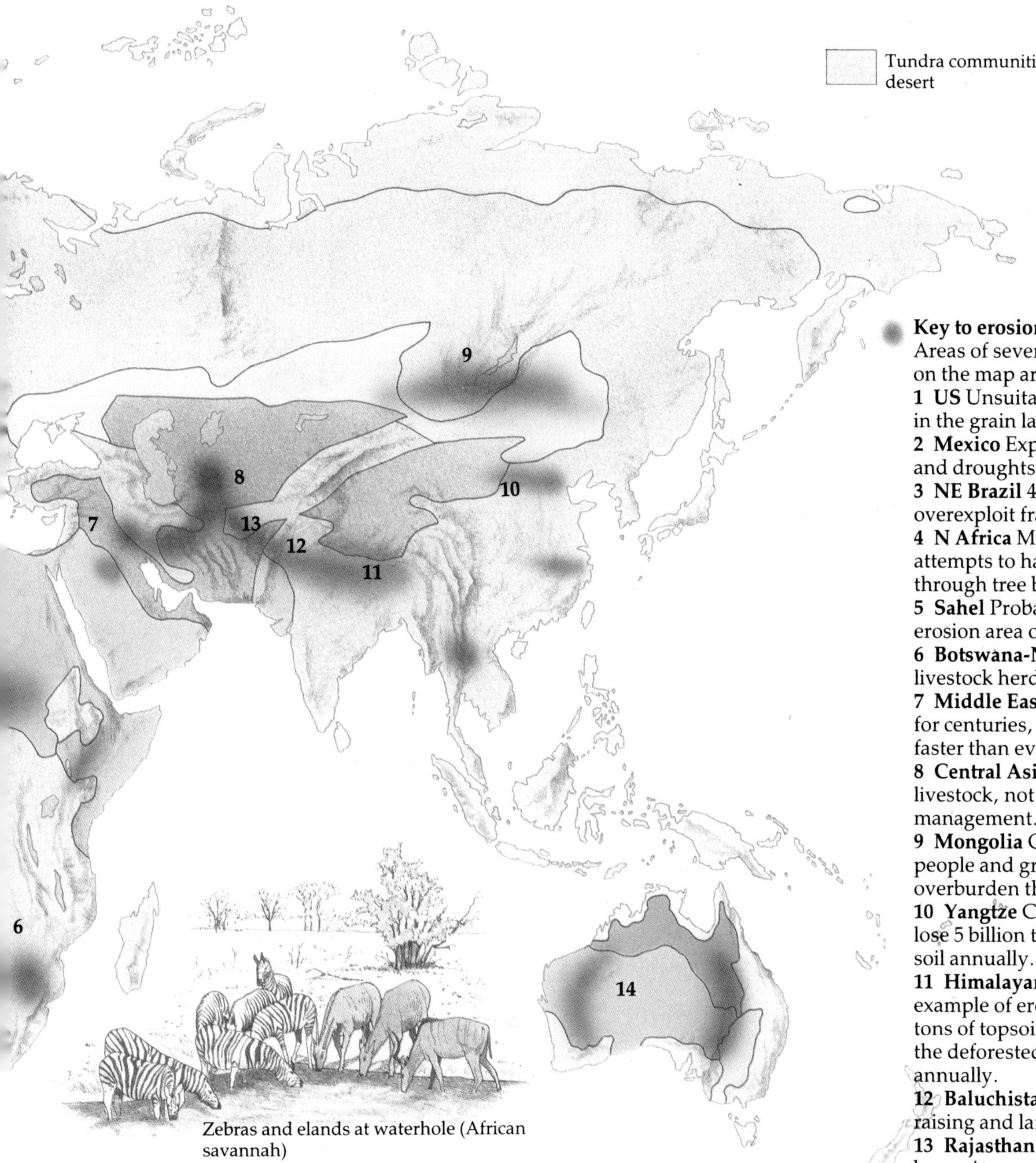

9

8

7

10

13

12

11

6

14

Key to erosion hotspots
Areas of severe erosion marked on the map are listed below.
1 US Unsuitable pressure on soils in the grain lands.
2 Mexico Experiencing erosion and droughts
3 NE Brazil 40 million people overexploit fragile lands.
4 N Africa Much erosion, despite attempts to halt the desert through tree belts.
5 Sahel Probably the worst wind erosion area on Earth.
6 Botswana-Namibia Excessive livestock herds accelerate erosion.
7 Middle East Erosion, a problem for centuries, now spreading faster than ever.
8 Central Asia Again, too many livestock, not enough management.
9 Mongolia Growing numbers of people and growing herds overburden the environment.
10 Yangtze China is reported to lose 5 billion tons of fine "loess" soil annually.
11 Himalayan foothills The worst example of erosion – 250,000 tons of topsoil are washed off the deforested slopes of Nepal annually.
12 Baluchistan Traditional stock-raising and large herds to the damage.
13 Rajasthan Droughts are becoming a permanent phenomenon.
14 Australia Long droughts, sometimes aggravated by excessive numbers of stock.

Zebras and elands at waterhole (African savannah)

Tropical grassland *Tropical grasslands lie between the desert and tropical forest zones. They have distinct wet and dry seasons. The wildlife, which must survive drought or migrate to find permanent water, often lives in huges herds or flocks.*

Cold desert *The cold deserts of central Asia, Patagonia and the great basin of North America are similar to the tundra in being too cold and dry for much of the year.*

Onager (Gobi desert)

55

vast number and kind of wild grazing mammals, which for sheer weight have no parallel in any other terrestrial situation. On migration, the herds of bison in North America, of wildebeest in Africa and of saiga in Asia were often described as limitless, passing a campsite for days in an uninterrupted flood. The smaller herbivores - the rodents, rabbits, grasshoppers and ants - are no less profuse.

It seems unnatural that an ecosystem should thrive under such treatment as the eating and the burning of its vegetation. And yet it does. Fires set by dry lightning sweep through the parched grasses, burning off any woody seedlings. The roots, stems, buds and seeds of the grasses and other soft plants lie safely beneath the mulch or soil, storing enough moisture and energy with which to start the growing season, stimulated by the elements released from the charred remains of their predecessors. Then, the wild hoofed animals graze, each species with slightly different food preferences so that no one plant loses out to another - except the woody seedlings, of course, relished by most wild herbivores. The ubiquitous burrowers enrich the vegetation by constantly turning over and fertilizing the soil.

If grasslands evolved under a regime of fire and grazing, then why is the practice of deliberate burning to promote pasturage for livestock so detrimental? The reason is less the burning itself than our lack of attention to the finer points of grassland ecology. Indeed, burning at the right season does make the grass grow, but it's all of a green illusion if it encourages *over*grazing. The great and varied herds of wild ungulates are migratory, which allows the pastures to recover during their absence, but domestic hoofed stock is usually confined to one place. The succulent grasses preferred by the few species humans keep are destroyed and replaced by less palatable plants, and trampling causes increased water run-off which desiccates and erodes the soil. Because there is now little tinder to burn, there are fewer fires to stop the encroachment of hardy scrub. In the more arid regions of the world, desertification sets in, particularly in Africa, but also in parts of North America, Eurasia and Australia.

The other main cause of the loss of natural grasslands is outright destruction in order to put the fertile soil under cultivation. I recently visited the Ukraine in the USSR, and looked over a fence surrounding 100 square kilometres of virgin land filled with waving feather grass. That's what's left of the steppe in *all* of Eurasia after centuries of cultivation. Canada and the USA went under the plough much more recently, but two-thirds of the Canadian prairies are gone, and America has lost almost half. Most of the large wild mammals exist in pathetic relict populations, with the notable exceptions of the Eurasian saiga and North American bison, saved at the eleventh hour by conservationists.

Of course, the world is grateful for these breadbaskets, but the Soviets' is much depleted, judging from what they have to import, and although America's is kept topped up today by expensive fertilizers, pesticides and irrigation works, the degree of soil erosion - which reduces annual productivity in one-third of the croplands - is alarming. Surely these wealthy countries could have used their grasslands more wisely.

Deserts

True deserts occupy about one-seventh of the Earth's land surface. They lie in regions that are naturally devoid of moisture, where the air is so cold or so far from the oceans it carries little rain, or where the rain is deflected by high pressure weather systems or mountain ranges. But land can be artificially deprived of moisture by removing its vegetation, and in the dry areas bordering true deserts, humans have done just that, creating conditions inimical to themselves, their crops, their livestock, and, incidentally, even to true desert inhabitants such as the addax. About a fifth of the Earth's land has undergone or is risking desertification.

CASE STUDY
Restoring the prairie

The vast prairies of Illinois are gone forever. Of 145,000 square kilometres of wild grassland there 200 years ago, barely a dozen now remain untouched by farming. Faced with this disastrous situation, Dr Robert Betz of Northeastern Illinois University has been recreating a new prairie. This ambitious project is taking shape within the accelerator ring of the Fermi National Accelerator Laboratory (Fermilab), on land owned by the US Department of Energy.

It began in a small way, on a four-hectare patch. The seed came from odd surviving corners and embankments where original prairie plants had somehow managed to survive. Each year, 10-20 more hectares of land were carefully prepared and sown until, ten years later, all 184 hectares of grassland within the ring had been restored.

So far, about 50 species of plants have been established in the Fermilab prairie, still a long way short of the 150-200 species that once flourished there. New seeds are regularly introduced from other wild places, and rare specimens are planted into the sward as seedlings. There are also hopes of introducing a variety of prairie animals to the site - a start has been made with pairs of sandhill cranes and rare trumpeter swans.

Dr Betz is now extending the prairie outside the ring using seed harvested from within. This brave venture may not be a genuine piece of the one true prairie, but it comes very close. It has to be an effort worth making for the sake of future generations.

Blue grama, a prairie grass (Bouteloua gracilis).

CASE STUDY
Serengeti grazers

The stability of a grassland ecosystem is dependent upon its grazers. Take away the grazers and the grasses are replaced by woody vegetation. Increase the number of grazers, and the grassland turns into a desert.

So sensitive is the savannah ecosystem to disruption, that when something goes awry, the effects can be seen to reverberate throughout the whole ecosystem. The Serengeti ecosystem is a case in point.

The Serengeti National Park in Tanzania covers an area of some 13,000 square kilometres - an area almost the size of Northern Ireland. Yet even in an area as large as this, the numbers of animals are a cause of constant concern. When an epidemic of rinderpest swept through East Africa in the 1880s, causing the death of huge numbers of domestic cattle and wild ungulates, the plains became deserted. Famine was rife, and even lions were forced to attack humans through shortage of food. The vegetation changed too - dense woodland grew where formerly there had been grassland, and thickets developed on abandoned cropland.

More than 50 years were to elapse before the rinderpest was finally

Aerial view of wildebeest and zebra. Kenya, 1980.

eradicated in the 1960s - a change which was to send still more ripples through the system. Removal of rinderpest led to a population explosion of wildebeest, which in turn caused a decrease in the number of buffalo due to the wildebeest trampling much of their food supply in the wooded areas. On the plains however, the wildebeest were seen to have a positive effect on the populations of Grant's gazelle, by reducing the competition between grasses and the herbs favoured by the gazelles. Giraffe have also benefited from the wildebeest, in that the latter have been indirectly responsible for an increase in the regeneration of acacia trees. The savannah ecosystem is one of the most difficult to maintain under "reserve" conditions. Whereas a large enough piece of forest can be contained within a buffer zone and will more or less look after itself, even an enormous piece of savannah depends on migrations from outside the protected zone. It is therefore very vulnerable to any problems its grazers might face while they are away from the reserve.

The response of various components of the Serengeti ecosystem to the removal of rinderpest.

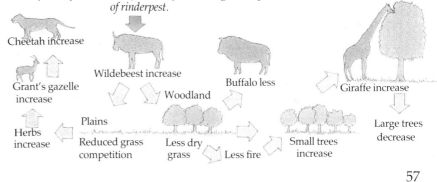

Cheetah increase

Wildebeest increase

Buffalo less

Giraffe increase

Grant's gazelle increase

Woodland

Herbs increase

Plains

Reduced grass competition

Less dry grass

Less fire

Small trees increase

Large trees decrease

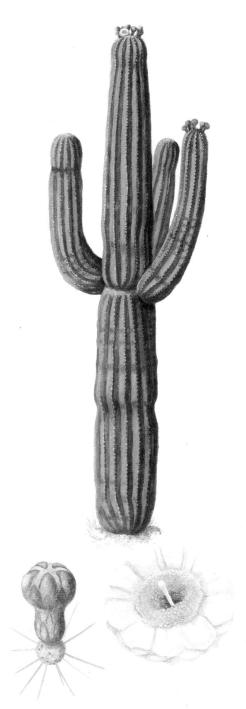

The giant saguaro cactus is vital to the lives of the animal inhabitants of the Sonoran Desert of the southwestern USA. Its massive trunk and arms support the nests of hawks and owls, and the holes excavated in its pliant green tissues by woodpeckers and flickers become the homes of countless other birds. Its blossoms, fruits and seeds are food for rodents, coyotes, bats, birds, ants and other insects. The Papago Indians made 12 different products from its fruit, including the wine used in a rain-making ritual.

Few deserts are literally rainless, so the popular notion of a desert as a sandy, barren waste is just not true. Even in the depths of the Karakum in Middle Asia, where the great mobile dunes shift as much as 20 metres a year, I have seen, on a morning in early spring, the daisy-chain tracks of innumerable creatures - darkling beetles, toadhead lizards, sand geckoes and gerbils - beneath the fiery orange and yellow blossoms of a shrub called the Thousand Suns. Seasonal rains, as sparse and erratic as they are, signal growth and reproduction, and the desert becomes a green and lively place.

But so inhospitable is the environment at the cessation of rain, that both plants and animals have evolved the means to resist or altogether avoid the heat and drought. Plants resist by having waxy or tiny leaves which reduce the rate of water loss, and by developing capacious tissues for long-term water storage. Animals resist by being nocturnal, resting in shade or burrows during the day, by using parts of their bodies (like big ears) to radiate heat and by concentrating their urine. They are also opportunistic feeders, satisfied with whatever's available at the time. Some plants and animals avoid the hot, dry season by becoming dormant. Plants grow and flower just after a rain, producing seeds capable of withstanding years of heat and drought. Some animals become torpid, and others follow the rain cycle, like plants, reproducing only during a rainy period, their eggs or offspring lying in suspended animation until the next one. Many animals simply migrate away from the desert when conditions are harsh.

For all the complex adaptations and interdependencies that have evolved to sustain life in the desert, desert ecosystems are no less fragile. Here evolution has been working at the limits of what most biological processes can stand in terms of temperature, moisture and nourishment. Just taking away a little shade can be devastating to seedlings that grow under a "nurse" plant or to animals that don't burrow.

Humans who are tempted to produce super crops in the desert by sinking wells or piping in water should be warned off by the desert's response. A lowered water table shrivels up the natural vegetation resulting in wind erosion, and high evaporation from the fields brings up salts that poison the topsoil. Why repeat the errors that are thought to have caused the collapse of the ancient civilization of Mesopotamia?

False deserts *are* lifeless, barren wastes. They are being created at the rate of 20 million hectares a year, at the expense of the fascinating true deserts and the lands at their margins. These could still be supporting a small population of nomadic pastoralists who, like the plants and animals, have developed ways of sustaining themselves in arid regions.

Tundra

In the north, beyond the belt of coniferous forest, lies the tundra, similar to deserts in lack of precipitation, but more fashioned by cold and dark than anything else, and ruled by what is known as the permafrost, the ever-frozen slab of subterranean earth. This arctic tundra comprises about 5% of the planet's land surface, while the other "tundras" found on mountains above the timber line and on the rim of the Antarctic take up less than a hundredth.

The permafrost defeats conventional farming and building, so the tundra hosts fewer people than any other ice-free land. However, this vast wilderness is not necessarily safe from human interference. The lure of mineral and petrochemical wealth has caused the North Americans and the Soviets to begin laying a network of tracks, roads, pipes, pits, settlements, garbage, factories - and oil spills - across their pristine north, and modern firearms and vehicles have turned the native peoples into super-hunters. It is too early to say what effect these developments are having on the tundra ecosystem, because they are so recent. Better to ask what is the inherent ability of the ecosystem to cope with disturbance.

CASE STUDY
Joyriders at large

Every week the California Desert suffers an invasion of joyriders. Off-road vehicles (ORVs) that can travel over sand - trail bikes, dune buggies, four-wheel drive vehicles, sail planes - are doing tremendous harm to the highly specialized plants and animals that live there.

Dune grasses, which not only help stabilize the dunes and retain moisture, but also serve as an important food source for many desert creatures, are being destroyed without a thought for their vital role in the desert food chain. Animals too are directly disturbed by ORVs. Besides losing their food supply, tortoises are killed by vehicles and their burrows collapse when they are driven over. The ORV also enables people to penetrate deep into the desert to collect tortoises that would otherwise have been out of reach.

The numbers of people visiting the California Desert just for fun increased nearly threefold between 1958 and 1973. It must now be many times greater. There are a million motorbikes, 200,000 dune buggies and 500,000 four-wheel drive vehicles used in the desert. This army takes part in organized ORV events in the California Desert every week during autumn, winter and spring. Unless these events are restricted, many desert animals and plants are doomed.

Dune buggies in the California Desert.

CASE STUDY
The addax - food in the desert?

All over the world, species that have not been "discovered" are becoming extinct. This tragic situation probably means that many potentially beneficial animals and plants will never be known. At the same time, there are known species, also facing extinction, whose potential is very great indeed.

One such creature is the addax, an antelope of the deep desert. Few large animals live in these regions; those that do are wonderfully adapted for survival in one of the most difficult habitats in the world.

Addax are formally classified as "endangered". In early years of this century they were quite common; one observer counted 400 in one day in the Sudan. As recently as 1974, 5000 addax were estimated to live in Chad, which is still considered to be their largest stronghold. Many places where they once roamed now have no addax at all; they are extinct in Tunisia, Western Sahara, Egypt, Libya and Algeria.

The irony is that these beasts could be a valuable food source in a part of the world where meat is hard to come by. All that is needed is a practical conservation programme.

One reserve for addax exists. It is in Chad, where civil war has been raging since 1978. The presence of armed forces in the desert - wanting meat and having the means to kill it - probably means the end of the world's largest protected addax population. Time is running out, but there is a ray of hope

The addax is a heavily built antelope, about 100 cm at the shoulder and weighing up to 150 kg. Its splayed, fleshy feet and long eyelashes are typical of a desert mammal. Addax live in a region where rainfall is less than 150 mm a year, and are said to be able to survive without water for a whole year.

in Niger. Twenty per cent of the world's addax live in the Aïr Mountain/Ténéré Desert region of northern Niger. The Niger government has set aside a huge area here, 8 million hectares, to be kept as a faunal reserve. With funds and expertise from WWF/IUCN, the population of 600 addax there may yet recover its former numbers.

The ancient Egyptians are known to have domesticated addax to some degree, and orphaned young addax do make tractable pets, but these antelopes could not be kept in the same way as even goats. They need space to wander in search of food, shade and water in their own way. Their reproduction is slow: a single calf is born after 8-9 months gestation and does not mature for 2-3 years. Their life span is up to 20 years though, and they need no special help in time of hardship, which is often when traditional domestic cattle must either be slaughtered or eat and drink valuable reserves. A great deal is still unknown - particularly how addax manage to cope without drinking - but this animal is well worth conserving, even if it is only for what we, the human race, can get out of it.

Arctic fox

Snowy owl

Lemming

Purple saxifrage and arctic poppy

In a system characterized by quantity of individuals and not diversity of species, tundra food webs are simple and direct. Small wonder that when the lemming population crashes (because the prolific little rodents have eaten all their food) so does the fox's and owl's. Still, extinctions are local, and lemmings and their predators, recruited from the vast territory of the tundra, eventually regain their numbers.

Because of the permafrost below and the low temperatures and abrasive winds above, the tundra landscape is most peculiar. Alternate freezing and thawing of the top layer of soil, the cracking of rocks and the intrusion of ice wedges model it into an incredibly varied microrelief. During the growing season the soil is kept chilled by the permafrost, and in the innumerable depressions it stays waterlogged, because the permafrost blocks drainage. In spite of the low precipitation, the tundra in summertime becomes a rather wet maze of trickles from thawed soil and snowbeds, and the microrelief channels these into meandering streams and undrained pools or marshes.

Fewer species of plants live in the tundra than elsewhere, and they stay short and grow slowly. Birches and willows are reduced to shrubs, and the ground is a lumpy jigsaw puzzle of mosses and lichens (small patches of which may be 100 years old) and grasses, sedges and other soft plants. Seed germination is so chancy that most reproduction is vegetative; the profusion of summer flowers is the product of many seasons of plants saving their energy.

The thick mat of vegetation actually protects the permafrost to some extent. Destruction of this insulating plant blanket causes the ground to thaw out more and to settle, resulting in erosion of the bare soil if water is channelled through the new depression.

Like plants, there are fewer animal species living in the tundra than elsewhere, even at the height of summer when millions of waterfowl and waders fly up from the south to breed, and the air, black with flies and mosquitoes, rings with the hoofbeats of reindeer or caribou. Among the few hardy creatures that stay the year round are lemmings, musk oxen, arctic foxes and hares, snowy owls and ptarmigans. Populations of these animals have long suffered natural calamities (*see left*), but in time they always bounce back. Clearly, part of the tundra ecosystem seems to be robust, although artificial interruptions of population cycles have not yet been widespread enough to determine any ultimate effect.

Another component of the tundra ecosystem - the migratory animals and their feeding and breeding grounds - may not be as resilient. Intensive hunting and interference with migration routes have certainly happened (as with caribou and some waterfowl), but their long-term effects on the tundra have not been well-studied. Finally, the most fragile part of the ecosystem - the delicate balance between permafrost and the slow-growing vegetation cover - so far seems to have a localized and self-contained reaction to disturbance.

Happily, the rush to utilize the resources of the north preceded the growth of public awareness by only a few years. Perhaps, for once, human impact will be sensibly controlled before too much damage is done.

Rivers and lakes

The connection between land and water is closer than most people realize. Streams originate from rain and snow running off over the land or seeping through the ground. Lakes are also fed this way, as well as by streams and rivers. The parent waters bring what the land has to offer. From naturally vegetated land comes a paced and regular supply of water and nutrients; where the natural cover has been disturbed by humans, water is delivered in fits and starts, sometimes overloaded with soil or containing chemicals washed down from the farms and settlements that replaced the natural vegetation. Then there is the practice of using water directly to rid human homes and industries of their waste. More ominous still is the pollution of the air which acidifies the rain that falls directly into bodies of fresh water.

Flowing water and still water are two extremes of an ecological continuum. A brook and a pond are very different, but big rivers have quiet pools, big lakes have turbulent currents and flowing water feeds into and moves out of bodies of still water. The headwaters of a river are directly nourished from the land - from water coming over or through rich

CASE STUDY
Caribou and the Alaska oil pipeline

The Trans-Alaska Oil Pipeline is 1288 kilometres long. Started in 1974, it reaches from Prudhoe Bay on the Arctic coast across three mountain ranges, tundra and forest, to the port of Valdez on the North Pacific coast.

Work on the pipeline naturally caused disturbance to all species in the vicinity. Noise, pollution and all the concomitants of industrial activity were expected to disrupt the scene, and they did. Most of the effects were temporary, but some may be permanent.

One very permanent feature is 675 kilometres of elevated pipeline, made necessary by the high ice content of the permafrost soil. This was designed so as not to form a barrier to wildlife, but in practice it did not always meet that specification.

Caribou, whose migrations are crucial to their feeding and breeding patterns, were expected to be very nervous of the elevated pipeline. Where it crossed their migration routes, it was buried for several miles in an insulated sleeve to prevent thawing of the permafrost. The elevated pipeline has created problems for caribou that were not, however, foreseen. In particular, nursing females are very shy of it. The males do not have the same degree of fear, and it is thought that this difference may lead to a fragmentation of the herds. Many more years of careful observation are needed before the effects of this colossal encroachment into the tundra can be fully assessed.

Barren-ground caribou – afraid of the pipeline?

CASE STUDY
Healing the tundra

Tracks in the tundra - a permanent scar on the landscape.

Traffic in the tundra has been increasing ever since Henry Hudson landed in arctic Canada in 1610. The Hudson Bay Company, licensed in 1670, brought trade to this far-flung region, and the Hudson Bay Railway joined it to the industrial world in 1931.

Further encroachment into the tundra has largely been due to oil exploration. The expeditions have been large, expensive and well equipped. All this traffic has had its effect on the scenery. The wide open spaces have been disfigured by garbage; vegetation has been destroyed by fire; and heavy vehicles have left deep tracks that will march across the terrain for centuries.

When the US Navy came to Alaska in 1944 to try out equipment, they found they could only travel easily overland in winter when the ground was frozen hard. In summer, they had to scrape off the soft topsoil to reach permafrost as they went along. During the ten years they were there, it became clear that permafrost soils behaved like no others.

By the time that oil was discovered in Prudhoe Bay, a great deal of information had been gathered about the wildlife and topography of the tundra. This knowledge is now being put to practical use in trying to repair the damage left by earlier visitors.

Garbage, dumped oil cans, abandoned vehicles and the like are now being buried or otherwise removed. Though expensive, this is at least feasible. Other marks made by humans may even prove impossible to erase. Accidental oil spills have not only wiped out large areas of tundra vegetation, but have also penetrated the natural drainage systems, increasing the risk of fire in the summer. Track vehicles, too, have played their part; in a single journey, one vehicle can destroy plants which will take years, if ever, to re-establish.

The permafrost soil itself is the key to all tundra life. When its structure is damaged, a sequence of changes begins that cannot be reversed. A vehicle track can turn into a gulley, which will deepen and widen each winter until it becomes a ravine. Off-road travel has recently been banned in Iceland, and traffic on the Alaskan tundra is only permitted in winter, but the earlier tracks can never be erased.

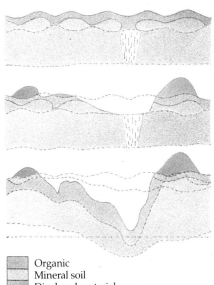

Organic
Mineral soil
Displaced material
Permafrost
Ice wedge

How the tundra soil structure is damaged by heavy vehicles.

Wetlands, lakes and rivers

Wetlands serve vital ecological functions, and teem with life. Yet we treat them as wastelands, suitable only for dumping rubbish and sewage or "reclamation".

Like great, self-cleansing sponges, swamps and marshes purify polluted water, and regulate the flow of rivers, acting as vast natural reservoirs. From lakes to mangroves, both fresh water and coastal wetlands support much wildlife, notably migratory birds, and act as nursery grounds for fisheries – millions of people depend on them for their livelihood.

Wetlands are under siege from pressing human need for land or energy – but hydroelectric dams or reclamation can backfire on industry and agriculture, causing immense environmental problems. Recognition of this is now boosting wetland conservation.

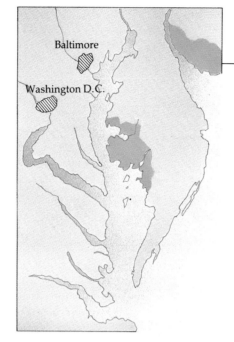

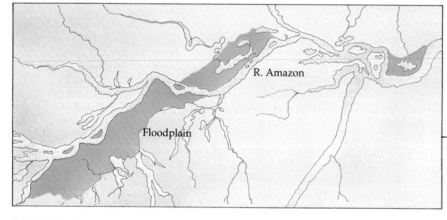

Chesapeake Bay (above left) Estuaries, where rivers meet the sea, are incredibly productive. But Chesapeake Bay is sick. Its famous crab and oyster fisheries are declining and the numbers of sea fish that spawn in its shallow waters are falling. The problems are pollution by herbicides, fertilizers, sewage and excess silt, which destroy the vital marshes, seagrass beds and seaweeds.

Amazonia's flood forests *Thousands of square kilometres of forest bordering the Amazon flood every year as the map (above left) shows. Shoals of fish feed and breed among the trees during the flood season and support important fisheries. Deforestation ruins this productive ecosystem. At the same time, dams are built in Amazonia which will cause permenent flooding and destruction of the forest. Erosion will then set in and the dams will silt up.*

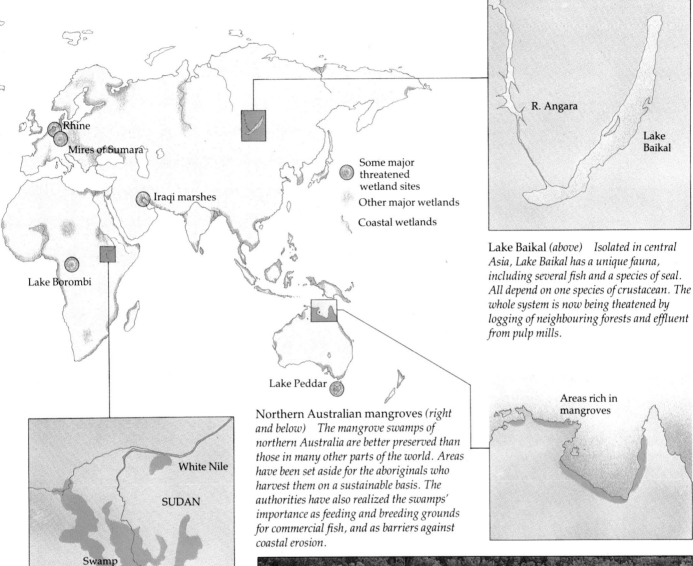

Rhine

Mires of Sumara

Iraqi marshes

Some major
threatened
wetland sites

Other major wetlands

Coastal wetlands

Lake Borombi

R. Angara

Lake
Baikal

Lake Baikal (*above*)   *Isolated in central
Asia, Lake Baikal has a unique fauna,
including several fish and a species of seal.
All depend on one species of crustacean. The
whole system is now being theatened by
logging of neighbouring forests and effluent
from pulp mills.*

Lake Peddar

White Nile

SUDAN

Swamp

Northern Australian mangroves (*right
and below*)   *The mangrove swamps of
northern Australia are better preserved than
those in many other parts of the world. Areas
have been set aside for the aboriginals who
harvest them on a sustainable basis. The
authorities have also realized the swamps'
importance as feeding and breeding grounds
for commercial fish, and as barriers against
coastal erosion.*

Areas rich in
mangroves

Sudd swamplands (*above*)   *The Sudd
swamp is the home of the world's largest
remaining population of large mammals as
well as possibly the largest concentration of
waterbirds in Africa. It is also the home of
tribes of nomads. All were threatened by the
digging of the Jonglei Canal through the
swamp which was to speed the flow of water
down the Nile. If the canal had not been
abandoned before completion, the Sudd and
the lives of its inhabitants would have been
damaged irrevocably.*

soil and from branches and leaves blowing in. In a lake the nutrients derived from land are utilized by the aquatic plants, and they themselves die and decompose, adding nutrients to the whole. Flowing waters are well-oxygenated, whereas in a lake oxygen is distributed in layers. There's a lot near the surface, not only because of air contact, but because the plants live there, producing it by photosynthesis. Near the bottom, however, where the detritus collects, the decomposers use it up. The kinds of organisms to be found in fresh waters are closely tied to the availability of oxygen.

The ability of fresh waters to cleanse themselves depends on the nature of the pollution. Natural organic substances received in unnatural quantities will eventually decompose if the amounts are not too great, but an unusually heavy load can make the ecosystem "backfire" (*see left*). Other "natural" water pollutants include the heat from industrial processes and increased amounts of soil from upstream erosion, both of which deplete the oxygen supply. Heavily silted rivers cause problems by harbouring disease organisms, clogging dams and reservoirs, blocking irrigation canals and ruining deep water ports and coastal fisheries.

"Unnatural" pollutants like pesticides and plastics are damaging in other ways. Not only are they more toxic than natural ones, but worse still, they're not readily decomposed. So, as well as directly poisoning organisms, they creep through the food web, becoming more concentrated at each stage. Some natural substances seem to act like synthetic ones if they're applied at abnormal levels. Aside from the direct toxicity of petroleum products and heavy metals, they have been shown to interfere with photosynthesis and reproduction, and cause cancers.

When the use of such substances is discontinued, water systems eventually flush themselves clean (at least locally), but, again, the system may have already backfired, and only with help can it be restored.

The planet's fresh water supply is virtually limitless, thanks to the ongoing cycling from ocean to air to land and back (*see p.22*), but from the human perspective, it's unevenly distributed in time and space. Some countries are blessed with lots of water, others have little, and unlike the salmon which travels up and down thousands of kilometres of rivers, we use water within national boundaries. Any abuse becomes the problem of the communities, human or otherwise, situated downstream or on the opposite shore.

A classic example of an ecosystem "backfiring" is what happens when phosphate detergents are dumped into lakes. Phosphorus stimulates the algae to grow in a blanket across the surface. This cuts off light to the plants below, interrupting photosynthesis, and when the heavy blanket itself begins to decompose, the lake slowly suffocates, undergoing premature eutrophication.

Wetlands

Wetlands literally mean just that - places where land and water meet and mingle. Here are some of the richest ecosystems in the world. They are charged by aquifers, soil moisture, rivers, lakes, oceans, rain and snow, and the water can be fresh, brackish or salt. The vegetation is water-loving and, therefore, the animals are more or less water-reliant. An estuary, where a river meets the sea, takes pride of place among wetlands, for its productivity is due to what the river *and* the tides wash into it.

Wetlands are so varied that their ecology is complex, but, using water as the vehicle, they all derive nourishment from land, using it for their own prodigious plant growth which in turn enriches the ecosystem. Further enrichment comes from the incredible number of animals attracted to wetlands. Migratory waterbirds use them as wintering or summering grounds or just as lay-bys, marine fish use them for nurseries, and many rare and endangered species have found sanctuary in them. To countless creatures from insects and shellfish to moose and manatees, they're simply home.

Because wetlands are so numerous and diverse, it's difficult to calculate their original and present extent on a global scale, but they have certainly been under attack for centuries. What was a wetland but a breeding ground for mosquitoes and an obstacle to progress? But now, half the wetlands of the USA and much of those of Europe have been

CASE STUDY
Pulp mills on Lake Baikal

One of Lake Baikal's celebrated inhabitants.

One-fifth of all the world's fresh surface water is in Lake Baikal in the USSR. Home to over 2000 species of plants and animals, it contains 23,000 cubic kilometres of water, and is up to 1620 metres deep. Normally a body of water this size can absorb a great deal of contamination without appreciable change, but now even Lake Baikal is becoming a casualty of large-scale human activities.

Industry has been steadily growing on its banks and on the banks of its feeder rivers. In addition to the thousands of tons of silt that are washed into it each year, the lake takes in agricultural chemicals, dust and gases from factories and vehicles, and oil from ships upriver. The most serious pollution, however, comes from the effluent poured out by two huge pulp and paper mills. Feeding these factories with timber will clear 50,000 hectares of forest for every year they remain in operation. Cutting down the woodland adds even more contamination in the form of silt from soil erosion, together with a variety of pollutants leached from millions of floating logs.

The consequences of this massive abuse of Lake Baikal could have been predicted. Apart from wholesale deaths of smaller organisms in coastal water, fishes in the lake are growing more slowly as the load of pollutants increases. The famous Lake Baikal seals, too, are showing similar symptoms.

As well as providing fresh water, Lake Baikal is an important fishery and its plight has caused concern at the highest levels both nationally and internationally. It takes at least 400 years for a complete change of waters to occur naturally and we can only hope that the new protective measures have not been taken too late.

CASE STUDY
Cleaning up the Thames

In 1981 a salmon was pulled out of the Thames and made history. One of seven caught there that year, it marked a milestone in the convalescence of London's great river.

Twenty years before, Londoners shunned the banks of the Thames in summer. Every drop of thick stinking water that oozed past carried the weight - and smell - of a thousand years of urban pollution. And under the surface, the river was all but dead. A 45-mile stretch contained hardly any oxygen at all. Without oxygen, the normal processes of decay are arrested. Instead of mud, the bed of the Thames consisted of layers of festering refuse.

In 1949 a thorough study of the state of the Thames was begun. Its aim was to identify the cause of the river's sickness and to suggest possible remedies. The conclusion reached after 15 years of intensive research suggested that the key to the problem was the very low oxygen content of the water.

There were a number of contributory factors, but top of the list was sewage. A healthy river takes its normal complement of decay in its stride, but the sheer quantity of sewage being dumped into the Thames was far too much for it to handle. The sewage clearly had to be more broken down before entering the river.

Another factor affecting oxygen levels is temperature. Warm water holds less dissolved oxygen than cold water. London's power stations had been heating the river by discharging warm effluent and so, if some alternative could be worked out, this would also help to improve the situation. Chemical effluents, too, from a procession of factories along the lower reaches, were putting more stress on the ailing river. Higher standards on the management of factory wastes would have to be set and enforced.

Work began tentatively in 1959, and gathered momentum during the '60s and '70s. In particular, sewage management was dramatically improved. New treatment plants were built, some of the old ones were modernized and others were scrapped. During this time, samples of the river's water showed a steady improvement in oxygen content.

Fish began to return to the river. About 100 species have so far been recorded, and the first salmon to be seen in the River Thames for over 60 years was caught in 1974. The seven salmon caught in 1981 gave even greater cause for celebration. Young salmon had been released into the upper reaches of the Thames in 1979, and these seven were the first to get to the sea and back via London. The waters of the Thames can now be truly said to be fit for the king of fish. Only time will tell whether London's river is finally cured, or only in remission.

The salmon – a welcome return to the Thames after an absence of more than 60 years.

converted. Declines in water quality, flood protection, fish and game resources and populations of rare wildlife have been demonstrably linked to these losses. On the whole, the value to the public at large of wetlands *as they are* is much greater than that of the so-called "reclamation" schemes. Yet in spite of past experience, only one in 20 of the world's major wetland conversion projects completed or under way in 1985 was first assessed for its ecological costs.

As well as wholesale destruction, wetlands are vulnerable to the threats facing any aquatic habitat, such as chemical pollution and siltation. They can be damaged by any activity, (e.g. damming and dredging) which alters the water flow on which they rely.

Some of the benefits of preserving wetlands and the consequences of losing them are specific to the kind involved, which for the sake of convenience can be separated into inland (fresh water) and coastal ecosystems.

Fresh water wetlands Fresh water marshes and swamps are found "where streamlets meander", as behind beaver dams and along low floodplains, and at the edges of lakes made shallow by sluggish inflow and outflow and the natural build-up of rooted vegetation.

A remarkable feature is their ability to absorb certain shocks. Natural organic pollution is dissipated in the fine network of water channels, where the myriad tiny creatures that inhabit the backwaters decompose it and the myriad plants welcome it as fertilizer. Cities as different as Vienna and Calcutta have long relied on nearby wetlands as nature's free sewage treatment facilities.

Upstream flooding, natural or otherwise, is gentled by the spreading out of the heavy water flow and the silt in downstream wetlands. The US Army Corps of Engineers, once notorious for straightening rivers to "prevent" floods, now recommends that flood control is best achieved by simply protecting wetlands. Furthermore, attempts to regulate natural waterflow often have tragic consequences, as witness the Aswan Dam in Egypt (*see p.156*). Correcting the mistakes, if possible, is expensive, but necessary. Florida's Kissimmee River will be *unstraightened*, at a cost of up to $200 million, in an attempt to restore parts of the stunning Everglades National Park which have dried up and to secure Miami's water supply.

Both plants and animals native to fresh water wetlands are well worth harvesting. Such an unappetizing plant as water hyacinth can be turned into fertilizer, animal fodder, methane gas and pulpboard, and half a hectare of cattails can yield over 35 tons of protein-rich flour. The fish that rely on the Amazon floodplain (*see p.113*) account for most of the protein intake of the local people, and the trade in pelts of such water-loving animals as nutria, muskrat and mink provides income to rural communities in the USA and the USSR.

Finally, recreation and tourism are burgeoning on inland waters, not just in places like Massachusetts where "marshview" lots have been selling for nearly $150,000 per hectare, but also in the tropics. One of the greatest moments of our wildlife tour of Zambia was flying low over the Kafue Flats to glimpse the herds of lechwe, the little waterbucks found only on the rich marshes created by the Kafue River.

Coastal wetlands Around gently sloping sea shores grow salt marshes and, in warmer regions, mangrove swamps. Where a river braids its way down through marsh or swamp, the mix of waters and organic matter from the land with those of the sea makes for one of the most productive ecosystems in the world. Plant debris is continually washed into the water and finely "milled" by crabs, molluscs, insect larvae and worms, and further broken down by bacteria and fungi into a nutritious base for microscopic plants and animals, the plankton. The whole Lilliputian broth makes coastal wetlands prime habitat for creatures highly prized and priced for our tables, like scallops, mussels and oysters, which feed by

Because decomposition and subsequent release of nutrients are so hampered by the cold, still water of bogs and fens, they are the least productive of wetlands. They do, however, foster an unusual assortment of wildlife, including the rare white-fronted goose. The main threats to bogs and fens are from peat cutting and drainage.

Zambia's Kafue Flats

The Kafue National Park in Zambia was recognized as an important site for wildlife in 1951. It covers over two million hectares of land around the floodplains of the Kafue River and its tributaries in southern Zambia.

The Kafue River is a main tributary of the Zambezi. Before it falls steeply through a deep gorge to enter the Zambezi, the river meanders across a wide floodplain, known as Kafue Flats.

Kafue Flats used to be a haven for wildlife. Submerged for several months a year by the annual floods, it provided a feeding ground for over 400 species of birds, from ducks, geese and waders to fish eagles and the world's largest group of wattled cranes.

When the floodwaters receded each year, the mudflats grew a rich crop of grasses which then fed zebras and wildebeest. Large herds of lechwe grazed in the wetter places, and crocodiles and hippopotamus also lived in and around the water. Aquatic life, too, was abundant and formed the basis of a good fishing industry.

The greatest threat to wildlife at that time was hunting, legal and illegal. Even after the flats were declared a national park, poaching had been difficult to control. But now the flats face a threat that might well make poaching impossible. Two large power-dams are in operation on the Kafue River, one above and one below the floodplain. The first

effect of damming the river has been to reduce the fluctuations of water level that were the basis for the region's ecology. Instead of alternate flood and mud, most of the eastern shore is now permanently flooded. Here, the seasonal grass growth has been lost to permanent aquatic vegetation in the water and thickets of marsh species on the moist margins. Elsewhere, the floodplain is steadily drying out, permitting scrub and woody

Wattled crane

Kafue floodplain at dawn.

growth to become established. In place of a large area that was alternately flooded and grassy, there is now a permanent shallow lake surrounded by rushes and woody higher ground.

Zambia's need for power cannot be ignored, since it is the country's most marketable export. These dams enable the country to produce a surplus of electricity which can be sold to its neighbours. The difficulty here is that of reconciling economic necessity with environmental value, for the interests of the hydroelectric plant seem to be completely at odds with those of the existing environment.

Theoretically, it should be possible to operate the upper dam to permit controlled flooding of the flats. This would mean that a smaller flow of water would be available to the hydroelectric plant; much of that water would also be permanently lost to use as it would evaporate from the large surface area of the flooded flats. It is this same argument that prevents the use of the Kafue River for irrigation of the land on the floodplain which is now available for cultivation.

It seems that a change in the wildlife of Kafue Flats is bound to occur, unless there is a change in the economic priorities of Zambia. Ultimately, the fate of Kafue Flats is dependent on the economy of the rest of the world.

filtering particles from the water, and prawns and big crabs, which pick out what has settled to the bottom. They are nurseries to young fish, which eat anything that fits into their tiny mouths, and grow up to become no less that two-thirds of the world's catch!

One reason why a large number of sedentary and slow-moving organisms take up residence in coastal waters is for protection. Although natural deltas and coastlines are subject to redesign by severe storms, their marsh or mangrove vegetation makes them better suited to buffer damage and erosion than their cleared or "reclaimed" counterparts. A tragic example is the story of a lovely South Sea island surrounded by mangroves. The mangroves bred mosquitoes, so they were cut down. After the next hurricane, all that was left was a pile of sand the size of a hearth rug - no buildings, no trees and no people.

As well as coastal wetlands cope with natural disturbances, they do not fare well with artificial ones. Like fresh water wetlands, they can absorb a certain amount of organic pollution. But it's a rare river that finally comes to sea and dumps only a slightly heavier burden of silt and nutrients. And, increasingly, industry and people have tended to move to the coasts, especially to estuaries which offer harbour to ships. Destruction of coastal wetlands in industrialized countries is now due mostly to direct pollution and "reclamation".

Having learned from the past, public concern for wetlands in developed countries has grown enormously, but still not enough to stop the piecemeal destruction encouraged by the quick profits to be had in selling real estate or farming suddenly valuable crops. The British government actually subsidizes up to 80% of the drainage costs to a farmer, even on sites that have already been given a certain measure of legal protection! Worse still, outdated methods of drainage and reclamation, agricultural production, pest control and waste treatment are increasingly being offered to and taken up by developing countries. As incredible as it seems, it looks like environmental history is going to repeat itself at the expense of many of the last pristine wetlands in the world.

Oceans and seas

The marine environment takes up most of the space on the planet - if the mighty Amazon were to flow for a hundred millennia, only half the oceans would be filled. But, as we've seen, the separation between sea and land is not a definitive one. Coastal waters are enriched (or impoverished) by what happens on the shores and up the rivers, and even ecosystems often thought of as strictly marine are influenced by terrestrial as well as maritime events.

The intricate limestone structures found in tropical and subtropical shallows are made of layer upon layer of the skeletons of tiny colonial animals called corals which are related to sea anemones. The depth and clarity of the seas must be such that the living corals receive plenty of sunlight, for they are "fed" during the day by the photosynthetic algae embedded in their tissues. At night they feed themselves, extending their delicate tentacles to trap plankton.

For a dazzling display of shapes, colours and textures, no other community on Earth can rival the coral reef ecosystem. The finest reefs I have ever seen are off the west coast of Madagascar, where it looks as though the sea bottom is covered in a three-dimensional Persian carpet strewn with jewels and flowers. The firm coral beds, pierced through with tunnels and recesses, provide anchorage and shelter for an infinite variety of creatures, and the wigs of algae that perch on the coral are good grazing grounds for snails and sea urchins. Many animals feed on the coral itself, and, of course, on each other. Needless to say, the food web on a coral reef is complex.

But the reef does not exist on its own. It relies on tides and currents to bathe it in water of just the right temperature and salinity and to bring in

CASE STUDY
Mangroves

Mangroves grow in muddy tidal waters, alternately washed by salt water and fresh. Their extraordinary roots overcome the disturbance of tides and currents that few other trees can tolerate. But they are not merely a botanical curiosity. The sheer volume of mangrove forests demands attention. The coastline of tropical Africa is fringed by 3.5 million hectares, tropical Asia by over 6 million, and South America by 5.75 million.

Human exploitation of these areas is crude, as usual. The trees themselves are felled for firewood, and the tidal zones where they grow are reclaimed for agriculture or used as building sites. Thousands of hectares are destroyed by pollution or diversion of watercourses.

The uses and values of the mangrove forest are rarely appreciated by decision makers or planners. As well as stabilizing the shifting mud and reducing coastal erosion, the mangrove forest forms the basis of a food chain that supports offshore fisheries. Mangrove leaves which fall into the shallow estuarine waters provide valuable nutrients for a key group of detritus consumers, which in turn provide food for fish and seabirds alike. Some of these fish form a major part of the diet of local people.

The mangrove forest is, in effect, a nursery for coastal marine life. When the mangroves are destroyed, the whole system goes with them.

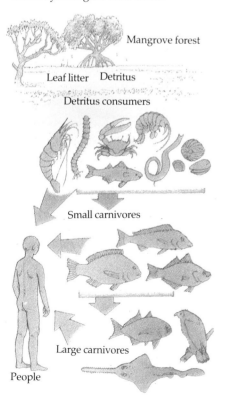

CASE STUDY
The Camargue

Flamingos of the Camargue.

Lying between Petit Rhône and Grand Rhône on the Mediterranean coast of France, the Camargue is one of the three most important coastal wetland areas in Europe. Originally recognized as an outstanding site for breeding and wintering birds in 1927, its significance has grown as other coastal wetlands have progressively disappeared under the cloak of cultivation. Today, the Camargue provides hospitality for a staggering number of birds. The flamingos, for which the region is famous, may reach 10,000 in an exceptional year, and there are around 1600 pairs of terns, about half that number of avocets, and some 400 pairs of purple herons.

The key to all this bird life is the mud flats themselves. Waters here range from fresh to salt, with many variations of brackish in between. The landscape, too, is varied enough to accommodate wild boar and foxes, as well as many other smaller mammals, reptiles and amphibians.

A buffer zone against the outside world is provided by a wide band of farmland. Of the 85,000 hectares that make up the Camargue National Park, only the seashore and the inner nature reserves (adding up to 20,000 hectares) are strictly protected. Much of the rest is leased by farmers.

Any problems the farmers have are inevitably passed on to the reserves. If the farmers find that their land is not giving a satisfactory return, they may turn to speculative ventures. Increased cattle stocks can damage the marshes; fish farming deprives many waterbirds of their natural habitat by raising the water levels. The reserves and their inhabitants can also cause headaches for the farmers. Drought in Africa in the winter of 1977 drove very large numbers of birds north. When they reached the Camargue, they found it was flooded - and the flamingos made for the surrounding rice fields. Bird-scaring devices now help to keep them away from crops, and trip-wires deter cormorants from raiding fish farms, but other problems are bound to arise.

The maintenance of the Camargue is a dynamic problem requiring constant vigilance. Research is an important function of the reserves there. Besides the Man and Biosphere reserve (*see p.84*) of 13,000 hectares, which is administered under the Ministry for the Quality of Life, there is a smaller 2000-hectare reserve which is independently run by the Fondation Tour du Valat. The research done by both establishments is largely complementary, though Tour du Valat is particularly concerned with the effects of outside influences.

The Regional Park of the Camargue, situated in the Rhône delta, occupies the whole area south of the town of Arles.

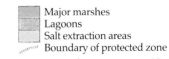

Major marshes
Lagoons
Salt extraction areas
Boundary of protected zone

THE STATE OF THE WILD
The ocean wilderness

Twenty or thirty years ago, the world's oceans were seen as the great food resource of the future. Shoals of fish would be herded and cropped to provide protein on a sustainable basis as cattle and sheep are on land. Instead, what has happened is that fish have continued to be hunted, like wild game, but with increasingly sophisticated "weapons". The result has been a collapse of one fishery after another with little thought for the future.

The establishment of Exclusive Economic Zones (EEZs) by coastal states for up to 300 kilometres is at least a step in the right direction. By protecting the habitats critical for fisheries and setting quotas for catches, coastal states are assured of both a regular protein supply and often a substantial income.

Incidental victims *(above)* *When the fish that usually formed their diet failed, humpback whales were forced to feed close to the Newfoundland shore. Many were caught in fishing nets, but some were freed. Every year fishing nets catch and drown uncountable numbers of marine animals, from seals and dolphins to seabirds and turtles.*

A fragile ecosystem *(left)* *The abundance and variety of fish and other animals in a coral reef demonstrate that it is the marine equivalent of a tropical rainforest on land. There is an enormous diversity of species, but like a rainforest, it is a fragile ecosystem that is easily destroyed. Once a reef is dead, fisheries are lost and the coast can be eroded as storms are no longer checked.*

One ocean, one habitat

Although the world's oceans form one huge body of water, as shown by this whole ocean projection, they are by no means uniform. Swirling currents and differences in temperature, salinity and depth form barriers to movements of marine life. Even powerful mammals such as the humpback whale are restricted to discrete populations, rarely straying from their traditional breeding and feeding areas.

The greatest concentrations of minute phytoplankton (and therefore of marine life feeding on them) are found along the shallow coastal zones, around reefs, and at upwellings of deep water. However, these areas of high productivity also tend to be the most severely affected by pollution. At least 83% of all marine pollution derives from land-based activities, much of it in the form of oil, sewage, heavy metals and persistent pesticides.

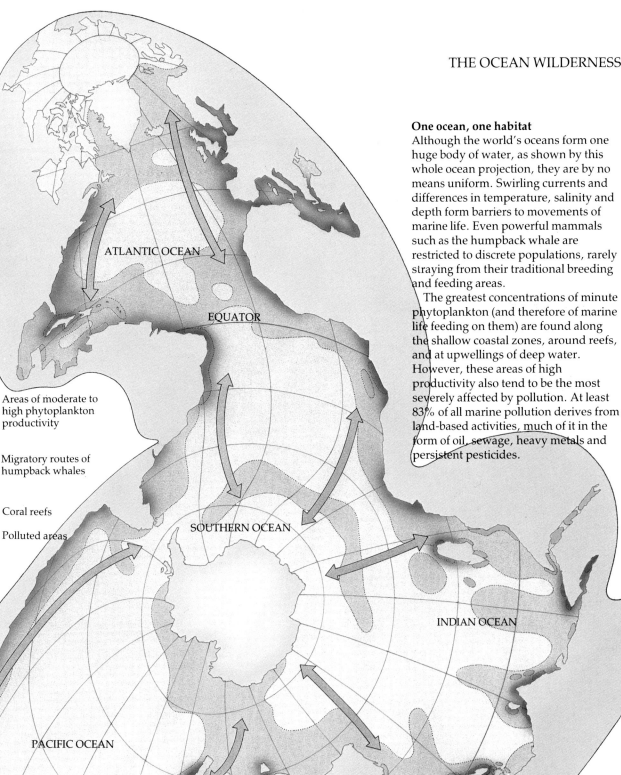

Areas of moderate to high phytoplankton productivity

Migratory routes of humpback whales

Coral reefs

Polluted areas

ATLANTIC OCEAN

EQUATOR

SOUTHERN OCEAN

INDIAN OCEAN

PACIFIC OCEAN

The ocean covers two-thirds of the planet's surface – and across the greater part of this vast wilderness humans still exploit and damage wild resources without restraint.

just the right mixture of plankton and nutrients from adjacent seagrass and algal beds. Too "rich" a mixture, say from sewage or fertilizer run-off, has the same effect as in other aquatic ecosystems by promoting algal blooms which suffocate the reef organisms. However, the greatest indirect threat to coral reefs is the erosion caused by human activities. Turbid waters laden with silt and sand from deforestation and harbour dredging not only cut off light and oxygen but also clog the feeding mechanisms of many reef creatures.

How other pollutants, such as pesticides, heavy metals and oil, affect reefs has been less well-studied, probably because, so far, tropical waters have been spared them. But current research has shown that some coral species die within 24 hours in just a 1:10 million dilution of a herbicide and that coral-eating snails readily concentrate the herbicide in their tissues. With this level of sensitivity plus the complexity of reef food webs, the impact of modern pollutants, now becoming widely used in tropical countries, is likely to be dramatic. However, the current drama is the direct destruction of entire reefs by mining for lime and "fishing" with explosives.

A little further out from the coasts, particularly off the western sides of continents, are natural "upwellings", where nutrient-laden deep waters are pulled up periodically by strong surface currents. These areas are even more productive than reefs or estuaries, so it's not surprising that half the world's fish catch comes from upwellings, although they account for only a hundredth part of the ocean.

By comparison to coastal ecosystems, the open ocean itself is robust. The very immensity and the relative scarcity of organisms have meant that the high seas have taken human chemical abuse without much ecological comment to date. Toxins dumped at sea or carried out by the currents and winds are taken up by the plankton, whose bodies and faeces settle quickly to the ocean floor, but degrade only very slowly because of the low temperatures. Since it is likely that world production of toxins will increase faster than pollution controls can be imposed, the vast oceans will quietly continue to store up toxins for a long time to come, with unknown implications.

One open ocean development gives pause for thought, however. Mining the deep seabeds stirs up bottom sediments which cloud the water and only slowly drop back. How these turbid "plumes" affect the plankton is in dispute, but whipping up a brew of toxins could be catastrophic, especially if it occurred near an area of upwelling. Moreover, trying to clean up the seabeds once they are fouled would be impossible. The oceans are just too big.

The polar regions

The northern and southern polar regions are reverse images of each other. The Arctic is an ocean mostly covered in ice made from sea water and surrounded by land, whereas the Antarctic is a land mostly covered in ice made from snow and surrounded by a cold ocean. These contrasting configurations account for some of the major ecological differences between the regions and the kinds of impact that human activities can have on each. But in both, the perpetual cold and the great seasonal variation in productivity, owing to the long dark winter and the brief summer sun, mean that the number of species of plants and animals is low, but the number of individuals is, at times, enormous.

The Arctic is a region of interdependent terrestrial and marine ecosystems. Birds feeding at sea come back to nest on the tundra, polar bears and arctic foxes wander over the frozen ocean waters in winter and the meandering rivers of the continents eventually drain into the Arctic Ocean which is relatively small - only five times bigger than the Mediterranean. The indigenous people have a long history of sustainably utilizing the living resources of the Arctic. Now, modern methods of

CASE STUDY
Garbage in the seas

Early mariners, throwing slops overboard, hardly made a mark on the oceans. Thousands of ships sank with hardly a ripple, adding a mere pimple here and there to the seabed.

As the human race has multiplied, so has its garbage. If that garbage were simply natural, the oceans could still handle it. Three-quarters of the Earth's surface is sea, after all. It is the nature of our garbage that causes problems.

Supertankers circle the world, carrying millions of gallons of oil. A shipwreck can pollute miles of coast and kill thousands of seabirds. But even this disaster is relatively temporary. In time, the oil will break down and the environment will recover.

Plastics, however, are not meant to break down - and they don't. Every scrap of plastic dumped in the ocean will remain there, forever. Every tide drops its flotsam of plastic on the foreshore - only a minute sample of the contents of the sea.

Plastic fishing lines can and do kill seabirds. Turtles think plastic bags are jellyfishes, and die with stomachs full of them. Even a 12-metre sperm whale has been found dead with 50 plastic bags jammed in its throat. The numbers of plastic-related deaths are hard to estimate, but over two million seabirds and 100,000 mammals are known to die every year. The plastic plague is carried all over the world, even to the Antarctic.

Disposal at sea of plastic is prohibited by the International Maritime Organisation (IMO) protocol, but enforcement is virtually impossible. The only solution seems to be to ensure that plastics do not get on to ships in the first place.

Gannet killed by fishing net.

CASE STUDY
Mining coral reefs

Loading corals into a container van in the Philippines.

Coral reefs flourish in tropical waters at temperatures between 25° and 29°C. They need sufficient light to grow, which restricts their development to shallow waters, often close to land.

Coral reefs rank among the most biologically productive and diverse of all ecosystems. The numerous different corals, sheltering shoals of bright fish, are the furniture of offshore life. At the same time, the sheer mass of a reef forms a buffer zone between the beach and the ocean, and thus protects the land from erosion.

Unfortunately, one of a coral reef's many attractions is the fact that it is made out of limestone. Many local communities have made use of coral for practical purposes. Cut into slabs, it makes a good building material; ground up into powder, it makes polish; when burnt, it yields pure lime. The lime industries of many tropical countries are founded on coral.

In Bali, reefs have been so badly damaged by coral miners supplying the lime kilns there that the coast is being seriously eroded by wave action. Where living coral is cut, the mess in the water kills the remaining coral and all the other reef inhabitants. Ironically, Bali's growing tourist industry depends largely on the beauty of the reefs that are in the throes of destruction.

Coral reefs are highly exploitable commodities. Their greatest value, however, is in the intact form. Smashing a coral reef for its raw materials is an extremely short-sighted use of it - rather like smashing the best china for crocks to put in the flowerpots. With tourism likely to prove an ever-more valuable resource for tropical coasts, this waste is already being regretted in some areas.

When conserving coral means putting traditional industries out of work, however, careful planning is very important. Sri Lanka is at present attempting one of the developing world's most advanced coastal management programmes. About half of Sri Lanka's population lives in coastal areas, and in some of these regions coral mining and calcining are important industries. Some reefs have been very badly damaged. The Sri Lankan government is compensating 10,000 people in one region for loss of employment as a result of its prohibition of reef mining.

exploitation of these and non-renewable resources, like oil and minerals, are in full swing on land and sea.

The Antarctic ecosystem is essentially marine. The waters surrounding the single land mass cover ten times the area of the Mediterranean, and the ice-free rim is less than a tenth the area of the arctic tundra. Only two species of flowering plant and a few lichens, mosses, mites and insects actually live there. Seals, seabirds and penguins pack the limited shorelines during the breeding season and spend the rest of the time in the sea or on the floating ice packs.

"Ownership" of the Arctic is conveniently split among the north-ernmost countries, but in Antarctica there have been disputes since early this century when Argentina staked the first claim. However, a treaty was signed in 1959, and 12 nations have been peacefully exploring and studying the last virgin continent, in what is often cited as a shining example of international cooperation. It's true that people do cooperate, but now that the commercial value of the Antarctic has become apparent, so have the cracks in their shining armour.

Probably oil, certainly minerals and definitely huge stocks of fish and krill are straining the Treaty. Agreement on updating fishing regulations is stonewalled because the Soviets have not supplied the data on their catch for the last 15 years, and the French have begun work on an airstrip in Terre Adelie in flagrant breach of the terms of the Treaty.

Humans have been about in the Arctic longer than in the Antarctic, and so threats to the ecosystem there are viewed by some as more critical. Many living marine resources have already collapsed from overexploita-tion. If the expected level of oil exploitation is met, risks of spills and blow-outs will be tremendous. The preference for using ships rather than pipelines for transport makes economic sense, but further increases the chances of leakages into the sea.

Oil does peculiar things with ice. A slick creeps under the ice pack, and tiny oil droplets become embedded in the pack as the water freezes in the winter. Aside from the impossibility of cleaning up this "mix", the gloomiest prediction is that the affected packs will absorb more heat under the summer sun, melt and thereby alter the climate of the whole northern hemisphere! Whatever the global effects, a widespread presence of oil, so slow to degrade in the cold, would cause irreversible damage to the marine and shoreline communities of the Arctic.

In the Antarctic, there is a further ecological concern about the ice packs, should oil extraction and transport become a reality. Specialized forms of algae living on the undersurface of the packs are thought to account for a fifth of the primary production in Antarctic water. Exactly how oil in packs would influence this basic component of the marine food web is not clear, but there's reason to think that it would cause a major disruption.

Islands

Islands are at once both poor and rich - poor in the number of different species they can hold, but rich in the sense that many of their plants and animals are endemic, that is, like fabulous gems in a private collection, they're found nowhere else in the world.

Species diversity and endemism are determined primarily by the age of the island and how far it is from the mainland. A young, remote island, such as a volcanic cone newly risen out of the depths of the ocean, is less likely to have received visitors and received them hospitably than an older island lying near, and maybe once connected to, a land of potential colonists. On the other hand, on an old, remote island, there has been enough time for the few colonists that did make it to adapt to any environmental peculiarities and to try out new niches before having to compete with or protect themselves from latecomers. Descendants of the original colonists gradually evolve into new species, unique to the island.

South America

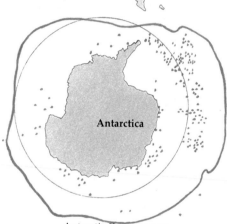

Antarctica

Antarctic Convergence

Red dots show main known concentrations of krill

The band of water called the Antarctic Convergence is the ecologically defined northern boundary of the region. This is where cold bottom currents coming off the ice from the south are mixed with warm cur-rents from the north by circumpolar winds, creating upwellings of nutrients. Here the phytoplankton "bloom" in summer, feeding the incredible numbers of zooplankton and krill, which in turn are eaten by fish, penguins, seals and, until their near-exter-mination by the end of the '60s, the large whales.

Getting oil out of the Arctic

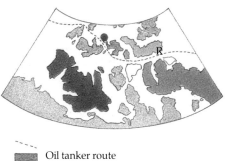

Canada's Northwest Territory and the proposed oil tanker route.

Oil tanker route
Cameron Island
Melville Island
Devon Island
Bathurst Island
Victoria Island
Baffin Island
● R Lancaster Sound, refuge for wildlife
Oil reserves

All the indications are that there will be more major oil finds within the Arctic Circle very soon. Before regular transport of oil through arctic waters begins, it would be as well to consider some of the consequences.

There are two possible transport options: ship and pipeline. A ship has already been tried. The *MV Arctic*, an icebreaker converted into a tanker, managed four knots though ice half-a-metre thick. Even at this rate, it could only penetrate these waters for a few weeks of the year. Plans are already under way for storing a year's yield of oil on Cameron, an island that is only accessible two years in every three.

Even large icebreakers can be damaged by icebergs. No pipeline could ever be considered safe, either. The ocean floor shows gashes two metres deep cut by passing icebergs.

The consequences of an oil spill in the Arctic Ocean would be very serious indeed. Apart from the effect on the ice itself, oil breaks down painfully slowly in sub-zero temperatures. It would stay around for years, possibly travelling far from the original spill site. Oil in the Lancaster Sound would cause huge mortality to the eight million seabirds and many seals that seek refuge there.

Our knowledge about the effects of major ecological disruptions has all too often been a baptism by disaster. In the Arctic, the chances are that knowledge gained from one disaster could be knowledge gained too late to use.

The krill harvest

Krill feeds Antarctic whales, fish, seals, squid and seabirds. It is now increasingly being harvested by people. Factory ships from Japan, the USSR and other countries take up to 500,000 tons a year. Such a plentiful supply of protein can be expected to be increasingly exploited by humans.

The quantities of krill in Antarctic waters are prodigious. It has been estimated that, in 36 million square kilometres (the extent of its summer range), the summer stock of krill would amount to 650 million tons. It would seem that the Antarctic thus represents an endless supply of food for the overpopulated human world. But the effects of tapping even 500,000 tons are unknown. Many other apparently bottomless stocks have proved all too vulnerable to human depredations.

One big unanswered question is how fast the krill can multiply. Their growth rate is not known, nor is their life span or breeding rate. These data are crucial in estimating the size of the krill harvest. Then there is the effect on other krill-eaters, many of which are of commercial importance – virtually every other vertebrate of Antarctica depends on krill.

The Antarctic is a difficult place to work in. Data are hard to come by and hard to interpret. A sample of krill taken from the middle of a superswarm would suggest that the ocean was nothing but krill soup, yet they may be very scarce in another patch of sea. In order to give an accurate picture, observations and measurements must be continued for many years, on all Antarctic life and in all seasons.

Antarctica is a region of great international attention nowadays. The Antarctic Treaty of 1959, which gave a number of nations the right to use territory there, worked well in the early years. There is now much more at stake than there was in 1959. Oil, minerals and the krill are straining the Treaty. Many international organizations are pressing for new forms of agreement, according to their several requirements. In the midst of this international muddle, the krill are still being harvested and the researchers are still researching. Handled sensibly, krill could be a precious resource. Mismanagement could have disastrous consequences for the Antarctic, and for ourselves. It seems to be a race whose outcome may not be known for years.

Krill forms the vital link in the Antarctic food web.

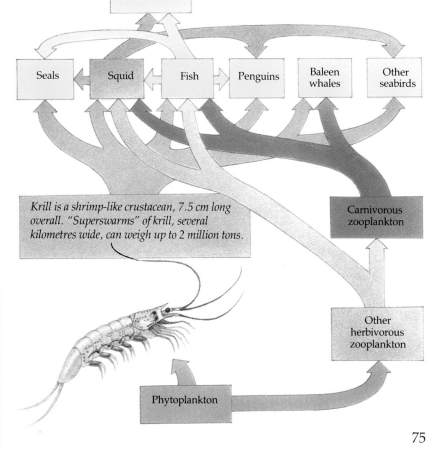

Krill is a shrimp-like crustacean, 7.5 cm long overall. "Superswarms" of krill, several kilometres wide, can weigh up to 2 million tons.

Islands – evolution in isolation

Left undisturbed, islands are biological treasure-houses. Isolated from the mainland, the endemic plants and animals have evolved into new species to fill the various habitats, often in the absence of mammalian predators. Consequently the native species, while unique to one island, are also extremely vulnerable to extinction, because of the small size of their populations and the lack of any defences against introduced predators.

The islands on the map that fall within the continental shelf were at one point connected to the mainland, and this is reflected in the diversity of their floras and faunas. Oceanic islands, however, have had to recruit their fewer species entirely from immigrant stock.

Undisturbed islands are treasure-houses of unique species. But they are not left untouched, and their fragile systems perish under the impact of introduced species and human activities.

Endemic taxa 52

58%

2%

65 km

Balearic Islands *The Balearic Islands, Majorca and its neighbours, are holiday resorts where the coast, in particular, has been developed to cater for a seasonal influx of visitors. As well as habitat destruction, there are problems of pollution and disturbance. Of the 52 endemic plant taxa, well over half are threatened with extinction. Luckily, the countryside inland is relatively untouched, otherwise the situation could be much worse.*

Endemic taxa 11

9%

91%

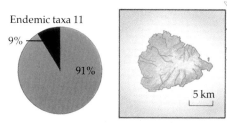

5 km

Ascension *Ever since Ascension was occupied by the British Navy in 1815, the island has been a military base. Crops and domestic animals, introduced by the sailors to provide a regular source of food, posed great threats to the wildlife. The present garrison on Ascension, however, causes no damage, as most of their supplies are imported.*

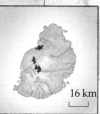

16 km

7%

79%

Endemic taxa 280

Mauritius *Mauritius lost many of its native species when its forests were replaced with sugar cane plantations and other crops. For instance, many endemic swallowtail butterflies became extinct although one,* Papilio manlius, *manages to survive in citrus plantations. Today, all but 14% of the endemic plant taxa are endangered.*

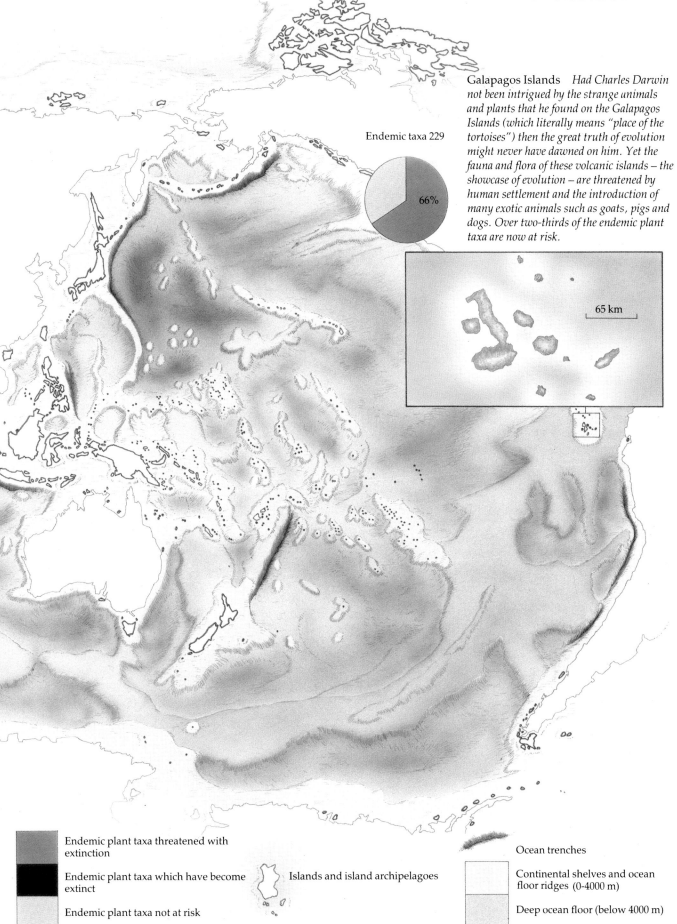

Endemic taxa 229

66%

Galapagos Islands   *Had Charles Darwin not been intrigued by the strange animals and plants that he found on the Galapagos Islands (which literally means "place of the tortoises") then the great truth of evolution might never have dawned on him. Yet the fauna and flora of these volcanic islands – the showcase of evolution – are threatened by human settlement and the introduction of many exotic animals such as goats, pigs and dogs. Over two-thirds of the endemic plant taxa are now at risk.*

65 km

Endemic plant taxa threatened with extinction

Endemic plant taxa which have become extinct

Endemic plant taxa not at risk

Islands and island archipelagoes

Ocean trenches

Continental shelves and ocean floor ridges (0-4000 m)

Deep ocean floor (below 4000 m)

Number of species of reptiles and amphibians

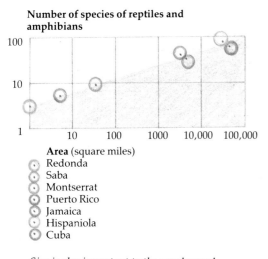

Area (square miles)

- Redonda
- Saba
- Montserrat
- Puerto Rico
- Jamaica
- Hispaniola
- Cuba

Size is also important to the number and kinds of species an island can contain. Small islands offer fewer resources than large ones in terms of shelter, nourishment and, simply, space. Animals that need roomy territories, like the big carnivores, have never successfully established themselves or evolved on small islands.

Dodo skeleton,
Tring Museum, UK.

The beak and foot of this reconstructed skeleton are some of the few remains left of the dodo, the most famous of extinct animals. It was safe on its island home until humans and their domestic animals arrived.

In certain combinations of size, age and isolation, islands are extremely sensitive to disturbance. Natural calamities, like hurricanes, can decimate whole populations of animals on small islands. The arrival of a mammalian predator on an island whose fauna evolved without one is catastrophic. Picture the poor old dodo, unable to fly away and probably not even trying to waddle away, when the first ships with hungry sailors landed on Mauritius.

The latecomers to islands, on the evolutionary time-scale, are ourselves. The native plants are usually overrun with the foreign "weeds" we bring in. Of the native animals, some are overhunted and most are unable to adapt to the radical changes brought about by farming, building and industry or to hold their own against our highly competitive or predatory "familiars" (the ubiquitous dogs, cats, goats, pigs and rats). They retreat to ever-smaller corners in ever-smaller numbers to the point of no return. Of all the birds that have become extinct in the last 200 years, most were native to islands!

It is difficult to estimate the present degree of disturbance to island flora and fauna. Accurate catalogues of species and their life styles began to be kept only a few hundred years ago by the "explorer-naturalists", but many islands were settled long before then. At least we now know something about Hawaii. Polynesians arrived there 1600 years ago, and recent studies of subfossil birds show that half the avifauna became extinct after that time and before the appearance of Europeans. Frequently, sailors released goats and rabbits on to islands (to set up a food supply for the next time their ships called), which then destroyed the natural vegetation and, therefore, an unknown number of the animals relying on it, before lists of native species were compiled.

The classic example of "exotic" animals running riot on islands is that of New Zealand, where unthinking Europeans, pining for home, actually imported 133 non-native bird species. About a quarter of these happily established themselves at the expense of seven native birds which became extinct and another 17 which are on the brink.

Not many islands have escaped human interference, but perhaps because islands are so self-contained, it is possible to halt and even undo some of the damage. New Zealand is at the forefront of island rehabilitation, and many islands are now receiving the attentions of governments and conservation organizations, some to be rehabilitated and others to be protected. For on the "unsuspected isle in far-off seas", as Browning's description runs, there still exist a few of the fabulous plants and animals that evolved when the world was innocent, and these refugees deserve our care, however late it maybe.

The "State of the Ark" today is reflected in microcosm by islands; the persistence of ecosystems over time, their fragility in the clumsy hands of the "latecomer", the environmental tragedies *and* a few recent successes for which we have been responsible. Research on island ecology has been the most relevant in deciding how to protect some of the last original timbers of our Ark.

Protecting the Ark

Ecosystems are the timbers of the Ark, and, as we've seen, many have been damaged or destroyed and still more are under threat. Guarding the Ark timber by timber may or may not be enough to stop her from sinking, but it's one of the only feasible options at the moment, so we must get on with it.

The notion of protecting habitats is not new. In 300 BC, a king of India declared certain forests as reserves in order to save wildlife; 1800 years ago the Emperor Hadrian set aside a reserve for the cedar forests of Lebanon; and in the Middle Ages, European royalty declared large tracts of forest off-limits to the general populace. The motivation behind these early "conservation programmes" was very likely inspired by a perceived threat

CASE STUDY
Round Island

An island is a natural reserve. Even the smallest island has a community that has settled into a way of life that requires little or nothing from the outside world. This is a two-sided coin, however, for the harmonious life of an island can be instantly wrecked by the arrival of just one foreign species.

Round Island is one such casualty. It is a volcanic cone with a land area of 151 hectares, situated 24 kilometres from the northern tip of Mauritius. Although it is now protected under the auspices of Mauritius, it cannot be described as a thriving community.

The former hardwood forest on the crown of the island has dwindled to a single tree, and the once-luxuriant palm savannah lies in scattered remains around the periphery, with only ten individuals still standing. This havoc was caused by the introduction of goats and rabbits about a hundred years ago by mariners planting live food stores along their trade routes.

The indigenous fauna of Round Island includes some reptiles that have disappeared from nearby Mauritius. Five of them, two geckos, a skink and two boas, are officially listed as endangered. Vegetation loss is serious for the lizards. One of the geckos, for example, feeds on the ground at night. During the day it rests in the leafy crown of a palm tree. Although the feeding ground may

remain, the loss of palm trees makes it impossible for this gecko to cope. One of the boas has only been seen twice in 20 years and is probably extinct. A casualty of the goat invasion, it used to burrow in loose soil and leaf litter in the forest but, with the loss of tree cover, the island has lost three-quarters of its soil through erosion. The remaining soil is at a premium; shearwaters, using all they can find for digging their nest burrows, are endangering the roots of the palms that grow there.

Seabirds have suffered from direct confrontation with humans. Four species breed here, one of them a very rare petrel. The nestlings have traditionally been collected for food by local fishermen. Nobody actually lives on the island, which has no source of fresh water other than rain, but conservationists visit it at intervals to monitor the situation.

Now human intervention has been redirected towards saving Round Island and helping its struggling populations to recover. The goats have been removed and the palms are showing signs of regeneration. Other plants native to Round Island are growing safely in botanical gardens, and three reptile species are breeding well in captivity.

The key to the regeneration of plants on Round Island will be the removal of the rabbits. Rabbits and goats between

Gully erosion on Round Island – a consequence of loss of tree cover.

them caused loss of vegetation through teamwork: the goats ate the mature growth while rabbits ate new growth. Now the goats are gone, the rabbits are still preventing the regrowth of woody plants.

Telfair's skink
Like all Round Island species, it is threatened with extinction due to the introduction of rabbits and goats.

79

THE STATE OF THE WILD
Protecting our heritage

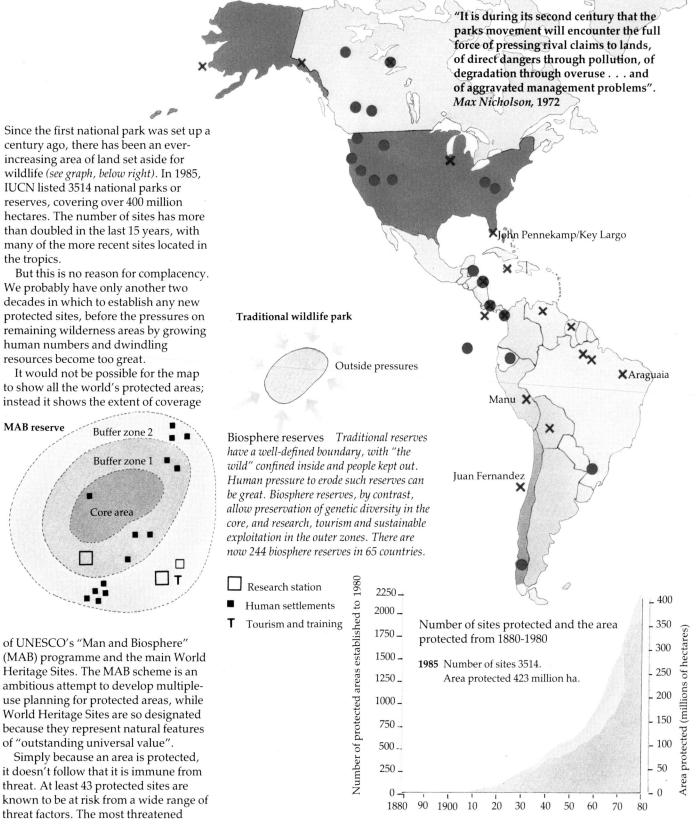

"It is during its second century that the parks movement will encounter the full force of pressing rival claims to lands, of direct dangers through pollution, of degradation through overuse . . . and of aggravated management problems".
Max Nicholson, 1972

Since the first national park was set up a century ago, there has been an ever-increasing area of land set aside for wildlife *(see graph, below right)*. In 1985, IUCN listed 3514 national parks or reserves, covering over 400 million hectares. The number of sites has more than doubled in the last 15 years, with many of the more recent sites located in the tropics.

But this is no reason for complacency. We probably have only another two decades in which to establish any new protected sites, before the pressures on remaining wilderness areas by growing human numbers and dwindling resources become too great.

It would not be possible for the map to show all the world's protected areas; instead it shows the extent of coverage

Traditional wildlife park

Outside pressures

MAB reserve

Buffer zone 2

Buffer zone 1

Core area

T

Biosphere reserves *Traditional reserves have a well-defined boundary, with "the wild" confined inside and people kept out. Human pressure to erode such reserves can be great. Biosphere reserves, by contrast, allow preservation of genetic diversity in the core, and research, tourism and sustainable exploitation in the outer zones. There are now 244 biosphere reserves in 65 countries.*

☐ Research station
■ Human settlements
T Tourism and training

John Pennekamp/Key Largo

Araguaia

Manu

Juan Fernandez

of UNESCO's "Man and Biosphere" (MAB) programme and the main World Heritage Sites. The MAB scheme is an ambitious attempt to develop multiple-use planning for protected areas, while World Heritage Sites are so designated because they represent natural features of "outstanding universal value".

Simply because an area is protected, it doesn't follow that it is immune from threat. At least 43 protected sites are known to be at risk from a wide range of threat factors. The most threatened ones are named on the map.

Number of sites protected and the area protected from 1880-1980

1985 Number of sites 3514.
Area protected 423 million ha.

Number of protected areas established to 1980

Area protected (millions of hectares)

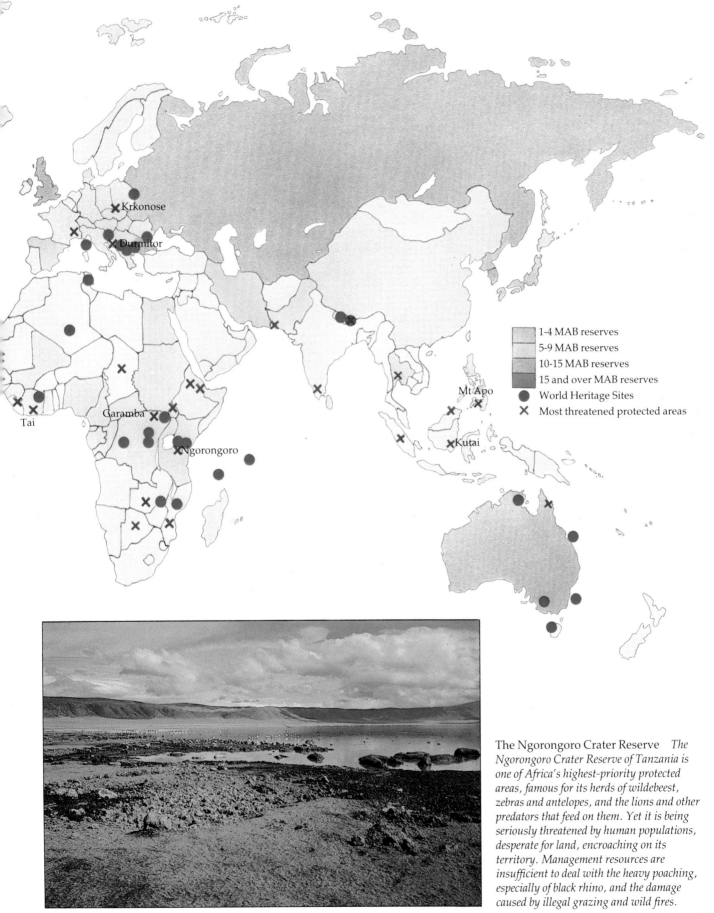

Krkonose

Durmitor

Tai

Garamba

Ngorongoro

Mt Apo

Kutai

1-4 MAB reserves
5-9 MAB reserves
10-15 MAB reserves
15 and over MAB reserves
● World Heritage Sites
✗ Most threatened protected areas

The Ngorongoro Crater Reserve *The Ngorongoro Crater Reserve of Tanzania is one of Africa's highest-priority protected areas, famous for its herds of wildebeest, zebras and antelopes, and the lions and other predators that feed on them. Yet it is being seriously threatened by human populations, desperate for land, encroaching on its territory. Management resources are insufficient to deal with the heavy poaching, especially of black rhino, and the damage caused by illegal grazing and wild fires.*

The theory behind the design of nature reserves is that the larger the breeding population of a species, the less likely is the species to become extinct.

Each of the reserve designs shown on the left will preserve larger breeding populations than the one on the right.

Some practical considerations, however, warn against "putting all your eggs" into one reserve, even a large one, because a single disease could wipe out the breeding populations, and against the use of corridors through dense human settlements because of the difficulties of controlling poaching and contact with diseased domestic animals along the long, exposed borders.

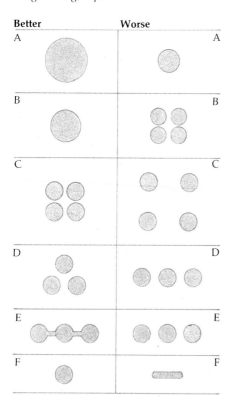

to resources, but the resources were intended for use by a privileged few. Perceptions changed radically with the Industrial Age, when so many wild places were laid to waste with astonishing rapidity. In 1872 America created the first national park for "the benefit and enjoyment of the people", and by the 1920s every continent boasted them.

Only recently, however, has the concept of preserving areas for their wider virtues as ecosystems been accepted. It was finally realized that ecosystems themselves are the "protectors" of renewable and potential resources and the "defenders" of environmental stability beyond their obvious borders.

How to put the concept into practice is not so simple, for ecosystems along with their human neighbours are so vastly different from one another. A rainforest reserve will take up more space than one in a temperate forest because its components are more widely dispersed. And whereas some people can buy food for a picnic in a national park, for others, the main meal is often "bushmeat" (*see p.107*). If their village is near a protected area, bushmeat is no longer on the menu (legally, anyway), which understandably causes resentment.

Successes and failures in modern efforts to preserve ecosystems are all related to the particulars of the situation. For example, the attempt to save a bit of the rainforest where the Panama Canal was built has been a *qualified* success. A few years ago we made a film on the beautiful reserve of Barro Colorado Island, which was created when the Panama Canal was flooded. We filmed everything from leaf-cutting ants and fig wasps to three-toed sloths and howler monkeys, and at the end of the day, exhausted but pleased with our rendition of the diversity of life in a rainforest, we would relax on the veranda of the Smithsonian research station while inquisitive tapirs tiptoed around us in the evening gloom. But we didn't see it all. Since Barro Colorado became isolated in 1914, large predators, like the jaguar, have died out because of lack of space, and a number of ground-nesting birds have died out because omnivores, like peccaries and coatis, and grazers, like tapirs, proliferating in the absence of predators, robbed and trampled the birds' nests.

Ideally, a reserve has to be very large to keep an ecosystem intact. Depending on the ecosystem, however, there does seem to be a minimum critical size at which stability is maintained. Given the kinds of human pressure on the environment in certain countries, large reserves aren't always possible, but the relative positioning of several small reserves and the use of corridors between them should offset the high extinction rates characteristic of small areas, and cater for such creatures as elephants. Reserves should also be carefully sited to include regions where species diversity is exceptionally high in order to protect as yet undiscovered resources. And all different types of ecosystems within a country should be well represented in that country's network of reserves. Finally, as defenders of environmental stability, ecosystems should be preserved intact in watersheds, along watercourses, on coasts, around cities and amongst farmlands.

All these wise conservation measures sound as if a whole country would have to become a reserve, leaving no room for its own people, but this is not so! In any case, the new thinking in modern reserve planning and management is that it is not necessary and, indeed, not desirable, for *all* reserves and their resources to be closed to human beings. Strategies of "rational" and "multiple use" are being pioneered in many reserves today.

Biosphere reserves - a new approach

The current revolution in how we guard the timbers of the Ark is not so much about the size or shape of reserves or where they're located, but about their boundaries. Drawing a line on a map and saying "protection stops on this side, and on that side people can use the land as they like" is no longer done by responsible environmental planners.

CASE STUDY
Devil's Hole pupfish

There aren't many fish in the desert. The few that are found there are the best possible proof of the tenacity of life on this planet. Isolated in scattered remnants of water since the last Ice Age, each of these little fish represents thousands of years of lonely survival.

Nine species of pupfish live in Death Valley in the Nevada Desert. Now the hottest and driest part of the USA, Death Valley was once a large lake, and these fish are all that is left of lake and river species from that time.

One of the best-known is Devil's Hole pupfish. Just one limestone pool, 20×3 metres, is the only home this unique fish has. It is highly specialized for life there, which is not surprising since the pool has moulded its evolution for over 10,000 years. Any sudden change in the pool will mean extinction for the pupfish.

The main threat to Devil's Hole comes from drainage. Water levels fell in the early 1970s due to extraction of water by irrigation. The plight of the pupfish was brought before the US Supreme Court in 1976 and, eventually, the water levels were made legally secure by creating a reserve. Pollution is an ever-present danger; even the accidental death of a cave diver might cause a pollution hazard. The situation is constantly monitored, however, and with time, it is hoped that the present population will gradually rebuild its size to the 900 estimate of the pre-pumping days.

A dwarf species of fish, Devil's Hole pupfish grow to only 28mm. Their movements during the day are largely in response to temperature changes. They spend the night in cool shallow water, moving into warmer, deeper water at dawn to feed. They return to the shallow water during the day as it heats up, but when this water becomes too warm in the afternoon, they move back into the deeper water again. They return to the shallow water at night to rest.

CASE STUDY
How small can a reserve be?

In the heart of the Brazilian jungle an experiment is being conducted that could influence the future of all forest reserves. The object of the experiment is, briefly, to define the smallest workable size for a rainforest reserve. It is broadly true that a large area will contain more species, with a better chance of survival, than a small area. Large and small are comparative terms that have no measurable dimensions, however, and Dr Thomas Lovejoy is hoping to learn more about the spatial needs of forest species.

In order to gather the greatest amount of useful data, 23 test areas have so far been established. Eight consist of a single hectare, eight of 10 hectares, four of 100 hectares, two of 1000 hectares, and one is an area of 10,000 hectares. Some of the smaller ones are isolated from the surrounding forest, and have previously been observed while they were part of the intact forest, while the rest remain connected to the forest.

Selected species in isolated areas are regularly counted, and the numbers compared with those in non-isolated areas, or with the same area before isolation. Eventually these observations should provide much information about the needs of many of the animals and plants within the test zone.

One important question is whether the broad variety of species is likely to suffer in an isolated reserve. Early

Plants and animals are being studied in undisturbed forest areas in Brazil. When all but isolated patches of forest remain after forest clearance, then some plants and animals will be studied again, to see what effect isolation has on forest species diversity.

observations show that deep-forest species are indeed lost from small reserves, and quite quickly. Butterflies, in particular, have been found to desert all but reserves of over 100 hectares. Whilst the light-loving butterflies increase, the shade species are lost.

This is the "edge effect", which is of very great importance in an isolated reserve. All the species that inhabit forest edges benefit from isolation, since there will be edges where there were none before. Conversely, when the distance from edge to centre is small, as it is on a small reserve, it may be intolerably small for deep-forest species. It will clearly be important to eliminate the edge effect, by surrounding a reserve with a buffer zone, to preserve the balance of edge and shade species.

Trees suffer from the edge effect, too. More trees die and fall in isolated small areas, due to increased exposure, increasing wind penetration and lowering humidity.

As more data become available, these effects should become more clearly defined, helping to build a data base on which to plan better reserves.

The broadest and boldest approach to protecting ecosystems is UNESCO's Man and Biosphere (MAB) programme. A "biosphere reserve" is one that contains a "core" of true wilderness, large enough for plants and animals to maintain their natural numbers, which is surrounded by one or more "buffer" zones. In the buffers, the human presence ranges from light resource utilization, such as wood-gathering or occasional hunting, to established settlements, be they North American ranches or the communal longhouses of Siberut. The reserve is run on an integrated basis, with open dialogue and decision-making among the scientists, local people and managers. Scientists collect basic information on the "wilderness" and how it is progressively altered by human activities, which is then related to the needs of the people. By common consent, a compromise is reached on a plan to ensure a harmonious and sustained relationship between the people and their environment.

The aim of the biosphere reserves programme is to encompass several areas in each of the world's biogeographic provinces (the number of such provinces has been estimated at 193) and to form a global network for the rapid interchange of information and ideas on the sustainable use of natural resources. Not surprisingly, such an ambitious scheme has experienced many problems and much criticism. For one thing, most newly named "biosphere reserves" have involved lands already protected (as national or regional parks, wildlife sanctuaries and the like). Entrenched, sometimes rivalrous managers and administrators haven't often welcomed the changes suggested by outsiders. Another problem is money. Although the biosphere reserves are supposed to be financed by the countries concerned, little has been allocated beyond the budgets for managing "pre-biosphere" lands. Finally, there is human selfishness that leads to lack of communication and friction. The scientists concentrate on their own projects, the managers on their own paper plans and the local people on their own circumscribed needs. The breadth of vision possessed by the originators of the MAB concept is not easily learned.

The more general view of parks and reserves as keystones in balanced resource management strategies seems to be only half-heartedly accepted by the world's politicians. There are about 3000 parks and reserves occupying four million square kilometres of land, plus an unknown amount of wilderness under private or provincial protection. Let's say the total is five million square kilometres. Even if all this were properly managed (which it is definitely not), and even if the figure trebled by the turn of the century (which is difficult to say, given the pressure of human population), little more than 10% of the world's land surface would be expected to shore up the terrestrial environment. More terrifying still is the prediction that by the year 2000 the rest of the land will have been converted to other uses, making it impossible to create any more parks or reserves.

There are rays of hope, however. Half of the 3000 nationally protected sites were created in the last 15 years, many of them in the developing countries. Furthermore, a few biosphere reserves have been remarkably and *demonstrably* successful, so much so that it's inconceivable that the idea won't "catch on". And if enough of the "other uses" to which wild places will be put over the next 15 years can be applied in the context of biosphere reserves, then perhaps the Ark *will* sail through the 21st century.

Cashing in on the tourist

Some people in government still do not grasp the difference between short-term gain and long-term loss in how the environment is treated nor understand the vital role that intact ecosystems play in sustainable resource management. If they consider protecting the environment at all, they insist that the environment pays its own way, and therein lies the *raison d'être* of many national parks and reserves. Tourism is big business.

CASE STUDY
Siberut - paradise regained?

It is so much easier to destroy than to conserve. In all the centuries that humans have been trying to protect threatened natural resources, each attempt has produced new problems to be solved. It is easy to point to the reasons for past failures but not so easy to get it right, even now.

Seeing people as a part of the process of nature rather than divorced from it is the concept behind the creation of the Man and Biosphere (MAB) reserves. The island of Siberut in Sumatra is one of the most recently named MAB reserves. The island itself, an area of about 4500 square kilometres, lies a hundred kilometres off the coast of mainland Sumatra. Primarily rainforest, with no dry season, the flora of the island is extremely rich in endemic species. Half a million years of isolation from the mainland have given the island a unique fauna, too, including four endemic primates.

This rainforest paradise has not existed in isolation from humans, however. People have probably lived on Siberut for thousands of years. The 18,000 people who live there now represent one of the oldest Indonesian cultures. The traditional life of this culture was closely related to the forest, with an animist religion and many hunting taboos. So perfect was the balance on Siberut that, until missionaries came to the island and began to "improve" the life of the people there, the forests were virtually untouched.

Within a few years of the outside world's "discovery" of Siberut, the whole structure began to crumble. Pressure was put on the people to abandon their traditional wooden halls in the forest in favour of villages of little huts near the coast, while the forests and mangroves were exploited by logging. Sago palm cultivation was replaced with sawah (flooded-field) rice, a crop which is incompatible with the forest ecosystem, and social and cultural traditions were abandoned. It seemed that, without some form of swift action, Siberut would become a paradise lost.

Fortunately, an action plan has now been formulated. Initially, three zones have been established, to take account of three vital components of the island's life: natural, social and economic.

The "development" zone of 250,000 hectares will be the area where logging is permitted. This zone is already occupied by the bulk of the population, and

Sakuddei man stripping bark on Siberut.

Proposed system of zones for Siberut.

Development zone ——————
Traditional use zone ——————
Proposed nature reserve ——————

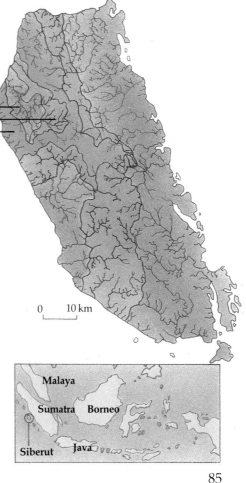

0   10 km

Malaya

Sumatra   Borneo

Siberut   Java

includes much of the forest already damaged by logging. Further activity is not expected to encroach on virgin land.

Another 100,000 hectares is designated as the "traditional use" zone. Here, the island people will live and, hopefully, recover their old skills of living with the forest. This zone will effectively serve as a buffer zone.

The nature reserve zone of 50,000 hectares is comparatively small. Extending from the north-western coast into the heart of the island, it will be sufficiently large to protect the plants and animals contained within it. Traditional uses will be allowed within the zone, provided they are not considered detrimental to the ecosystem.

The plan for Siberut, ambitious as it is, is only just beginning to take shape. Its future is in the hands of unknown managers and governments.

A clever calculation based on the numbers of visitors to Amboseli Park and how much time they spent viewing wildlife, demonstrated that the value to Kenya's economy of the tourists's favourite animal - a live, fully grown maned lion - is over half a million dollars per lion! (By comparison, a lion shot for sport is worth $8500 and a skin about $1000).

Second only to oil in international trade, tourism turns over nearly $100 billion a year. Much of this is generated by travel for cultural interest within the developed countries, which, in fact, accounts for only a fraction of their national revenues. But in many developing countries, tourism is a major source of revenue, and the "feature attractions" do not even have to be constructed. They are the clean beaches and dazzling reefs, the remote and peaceful mountains and the profusion of wildlife, lost forever from the lands at home.

A few years ago, tourism was hailed as the "smokeless industry" that would provide local employment and country-wide services, such as roads, airstrips and hospitals. But the way tourism has developed to date, it has fallen short of these happy expectations. Damage to reefs by snorkellers standing on them for a rest or taking home "just a piece of coral and a few shells" is a serious problem in the Caribbean, as is the disappearance of beaches under hotels. Deforestation in Nepal is attributable to the fuelwood collected to service intrepid mountain trekkers, and compaction of soil by the heavy use of off-road vehicles has caused erosion and vegetation damage in the game parks of East Africa. Declines in wild animal populations in many protected areas result from poaching by local people, who consider they've been denied a traditional food source, and disturbance by tourists, who never stop to think that chasing animals to photograph them might be harmful.

One problem is that less than maximum use has been made of local "resources" in developing a park for tourism, which leads to local resentment. Why bring materials, workers, guides and even managers from afar when they're all on the doorstep? Certainly, the social and economic implications of such a strategy must be considered, but it can work, as shown in Benin in West Africa where visitors are delighted with the simple camps built of local materials and in Nepal and Thailand where villagers have been trained as park managers or guides.

Another problem is simply poor planning, no doubt some of it stemming from the fact that park administration has been occasionally handed over to the tourist industry, which is not renowned for its expertise in ecology and conservation! Had the development of Amboseli been designed around animal and human ecology from the outset, disturbances within the park and dissatisfaction among the Masai outside could have been avoided. Today there are plans to manage wildlife on expanded, overlapping ranges. The Masai will be compensated for losses when wild ungulates move through their pastures, until the relocation of visitor facilities outside the park proper begins to stimulate the local economy directly. The dispersal of tourists will also serve to reduce pressure on the soils, vegetation and animals within the park itself.

Tourism should be viewed as an ecological phenomenon. Tourists are like a new species invading an island. Because they are flexible, they are inclined to overrun the whole place, but if they are to persist on the island as they found it, they must settle down in a niche and behave themselves. The resident "species" - the local people and the wildlife - may have to make some adjustments to accommodate the new neighbours, but eventually they should be able to use them to their mutual benefit.

There is something niggling at the back of the mind about tourism, however. A park *should* be established for the sake of preserving an ecosystem. If tourism can meet the costs, that's fine. But what happens if the tourist dollars ever dry up? Will governments have the foresight and courage to try to save their parks, which may well be among the last timbers of the Ark?

CASE STUDY
Bonaire Marine Park - can conservation and tourism co-exist?

The difficulty with "selling" conservation is that long-term benefits are less attractive to business interests or local populations than quick returns. When tourism is involved, however, the chances are better. Where a site's attractions depend on its natural beauty, conservation and profit can go hand in hand. That this does not always happen is due to either greed or mismanagement. Greed cannot be cured, but management can be better advised.

Many Caribbean islands have been ruined by the tourist trade - hotels, marinas and all the paraphernalia of people at leisure. But one island, Bonaire, is making a determined effort to preserve its assets.

The greatest asset of Bonaire is its extensive coral reef. This, together with the mangrove forests and seagrass beds, forms the basis for the local fishing industry. The islanders traditionally harvest conch, spiny lobster and turtles, as well as a variety of reef fishes. The territorial waters are owned by the island government together with 60% of the coastal land. The government has been concerned with conserving the fishing industry since 1961, starting with controls on catches of spiny lobster and turtles, and banning spearfishing in 1971.

During this time a tourist industry geared towards diving and underwater photography had been growing. The accessibility of the reefs made them vulnerable to disturbance, but because the dive operators demonstrated a conservation-oriented attitude, activities such as spearfishing and collecting were restricted. This was the situation when the Caribbean Marine Biological Institute (CARMABI) embarked on a coral reef research programme in 1970.

The Bonaire Marine Park was established in 1979 as an IUCN/WWF project, with funds from WWF and the Netherlands. It covers an area of 2600 hectares, including all waters from high tidemark to 60 metres deep around the islands of Bonaire and Klein Bonaire (which is privately owned).

The extent of the reserve and the involvement of marine biologists in all aspects of its development and management are exceptional. Tourism and research seem to be compatible here. Two strict reserves, where diving is

prohibited or limited, have been established, and the island government has powers to close any area that shows damage.

Greater tourism has brought its problems, however. Yachting and boating may damage the reef, as may inexperienced divers. The inevitable hotel and marine development may also give rise to disturbance, and damming a river has affected the mangroves. The situation is being constantly monitored, though, and income from tourism is a necessary part of the cash flow for conservation.

Bonaire Marine Park seems to have all the ingredients for success: the will is there, funds and expertise are available, and there is legal power to protect the site. It should stand the best possible chance.

Diver exploring coral reef. Inexperienced divers can break and damage corals unintentionally.

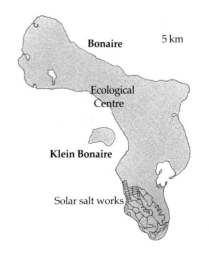

Lechwe at sunset on the Kafue Flats, Zambia

CHAPTER THREE

The State of the Species

Living beings are the parts of ecosystems that most people know about. Because of this, popular awareness of the "State of the Ark" often revolves around discussions of how many condors are left in California or whether the giant panda will survive the bamboo shortage in China. Professional ecologists may snigger a little at what they consider a limited understanding of the broad issues in their field, but without this public concern, the Ark would be in an even sorrier state.

The lynchpins of ecosystems are the species themselves. The top carnivores are the obvious ones, for pulling them out creates great instability in food webs, which may or may not readjust satisfactorily. But other key species are more "subtle", like the humble ribbed mussel which lives in the southeastern American salt marshes. Decomposing bits of marsh grass are swept out to sea by the tides, filling the water with phosphorus-rich particles, but in less than three days, *all* the particles are filtered by the mussel and firmly deposited in the mud. The mud-feeders then release phosphorus to the water in a form usable by the marsh grass and plankton, which in turn feed fish and other creatures, whose droppings fertilize the marsh grass. Remove the mussel, and the whole salt-marsh ecosystem collapses.

The phrase "the conservation of genetic resources" simply means that there are wild plants and animals whose characteristics we know little or nothing about at the moment, but which had better be saved because one day we may want to call upon them to improve our lot in life. The vitality of agriculture, medicine and industry continues to rely on discovering the secrets of nature, like the perennial, disease-resistant strain of wild maize which was recently found growing on a remote mountain in Mexico.

The characteristics of plant and animal species that will prove so vital to our future are not salvageable by test-tube tactics. They appear, persist and disappear by the processes of nature, and these require large breeding populations to sow "good" genes and weed out "bad" ones in relation to the environment in which the population lives. Much research is being devoted to the artificial preservation of large breeding populations and even to genetic engineering, but the most reliable way to ensure a steady supply of genetic resources is to let species get on with their breeding in the wild.

How are the members of the Ark's crew faring? The answer is complicated because we don't even know how many species exist, and with rampant habitat destruction, species are disappearing before they're discovered. Of the species we do know about, there's still much to learn of their distribution and status in the wild. Some of them, however, are clearly on the brink of extinction, brought to the edge by their fellow crew members, ourselves.

The Plant Kingdom

Plants feed us, doctor us, clothe us, supply industries and fuels, and provide home and health for all living creatures. The green cover of the planet sustains the very air we breathe, the soils and water we use, and the stability of climates.

Yet we know all too little about them. To date, we have identified about 380,000 species, and of these about 10-15% are threatened. But new species are being discovered all the time, and we are only just beginning to perceive and document the causes of plant decline.

Today the accelerating destruction in process is forcing the planetary flora into retreat, with untold consequences for all of us.

Bee orchid

Orchidaceae c.18,000 spp (RD 712)
Ornamentals

Palmae c.2800 spp (RD 546)
Date, fibres, oil, timber

Date palm

Leek

Liliaceae c.3500 spp (RD 495)
Ornamentals, leeks, onions

Wheat

Rubiaceae c.7000 spp (RD 524)
Coffee, quinine, ornamentals

Cinchona (quinine)

Graminae c.9000 spp (RD 460)
Cereals, rice, sugar, fibres

RD = No. of species listed as threatened in *Red Data Books*

Leguminosae c.17,000 spp (RD 941)
Pulses, forage, soil nitrogen

Euphorbiaceae c.5000 spp (RD 487)
Rubber, cassava, castor oil

Wood spurge

Rosaceae c.2000 spp (RD 111)
Apple, peach, pear, plum, herbs

Crab apple

Compositae c.25,000 spp (RD 1430)
Artichoke, endive, sunflower

Globe artichoke

Cruciferae c.3000 spp (RD 443)
Cabbage family, forage, spices

Cabbage

Angiosperms c.250,000 species
These are the flowering or "higher" plants. Some important families are shown below.

Orchids and lilies are valuable commercially but often threatened in the wild; the lily family also offers onions and other crops. Palmae include tropical trees and climbers (rattans), many of which yield multiple products; the date palm has sustained whole societies for millennia. Grasses (Graminae) are a dominant group of immense value in ecosystems; they provide all our staple cereals. Compositae are spread throughout the world too, from asters to artichokes. The pea family includes the protein rich beans and pulses; many leguminous plants have nitrogen-fixing bacteria in root nodules which enrich the soil. The potato family (Solanaceae) also yield tomatoes and other foods; many are valuable medically. The Rubiaceae give us coffee and quinine, the Euphorbiaceae or spurge family offer rubber and cassava, castor oil and succulents. Crucifers, besides many familiar wild flowers, provide the cabbage family and other important vegetables. The Rosaceae bring apples, peaches, strawberries, perfumes and the rose itself.

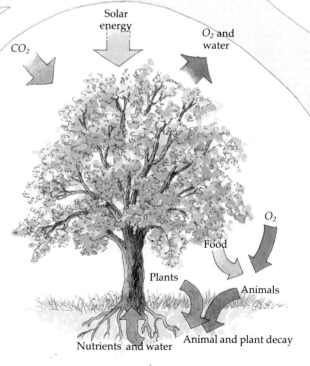

Solar energy

CO_2

O_2 and water

O_2

Food

Plants

Animals

Nutrients and water

Animal and plant decay

The life-giving role of plants
Plants are primary producers, sustaining all other life-forms. The chlorophyll which makes them green enables plants to manufacture carbohydrates from carbon dioxide, air and water using solar energy and nutrients from the soil. In photosynthesis, plants release the free oxygen all *air-breathing creatures need. Animals use this oxygen to metabolize the plant carbohydrates they eat, releasing carbon dioxide in the process. Dead organisms return their nutrients to the soil, to be broken down, and used once again by plants in their alchemy of life.*

Weymouth
conifer

Lady fern

Rhynchostegium confertum

Gymnosperms c. 750 species
This group of flowerless but seed-bearing species includes the cycads, and the conifers – mainly evergreen and fast-growing trees of immense economic value for their timber, pulp, resin and turpentine. Conifers mantle the subarctic zones in the boreal forests. Among the gymnosperms are some of the greatest and oldest plants of the kingdom – giant sequoias reaching up to 120 metres and weighing 6000 tons and bristlecone pines over 4000 years old.

Pteridophytes c.13,000 species
These are the ferns and fern allies which, like other "lower" plants, use spores to reproduce. They occur mainly in moist regions, especially the rainforests. The majority are true ferns (about 12,000 species), ranging from the familiar waist-high fronds of temperate woods to the giant tree ferns of the tropical forests, which can reach 20 metres. The remainder, the fern allies, include the horsetails and club mosses.

Bryophytes c.16,000 species
Mosses and liverworts, though often small and inconspicuous in colder regions, can be spectacularly large in the tropics. Damp-loving, spore-producing plants, they play vital ecospheric roles in breaking down exposed rock and dead wood to form soil, in covering and stabilizing that soil and retaining moisture, and as the principal base of food chains in subarctic ecosystems. Sphagnum mosses are valuable commercially as they provide peat.

Algae c.25,000 species
Ranging from the giant kelps of the Pacific to single-celled plants which mist the surface, sunlit layers of water, algae are mostly aquatic species, and of crucial importance to the ecosphere. It is estimated that marine algae (green plankton) produce 70% of atmospheric oxygen. The economic potential of algae is largely unrealized, though seaweeds are already used for alginates, fertilizer, animal feeds and food in some areas.

Kelp

Lichens c.18,000 species
These remarkable plants are not really one organism, but two – a fungus and an alga living in symbiotic association. The alga uses sunlight to photosynthesize, the fungus decomposes dead matter, and together they thrive. Lichens are highly sensitive to airborne chemicals, and so are increasingly used as pollution indicators. They also provide excellent natural dyes, but are threatened through over-collection in some regions.

Caloplaca thallincola

The bar chart shows, from tallest to shortest:

- 210 Elimination of special habitats
- 173 Drainage of habitat
- 172 Abandonment of land use
- 155 Landfilling and grading
- 123 Alteration of land age
- 112 Strip mining, topsoil removal
- 99 Impacts, e.g. trampling
- 89 Herbicides
- 81 Clearance, weeding, fires
- 69 Dredging rivers and lakes
- 67 Plant collection
- 56 Water eutrophication
- 42 Discontinuance of periodic soil disturbance
- 31 Water pollution
- 20 Urbanization of villages

Fungi c.50,000 species
Since they possess no chlorophyll, and thus are not green and do not photosynthesize, fungi are not true plants. Neither are they animals. Fungi are decomposers, vital in the life chain to release nutrients from dead organic matter and recycle it back into use. Most are microscopic, except the familiar toadstools and mushrooms; many are of value, from the yeasts used in baking and brewing to the Streptomyces *and* Penicillium *important to medicine.*

Russula vesca

Causes of decline
The planet's flora is at risk. Various estimates put the number of species in danger of extinction by 2000 AD at 25,000 to 40,000. Regionally, it ranges from 8% threatened in the USA or Australia to 17% in Europe overall. The table above lists the 15 most important "ecofactors" in this decline and illustrates their impact on the flora of one area, West Germany (31% threatened), in order of numbers of species affected by each pressure.

The plant treasury

The much touted Green Revolution has been only a skirmish in which some say we actually lost ground. The reason is that the "miracle" strains of wheat and rice were developed and applied with little attention to basic ecology and genetics. They needed much pampering, and so failed in regions where the environment was not suitable or intensive husbandry not possible. They were very inbred, which means that variation among the genes of each of the strains was extremely limited. Among a huge wheat field, for example, not a single plant was likely to possess the genetic make-up that might help it and its offspring resist pests and diseases.

Today we're on the verge of another green revolution, one much more far-reaching than that of the '60s, because we are realizing what the world's estimated 600,000 wild plant species have to offer, not only nutritionally, but also medically and materially, and in unsuspected ways as well. Over half the food eaten by humans comes from just three plants - wheat, rice and maize - and most of the rest from fewer than 20 others, yet there are 75,000 species known to be edible, many of them nutritious, like the beans of the Kalahari desert and the lake algae of Mexico and Chad. Continual improvements to the major crops are reliant on cross-breeding with their wild relatives. This requires, as does the development of new crop species, that wild stocks be large enough to provide a diverse genetic base on which to experiment with desired characteristics, such as high yields, disease and pest resistance, palatability (to humans and livestock), marketability, and economical methods of distribution. Sufficient stocks of plants are also needed to introduce or simply to maintain the hardy traditional cultivars (plants that are sown, but not selectively bred) important to many groups of people, from the unusual strains of rice grown in the Himalayan foothills to Ethiopian peas and barley.

Over 40% of "modern" medicines are derived from natural sources, mostly plants, and over three-quarters of the people living in rural areas rely on traditional herbal medicine. Although some 20,000 plants have been identified as having medicinal properties, only a fraction have been thoroughly examined. Of those that have, the pay-off has been high: atropine, curare, digitoxin, diosgenin, morphine, quinine, reserpine and vincristine.

New, less costly techniques for the analysis and extraction of medically active plant compounds has shifted the emphasis in drug research towards searching through nature's vast pharmacopoeia. The search is made easier by the new field of ethnobotany, whose practitioners turn to village healers and ancient literatures for information.

Our most "intimate" association with plants is in eating food and taking medicine, but no less important has been our reliance on them for construction material and fuel. Industry began with living plants, the trees, and then moved on to the non-living - coal, oil and gas formed millions of years ago from dead organic matter. These resources are in finite supply, and so industry is beginning to look back to living plants as new sources of not only fuels, but also oils, waxes, gums, rubber, textiles, pesticides and building materials.

Judicious use of plants will allow us to benefit from lands and waters normally considered worthless. The 1250 species of naturally salt-tolerant plants, the halophytes, can be grown on saline soils, including those made saline by bad irrigation practices, and can even be irrigated with sea water. Not only have they enormous potential as agricultural, medical and industrial products, but also in rehabilitating badly degraded lands along coastlines and at desert margins. Perhaps the most innovative research into plants that can use "worthless" water concerns the disposal of raw sewage. In an experiment in India, a grove of eucalyptus trees watered with sewage grew bigger and faster than a grove watered from a well,

The reawakening of interest in traditional, usually plant-based medicine is now worldwide. Research into plant drugs new and old is increasing, and the World Health Organisation, through its Traditional Medicine Programme, is supporting the integration of local healers and healing systems into mainstream health care, especially in developing countries. The book of herbalism in the West, however, is not without its dangers. As products flood the health stores, legislation and research lag behind, putting the consumer at risk. One example is mistletoe - a plant with an ancient place in European culture. Mistletoe can cause gastro-enteritis - yet commercially it is available as a dried herb tea. It should not be sold to the lay-person, though it does have valuable curative properties in controlled use.

CASE STUDY
Amaranth - mystical crop of the Aztecs

Amaranth is a poet's name for a fabulous, immortal flower. Better known in the West as love-lies-bleeding, this beautiful plant was once the Aztecs' most widely cultivated crop.

The almost complete disappearance of the amaranth from the world's larder was due to its incidental use as a dye. The red colouring made by the Aztecs from its flowers was closely associated with their religious ceremonies. When Hernán Cortés arrived in Mexico in 1519, he banned the growing of amaranth as part of his oppression of the Aztec religion. Cultivation persisted in isolated communities, but it was never again grown on a large scale.

Not until the 1970s, that is, when American researchers, suspecting its possible worth, began experimental cultivation. There are many properties of this plant that make it an exciting agricultural prospect. Although not a grass, it produces huge quantities of seed with an exceptionally high percentage of lysine-rich protein that cannot be matched by grains. In terms of cultivation, too, amaranth thrives in a dry, hot climate where grain is hard to grow, and is extremely efficient at converting water and sunlight into energy.

Of all the mysteries left behind by the Aztecs, this one at least has been solved. The scene now looks set for amaranth to make a triumphal re-entry back into the modern age, as a major food crop.

Amaranthus caudatus, *a native plant of Peru. Of the 60 species of* Amaranthus, *three produce massive seedheads some 30 cm long and 15 cm across, laden with thousands of tiny seeds.*

CASE STUDY
Dioscorea - India's contraceptive plant

Dioscorea – *India's answer to the contraceptive pill.*

Modern medicine is not all genetic engineering and advanced chemistry. In spite of the publicity given to these techniques, plants are still the mainstay of pharmacology.

With the world's human populations growing ever larger, and space becoming ever scarcer, the need for contraception has never been more pressing. One possible solution is growing wild in northern India. This is the plant *Dioscorea deltoidea*, a valuable source for a number of steroid drugs. Its tubers contain a high concentration of diosgenin, a cortico-steroid used in the production of cortisone and progesterone.

Traditional uses of dioscorea, based on its saponin content, have included washing wool and hair, treating body lice, and expelling parasitic worms. More recently, however, the extraction of diosgenin has developed into a considerable industry.

Most of India's steroid production is now based on dioscorea. *Dioscorea deltoidea* is one of two species exploited in India, and there are three more species growing in Mexico that also give a good yield of diosgenin. The genus is, in fact, a very large one of up to 800 species, and also includes the yam plant. About one-tenth of the species grow in India.

In the period between 1960 to 1974, 8000 tons of dry dioscorea tubers were harvested in India. The total stock of tubers left growing in the wild in India probably only amounts to 15,000 tons, and the demand continues to increase. All the dioscorea used is collected from the wild, and India also imports supplies from Mexico, though this is heavily taxed by the Mexican government.

The value of dioscorea is clearly appreciated. It is not likely to die of neglect, but there is a grave danger to wild populations from *ad hoc* collection. Restrictions do exist, which should protect wild populations from extinction, but these cannot distinguish high-yielding strains from less valuable ones. Because wild plants are very variable, the diosgenin yield is not consistent from one plant to another. It has already been suggested by one research team that the higher-yielding strains of dioscorea are disappearing, and this could become a significant problem in the future.

Various projects are under way to improve the yield of diosgenin. One of the most promising lines of research is tissue culture, by which very high-yielding material could be propagated indefinitely. This could take some pressure off the wild dioscorea of India, as well as helping to distribute the centres of production more widely within the country.

Plant diversity

Only in recent years has the world come to realize the full scope and importance of the natural resources offered by the plant world, or the extent to which we are losing them and the vital need to preserve them.

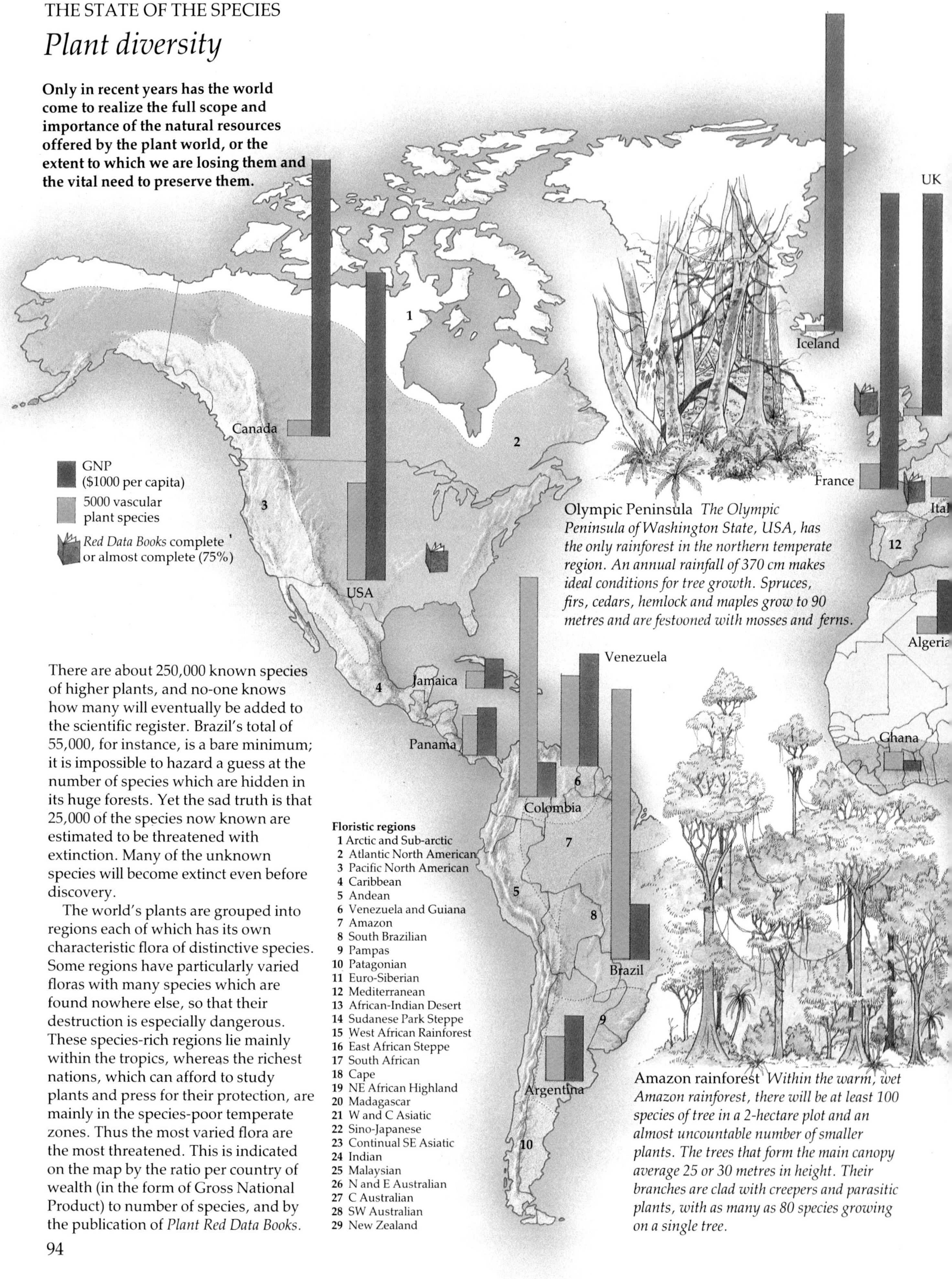

GNP
($1000 per capita)

5000 vascular
plant species

Red Data Books complete
or almost complete (75%)

There are about 250,000 known species of higher plants, and no-one knows how many will eventually be added to the scientific register. Brazil's total of 55,000, for instance, is a bare minimum; it is impossible to hazard a guess at the number of species which are hidden in its huge forests. Yet the sad truth is that 25,000 of the species now known are estimated to be threatened with extinction. Many of the unknown species will become extinct even before discovery.

The world's plants are grouped into regions each of which has its own characteristic flora of distinctive species. Some regions have particularly varied floras with many species which are found nowhere else, so that their destruction is especially dangerous. These species-rich regions lie mainly within the tropics, whereas the richest nations, which can afford to study plants and press for their protection, are mainly in the species-poor temperate zones. Thus the most varied flora are the most threatened. This is indicated on the map by the ratio per country of wealth (in the form of Gross National Product) to number of species, and by the publication of *Plant Red Data Books*.

Floristic regions
1 Arctic and Sub-arctic
2 Atlantic North American
3 Pacific North American
4 Caribbean
5 Andean
6 Venezuela and Guiana
7 Amazon
8 South Brazilian
9 Pampas
10 Patagonian
11 Euro-Siberian
12 Mediterranean
13 African-Indian Desert
14 Sudanese Park Steppe
15 West African Rainforest
16 East African Steppe
17 South African
18 Cape
19 NE African Highland
20 Madagascar
21 W and C Asiatic
22 Sino-Japanese
23 Continual SE Asiatic
24 Indian
25 Malaysian
26 N and E Australian
27 C Australian
28 SW Australian
29 New Zealand

Olympic Peninsula *The Olympic Peninsula of Washington State, USA, has the only rainforest in the northern temperate region. An annual rainfall of 370 cm makes ideal conditions for tree growth. Spruces, firs, cedars, hemlock and maples grow to 90 metres and are festooned with mosses and ferns.*

Amazon rainforest *Within the warm, wet Amazon rainforest, there will be at least 100 species of tree in a 2-hectare plot and an almost uncountable number of smaller plants. The trees that form the main canopy average 25 or 30 metres in height. Their branches are clad with creepers and parasitic plants, with as many as 80 species growing on a single tree.*

Canada

USA

Jamaica

Panama

Venezuela

Colombia

Brazil

Argentina

Iceland

UK

France

Italy

Algeria

Ghana

94

	Species	Extinct	Endangered	Threatened
Europe	11,500	20	120	2300
S. Africa	23,000	40	110	2100
Australia	25,000	120	200	1700
USA	20,000	90	840	1200
Mauritius	230	20	60	650
USSR	21,000	20	160	70

Threatened plants *The IUCN database shows the serious plight of the world's plants. In the areas listed on the left, the flora have been fully monitored. Yet Australia has many more species to be discovered, and the situation is worse in developing countries where the plants have not been so well studied. The flora of islands such as Mauritius are particularly vulnerable.*

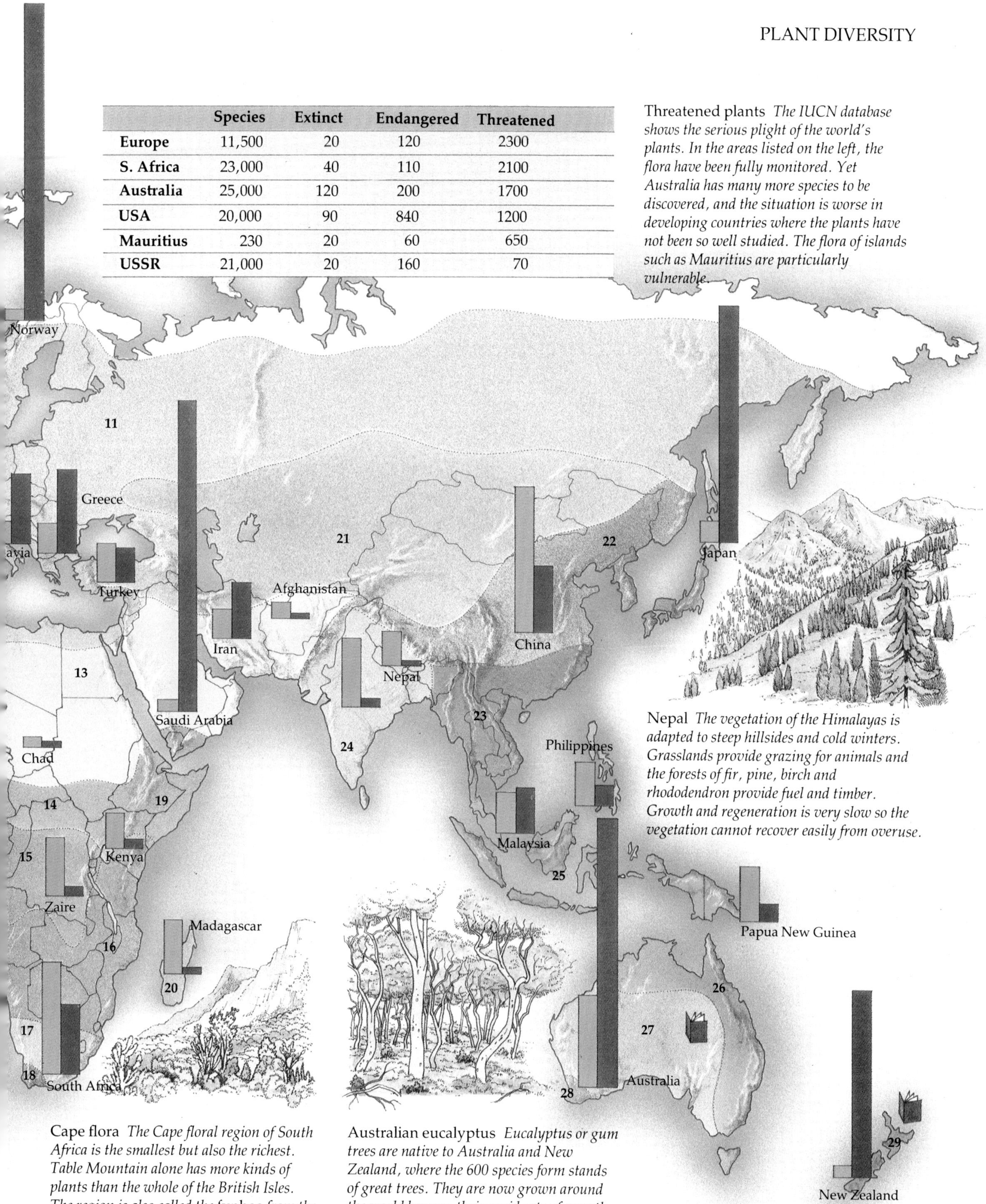

Norway

11

Greece

avia

Turkey

Afghanistan

21

22

Japan

Iran

Nepal

China

13

Saudi Arabia

Chad

24

23

Philippines

14

19

15

Kenya

Malaysia

25

Zaire

16

Madagascar

20

Papua New Guinea

17

26

18

South Africa

27

Australia

28

29

New Zealand

Nepal *The vegetation of the Himalayas is adapted to steep hillsides and cold winters. Grasslands provide grazing for animals and the forests of fir, pine, birch and rhododendron provide fuel and timber. Growth and regeneration is very slow so the vegetation cannot recover easily from overuse.*

Cape flora *The Cape floral region of South Africa is the smallest but also the richest. Table Mountain alone has more kinds of plants than the whole of the British Isles. The region is also called the* fynbos *from the number of fine-leaved plants, which include over 600 heaths.*

Australian eucalyptus *Eucalyptus or gum trees are native to Australia and New Zealand, where the 600 species form stands of great trees. They are now grown around the world because their rapid rate of growth makes them ideal for windbreaks and firewood supplies.*

In spring, the 200 or so grizzlies of Montana's Glacier National Park like to dine off cow parsnips growing on the high slopes. Park authorities are anxious to keep away trampling backpackers, who damage the plants. To find out where the cow parsnips are flourishing each year, and so which trails and campsites to close for spring, they use survey data from the Landsat satellite, passing overhead every 18 days.

In the USA, large tracts of undeveloped arid land have been planted with jojoba, whose bean produces a machine oil as fine as that from sperm whales. This helps industry, and takes pressure off the endangered, though now protected, whale. But how many wild plants and animals of arid lands will be threatened by this means of saving the whale?

and, surprisingly, harboured few mosquitoes or foul odours! Clearly, the researchers had taken lessons from wetland ecology (*see p.66*).

The revolution in attitudes towards how and which plants are useful is not without its blind spots. Sustainable use of living resources implies that they're managed wisely, like someone who happily lives on interest dividends by keeping a careful eye on capital investments. But wise management is not necessarily the watchword for utilization of plant resources today.

The threats to plants

Traditional cultivars, themselves rich in genetic material, were nearly squeezed out of existence by the mass planting of "super crops" in the early days of the Green Revolution. Scientists have since crossed the super crops with traditional variants, but the improved strains are so widely monocultured that the range of traditional cultivars is still threatened.

Some pharmaceutical companies and people who collect for them are in danger of killing the goose that lays the golden egg by gathering up such enormous quantities of medicinal plants that they obliterate wild stocks in some areas and severely deplete them in others, as has happened with *Dioscorea* and other Indian plants. Although ginseng is cultivated, it is terribly threatened by overcollecting in the wild in China and the USA. Loss of the genetic variation in these wild stocks could prove detrimental to the ginseng industry.

More alarming than the activities of pharmaceutical companies are the people who collect plants as one would collect stamps or coins. The hobby has stimulated a multi-million dollar trade, and for plants not widely propagated, the attack on their wild populations has been devastating. In addition to collecting, other forms of direct exploitation are threatening many plant species, like the wild relative of the olive in Niger which is cut to feed cattle, and the forest trees of Malaysia and Indonesia that are felled for their fruit because it doesn't drop when ripe - and, say the consumers, because the trees are too tall to climb anyway.

Another threat involves the plants and animals newly introduced to a region, especially on islands, where the native plants have had no evolutionary experience in resisting exotic competitors or predators (*see p.78*). Among the most stubborn "carpet-bagger" plants are the prickly pear that has invaded over 24 million hectares of Australia, and the lovely lantana, with its tiny pink and yellow blooms, but which is not so lovely in Hawaii where it has overtaken the habitats of many endemic plant species.

Plants are even threatened by "nature lovers", including well-meaning conservationists. Maybe hikers can be forgiven the damage they do, because improper planning of trails and lack of supervision are really at fault. However, tales of two animal conservation projects do take the breath away. As a protective measure, the Cretan ibex (a rare wild goat) was introduced to an island off Crete, where it ate all but three individuals of an unusual endemic dwarf shrub. And in a bison reserve in America, all thought was for the bison which, allowed to roam freely, ate up a valuable strain of wild grape.

But by far and away the greatest single threat to wild plants is simple to tell - the progressive degradation and loss of habitats described in Chapter 2, from the grubbing up of hedgerows in Britain to the pulping of entire rainforests. Ironically, large-scale cultivation of wild plants for newly discovered uses has led to massive clearance of natural vegetation, as with the jojoba bean in the USA.

Outright destruction is happening fastest in the developing countries, in places that ominously coincide with regions of maximum plant diversity (*see p.94*). And in these regions too live the tribal folk, just as threatened as the plants and animals around them, and the only people to know what, how and when to collect and use the plants that we may need.

The mountain forests of Tanzania

African violet is one of the best-known of all houseplants. It is so widely cultivated that the world trade of this one plant is put at about $30 million a year. But the wild African violet, listed as one of the 12 most endangered plants on Earth, is not doing so well. Its forest home in the Usambara Mountains is shrinking year by year to feed the cooking fires of Tanzania.

African violet is not the only plant in danger of extinction in this corner of the world. The mountains of Tanzania (particularly those to the east) have an especially rich flora. Although less than 2% of the country is wet enough to grow rainforest (a total land area of 16,000 square kilometres), as many different species of plants grow here as in the whole of Kenya, Malawi, Mozambique and Uganda put together.

These eastern forests are also botanically unique. Probably 25 million years old, it has been estimated that they contain over 2000 different species of plants, at least 500 of which are endemic. Among the better-known plants to have come out of this region are 18 of the 20 known species of African violet, 53 of the 109 known species of busy lizzie, 16 species of coffee (of which 10 are endemic), and the African primrose. There is also a tree that yields a timber so enduring that it can be buried without damage; a spectrum of fruits and spices that have no common name in English; and an enormous variety of locally used medicinal plants.

These forests are being cut down. Because wood is so scarce in Tanzania, there is a great shortage of fuel and this, incredibly, is the forest's destiny. All the richness of vegetation, the potential wealth of valuable plants, could go up in smoke. The timber is also in demand for building material. There are pine plantations, but the country is too poor to afford the wood preservatives needed to make softwood fit for use.

There is also a shortage of water. Forest, mountains and water go together in this arid land. Where mountainous slopes are denuded of trees, the catchment of rain is damaged along with the slopes. Loss of trees is slowly but surely cutting down the available water.

It is very clear that the deforestation of Tanzania will bring no benefits to the growing population. Development aid is urgently needed. Some assistance has come from Finland, in the form of help to

Eighteen of the 20 known species of African violet are found only in Tanzania.

Nearly half the world's known species of busy lizzie come from the Usambara Mountain region. Only nine have so far been used by plant breeders.

There are approximately 40 species of coffee worldwide, of which 16 are found in the forests of Tanzania. Their potential usefulness has not yet been explored.

build sawmills and, however well-intentioned, this ill-advised gesture has simply accelerated the pace of forest destruction.

In 1986, an EEC/IUCN project was launched to try and find ways to resolve the problems. Among the aims of this project is the establishment of a reserve area where constructive forest exploitation can be developed. There will also be assistance with land use, marketing crops, supporting watershed systems, and promoting village-level activities. Some strict reserves will also be established.

If the richness of life in the mountain forests of Tanzania can be used properly,

it could be the key to a new economic future for the country. The few native species that have so far been exploited are paying handsome dividends. The world coffee industry is worth $12 billion a year, and many wild varieties growing in Tanzania have hardly been described, let alone studied. The drugs industry gets 40% of its sales from wild plants, making $40 billion annually, and the promising medicinal potential of the forests still awaits investigation.

The Animal Kingdom

From microbe to mammal, the animals of the Ark are linked together in close interdependence with each other, with us, and with their living environment. We still have little knowledge of this complex web of life, or the damage we are doing to it.

Scientists study the Animal Kingdom in various ways, and these can yield very different levels of understanding. Traditionally, we have described it in terms of different species – their numbers and division into related groups, using the familiar definitions of vertebrate or invertebrate, mammal, or bird. Species listings have been the main basis for *Red Data Books* of threatened wildlife.

An alternative description is by what we call "trophic levels", a hierarchy of feeding levels from herbivore to carnivore, and of the resultant flow of energy up food chains from the primary producers, plants, to the highest consumers, the predators. Understanding trophic levels brings home the significance of that relentless threat to wildlife – habitat destruction.

Ecologists are even more interested in studying animals in communities, and the complex webs of inter-relationships that bind them together. If these links are broken by loss of one thread, there is a knock-on effect throughout the whole community.

When threats to species, to trophic levels and to life webs are taken all together, the pressures of habitat loss, overexploitation, pollution, and general upsetting of systems by our human actions are seen to have grim consequences. The few species listed in *Red Data Books* pale into insignificance beside the estimated number of overall threats to the Animal Kingdom.

Trophic level

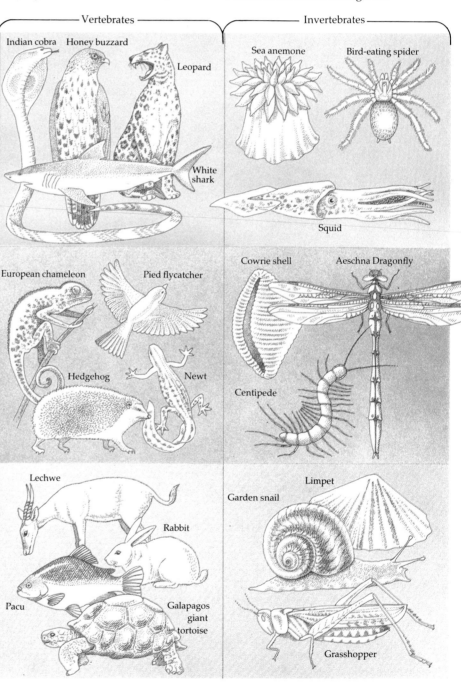

| Vertebrates | Invertebrates |

Tertiary consumers
(top carnivores)
Top carnivores are at the head of food chains, and vulnerable to their disturbance. A decline in populations at this highest trophic level warns of trouble in the whole system. They tend to eat secondary consumers, but may also eat herbivores, and generally prey on lower levels. Hawks, for instance, will consume smaller birds but also include beetles in their diets.

Indian cobra Honey buzzard Leopard White shark Sea anemone Bird-eating spider Squid

Secondary consumers
(invertivores/primary carnivores)
At intermediate trophic levels are found the secondary consumers which dine mainly off the plant eaters. These include the invertivores – from spiders eating crickets to birds eating slugs – and the primary carnivores, feeding on smaller herbivorous mammals, birds, reptiles and fish, plus many mixed feeders. Secondary consumers are more numerous than top predators.

European chameleon Pied flycatcher Hedgehog Newt Cowrie shell Aeschna Dragonfly Centipede

Primary consumers
(herbivores)
At the lowest trophic levels in the Animal Kingdom are found the grazers, fruit and nectar eaters, and other creatures which feed directly off plants – the primary food producers. Herbivores range from elephants to zooplankton, and include litter feeders. Primary consumers in a system total a greater number and bulk than the higher levels which prey on them.

Lechwe Rabbit Pacu Galapagos giant tortoise Limpet Garden snail Grasshopper

Omnivores and adaptive feeders

Omnivores show little dietary specialization, selecting widely from plant and animal prey. They are found throughout the Animal Kingdom, from insects and fish through to pigs, primates and, of course, humans. Because they are less tied to any special food item or location, omnivores are less vulnerable to change – indeed, they can take advantage of it. Such responses may be ecologically and evolutionarily adaptive, allowing rapid leaps in development and exploitation of ever-wider resources. Humans, one of the most adaptive species, are omnivores par excellence – and the ultimate predators on all food chains. They are the most dangerous creatures of the whole Animal Kingdom.

Proportions of animal groups

It is surprising how little we know about the true extent of the Animal Kingdom. The pie charts below show species so far identified – nearly one and a half million, of which most are invertebrates, hugely outnumbering the better understood vertebrate groups. But estimates of unknown invertebrates yet to be discovered range from 2 to 30 million more!

Food chains and energy flow

Plants make energy available to the community, herbivores eat them, and they in turn are eaten by carnivores, which are eaten by larger ones. At every step the energy transferred is less, sustaining a smaller biomass of species at each higher trophic level. This is a much simplified food chain concept. In real life, however, things are more complex. Food chains are really food webs, and few animals feed from only one, lower level. Moreover, many organisms die of causes other than predation, their remains supplying energy to detritus feeders.

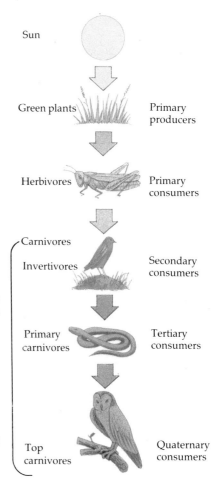

Sun

Green plants — Primary producers

Herbivores — Primary consumers

Carnivores / Invertivores — Secondary consumers

Primary carnivores — Tertiary consumers

Top carnivores — Quaternary consumers

Estimated unknown invertebrates 2-30 million

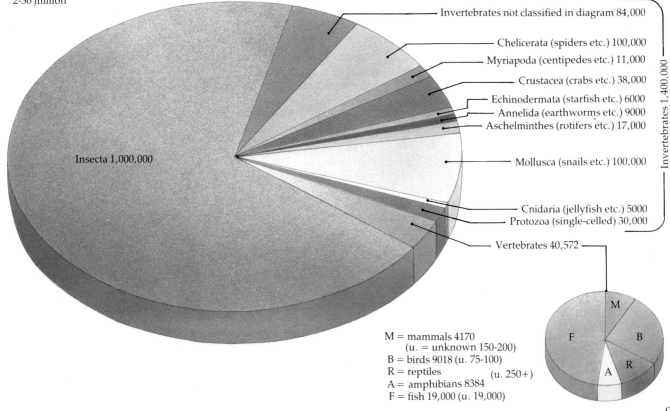

Invertebrates not classified in diagram 84,000
Chelicerata (spiders etc.) 100,000
Myriapoda (centipedes etc.) 11,000
Crustacea (crabs etc.) 38,000
Echinodermata (starfish etc.) 6000
Annelida (earthworms etc.) 9000
Aschelminthes (rotifers etc.) 17,000
Mollusca (snails etc.) 100,000
Cnidaria (jellyfish etc.) 5000
Protozoa (single-celled) 30,000
Insecta 1,000,000
Invertebrates 1,400,000
Vertebrates 40,572

M = mammals 4170
    (u. = unknown 150-200)
B = birds 9018 (u. 75-100)
R = reptiles (u. 250+)
A = amphibians 8384
F = fish 19,000 (u. 19,000)

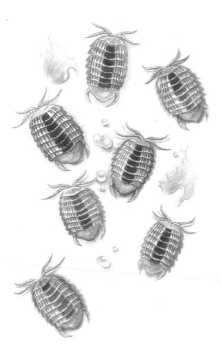

The Socorro isopod, a small creature related to the wood louse, is found only in New Mexico, USA, in an abandoned bath house fed by a hot water spring. It probably lived in a marsh maintained by three local springs, but most of the water from these has been diverted to a nearby town and the marsh has dried up. It and its habitat are protected by federal law in the USA, and a plan for its recovery has been implemented.

Billions of bugs

Invertebrates - the animals without backbones - outnumber vertebrates 20 times in terms of species and outweigh them by much, much more. Not surprisingly, then, they are found throughout all ecosystems at all heterotrophic levels and play all the roles, both major and minor, as herbivores, carnivores, parasites and scavengers. Many are detritivores, forming the vital link between organic matter and the bacteria and fungi (each of which comprises a living Kingdom on its own), that decompose it into the elemental molecules on which all life is based. As pollinators, invertebrates are responsible for the survival of more than two-thirds of the flowering plants, and as tillers, they prepare the soil for plant growth. Many other animals and even some plants and fungi rely directly on them for food. They are among the most cosmopolitan of animals (houseflies) and the most parochial (the Socorro isopod) and, to humans, the most vexing (mosquitoes), frightening (tarantulas), dangerous (cone shells), indispensible (earthworms), delicious (lobsters) and beautiful (butterflies).

It is difficult to describe the wild status of these eclectic and fascinating creatures, because they have received relatively little attention from conservation biologists, who tend to concentrate on higher plants and vertebrates - the first *Red Data Book* on invertebrates was published only in 1983. And, until quite recently, invertebrates have been neglected in conservation projects, sometimes to their cost. In one British woodland, 14 of its 17 species of butterfly became extinct soon after it was declared a nature reserve, because management did not take into account their habitat requirements.

The direct human-invertebrate association goes back a long time: gathering honey from bees' nests and *fruits de mer*, making silk from moth larvae and dye from bugs, dressing wounds with spiders' webs, using shells as money, vessels and ornaments, and keeping crickets for the pleasure of hearing their songs. Negative aspects of the association include the damage invertebrates do to our crops and constructions, and the human and livestock illnesses they transmit or cause directly. But for an ever-increasing number of these problems, remedies have been discovered among the invertebrates themselves. Biological control involves the introduction of carefully chosen predatory or competitive species that reduce the "pest" population with none of the dangerous ecological side-effects that invariably accompany chemical control. Other modern uses of the invertebrate "resource" lie in medicine and industry. The inhabitants of coral reefs are being screened for compounds to treat cancer, cardiovascular disease, hypertension and flu, with promising results, and research on fireflies has aided the development of a heatless illumination.

How invertebrates function in ecosystems is less well-studied than for vertebrates, with the possible exception of the pollinators. Without the services of such insects as bees, wasps, butterflies, moths, beetles and even flies and mosquitoes, most domestic and wild plants would disappear. Less obvious but equally vital activities are carried out on and in the ground by worms, millipedes, snails, insects and their larvae, which work up the litter into a state suitable for rapid decomposition by the microbes, and at the same time help aerate the soil and regulate its moisture content. In wetland and aquatic ecosystems, various crustaceans, like crabs and waterfleas, are also important detritivores. In rainforests and grasslands, it is particularly the leaf- and seed-gathering termites and ants which form a major link in the nutrient cycle. The wood ants of temperate zones also act as insect predators and honey "middlemen". They quickly suppress outbreaks of tree pests, and the surplus of honeydew they take from aphids is used by bees. Ants from one nest in Germany collected 200 litres of honeydew in one summer.

As it is for plants, the major threat to the world's invertebrates is habitat destruction. Of all species of organisms living in rainforests, 85%

CASE STUDY
The beetle and the bushfly

The dung beetle - a natural enemy of the Australian bushfly.

When cows were brought to Australia, nobody gave much thought to what would become of their droppings. In a hot, dry land, cowpats do not decompose in the same way as they do in rainy climates. They become hard, brittle and dry, and can take up to three years to break down. With 30 million head of cattle, each dropping 12 cowpats a day, the total of 131.4 billion cowpats a year is enough to cover a million hectares of land.

On top of all these cowpats, ever since the cattle arrived, the Australian bushfly breeds. The crust on a single cowpat can - and often does - accommodate 500 bushfly larvae. This biting fly was considered to be an inescapable part of the joys of the bush. Nobody questioned its presence, until Dr George Bormemissza saw the illogic of an assumed "native" creature depending on an introduced species.

Where wild cattle live in hot, dry climates naturally, their droppings are used up by dung beetles. Australia has its dung beetles, but they are adapted to feed on marsupial droppings and find cowpats too difficult. In 1967, a programme to introduce cattle-dung beetles into the Australian bush was begun. Twenty species were selected, from a variety of sources, and they are now firmly established. As hoped, the bushfly is indeed succumbing; areas once made intolerable by flies now have only a few.

The secret of the dung beetles' devastating effect does not lie merely in its ability to bury dung. When a dung beetle starts to work on a cowpat, it disturbs the crust so that any fly larvae there sink into the middle and drown.

CASE STUDY
The worms turn

The importance of earthworms was established by Charles Darwin in 1881. Gilbert White, writing in 1777, observed that the earth *"without worms would soon become cold, hardbound and void of fermentation; and consequently sterile…"* Since then, the rôle of worms in maintaining soil fertility has been taken for granted. In very recent times, however, it seems to have been largely forgotten.

On average, earthworms account for about 12% of the weight of animals in the soil of a meadow. The amount of soil they bring to the surface in worm casts has been estimated at between 1.2 and 15 tons per hectare per year. This is only a small proportion of the soil shifted by worms, however, since most species deposit casts in their tunnels. Tunnels and casts are formed as the earthworms burrow through the soil, taking in both soil and the organic debris it contains and excreting soil and "digested" organic matter.

Earthworm activity improves soil texture, surface infiltration and drainage. An old farmer's adage "too much lime makes a rich father and a poor son", refers to lime's inhibiting effect on earthworms; reducing worms eventually reduces soil fertility.

Traditional cultivation used manure for fertilizing the soil. Now chemical fertilizers are applied, in proportions calculated to provide for the specific needs of a particular crop. This takes care of the immediate needs of the crop, certainly, but does nothing to improve or even maintain the soil condition.

The organic matter worms feed on, though abundant in manure, is completely absent from chemical fertilizers. Where these are used, the number of worms in the soil is reduced. Organic content of arable land is further depleted by the new practice of repeatedly sowing the same crop. Where rotation once helped to control disease, now every scrap of organic material must be collected and burned to prevent persistent pests and diseases.

It is hard to say whether modern farmers consider worms to be of any importance to their operations. They can lay land drains and "soil improvers" as and when they wish. But the growing industry of worm farming is founded on the fact that there is more to worms than a mechanical tilling service. It has been found that when soil passes through a worm it becomes a better growing medium. Worm casts show improved water retention, and elements such as nitrogen, phosphorus, potassium and magnesium are present in an easily available form. In some way, worm casts encourage root growth and inhibit "damping off". These effects have not yet been fully investigated, but tests conducted so far have produced excellent results.

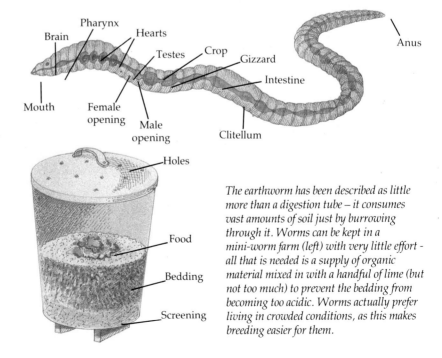

The earthworm has been described as little more than a digestion tube – it consumes vast amounts of soil just by burrowing through it. Worms can be kept in a mini-worm farm (left) with very little effort - all that is needed is a supply of organic material mixed in with a handful of lime (but not too much) to prevent the bedding from becoming too acidic. Worms actually prefer living in crowded conditions, as this makes breeding easier for them.

Invertebrates – the teeming millions

Invertebrates contribute to the maintenance of the biosphere through their role in the cycling of nutrients – they eat the living or dead tissues of plants and animals, and with their ceaseless activity break down organic material in the soil. They also form major links in the food webs of larger animals, and are of direct importance to humans – as food or as pollinators of crops, as disease organisms and pests or as the natural controllers of pests.

How many invertebrates are threatened with extinction? It is difficult to estimate the true numbers that may exist, let alone the percentage that may be threatened. One survey suggests that there could be 12,000 species of beetles in a single hectare of tropical forest canopy, indicating a potentially massive species loss through present forest clearance. Some scientists, notably Norman Myers, believe that half the world's insect species – most of them undescribed – will disappear in the next 25 years. Examples of known endangered invertebrates, and the threats to their survival, are depicted on the map. The underlying grid, *right*, provides a scale against which the numbers of known and unknown species can be compared. Estimated numbers of invertebrates vary hugely, from 2 to 30 million. We have used the conservative figure of 10 million.

Often overlooked but always with us, the teeming millions of invertebrate animals, in all their diversity, form a base without which other forms of life cannot survive.

Avalon hairstreak butterfly
The Avalon hairstreak butterfly is confined to Santa Catalina Island, California. This makes it interesting to zoologists studying evolution, ecology and genetics, but also makes it vulnerable to extinction because it is very close to a major conurbation. It could also be at risk if its nearest relative, the gray hairstreak, a wide-ranging North American species, became established on the island. This species could either outcompete the Avalon hairstreak or hybridize with it.

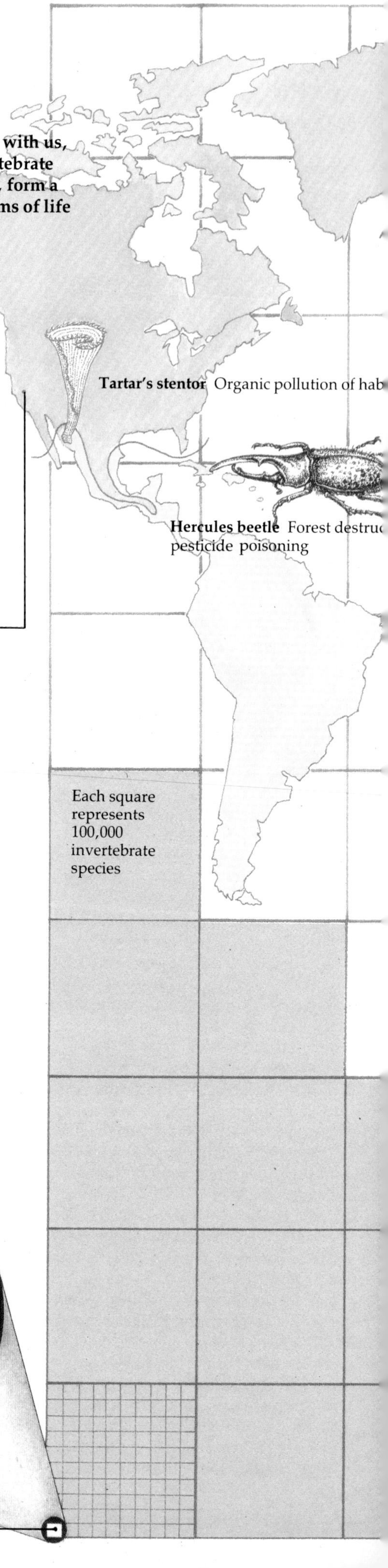

Tartar's stentor Organic pollution of hab

Hercules beetle Forest destruc
pesticide poisoning

Each square represents 100,000 invertebrate species

1,400,000 known invertebrate species

10,000,000 (estimated) unknown invertebrate species

■ Species in *Red Data Books*

Biogeographic realms

Nearctic (56)

Neotropical (11)

Palaearctic (48)

Africotropical (8)

Indomalayan (6)

Oceanian (18)

Australian (29)

Antarctic

Pacific Ocean (19)
Atlantic Ocean (7)
Indian Ocean (13)
Mediterranean (3)
Caribbean (3)
Red Sea (4)

Numbers in parentheses indicate number of invertebrate species listed in the *Red Data Books*

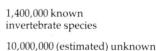

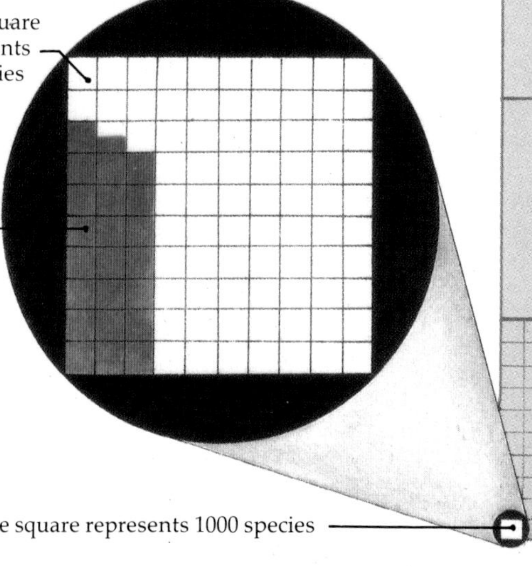

One square represents 10 species

225 species in *Red Data Books*

One square represents 1000 species

Medicinal leech Overcollection, habitat destruction

Peripatus Habitat disruption

Ground beetle (*Calosoma sycophanta*)
This 25-millimetre beetle lives in many parts of Europe and northern Asia, where both adults and grubs feed on tree-dwelling caterpillars. Its numbers have declined seriously in many countries, but it has been introduced to North America to help control caterpillar pests like the gipsy moth.

Giant weta Introduced predators, habitat destruction

Robber crab
The robber or coconut crab is probably the largest terrestrial arthropod in the world. Frequently weighing over 3 kilograms and measuring 1 metre across the legs, this hermit crab lives in burrows on many islands in the Indo-Pacific region. Its larger size makes it attractive to humans both as a source of food and as curios for the tourist trade. However, intensive hunting has reduced its numbers so severely that in some places its collection is banned or regulated.

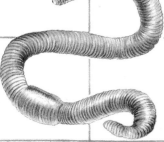

South African giant earthworms
It is odd to think of earthworms as being threatened with extinction but many South African earthworms have restricted ranges and cannot withstand habitat changes. The biggest earthworm in the world,
Microchaetus microchaetus, *which may reach 7 metres in length with a diameter of 2-3 centimetres, is being exterminated by the lowering of the water table and desertification caused by overgrazing. It is in our interests to protect these earthworms, as they condition the soil and their casts help to reduce erosion.*

Termites in tropical forests are actually nourished by the fungus and bacteria growing on the plant matter they eat. The drying out and warming up that occurs with selective logging of a forest is enough to slow the decomposers' attack on the litter, which makes it less palatable to the termites, threatening their survival.

Farming is one possible solution to the threat of overharvesting of edible invertebrates. European snail farming has had limited success so far, but the future looks better for the Indo-Pacific giant clam, which is the only "phototrophic" creature known that could become a "farm" animal. Most plants are phototrophic - they use the sun's energy to make their own food - and so is the giant clam by virtue of the algae-like organisms that live in its mantle. Young clams are hatched and grown in tanks, and when they're big enough to survive predation, they are "planted" out on the reef, needing nothing but clean water and sunlight until harvest. These techniques are being used to re-establish the giant clam in the waters of Guam, where it had recently become extinct.

have never been named, much less studied, and most of them are invertebrates. With the loss of these forests, in which plant and animal distribution is patchy and localized at best, whole species of invertebrate are disappearing, their secrets never to be known. But even with less drastic disturbance to rainforest, the invertebrate fauna is affected. In a forest in Sarawak, over half the species of termites had disappeared less than a year after the loggers had moved through.

In Europe, the drainage of wetlands has caused the precipitous decline of 16 species of butterfly and numerous dragonflies, and the felling of mature woodlands or "tidying" them by removal of dead and dying timber has endangered the ants and other forest insects. British bees, and consequently, bee-keepers and the farmers whose crops rely on bee pollination, are suffering from the ploughing up of hedges and meadows. There are fewer wild flowers from which honeybees can gather nectar and fewer nesting and overwintering sites for bumblebees (which are even better pollinators than honeybees).

More research has been done on the insects than on other European invertebrates, and so tentative assessments of their status have been made - 6000 are thought to be facing extinction. If this number of insects is in trouble, how many more worms, snails, spiders and the like, which share the same habitats in Europe, are threatened?

Second only to habitat destruction in the plight of invertebrates is the injudicious use of chemical pesticides. The dangers of pesticides are so obvious, it seems no-one could miss them; but some people still do not seem to grasp the fact that most pesticides are designed to kill invertebrates, so their effects go way beyond a targeted caterpillar or weevil. Ecologists have re-christened them "biocides" because of their direct toxicity to so many life forms, including worms and other beneficial soil organisms and predatory insects which have proven to be better controllers of crop pests than pesticides. Possibly, the notoriety given to DDT by Rachel Carson's book, *Silent Spring*, published in 1962, led to its banning in the USA in 1972, but just a few years later, an official of no less an august body than the Environmental Protection Agency was heard to complain about the new law. He recalled that people used to put their beehives under the flight paths of the crop sprayers, which would kill more of the mites that infested the hives than the bees themselves! As bees' high sensitivity to pesticides is well-known and their role in crop pollination is as indisputable as the law of gravity, the mind boggles at such a statement. Perhaps an infinitesimal advance in ecological awareness was made a few years later, when a control programme was mounted against grasshoppers in Wyoming, not with DDT of course, but with one of the many insecticides known to be toxic to bees. It was announced that "all bees will be removed before spraying". Honeybee hives were indeed removed, but as many as 50 species of wild bee, which are responsible for pollinating the native flora, were left behind.

Because invertebrates respond so dramatically to changes in their physical and chemical environment, we have found yet another "use" for them - as indicators of environmental quality. Their sensitivity and short life cycles permit early detection of even subtle habitat alterations - in fact, as soon as the next generations of indicator species are scheduled to appear. The Nature Conservancy Council of Britain has published maps of what species of dragonfly should be found in "healthy" habitats, and biologists and amateurs alike are using them to assess the quality of the British countryside.

The other main threat to invertebrates is direct overexploitation. Butterflies and shells have always been collectors' items, but the attentions of enthusiasts and commercial traders are increasing. Certain crustaceans and molluscs, once commonplace on the table, have been turned into expensive delicacies by overharvesting. Populations of the edible snail of Europe (*escargots*) and the giant clam of the Indo-Pacific have already undergone declines and local extinctions throughout their ranges. The

CASE STUDY
Collectors cash in on rarity

It is a great misfortune to be beautiful. The human desire to possess beauty extends to every corner of the natural world. In all cultures, and through all ages, pretty things have been collected for personal adornment, interior decoration, and as a form of wealth.

There is no limit to the efforts some people will make to acquire a special treasure. The harder it is to find, the greater its value, and so the more desirable it becomes. A rare seashell, butterfly, or even beetle, becomes more valuable as it approaches extinction, and conservationists are likely to be outbidded by market forces.

Many vertebrate species have fallen victim to the possessiveness of egg collectors, fish fanciers and falconers in the past. The collectors of invertebrates are equally insatiable, publishing their own trade papers and dealing in black markets. One of the most sought-after butterflies is also the world's biggest, the Queen Alexandra's birdwing. This magnificent endangered creature lives in the forests of Papua New Guinea. The government there has blazed an exemplary trail of wildlife conservation, in combination with the exploitation of commercially valuable species. This butterfly has been protected since 1966 from unauthorized collecting, and the organization controlling insect farming and trading on the islands estimates income from this industry at $50,000 a year. Unfortunately, protection from collectors is not enough, and Queen Alexandra's birdwing remains endangered due to loss of habitat through forest clearance.

Other insects in other places are equally endangered by collecting plus habitat loss. Probably 10% of all swallowtail butterflies in the world are in danger of extinction, and the status of most beetles is not even known. One beetle that has attracted some attention is the iridescent *Carabus olympiae* of the Italian Alps. Collectors thought they had exterminated it in 1928, but it somehow survived and was found again in 1942. A programme of captive breeding is at present keeping up the numbers of wild beetles, but only by protecting its habitat will its long-term survival be assured. Even though a special protection bill was passed in 1983, collectors will still pay over $300 for a dead specimen.

Marine animals are less accessible than land animals. They also have a much larger area to hide and breed in,

and are thus less likely to suffer extinction at the hands of collectors. Nevertheless, the scale of trade in seashells, corals and other decorative marine creatures is so colossal as to be causing some concern. It is hard to estimate the full size of the seashell trade, but it ran to well over 40,000 tons worldwide in 1977.

The income generated by exporting seashells is important to many small countries whose chief resource is a warm sea. The effects of shell collecting on the environment as a whole have not been assessed in most of these places. Where observations have been made, the situation seems to vary from sustainable to disastrous. Loss of triton shells from the Indo-Pacific region has caused

The sale of shells in shops and on stalls is only the tip of the iceberg. The bulk of the trade, the massive export of thousands of tons of shells by large trading companies to markets in the West, is unseen.

plagues of their normal prey, the crown-of-thorns starfish, which have wrecked coral reefs. On the other hand, the collection of hundreds of tons of capiz shells in the Philippines does not yet seem to have had any significant effect. The impact of collecting here seems to depend on whether target shells are important links in the marine food chains. Removal of a key species, be it a food source to other organisms or a major predator, can disrupt the balance of the whole ecosystem.

Indonesian coconut or robber crab is collected in boatloads by the Sulawesians; practically all meat, since it has lost the habit of carrying around a shell, it grows to the size of a newborn baby! Sadly, it is unlikely to be able to sustain such heavy cropping.

Animals with backbones

The very ancient lineage of our own group, the vertebrates, demonstrates our humble beginnings. We share a common ancestor with the starfish.

Although vertebrates number less than one-twentieth of all other known animal species, they are only slightly more restricted in terms of where they live on the planet and they perform in just as many ecological roles. The best-known groups are fish, amphibians, reptiles, birds and mammals, each of which probably every privileged child has kept as a pet - guppies, tadpoles, turtles, budgies and cats. But many wild relatives of our childhood companions have been put on the list of species threatened with extinction. How they've come to be listed and the magnitude of loss the world will feel when they pass away is the most stunning condemnation of our own species, next to the continued development of nuclear weapons.

Past vertebrate extinctions, either before our time (the dinosaurs) or even during our early days (the megafauna of the Pleistocene), occurred at a rate measured in millennia from the time of species abundance to extinction, whatever the cause. Today we measure it in decades: the Steller's sea cow of the far northern Pacific disappeared within 27 years of its discovery in the 18th century, and since 1750 more than 60 species of vertebrate have died out in the USA.

It is difficult to say when "modern" extinctions started. The conventional date is from the Age of Exploration, about 400 years ago, but extinction rates were high just prior to that time in places like Madagascar and New Zealand. These are islands, where extinctions are undoubtedly accelerated, but they are very large, and the ultimate causes of their extinctions reflect what began to happen everywhere after 1600 - first and foremost, habitat alteration, but for certain species, sudden obliteration by overexploitation.

Until fairly recently, intact habitat was still available to most animals, yet even so, such creatures as the quagga (a zebra with stripes only in front) and the famous passenger pigeon died out rather suddenly at the hands of the modern overkillers. Today the pressures of overexploitation are grave and ever-growing, and degradation or loss of habitat provide the final push over the edge - for once a species' numbers drop and there is not enough suitable space in which to recover them, extinction is inevitable.

We are well aware of the details of the exterminations of the last few centuries and of the implications of the losses in terms of ecosystem stability and genetic resources; yet we still continue to be directly responsible for the decline of many vertebrate species. Few wild animals would be threatened today if they were taken only for immediate human needs. Instead they're killed for luxury markets in meat and skins and for trophies, souvenirs, decorations, jewellery and aphrodisiacs, and incredible numbers of vertebrates, large and small, are captured alive for menageries, pet shops and laboratories - there to suffer and die from neglect or invasive experimentation. There are laws now regulating many of these activities, especially in the trade of live threatened species and their dead parts (*see p.136*), but in some countries authorities are easily persuaded to turn a blind eye to infringements and in others the legislation is weak or outdated. A number of developing countries still classify some of their very rare animals as "vermin". Some of the most horrific animal slaughters occur because it is thought, usually erroneously, that by eradicating large predators and herbivores or those animals which carry diseases, we protect ourselves, our livestock and crops and "our"

CASE STUDY
The insatiable demand for bushmeat

People have to eat. In many parts of Africa, the traditional way to get meat is to go out and kill something. This game is called bushmeat, and is an important component of national diets. It is not always easy for game wardens to distinguish between subsistence hunting for bushmeat and poaching for profit. Indeed, the bushmeat market itself is something of an industry; it makes a profit for the hunters and middlemen, but at the same time could be regarded as a means of subsistence in the national sense.

Prohibitions on poaching in colonial times usually included bushmeat. This weakened the legislation and often led to its evasion because it was seen as unreasonable. On the other hand, poachers have benefited from the confusion. What is needed now is a clear policy to take account of the needs of people as well as those of wildlife. Nobody will benefit if the stocks of bushmeat are overhunted. The sensible course would be to regard bushmeat as a renewable resource, to be managed and controlled for optimum return.

Bushmeat is not some anonymous creature running around in the bush. It is antelopes, monkeys, rodents, bats, porcupines, wild pigs, lizards and many other species. Some species are in great danger of extinction from being overhunted; others, like the manatee and pigmy hippopotamus of Ghana, have already been exterminated.

The sheer volume of the bushmeat market makes it hard to believe that anything can still survive in the bush. In Ghana, it is estimated that 75% of the population depend on wild food. During a period of 19 months (from December 1968 to June 1970), Kantamanto Market in Accra handled nearly 158,000 kilograms of bushmeat from 13 species of animals. In Botswana, the annual consumption of bushmeat is estimated to be over 9 million kilograms. This has enabled Botswana to export $2.5 million worth of spare beef that would otherwise have been eaten locally had bushmeat not been available. At the same time, export of game skins is worth $280,000 a year. Bushmeat is obviously a valuable resource.

Some species clearly cannot breed quickly enough to make up for the high level of hunting, and these simply must be protected or they will become extinct. Many of the favoured species, however, are comparatively efficient breeders. One

way these species might be protected is by establishing areas where culling can be controlled.

Game farming has been tried by many landowners in South Africa. It has not proved profitable unless it has been coupled with some form of "safari" industry. Land in South Africa is largely privately owned, however, as is the case in Zimbabwe and Namibia. A national effort, such as might be possible in Ghana and other African states with little private landownership, might be more cost-effective.

Another possibility is to raise some species in full captivity. Though not very successful with the larger ungulates, it has been tried with good results on a number of rodents in Ghana. Some species, in particular the cane rat and the giant rat, are very popular as bushmeat. Cane rats, which can be fed almost

Warthogs, pictured here at the Msinga waterhole on the Mkuzi Game Reserve, South Africa, are a popular item on the bushmeat menu.

entirely on elephant grass, will breed quickly enough for a "tame" generation to be obtained quite soon and, once this is achieved, settle down well as cage animals.

Whatever measures are taken to protect Africa's wildlife, it is essential that the principles should be fully understood by the people who will be affected by them. Many of the traditional attitudes towards the wild, incorporating taboos and customs that helped to protect hunted species, have been lost as the pattern of life has changed. A renewed sense of stewardship is evidently called for if Africa's rich wildlife assets are to be safeguarded.

Vertebrates – threatened on all fronts

Vertebrates are familiar, eye-catching and popular. People are willing to donate time and money to protect them – from pandas, whales and elephants to otters and hedgehogs, even lizards or frogs. But the impact of human progress belies our concern – the "wild animals" of our childhood may be the extinct species of our old age.

Compared with the uncharted millions of invertebrates, vertebrates are fewer, much more visible, and consequently better known. We also know much more about the conservation status of many vertebrates. But the picture is not a happy one. All round the world, declining population figures reveal alarming trends in the numbers of species that are in danger of becoming extinct, or have become extinct. Loss of habitat and overhunting are the main threats.

Vertebrates comprise mammals, birds, reptiles, amphibians and fish, and endangered examples of each group are shown on the map. The proportion of threatened mammals for each biogeographic realm is also given. The total in each pie-chart excludes bats, rodents and insectivores, as they are insufficiently documented. Worldwide, we can say that about 25% of the better-known mammals are threatened.

Numbers of threatened vertebrates for seven sample countries are given in the bar-charts. Amphibians have been omitted because of lack of data.

Percentage of mammals threatened

Threatened vertebrates
Birds
Mammals
Reptiles

Nearctic
Neotropical
Palaearctic
Africotropical
Indomalayan
Oceanian
Australian
Antarctic

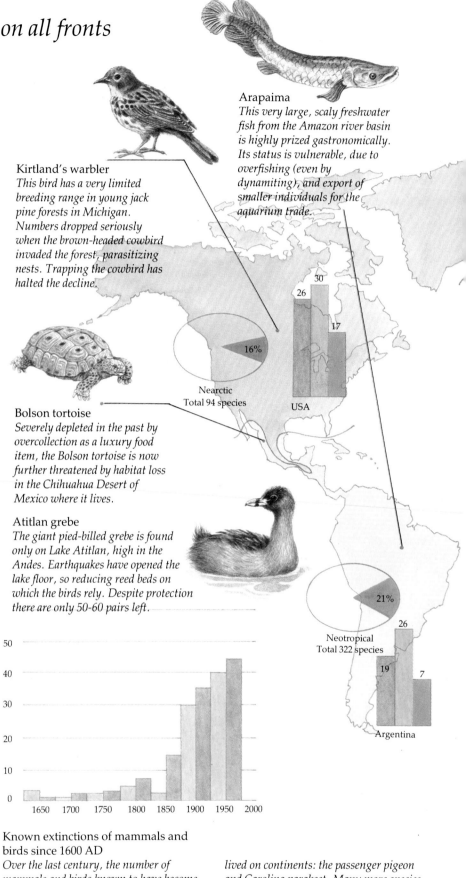

Arapaima
This very large, scaly freshwater fish from the Amazon river basin is highly prized gastronomically. Its status is vulnerable, due to overfishing (even by dynamiting), and export of smaller individuals for the aquarium trade.

Kirtland's warbler
This bird has a very limited breeding range in young jack pine forests in Michigan. Numbers dropped seriously when the brown-headed cowbird invaded the forest, parasitizing nests. Trapping the cowbird has halted the decline.

Bolson tortoise
Severely depleted in the past by overcollection as a luxury food item, the Bolson tortoise is now further threatened by habitat loss in the Chihuahua Desert of Mexico where it lives.

Atitlan grebe
The giant pied-billed grebe is found only on Lake Atitlan, high in the Andes. Earthquakes have opened the lake floor, so reducing reed beds on which the birds rely. Despite protection there are only 50-60 pairs left.

Nearctic
Total 94 species

16%

USA

26 · 30 · 17

Neotropical
Total 322 species

21%

26 · 19 · 7

Argentina

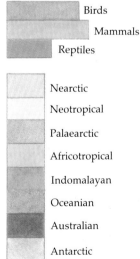

Known extinctions of mammals and birds since 1600 AD
Over the last century, the number of mammals and birds known to have become extinct has risen sharply. Most of these lived on islands and their numbers were never great. Of recently extinct birds, only two lived on continents: the passenger pigeon and Carolina parakeet. Many more species exist in very low numbers and may become extinct soon.

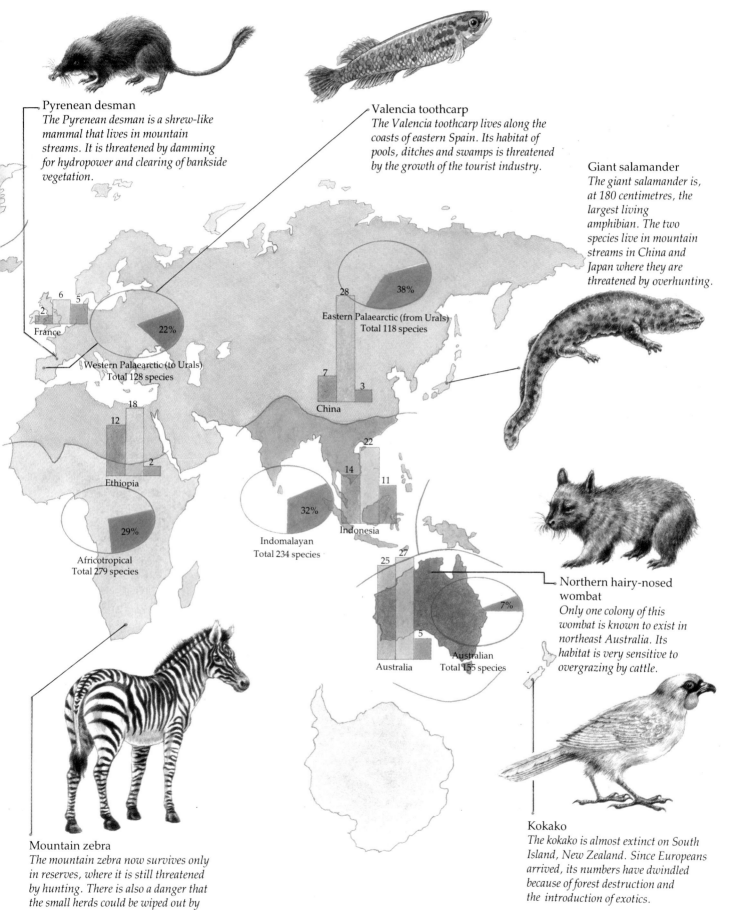

Pyrenean desman
The Pyrenean desman is a shrew-like mammal that lives in mountain streams. It is threatened by damming for hydropower and clearing of bankside vegetation.

Valencia toothcarp
The Valencia toothcarp lives along the coasts of eastern Spain. Its habitat of pools, ditches and swamps is threatened by the growth of the tourist industry.

Giant salamander
The giant salamander is, at 180 centimetres, the largest living amphibian. The two species live in mountain streams in China and Japan where they are threatened by overhunting.

28   38%
Eastern Palaearctic (from Urals)
Total 118 species

22%
France   6   5   2
Western Palaearctic (to Urals)
Total 128 species

7   3
China

18
12   2
Ethiopia

29%
Africotropical
Total 279 species

22
14   11
Indonesia

32%
Indomalayan
Total 234 species

25   27
5
7%
Australia
Australian
Total 155 species

Northern hairy-nosed wombat
Only one colony of this wombat is known to exist in northeast Australia. Its habitat is very sensitive to overgrazing by cattle.

Mountain zebra
The mountain zebra now survives only in reserves, where it is still threatened by hunting. There is also a danger that the small herds could be wiped out by drought or anthrax.

Kokako
The kokako is almost extinct on South Island, New Zealand. Since Europeans arrived, its numbers have dwindled because of forest destruction and the introduction of exotics.

game animals. Some American state governments pay out thousands of dollars a year in predator "bounties", and then, when the predators are gone, they have to spend enormous sums on rodent control programmes.

The public's favourite animals are the spectacular and colourful mammals and birds, which in fact are the ones most likely to be overhunted. This gives the impression that direct exploitation is the greatest danger for wildlife. But a recent calculation based on the *Red Data Books* shows that whereas under half are threatened by direct killing or capture, over two-thirds of the vertebrates listed are threatened mainly because of deterioration of their environment.

No room to survive

Habitat degradation occurs not only with the gradual loss of natural features as by logging out trees or draining marshes, but also by unnatural living additions to communities. Any exotic species - plant, animal or a microbe causing an unfamiliar disease - can put pressure on any resident species, but some of the most dramatic effects are seen in the vertebrates. The rampages of introduced predators are straightforward, like the Asian mongooses brought to the Caribbean where they have devastated the native mammals and birds. But there are many ways in which uninvited species "run down the neighbourhood", forcing the resident vertebrates into decline. The problem is most acute on small islands, but it is clearly observable in larger areas. The eastern bluebird of North America has dwindled in numbers because introduced starlings and sparrows take the best nesting holes, and the charming Russian desman, an aquatic insectivore with a long whiffly nose, is in retreat because the introduced muskrats take the best nesting sites on the banks. The classic cases of lost competitions between wild and introduced animals are those of wild ungulates vying for water and pasturage with livestock. The remnant populations of the Prezewalski's wild horse, which once roamed the Asian steppes, were last seen wandering further into the mountains of Mongolia as domestic stock crowded their waterholes.

Vertebrates are the most well-known victims of habitat pollution. Many seabirds have died from contact with spilled oil, and the notorious Mississippi fish kills were caused by run-off and dumping of pesticides into the river. Such pesticides and similar compounds work their way up the food chains to the top vertebrates, not necessarily killing them, but greatly interfering with their reproductive capabilities. The often-cited examples are the birds of prey which accidentally crush their own eggs because the shells have been thinned by the effect of DDE (a product of DDT). Although use of DDT has been restricted for some time in developed countries, similar compounds have been found in the blubber of fish-eating seals of the Baltic, and the seals are now experiencing abnormal pregnancies.

Outright destruction of habitat is forcing the vertebrates into ever-smaller corners of the planet, along with the other animals and the plants, of course, but because vertebrates - the birds and mammals in particular - are the organisms most familiar to us, their crises have been the most avidly followed and best documented. There are only 50 Javan rhinoceroses left in one reserve on that island of rice paddies, and, as I write, only four wild California condors in the most populous state of the USA. But unnamed fish, frogs, lizards and snakes have no doubt preceded these creatures in the slide to extinction under fields, pastures, tarmac and buildings, as have untold numbers of invertebrates and plants.

On the other hand, we have witnessed some remarkable recoveries in populations of animals, like the Russian saiga, a curious goat-antelope creature, down to a few hundred in the 1920s, but back to its millions by the late '60s because of strict hunting controls, and the revival of birds of prey in Britain and North America because of the restrictions on DDT. However, the ultimate safety of these creatures from untimely extinction

CASE STUDY
Madagascar - an island under siege

There are no monkeys on Madagascar, but there are lemurs; there are no toads or salamanders, but there are plenty of frogs. Despite these gaps which characterize the Madagascan fauna, there is no shortage of animals, for every available niche has been occupied by a species which in most cases is found nowhere else in the world. Sadly, we know very little of the extraordinary plants and animals that live on this island, many of which will become extinct without ever having been "discovered".

When people first came to Madagascar, about 1500 years ago, they found an enormous island almost entirely covered in forest. In the forest was a multitude of fabulous beasts, quite different from the animals of Africa or anywhere else. There were three different giant flightless birds, two giant tortoises, and 11 species of giant lemurs, all of which are now extinct.

As the fourth largest island in the world, with an extremely varied landscape, it would be more appropriate to describe Madagascar as a mini-continent. It has mountains, rivers, lakes, deserts and, of course, forest. But the forest is itself diverse: the east of the island is constantly wet; in the west, there is a wet and a dry season; in the south, it hardly ever rains. Eastern forest is rainforest, western forest is deciduous, and the southern forest is thorny. This diversity is the framework on which the richness of fauna has grown, for it presents an infinite variety of habitats. This, plus 100 million years of isolation from the African mainland, gives Madagascar a flora, too, that is probably richer in species than any equivalent area on any continent in the world.

Regrettably, four-fifths of the Malagasy forest is now gone. Most of the centre of Madagascar is barren, with the remaining forests distributed in a patchy, broken ring around the coastal regions. Some 150,000 hectares of forest are cleared every year in a relentless pattern of shifting cultivation and uncontrolled burning and grazing, causing massive soil erosion and all its concomitant problems. Of the 10 million people living on Madagascar, 8.5 million of them directly depend on agriculture, and the population is growing at a rate of over 3% a year. It is easy to see how the forest is being wasted so quickly, but hard to understand why some more sensible management of resources has not yet

been established. At this rate, all the available forest will be gone within the lifetime of a child at school today. Unless alternatives are found, Madagascar will lose all its forests and, when these are gone, alternatives will have to be found anyway.

The island has always been very attractive to biologists. The Malagasy Academy was founded in 1904, and there are now many researchers, both Malagasy and foreign, working in the forest reserves. Conservation has also been considered for a long time. The system of Natural Reserves, covering about a million hectares, was created in 1927, and there was a forest code of 1930 that prohibited the clearance of virgin forest. The spirit has been there, if not the resources to back it up.

In 1970, international attention was focused on Madagascar's environmental problems. In the late 1970s, an office of the World Wildlife Fund opened on the island, and a number of research projects were started. IUCN's call in 1980 for governments to prepare National Conservation Strategies produced a comprehensive response from Madagascar.

The spirit is still willing, but the funds are lacking. In the meantime, more plants and animals become threatened with extinction. The Madagascar serpent eagle has not been seen for 55 years, and there are now probably fewer than 400 of the world's rarest tortoise, the angonoka, left.

Roughly twice the size of Britain, Madagascar is an extraordinarily diverse island of mountains, rivers, plains and forests. Within its forests a unique collection of unusual plants and strange animals has evolved.

The forests of Madagascar

- Dense rainforest
- Mountain forest
- Dry deciduous forest
- Spiny desert
- Savoka (secondary vegetation)
- Savannah and steppes

Artist's impression of the Aepyornis *of Madagascar. The biggest bird ever known, it unfortunately became extinct in the early 17th century.*

depends on their having the room to live and rear their young, then die by the "hand" of other members of the ecosystem for some reasonable purpose, but be back again with the next generation. Some "flagship" vertebrates, like pandas and gorillas, have inspired the setting up of nature reserves where, if properly managed and adequately protected, the waters run clear, plants grow, animals prosper and people engage in renewable harvests at the edges. We can consider ourselves welcome passengers on the Ark, if only we behave.

The plant eaters

Some herbivorous animals eat only grass, but others consume leaves, bark, sap, roots, seeds, fruits, flowers, nectar or pollen. Part of the energy stored in the plants is transformed into tasty herbivore flesh, which in turn meets the energy requirements of animals at the next trophic level, the carnivores. At midpoints in food chains, herbivores are well positioned to keep in balance or drastically alter life "above and below" them, as has been shown by the far-reaching ecological ramifications of rabbit deaths from myxomatosis in England and the surprising results of recent studies on fish of the Amazon.

However, the role of herbivores is not just one of eating and being eaten. Fruit (and nut) eaters are responsible for dispersing the seeds of plants, and animals that feed on flowers and flower parts are responsible for pollination (although not to such a degree as the insect pollinators). Certain plants, especially in the tropics, owe their existence to the hummingbirds, bats, rodents and even monkeys that visit their flowers. Small grass-eaters, like ground squirrels, voles, marmots and lemmings, actually encourage the growth of natural vegetation by enriching the soil with their droppings and keeping it well-drained with their burrow systems. Large herbivores, like elephants, rhinos, buffalos and hippos, have been nicknamed the "bulldozers", and it is thought that they created the mosaic of woodland and grassland so typical of Africa. The evolution of the large herbivores permitted the evolution of the large, social and intelligent carnivores - the lions, wolves and ourselves.

The grass-eating ungulates are the creatures on which we have most depended. They were the deer, antelopes, bison and mammoths and the wild horses, oxen, sheep and goats of prehistoric times, and now, their domesticated relatives. For many ancient cultures, the dependence was total. In the lore of the Kiowa Indians, the Great Spirit was said to have given the buffalo to the tribe for food and clothing, but warned that "if one day you see them perish from the face of the earth, then know that the end of the Kiowa too is near".

For today's societies, the dependence on herbivores seems less than total, if the domestic ones are not counted. After all, the devastation wrought on large "game" by modern firearms filled our bellies for a while and served to clear the way for crops and livestock. Those few that are left provide sport, trinkets, luxury foods and pretty photographs for certain people. But our dependence on wild herbivores as indispensible components of ecosystems, and their future value to us, are both greater than most of us realize, because these animals' rôles have been obscured by human activities. Removal of native herbivores can backfire immediately, as happened in the African tsetse control programmes (*see p.159*). Moreover, the productivity of some grasslands under current domestic stocking practices is below what it would be if the ecosystem were allowed its wild herbivores instead. But strong traditions, not easily modified, have built up over generations of land users - be they Australian sheep raisers or African cattle herders. Until recently, wild animals were pushed aside as humans spread across their pastures.

The major problem in Africa today is not the tsetse fly but soil erosion - arising from the herding of excessive numbers of *domestic* animals. And the major problem for African ungulates is that their

As population increase and cropland expansion continue, conflict between humans and animals over crop-raiding becomes more intense. In affluent societies, a certain amount of raiding may be tolerated, but in poorer tropical regions, the threat to farmers' incomes raises a corresponding threat to wildlife, especially the herbivorous primates, like baboons. Various techniques to control baboon raiding and so prevent attack on the animals are being tried - playback of baboon alarm calls, hot chili pepper sprays, even "taste-aversion therapy" using lithium chloride (an emetic) on maize crops. Results are inconclusive as yet.

CASE STUDY
Fruit-eating fish of the forest

Every year, when the waters of the Amazon and its tributaries overflow to flood an area of some 10 million hectares, millions of fish swim out into the floodwaters to feed in the forest. The fish feed on fruit and seeds dropped by the forest trees, while the trees depend on the fish to spread their seeds.

Only now, when some of the floodplain forest has been cut down, is the importance of this mutual dependence coming to light. For not only are the seed-eating fish missing their vegetables, but the hundreds of species of meat-eating fish that prey on them are also going short of protein, and the local fishing industries are collapsing.

Fish are a very important source of food for Amazonians; 75% of the catch comes from the floodplain forest and is nourished by it. One-third of all the protein eaten by the 700,000 people of Manaus comes from fish, and the most important food fish of Manaus is a seed eater. Satellite photographs show that there is now no large area of forest left standing within a 100-kilometre radius south of Manaus.

Huge areas of forest have been cleared to grow crops such as rice and for cattle ranching. In fairness to the developers, the fish-forest connection has only recently been revealed. But it does seem that the price the Amazonians will have to pay for rice and beef is far too high.

CASE STUDY
Echoes of myxomatosis

When myxomatosis arrived in Britain in 1954, it killed 99.9% of rabbits in some places. This had a dramatic effect on farming efficiency, which was estimated to have lost £50 million a year due to rabbit damage. It also had far-reaching effects on the wildlife of Britain.

With the loss of rabbits, the primary herbivores of the countryside ecosystem, seedlings of shrubs and trees were no longer checked and a great deal of woodland regenerated. Some permanent changes in woodland management became necessary as plantation trees began to seed themselves, often for the first time since a plantation had been established.

Grassland carried the brunt of the change, however. Where rabbits had been abundant, soft grasses in particular were heavily grazed and most grass species did not reach their full height or flowering potential. After myxomatosis, grasses grew taller and produced a great deal more seed. This had a dramatic effect on other plants. Freedom from rabbit grazing first of all allowed many plants to flourish, but grasses soon dominated and shaded out the smaller flowering herbs. Ragwort, a plant whose young shoots are eaten by rabbits, showed a great display of bloom for two or three years after myxomatosis, but then declined sharply. Although it was producing seed, the absence of rabbits scrabbling the soil had allowed the grasses to close ranks, preventing the seed from reaching the ground.

Changes in the pattern of vegetation has had repercussions for many animal species. The increase in grasses and other tall species has been blamed for a consequent reduction in numbers of sand lizards, stone curlews and wheatears, all of which prefer barer ground. Even the large blue butterfly might have been an incidental casualty of myxomatosis, due to the decline of the ant species that rears its caterpillars.

The interdependence of species in Britain's countryside is complex, and lines of causation are hard to unravel. It is clear that some species of animals declined after myxomatosis while others flourished, but the connection with rabbits is sometimes hard to trace. Field voles increased after myxomatosis, probably as a result of the increase in grasses. On the other hand, brown rats declined. Both would have suffered higher levels of predation by rabbit-hungry predators, but the rats would not have enjoyed an improvement in their habitat.

Rabbit predators also responded in different ways. Foxes, polecats and kestrels, able to change their food preferences to voles, increased in number, in spite of the shortage of rabbit meat. Stoats and buzzards, on the other hand, depended very heavily on rabbits and were hard hit by the loss of their staple food. Whatever the variation, however, the effects of losing the majority of Britain's rabbits spread far beyond the immediate target of myxomatosis. It changed the balance of nature forever in Britain's countryside.

Rabbit with myxomatosis.

The plant eaters

The fate of the bison foretold that of the wild game of today – hunted for meat, or driven from their range as competitors to livestock, the larger herbivores are threatened by direct attack. But for most plant eaters, the worst threat is habitat loss, and with it, loss of their special food supply.

Herbivores do not always confine their diet to plants – hummingbirds eat insects as well as nectar, and even giant pandas add meat to their diet of bamboo shoots. Specialists feeders tend to be more vulnerable. Some plant eaters have a diet that follows an annual cycle. Fruit bats, for instance, move from one ripening crop to another. If one crop is destroyed, the animals may starve to death before the next becomes available.

The decline of the rhino

The status of rhinos in Africa, once worldwide symbols of this continent, is alarming. Since 1980, black rhinos have decreased from 15,000 to less than 9000, while the northern white rhino, at a mere 20 individuals, is on the brink of extinction (see graph, left). Whereas rhinos once roamed freely over much of the African savannah, they now survive only where there is strict protection. The problem has been poaching, encouraged by the trade in horn in both North Yemen and the Far East.

In Asia, the three species – Javan, Sumatran and Indian – are in similarly reduced circumstances, with only about 50 Javan rhinos left, although this is double the all-time low of 20 years ago.

Below The southern white rhino, thanks to active management programmes, is the only rhino species which shows any signs of increasing its numbers.

Periodical cicada Forest clearance for farmland

Bonytail chub Loss of habitat due to river modification

Baird's tapir Forest clearance for agriculture, and hunting

Three-toed sloth Forest clearance

Huemul Loss of habitat due to agriculture and logging, and hunting

14,785

Black rhino — 8800

3920

White rhino (southern) — 3020

821

White rhino (northern) — 28

1980 — 1984

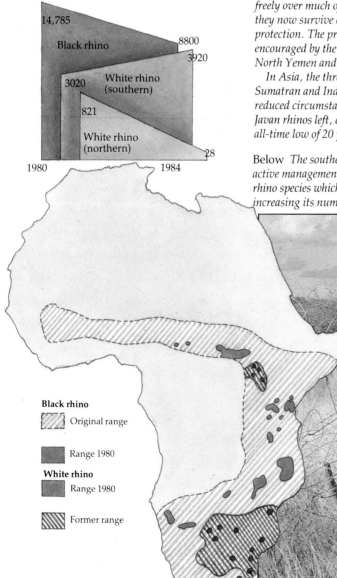

Black rhino

Original range

Range 1980

White rhino

Range 1980

Former range

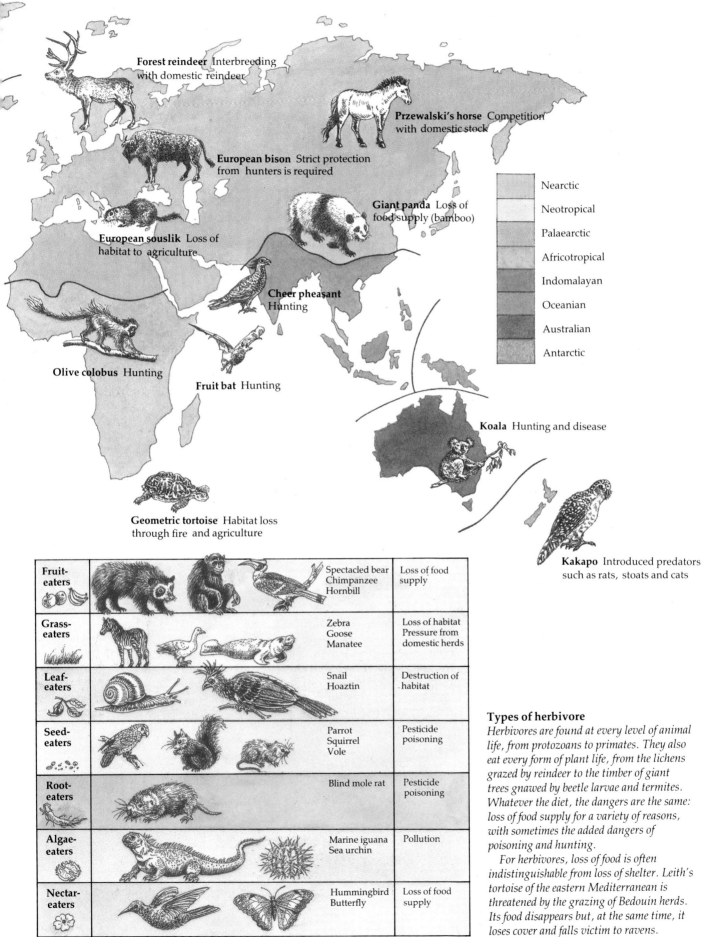

Forest reindeer Interbreeding
with domestic reindeer

Przewalski's horse Competition
with domestic stock

European bison Strict protection
from hunters is required

Giant panda Loss of
food supply (bamboo)

European souslik Loss of
habitat to agriculture

Cheer pheasant
Hunting

Olive colobus Hunting

Fruit bat Hunting

Koala Hunting and disease

Geometric tortoise Habitat loss
through fire and agriculture

Kakapo Introduced predators
such as rats, stoats and cats

| | | Nearctic |
| Neotropical |
| Palaearctic |
| Africotropical |
| Indomalayan |
| Oceanian |
| Australian |
| Antarctic |

Fruit-eaters		Spectacled bear Chimpanzee Hornbill	Loss of food supply
Grass-eaters		Zebra Goose Manatee	Loss of habitat Pressure from domestic herds
Leaf-eaters		Snail Hoaztin	Destruction of habitat
Seed-eaters		Parrot Squirrel Vole	Pesticide poisoning
Root-eaters		Blind mole rat	Pesticide poisoning
Algae-eaters		Marine iguana Sea urchin	Pollution
Nectar-eaters		Hummingbird Butterfly	Loss of food supply

Types of herbivore

*Herbivores are found at every level of animal
life, from protozoans to primates. They also
eat every form of plant life, from the lichens
grazed by reindeer to the timber of giant
trees gnawed by beetle larvae and termites.
Whatever the diet, the dangers are the same:
loss of food supply for a variety of reasons,
with sometimes the added dangers of
poisoning and hunting.*

*For herbivores, loss of food is often
indistinguishable from loss of shelter. Leith's
tortoise of the eastern Mediterranean is
threatened by the grazing of Bedouin herds.
Its food disappears but, at the same time, it
loses cover and falls victim to ravens.*

115

presence, albeit now confined to pockets and corridors of their former ranges, is seen to conflict with the wants of a huge and hungry human population.

There is need for compromise between people and animals, if we don't want to witness the animals' extinction nor make the futile attempt to live with the ecological disruptions we've caused. At one time we were dependent on the large herbivores. Why not see if we can revive the relationship? More efficient and less damaging use of native grasslands could be made by stocking mixed herds of wild and domestic animals. Remarkable discoveries in using the eland for milk and meat have been made by scientists in the USSR, and the Kenyan government has recently expressed interest in the research. And even the Australians have been studying the possibilities of running sheep and kangaroos together.

The invertebrate eaters

Most vertebrates do not fit neatly into the classic plant-herbivore-carnivore food chain. There are the omnivores, like badgers and baboons, which eat everything from roots and seeds, worms and insects to birds' eggs, "fleshy" prey and carrion; and there are other animals which avoid plant matter, preying only on creatures, but, as a group, display very diverse appetites. Most of these have catholic tastes in invertebrates, and so are best called "invertivores" - but some are not above taking the occasional vertebrate, including members of their own species, as large lizards do. The diets of some other invertivores are highly specialized. There are mammals that feed exclusively on worms, and birds that eat only snails. Flamingos strain small crustaceans with their oddly shaped bills, and anteaters lick up ants and termites through their tube-shaped mouths.

Invertivores seem to consume enormous quantities of whatever they eat, and if the prey is considered a pest from the human point of view, they are extremely valuable as pest controllers. Unfortunately, a number of these animals are also in great demand by people for food and sport - fish, frogs and gamebirds - and when the wild stocks are depleted, outbreaks of pests inevitably follow.

Most European countries have passed laws protecting their own invertivores from overexploitation, but do not hesitate to exploit other countries'. The international trade in frogs' legs is particularly important in the economies of southern Asia, although the frogs inhabit the paddies where they feed on insects injurious to rice.

In the developed countries, chemical pollution rather than overexploitation affects invertivore populations. Toxic chemicals, wide-spectrum pesticides included, can have a direct effect, of course, as they move through the food chains, but also an indirect effect simply by reducing the invertivores' food supplies. Although their parents are herbivorous, young gamebirds, like pheasant and partridge, eat the insects in grain and hay fields, and it is now widely known that chicks feeding in fields sprayed with pesticides die from starvation. Air pollution has been shown to affect the nesting behaviour of birds that feed on aerial insects. Fewer house martins nested in inner London in the 1950s than in the '60s when rigorous controls on smoke pollution were finally enacted, and there are fewer martins nesting around industrial plants than in industrial-free zones in Czechoslovakia (all other ecological factors, like access to water and nest sites, being equal). One likely explanation is that the aerial insects are killed by the air emissions.

More than anything else, however, it's habitat destruction that reduces invertivore populations. A few species are "attractive" enough to gain attention, like the beautiful bustards of Eurasia, colourful turkey-sized birds, that feed on grassland invertebrates and have all but gone as the steppes have been put to the plough, or the cuddly numbat, the dying emblem of western Australia, that's disappearing along with the wandoo

The frog business is thriving - India and Bangladesh alone have been exporting over 150 million frogs annually. Fears of malaria epidemics and declining rice crops (because there are fewer frogs to eat the mosquitoes and crop pests) have brought on the widespread use of insecticides, including the infamous DDT. The frog-exporting countries spend several times more on insecticides than they earn from the frog trade, while thousands of their people are suffering insecticide poisoning. (Over 300,000 people in developing countries fall ill every year to the toxic effects of pesticides.) The EEC is considering a resolution to ban the import of frogs' legs, while India is developing plans for the rational use of her frog resources.

CASE STUDY
Partridge chicks go hungry

Nearly all young birds are invertivores, even if they grow up into seed-eaters. In the arable fields of Britain, invertebrates are in such short supply that baby partridges are literally starving to death. Pesticide sprays, mainly intended to control aphids, are turning millions of hectares of the countryside into an invertebrate-free zone.

Partridge chicks feed mainly on three groups of insects. Top of the list are the plant bugs, followed by sawfly larvae and leaf beetles. None of these is in fact a target of insecticide sprays; they - and the partridge chicks that feed on them - are simply incidental casualties.

Many farmers are not prepared to take the risk of waiting to see whether a pest appears on the crop. They choose to spray very early in the year, as a prophylactic measure. This strategy has removed insects from the fields at the time when partridge chicks need them most. Another risk is posed by the mixing of spray cocktails, so that pesticides and fungicides can be applied in one operation. Unless the crop needs both treatments, there is lethal overkill. It is likely that fungicides are also insecticidal, although they do not eliminate aphids.

Farmers enjoy the sport that gamebirds provide. The concern of farmers for the plight of gamebird chicks is now leading to the establishment of pesticide-free headlands and field banks. This has significantly improved the survival of partridge and pheasant chicks on farms where it has been tried. It will undoubtedly also help other hard-pressed wildlife to weather the chemical warfare waged in Britain's backyard.

Newly hatched partridge chicks.

CASE STUDY
California sea otter: friend or foe?

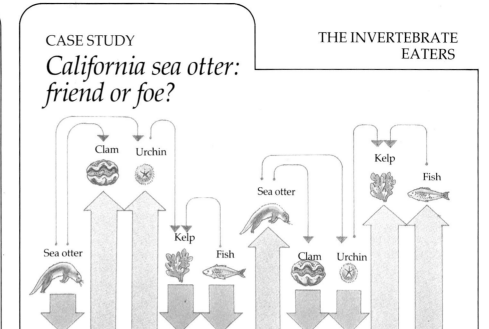

Ratio of sea otters to other coastal species before protection.

Present situation.

The sea otter is a delightful animal. Like the river otter, but larger, it frolics among the kelp beds and lies on its back to eat its dinner off its chest. Everything a sea otter does, it does with tremendous energy, and that includes eating. The only sea mammals without a layer of blubber to insulate them from the ocean's chill, sea otters need to spend a great deal of their lives simply feeding to keep warm. They even feed at night, each otter getting through over two tons of seafood a year.

Sea otters eat some fish and a wide variety of invertebrate prey. Urchins, abalones, crabs, snails, clams, sea cucumbers, and just about anything else they can find are gobbled up with relish. This has made them some enemies among both commercial and amateur shell-fishermen of California, many of whom probably wish that this creature was truly extinct, as was once supposed.

Heavily hunted for its fur for over 150 years, the California sea otter was practically exterminated in 1911. A small colony of survivors was found in 1937 and, with protection, the numbers have been increasing ever since. During the sea otter's absence, however, its staple food flourished and increased to a level that could support several commercial shell-fisheries.

There is a great deal of disagreement as to whether the sea otter is a pest or an endangered species. In California, the population before fur-trading was around 16,000. Now there are no more than 1700 animals on 160 miles of coastline. In Alaska, the numbers of northern sea otters are nearer 10,000,

and populations on the Russian coast are said to be near carrying capacity. Sea otters do eat large quantities of shellfish, but their position in the food chain is arguably beneficial. Some researchers consider the sea otter to be a "key species", i.e. one whose presence or absence makes a great difference to the environment. By eating sea urchins and shellfish, sea otters protect the kelp beds from damage. In the Aleutian Islands, regions with sea otters have been compared with similar regions where otters are absent. Where otters feed, very few sea urchins are found and the seabed is carpeted with kelp and other brown seaweeds. Where there are no otters, sea urchins carpet the seabed and there is scarcely any kelp. Barnacles and mussels are abundant in weedless regions, but the kelp beds support a greater wealth of fish and other life-forms.

In California, giant kelp is an important crop, with an annual value of about $20 million. Where there are no otters, the kelp harvesters spend much time and money trying to control the sea urchins. Where sea otters live this is not necessary.

The sea otter controversy has some way to go before the true balance of facts is established. In the meantime, however, many otters are trapped and drowned in fishing nets, together with sealions and harbour porpoises. They are also very susceptible to death by oiling, which destroys the critical insulation value of their fur. By and large, the survival of the California sea otter is still in the balance.

Invertivores – casualties of progress

The invertivores, midway in food chains, are threatened with decline, as their special habitats and prey are wiped out by human "progress". Yet many are valuable to us, as game and as natural pest controllers.

The teeming swarms of invertebrates are prey for a wide variety of creatures. Some invertivores feed on insects (insectivores) but many eat a range of invertebrates, and even small vertebrates. Typically, all are adapted to feed on very small species – whether, like baleen whales, they engulf masses of prey or, like chameleons and bats, they hunt individual creatures.

Invertivores are found among all animal groups, even the invertebrates themselves. Since their prey tends to be scarce in winter, invertivores are more commonly found in the tropics. Those that do live in temperate regions are often migratory, such as waders, warblers and whales. They feed on the abundance of prey in the north in the short summer, and then move back southward as winter sets in.

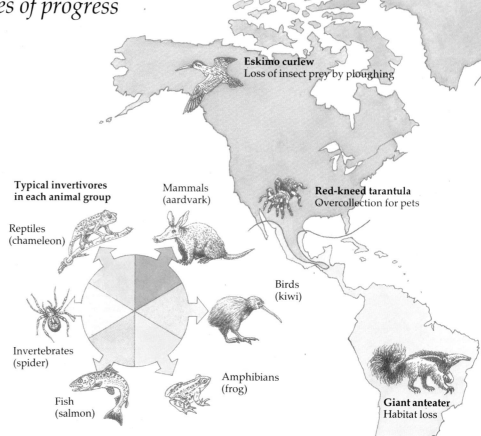

Typical invertivores in each animal group

Reptiles (chameleon)
Mammals (aardvark)
Birds (kiwi)
Amphibians (frog)
Fish (salmon)
Invertebrates (spider)

Eskimo curlew
Loss of insect prey by ploughing

Red-kneed tarantula
Overcollection for pets

Giant anteater
Habitat loss

Giant armadillo
Disturbance of forests

Decline of the greater horseshoe bat
Invertivores are particularly at risk when an important prey species is considered a pest by humans, and eradicated accordingly, by spraying or habitat clearance. The reduction in range of the greater horseshoe bat in Britain over the past century is shown on the map below; similar reductions have affected the species over much of Europe. One of the factors in this decline is the reduction of cockchafers *(a type of beetle), on which the bats especially feed in spring. Over the last 30 years, the pastures where cockchafer grubs live, and the woods where the adults live, have been cleared for cereals. Farmers have also been paid subsidies to spray the remaining pastures to get rid of the grubs, which eat the grass roots. The decline of the bats, of course, makes the cockchafer problem worse for the farmers.*

The hellbender of North America
A totally aquatic salamander which can grow to three-quarters of a metre long, the intriguing hellbender once lived in clear, oxygenated streams across the eastern United States. But pollution, channelling and damming have wiped out the species from much of its range.

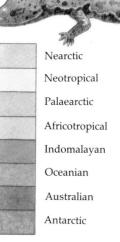

Range c 1870
Range today

Nearctic
Neotropical
Palaearctic
Africotropical
Indomalayan
Oceanian
Australian
Antarctic

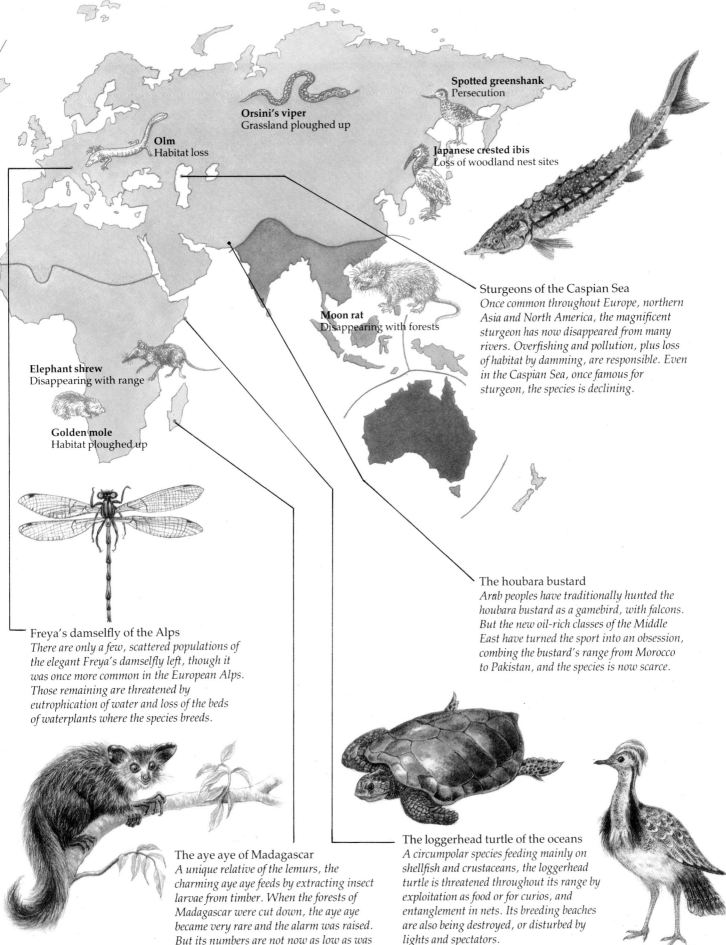

Spotted greenshank
Persecution

Orsini's viper
Grassland ploughed up

Olm
Habitat loss

Japanese crested ibis
Loss of woodland nest sites

Moon rat
Disappearing with forests

Elephant shrew
Disappearing with range

Golden mole
Habitat ploughed up

Sturgeons of the Caspian Sea
Once common throughout Europe, northern Asia and North America, the magnificent sturgeon has now disappeared from many rivers. Overfishing and pollution, plus loss of habitat by damming, are responsible. Even in the Caspian Sea, once famous for sturgeon, the species is declining.

The houbara bustard
Arab peoples have traditionally hunted the houbara bustard as a gamebird, with falcons. But the new oil-rich classes of the Middle East have turned the sport into an obsession, combing the bustard's range from Morocco to Pakistan, and the species is now scarce.

Freya's damselfly of the Alps
There are only a few, scattered populations of the elegant Freya's damselfly left, though it was once more common in the European Alps. Those remaining are threatened by eutrophication of water and loss of the beds of waterplants where the species breeds.

The aye aye of Madagascar
A unique relative of the lemurs, the charming aye aye feeds by extracting insect larvae from timber. When the forests of Madagascar were cut down, the aye aye became very rare and the alarm was raised. But its numbers are not now as low as was once thought.

The loggerhead turtle of the oceans
A circumpolar species feeding mainly on shellfish and crustaceans, the loggerhead turtle is threatened throughout its range by exploitation as food or for curios, and entanglement in nets. Its breeding beaches are also being destroyed, or disturbed by lights and spectators.

119

woodlands where it lives. But most species, like the invertebrates that they eat, are small and obscure, and among the lower vertebrates of the tropics - the fish, amphibians and reptiles - are simply unknown. Few people are inclined to take up their cause, and yet they could be as important in their ecosystems as any of the more popular animals, or be keeping secrets that could revolutionize medicine. But perhaps the lack of attention does not matter, for the animals that do get world press coverage are after all part and parcel of the invertivores' world. Preserving a tiger in the wild means preserving the habitat in which it lives.

The meat eaters

The nourishment derived from plants by the herbivores goes into letting them run, climb, fly and mate and into forming bone, fur or feathers. Only part of it is turned into flesh, which is why, generally speaking, there are fewer carnivores than herbivores, and why they require a lot of space to find enough food. The highest density of wolves in the USSR is no more than 70 animals per 1000 square kilometres, where they're supported by a population of about 800 wild boar. The American puma is a bigger, less sociable animal, and only ten of them can occupy 1000 square kilometres. The hunting territory of a pair of the huge African martial eagles is 200-300 square kilometres.

Because large carnivores live at low densities, their populations are highly sensitive to overhunting and to fragmentation of their habitat. As they are killed off or separated from each other, their chances of finding suitable mates become less and less, and recovery of populations (if they are allowed to recover) is slow.

So, too, is a whole ecosystem sensitive to the loss of its carnivores. The simplest example is what happens when a top carnivore is removed: the prey undergoes a population explosion, eats up its food supply and then starves to death. But as usual in nature, the simple example does not tell the whole story. The Everglades alligator, for instance, has a positive influence on its whole environment, and on many other species. Rampant poaching of alligators for their hides in the 1960s began to change the whole character of the Everglades.

Carnivores are the living endpoints of the food chains linked together by all the other members of the ecosystem. Healthy, stable populations of them indicate that all is well with their world.

Overhunting of large and medium-sized carnivores occurs for several reasons: for sport, trophies and pelts, and because of the threat they are believed to pose to ourselves and other animals. As "unsporting" as it was sometimes - the thrill of waiting up a tree to shoot down at a tiger lured by a tethered goat is beyond comprehension - sport and trophy hunting has been less of a factor than the others in the overall decline of the big carnivores. (An exception is the polar bear, which was in serious trouble from sport hunters until protected by international agreement.) The rarity of the spotted cats and the South American otters is due directly to the fur trade. Legal protection seems to have stimulated black marketeering, and many populations are still dwindling.

By far the most widespread and effective persecution of the carnivores has been because they're thought of as competitors ("vermin" is the word used by the persecutors), by taking the prey we want for ourselves, whether it's wild or our own domesticated stock. Furthermore, the big ones are perceived to be a direct menace to human life. All these views have been borne out in certain situations, but the situations are created by human tampering with nature. It should come as no surprise that the big cats turn to goats, cattle, dogs or people if their usual prey has been shot out or their hunting ranges fragmented. Something must obviously be done about a marauding predator, but translocation is not often an option, because there's no wild left. Extermination is the sad answer for which we have only ourselves to blame. But the desired proliferation of game

The Everglades alligator not only keeps in check the number of gar, a predatory fish which can decimate the populations of smaller fish, but also has a positive influence on many other species by excavating "gator holes", building nest mounds and maintaining trails. The deep holes, fertilized by the alligator's droppings and leftovers, support a rich aquatic life, and serve as the main refuges for aquatic species during droughts. The nest mounds are enlarged every year, eventually to form small islands where trees can grow. The trees support breeding colonies of herons and egrets, whose eggs and young are perhaps safe from racoons and wildcats because of the alligator guarding her own nest below. Gator trails, winding through the pools, keep the water from being choked by vegetation, thereby preventing the development of a marsh habitat.

Even the vultures belong

Andean condor

King vulture

Egyptian vulture

In the centre of Bombay, the Parsee Towers of Silence welcome the vultures which come to dispose of the dead. A similar custom was once also found among some American Indians.

The vultures of India and America, though they have similar habits and are remarkably similar in appearance, have evolved from quite different groups. American vultures are descended from the same line as storks, while the vultures of Europe, Asia and Africa are related to eagles and hawks. All share the more-or-less naked head and neck, powerful wings and rather weak legs and feet that are associated with their way of life. Their powerful wings carry vultures gliding, far and wide, patrolling high in the air in search of carrion. The naked head does not become befouled with blood, as feathers would, when plunged into a carcass.

The world's 20 or so species of vulture fit neatly into the food chain between hunters and decomposers. Different vulture species are adapted further to take a particular part of a carcass; at the end of the queue, the great lammergeier of Europe feeds almost entirely on bones and marrow.

However well adapted they might be, vultures are not immune from human persecution. Many species are threatened by habitat disruption, poisoning, and other ills brought by humans to their wide open spaces. Some reserves have now established vulture "restaurants", where entrails and broken bones are put out to help them recover from the ill-treatment caused by past misunderstanding.

The Russian wolf

Twice in this century, the long-suffering wolf has enjoyed a brief freedom from persecution whilst the people of Europe were busy fighting one another. Both these periods were associated with an increase in wolf numbers in the forests of Russia. Each time, the enlarged wolf population drew attention to itself by attacking domestic cattle, and was mercilessly hunted until the numbers fell again. Farmer and wolf, it seems, will never agree.

The USSR is the only nation where the wolves still live in any significant numbers. There are probably around 75,000 wolves in the whole of the country. In some regions local populations are increasing as controls have been relaxed; other regions offer a bounty, and there the numbers are falling. This situation is likely to continue, in a random fashion, together with an overall reduction in wolf territory due to human activity in previously unoccupied regions, although the inhospitable mountains of Caucasia, Middle Asia and Siberia will probably continue to provide sanctuary.

Recent years have seen an increase in the study of wolf ecology in the USSR. There are two main concerns: the effect of wolves on domestic animals, and their place in the wild. The diversity of the land inhabited by the Russian wolf has given rise to seven distinct subspecies. Two of these, the desert wolf and the tundra wolf, are especially vulnerable to hunters because they live in open country where they are easily spotted and shot from the air.

The task of evaluating the place of all these different wolves in their particular habitats is formidable. It is further complicated by the presence of feral dogs where wolf populations are small or absent. Wolves and dogs also interbreed, producing hybrids that are bolder and more aggressive than wolves. Where wolf populations have recovered from previous low numbers, wild dogs and hybrids disappear, and this fact may be an argument in favour of wolves.

The best argument, however, is the wolf's natural place in the ecosystem. There is now no doubt that the presence of wolves does little harm to a population of a wild prey species. Wolves prefer to take old, weak or sick animals, and this helps to keep the prey's breeding stock healthy. Populations of red deer and caribou have been seen to lose health when wolves were removed from their vicinity, and in one case a healthy moose population losing 50 animals a year to wolves was severely depleted by skin disease after the wolves were "controlled" by human intervention.

As more is learned about how wolves interact with their prey, it becomes more evident that wolves are not as evil as folklore would suggest. This improved understanding might well form the foundation for a new and improved relationship between people and wolves in the future.

Hunter with dead wolf.

The meat eaters

From lions and tigers to crocodiles, from eagles to bird-eating spiders and sharks, the meat eaters or carnivores are dramatic, "high profile" animals, much in the public eye. Many are well known and liked, or at least respected, others are feared. In practice, almost all are persecuted.

The survival of these "top predators" is a sign that the wildlife of an area is in good shape. Because of their position at the top of the food chain, carnivores are never very abundant. This makes them especially vulnerable to any disturbances further down the chain. Removal of their prey through destruction of habitat or disease (as happened when myxomatosis virtually wiped out rabbits in the UK) will affect them by reducing their numbers or forcing them to find alternative sources of food. Both consequences can have adverse effects on other species.

Contrary to what is sometimes said, predators do not control the numbers of prey. Rather, it is the numbers of prey which control the predator. True, if a predator is removed from the food chain, its prey may increase initially, but their numbers will level off as other factors such as availability of food and disease come into play. The role of the predator is often seen as a regulatory one; it actually helps to keep the prey population "healthy" by cropping the older and weaker individuals that would die of other causes. On the other hand, introducing predators to new habitats, especially islands, can lead to the extinction of defenceless species.

The map, *right*, shows examples of some threatened carnivores from around the world.

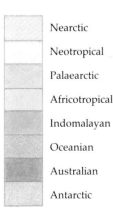

- Nearctic
- Neotropical
- Palaearctic
- Africotropical
- Indomalayan
- Oceanian
- Australian
- Antarctic

Polar bear Habitat loss, skin trade

Cougar Habitat loss, overhunting

Anaconda Skin trade

Giant otter Skin trade

Maned wolf Habitat loss, stock-taking

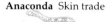

Skin trade

Persecution as stock takers

Persecution through fear

Loss of range to agriculture

Threats to carnivores

Threats to carnivores come in several forms. Many have skins which command high prices and make it worthwhile hunting populations to extinction. The high prices also encourage poaching and smuggling, despite vigorous attempts to protect the animals in reserves or by national and international laws.

As predators, carnivores have always been persecuted by farmers who need to protect their stock. Although attacks on livestock may have little effect on a global scale, a single raid by a wolf or a fox can have serious consequences for one farmer. Bounties are very often paid to get rid of "vermin", but when species become very rare and the remaining population needs to be saved, even promises of compensation for stock killed may not prevent the destruction of the last animals.

The concern about attacks on livestock is made worse by fear of attacks on human beings. Except in unusual circumstances, carnivores do not prey on people, but the isolated incident is sufficient for concerted attacks to be made on many meat eaters. Venomous snakes are the cause of many deaths, especially in crowded, tropical countries where people often go barefoot. However, the snakes' bad reputation has led to even harmless species being killed on sight.

Even if carnivores are given full protection from persecution, they will not survive if they have nowhere to live. The larger species especially require large hunting areas to supply sufficient prey for their survival. If the range is destroyed or fragmented, the predators will disappear.

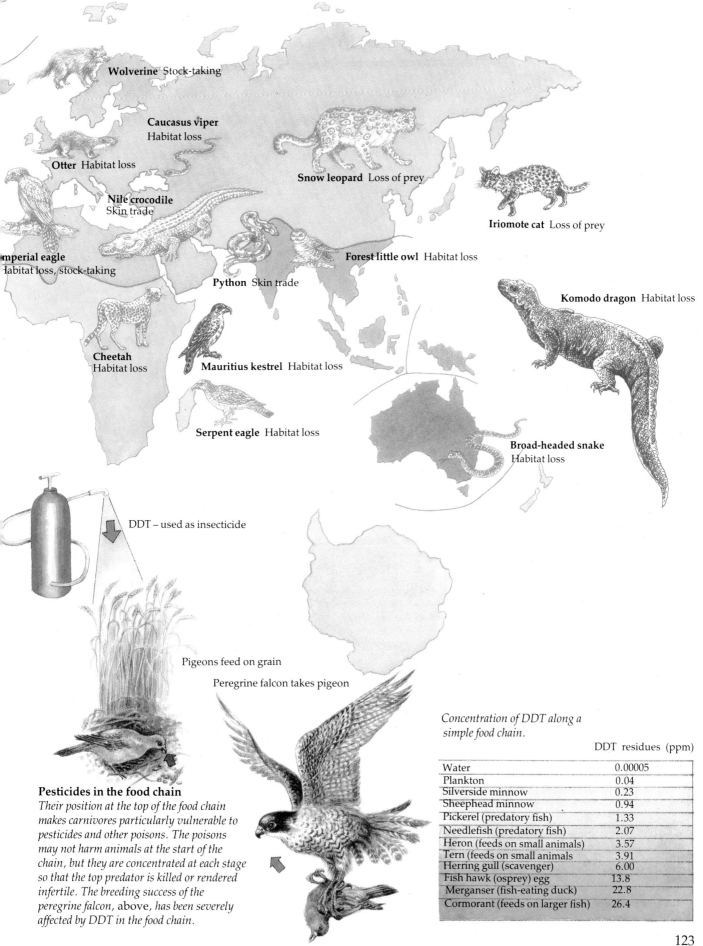

Wolverine Stock-taking

Caucasus viper Habitat loss

Otter Habitat loss

Nile crocodile Skin trade

Snow leopard Loss of prey

Iriomote cat Loss of prey

Imperial eagle Habitat loss, stock-taking

Forest little owl Habitat loss

Python Skin trade

Komodo dragon Habitat loss

Cheetah Habitat loss

Mauritius kestrel Habitat loss

Serpent eagle Habitat loss

Broad-headed snake Habitat loss

DDT – used as insecticide

Pigeons feed on grain

Peregrine falcon takes pigeon

Pesticides in the food chain

Their position at the top of the food chain makes carnivores particularly vulnerable to pesticides and other poisons. The poisons may not harm animals at the start of the chain, but they are concentrated at each stage so that the top predator is killed or rendered infertile. The breeding success of the peregrine falcon, above, has been severely affected by DDT in the food chain.

Concentration of DDT along a simple food chain.

	DDT residues (ppm)
Water	0.00005
Plankton	0.04
Silverside minnow	0.23
Sheephead minnow	0.94
Pickerel (predatory fish)	1.33
Needlefish (predatory fish)	2.07
Heron (feeds on small animals)	3.57
Tern (feeds on small animals	3.91
Herring gull (scavenger)	6.00
Fish hawk (osprey) egg	13.8
Merganser (fish-eating duck)	22.8
Cormorant (feeds on larger fish)	26.4

animals with the removal of the predator usually backfires - the weak and the sick appear and the vegetation begins to be overutilized. A sensible game management strategy is to leave some of the natural predators to do the job of keeping their prey healthy, and to crop the surplus game before the vegetation can be damaged. In parks and reserves, however, the balance between predator and prey has been upset time and again by the old-fashioned practice of controlling the predators to "safeguard" the prey. Unfortunately, the practice still occurs in some protected areas.

The creatures of the sea

Between 60 and 30 million years ago, mammals invaded the sea. Primitive ungulates gave rise to the whales and sea cows, and primitive carnivores gave rise to the seals and walruses, and a little later, the otters. The niches they developed in the marine ecosystem are somewhat different from those of their terrestrial relatives. Only the sea cows are true grazers of plant matter; some of the large whales "graze" the fields of plankton and tiny crustaceans. A number of them are full- or part-time invertivores: otters and walruses feed on molluscs and urchins, and some seals and whales include squid in their diet. But most of them prefer vertebrates, eating the flesh of fish, which, as in the case of the terrestrial carnivores, has brought them into head-on collision with the world's super-competitors - ourselves.

Many of the same pressures that faced the large terrestrial mammals (but which are now at least partly reduced by strict legislation, because there are so few animals left) confront their marine counterparts today. Since the seas are still "wilder" than the land and the high seas are governed by no nation, the attitudes of the people applying the pressures are rather like those of the 19th-century European colonialists: every species exists to be exploited and when stocks of one run low, there is always another to turn to, and any animal that interferes is classed as "vermin" to be killed on sight. Whether it is morally acceptable to harvest these species at all is another issue, very emotive and modern, which has sometimes obscured the facts that are required to determine exactly what the effects of the pressures are in order to devise rational regulations. One difference between the terrestrial and marine situations, however, is that there are no domesticated marine species; the human harvest of the fruits of the sea is directly reliant on wild animals - the scallops, oysters, mussels, crabs, lobsters and fish for our tables, the inhabitants of coral reefs that are proving so useful in modern medicine, and the multi-coloured little fish of tropical waters for our aquariums, as well as the large marine mammals.

The rise and fall (nearly) of big-time commercial whaling and sealing is well known. The industries chose the "best" species, and when stocks collapsed to the point of non-profit, moved on to the next, leaving behind pathetic remnant populations. The whaling countries clubbed together about 40 years ago to regulate their takes by setting up the International Whaling Commission, an organization with an extremely dubious record, for the members simply moved on to the next species, then the next and the next. The IWC finally declared a moratorium on all whaling after 1985, but several member nations, true to form, have simply declared themselves exempt. Harpoons are now poised at the smallest of the finback whales, the little minke, which is less than a third the size of its endangered relative, the blue whale.

Although the remnants of the species left behind by the whalers and sealers are legally protected from further exploitation, their fates, and indeed the fates of the more common species, are uncertain, for they all meet, directly or indirectly, with very powerful competition from the fishing industry. Fishermen believe that the marine mammals are ruinous to the trade by depressing fish stocks, damaging gear, eating the catch and the bait and wasting the fishermen's time. Certainly all the latter irritations

Ripples spread from the aquarium trade

Triggerfish, Sudanese Red Sea.

Threadfin coralfish.

Stocking a tropical aquarium may be expensive, but it is not difficult. It is not necessary to travel far in search of specimens, because there is a large network of suppliers that practically covers the world.

The size of the tropical fish industry is growing all the time. Some 400,000 ornamental marine fish worth about a million dollars are imported into Britain each year, and this is estimated to be only 3½% of the world market.

About 15% of all tropical fish imported into Britain are marine species. Although over half the fresh water species are specially bred for the aquarium trade, marine fish are almost exclusively taken from the coral reefs. Many different methods of capture are used, with many local variations. The most unscrupulous method of all is commonly used in the Philippines, where the tropical fish trade is very large. Divers there squirt a solution of sodium cyanide into a section of reef to dope the fish. They are then collected by suction (called "slurping") from the reef. Probably 90% of fish imported from the Philippines have been caught

this way. It damages their livers, leading eventually to death, though generally not before the fish have been sold to an aquarist.

Of all the marine fish that are caught, 10% die in transit, crammed into inadequately oxygenated plastic tanks, and another 5% die in similar conditions in warehouses and shops before they are sold. But the greatest mortality occurs in the aquarium, where 50% of all fish die within six months of purchase. Altogether, three-quarters of all fish taken from tropical reefs to delight the aquarist do not survive as long as a year.

The main causes of this appalling death rate are stress and disease. Stress comes from the effects of overcrowding and general bad handling that the fish are subjected to from the moment they are caught. Disease is frequently an after-effect of stress that did not kill the fish outright. Deaths in aquariums may be stress-related or simply due to the ignorance of the aquarist. In many cases, fish simply starve to death because the aquarist does not know how to feed them. Some fish, such as

butterfly fish, moorish idols and cleaner wrasse, are so difficult to feed that they ought not to be kept in amateur aquariums at all.

There are no regulations governing the movements of tropical marine fish into Britain. Thus, there is no existing framework on to which improvements could be attached. Improving the handling procedures, and outlawing some methods of capture, would certainly reduce the death rate. Apart from humanitarian considerations, if fewer fish died then fewer would have to be caught to replace them.

Although the seas are large, and marine creatures may seem inexhaustible, there is growing evidence that particularly popular species of reef fish become scarcer as the trapping season progresses. Seasonal bad weather may be all that has so far saved these declining species, but it is no real protection against consistent overfishing. The tropical fish trade brings in foreign currency to countries that have great need of it. They would be foolish to let greed now spoil the catch of the future.

The creatures of the sea

The creatures of the sea, from whales and seals to fish, crabs, squids, sponges and corals, have always been regarded as anybody's property, free for the taking – an endless resource which we, like early hunter-gatherers on land, could exploit without thought for the future. But the resource is not endless, as we are now discovering.

The wildlife of the sea is as rich and diverse as that on land, and just as closely linked together in food webs and communities. It is also just as vulnerable to habitat loss, pollution, disturbances, and overexploitation. As long as hunting methods were primitive, and the hunters few, little damage was done. But as soon as the number of hunters grew, and methods of capture improved, populations slumped – first the vulnerable whales and seals, and now the fish, turtles, seabirds, corals and molluscs.

Because the sea is no-one's property, control is difficult outside exclusive coastal fishing zones – and over these, wars have been fought. Even when groups of nations attempt to regulate fishery catches, seasons, nursery grounds or net sizes, it is all too easy for individual fishermen, or commercial fleets, even nations, to disregard the rules. Coastal waters are also most susceptible to pollution, again difficult to control, adding further threats to the rich communities of species there.

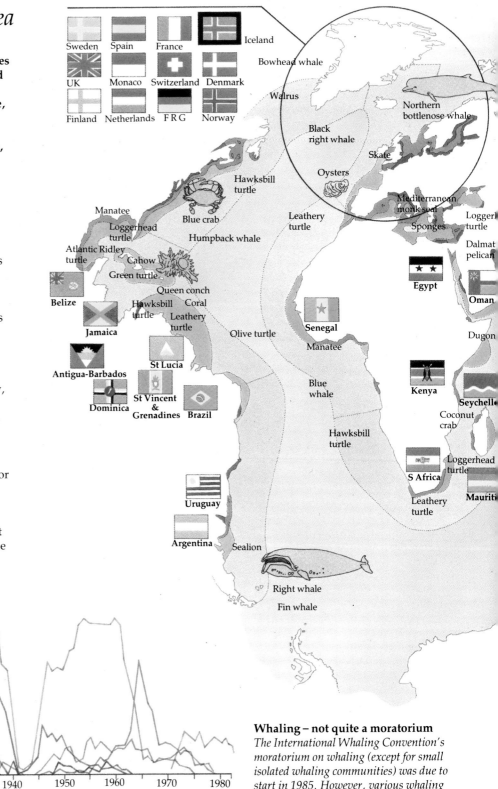

Decline and fall of the great whales
Unregulated Antarctic whaling led to a pattern of successive overexploitation of new species as old stocks crashed. The first whales to go were the largest – the humpbacks and blues. As these grew rare, the fin whale was hunted, and when it slumped too, the smaller sei. Finally, with the sperm whale barred, the failing industry turned to the little minke.

Humpback
Blue
Fin
Sei
Minke
Sperm

Whaling – not quite a moratorium
The International Whaling Convention's moratorium on whaling (except for small isolated whaling communities) was due to start in 1985. However, various whaling nations chose to evade the ban. The USSR, Norway and Japan objected to and so are not bound by it; Iceland and South Korea claim they are catching whales for "scientific purposes". The Philippines is merely ignoring the moratorium. Both the USSR and Norway may cease whaling soon; but Japan, still hunting the protected sperm whale among others, may only comply if forced to do so by boycott or legal pressures.

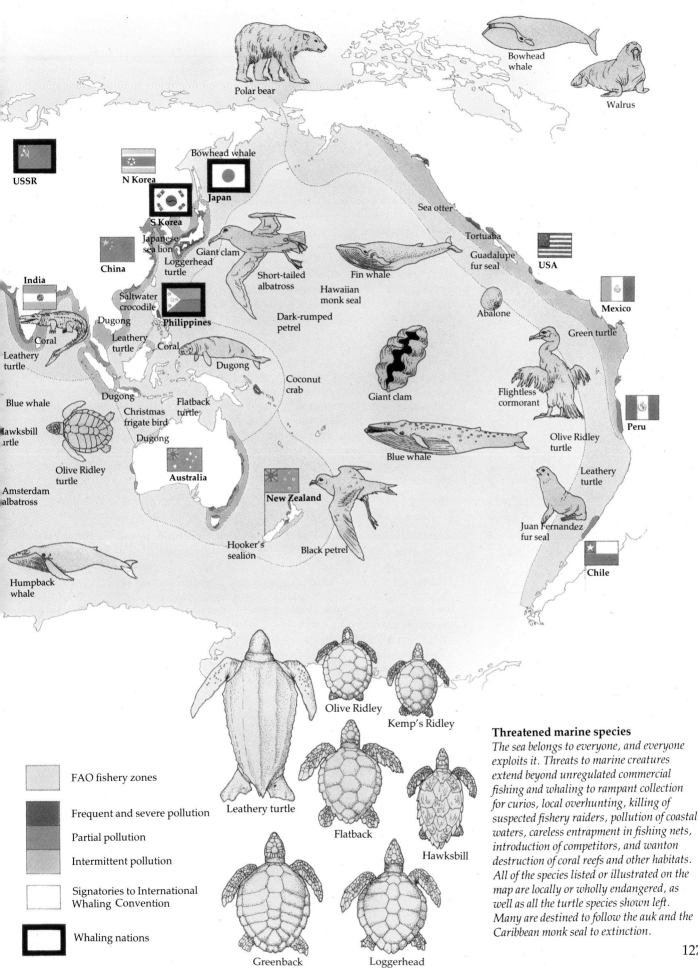

Bowhead whale

Walrus

Polar bear

USSR

N Korea

Japan

S Korea

Bowhead whale

Sea otter

China

Japanese sea lion

Giant clam

Loggerhead turtle

Short-tailed albatross

Fin whale

Hawaiian monk seal

Tortuaba

Guadalupe fur seal

USA

India

Saltwater crocodile

Philippines

Dark-rumped petrel

Abalone

Mexico

Dugong

Coral

Leathery turtle

Coral

Dugong

Giant clam

Green turtle

Leathery turtle

Blue whale

Hawksbill turtle

Dugong

Christmas frigate bird

Flatback turtle

Coconut crab

Flightless cormorant

Peru

Olive Ridley turtle

Olive Ridley turtle

Dugong

Blue whale

Leathery turtle

Amsterdam albatross

Australia

New Zealand

Juan Fernandez fur seal

Humpback whale

Hooker's sealion

Black petrel

Chile

Olive Ridley

Kemp's Ridley

Leathery turtle

Flatback

Hawksbill

Greenback

Loggerhead

FAO fishery zones

Frequent and severe pollution

Partial pollution

Intermittent pollution

Signatories to International Whaling Convention

Whaling nations

Threatened marine species

The sea belongs to everyone, and everyone exploits it. Threats to marine creatures extend beyond unregulated commercial fishing and whaling to rampant collection for curios, local overhunting, killing of suspected fishery raiders, pollution of coastal waters, careless entrapment in fishing nets, introduction of competitors, and wanton destruction of coral reefs and other habitats. All of the species listed or illustrated on the map are locally or wholly endangered, as well as all the turtle species shown left. Many are destined to follow the auk and the Caribbean monk seal to extinction.

127

have been experienced by many fishermen, but accurate information is difficult to obtain, and so their real effect on the industry is unknown. Furthermore, there is no evidence that marine mammals depress desirable fish stocks. In fact, the situation is probably the reverse: intensive commercial fishing of Alaska pollack has led to the decline of the fur seals of the Bering Sea, and there are fears for the tiny populations of humpback whales which rely on the already commercially collapsed stocks of capelin, a tasteless little fish used to make livestock feed. As the world's demand for protein grows, fisheries are casting their nets even wider to include non-traditional species of fish and invertebrates, once considered "fit" for only whales and seals, and now likely to be taken from their mouths.

The "casting of nets" literally poses another danger to marine mammals. Tens of thousands of seals and small whales, particularly the porpoises and dolphins, are accidentally netted and drowned in active or lost nets every year, and the number will rise, especially with the increase of gill-netting for squid in the open ocean. The effects on the commoner species can only be guessed at, but for species whose populations are known to be low, like Hooker's sea lion, Dall's porpoise, the little river dolphins, even sea cows and some larger whales, this "incidental" catch is potentially disastrous.

Finally, none of the marine mammals is immune from the habitat degradation which is dealing the final blow to so many terrestrial species. Loss of breeding beaches and inshore feeding waters to development and tourism, and the increase in coastal and oceanic pollution, have already had visible effects on some species. The Mediterranean monk seal seeks out the few remote islands left to it; heavy metals and pesticide residues have been found in the tissues of many whales and seals and linked to reproductive failure in some. The threat of oil pollution hangs heavy over all marine mammals, for simple contact with oil disrupts their buoyancy and ability to maintain their body temperatures.

Loss of staging posts

Animals know nothing of the lines we draw on our maps to define national borders or the boundaries of protected areas. For them, there are only mountains, seas, rivers or just a valley where the grass may be greener on the other side. Animals that undertake even short migrations can run into trouble. The quetzal, an iridescent greeny-gold bird with tail feathers like streamers, follows the different fruiting times of the wild avocados up the mountains, but the reserve created to protect the quetzal doesn't include all the avocado species in its diet, so it has to move out at certain seasons. The periodic tours around Sarawak by the bearded pig, whose populations erupt whenever there are bumper crops of illipe nuts and acorns, are likely to be cut short by the logging that not only removes the trees but disturbs their fruiting cycles. The cross-country treks of wildebeest and caribou take them in and out of reserves and across national borders, where wildlife policies on one side may not have been designed to complement the other.

The animals most difficult to protect are the long-distance migrants - the fish, turtles and whales of the sea and the flying creatures of the land. Birds, of course, but even butterflies and bats, make incredibly long journeys every year, and like any traveller, are more subject to natural disasters than stay-at-homes. They may never reach their destinations because they are killed or blown off course during storms; and if they do, natural disaster may await them. A large number of European birds overwinter in the African Sahel; after the drought of the early '70s, many never returned.

The greatest problem facing migratory animals is that they must move through places inhabited by *people* - of different laws, different environmental practices and different attitudes towards wildlife. Major conservation efforts - to protect the rivers where salmon spawn, beaches where

"BB touche pas à la tourterelle." "BB au secours des tourterelles." "BB vedette en Médoc." These were some of the headlines in French newspapers in May 1985 when Brigitte Bardot led demonstrations against the annual shoot of turtle doves on migration, as they passed through Médoc. A government loan was secured by the conservationists, but ignored by the powerful hunters. Without the direct involvement of the famous actress, it is doubtful whether the continuing campaign would have received much press coverage, despite the principles at stake.

CASE STUDY
Tangled up at sea

Dolphin caught tangled in net.

Modern fishing nets are extremely strong. They are rot-proof, maintenance-free, and very, very long. As well as fish, shrimp and squid, they catch and drown thousands of birds and sea mammals.

Tens of thousands of dolphins have been caught in purse seine nets, designed for tuna fishing, in the tropical Pacific Ocean. Nine thousand harp seals were killed in one year in North Atlantic cod nets. In the Gulf of Mexico, the world's most endangered turtles frequently become entangled in shrimp nets; fishermen there have been issued with Turtle Exclusion Devices in an effort to spare them. Over 2000 sea otters have drowned in wide-mesh nets off the California coast in 10 years; the use of such nets has now been prohibited throughout the California sea otter's range.

The worst carnage is probably caused by modern gill-nets. Made of synthetic monofilament, these nets are designed to entangle fish or squid instead of capturing them inside a pouch. Such invisible nets, which can trail 40 kilometres through the ocean, are a dreadful hazard to anything that swims. Known victims of gill-nets include 750,000 seabirds per year, 20,000 Dall's porpoises, 700 fur seals, and many small whales, all caught in North Pacific gill-nets set for salmon. Generally speaking, figures are not available for the great majority of incidental catches. Where figures are known, however, they are so high as to give grave concern for the innocent victims.

Gill-nets are also joining the rot-proof garbage of the oceans. Carelessly discarded, they will drift for years, entangling countless creatures indiscriminately.

CASE STUDY
Changing fortunes of the fur seal

The human animal is ill-equipped to face the cold. Since prehistoric times, humans have made overcoats from other animals' fur. In the frozen north, the Inuit have always depended heavily on the fur seals for warm and water-proof clothing as well as meat.

When traders came to Alaska, seal fur was one of their most valuable cargoes. Between 1786 and 1867, around 2.5 million seals were killed to satisfy the world's demand for skins. After the first 50 years of this bonanza, the earliest measures to protect future supplies were introduced. For 150 years since then, the fortunes of the seals have waxed and waned at the mercy of one policy or another.

The most important pieces of land in this story are the Pribilof Islands, which lie in the Bering Sea between Alaska and the USSR. It is here that 85% of all northern fur seals come to breed. Dominated by Russia in the early sealing years, the Pribilof Islands passed with Alaska to the USA in 1867. At that time, the number of seals was estimated at 2.5 million. The Pribilof Islands were declared a special reserve for fur seals in 1869, and a selective quota system was introduced to protect the breeding population. Despite revisions of quotas and fiercely contested prohibitions, the number of seals continued to fall due to pelagic sealing. This practice of taking seals at sea often accounted for up to double the number

allowed in the Islands' quota in some years.

By 1911, the numbers of seals had fallen below 300,000, and lack of success forced the pelagic sealers to give up. A total ban was enforced on pelagic sealing at this stage, in a joint agreement between Britain (for Canada), Japan, Russia and the USA. Under this agreement, only the Inuit, using traditional equipment, would retain the right to take seals at sea.

The fur seal population gradually recovered again until, in 1940, Japan claimed that seals were interfering with commercial fisheries. Quotas were increased, and a programme of research was begun at the same time.

Since 1945 the yearly kill has declined from over 60,000 males to less than 30,000. Measures to boost the population have not been successful. In 1950 the management of the Pribilof fur seal was regarded as a model of success, but there is now renewed anxiety about the future. The Bering Sea is heavily fished, and most of the scant evidence for the seals' decline points to a shortage of food. Another side-effect of fishing, accidental netting, may also be killing a large number of seals.

Although sealing is becoming less economically attractive as an industry, the Inuit of the Pribilof Islands derive most of their livelihood from the seals, and a ban on sealing would cause them intolerable hardship.

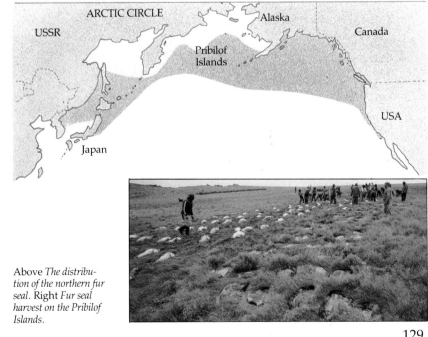

Above The distribution of the northern fur seal. Right Fur seal harvest on the Pribilof Islands.

Animals on the move

In a crowded world, the seasonal movements of animals pose a problem. How can populations that cross national boundaries be protected without some form of international legislation?

Migration is a means of exploiting two or more habitats. For the species to survive, all its habitats must be preserved and it must have the freedom to move between them. If any part of its route is restricted, then the species becomes especially vulnerable, as for instance when birds migrate along a coast or gather at a stopover.

The map shows the main bird migration routes, plus the routes of two particular birds (European stork and sanderling) and two fish (albacore and European eel).

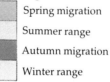

Albacore migrations up to 4 years

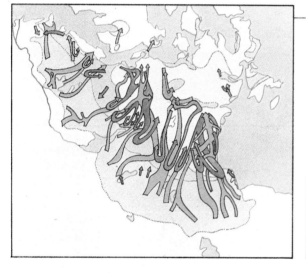

Spring migration

Summer range

Autumn migration

Winter range

Caribou

Caribou of arctic Canada migrate between two habitats – in winter they move south into the coniferous forests, and in spring they return northward to the tundra. Any disruption to their route, such as a new road or pipeline, could have dire consequences for herds already seriously depleted through overhunting.

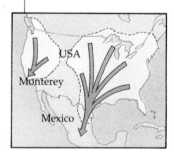

Monarch butterfly

The winter tree roosts of the monarch butterfly are an unforgettable sight. Clustered densely on evergreen trees in California, Florida and around the Gulf of Mexico, the butterflies remain relatively inactive until the spring. They then fly as far north as the Great Lakes, until the seasons dictate the reverse migration. Protection of their winter sites is vital for the conservation of the species.

Albacore migrations after 4 years
to Pacific Islands

Albacore
*The albacore is a kind of tunny
fish that lives throughout the
warmer seas of the Pacific. It has
a strange, double-loop migration
circuit, still little understood.
After 4 years, the fish abandons
the eastern Pacific loop in
preference for the western one.
The albacore is fished
commercially along the coasts of
California and Japan.*

European eel
*The European eel lives in fresh
water and, when fully adult (6
years), migrates across the
Atlantic to the Sargasso Sea to
breed. The larvae then make the
long trip back to Europe, the
stages in their development
(right) correlating with the
shading on the map. Eels on
migration may be halted by
pollution or dams, with
consequent loss of the
population.*

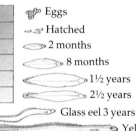

🐟 Eggs
➳ Hatched
⬭ 2 months
⬯ 8 months
⬯➝ 1½ years
⬯➝ 2½ years
Glass eel 3 years
Yellow eel 3½ years
Silver eel 6 years

Sanderling
*Sanderlings nest on the tundra
during the short Arctic summer
and migrate south for the winter,
some reaching well into the
southern hemisphere. Although
these birds can travel long distances without stopping, they
need to break their journeys at
estuaries to replenish their food
reserves. The preservation of
these rich halfway habitats is
vital for sanderlings and flocks of
many other migrants.*

―――― Main bird migration routes
―――― European stork
――― Sanderling

▨ Sanderling breeding grounds

▨ Albacore migrations

▨ European eel distribution

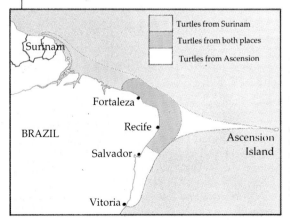

Turtles from Surinam
Turtles from both places
Turtles from Ascension

Surinam

Fortaleza •
Recife •
BRAZIL
Salvador •
Ascension
Island
Vitoria •

Green turtle
*Recent tagging experiments with
green turtles from Surinam and
Ascension have shown that they
migrate to the same nesting site
every 2 or 3 years to breed. They
then return to known feeding
grounds along the South
American coasts (or simply
disappear to unknown sites for
long periods). These turtle
populations are especially
vulnerable to any disruption of
their selected breeding sites.*

turtles lay their eggs or fields and forests where birds nest - are often wasted, either because the animals are hunted *en route* or because their starting and stopover points have been degraded or destroyed. Drought was only part of the problem for the European birds in the Sahel: the intensive spraying of pesticides wiped out the locusts which fed the white stork and some of the raptors, and heavy livestock grazing and fuelwood collecting wiped out the woodland and scrub habitat of numerous songbirds.

One difficulty in protecting migrants is simply not knowing their destinations. The numbers of the graceful roseate tern have dropped to under 600 pairs, although they are protected in their scattered nesting colonies around Britain, Ireland and Europe. Some ringed birds were recently discovered on the shores of Ghana in West Africa, along with spectacular flocks of other migratory birds, where small boys have "fun" catching them with snares and catapults. The Ghanaian government is now working closely with the Royal Society for the Protection of Birds (UK) and the International Council for Bird Preservation on a project to "Save the Seashore Birds", which involves an educational programme showing that the needs of the birds are integrated with the lives of the people. The terns follow the local fishermen, feeding on scraps, and the waders feed in the shallows created by the salt-makers.

It is more often the case that, even if the destination of a migratory species is found, protection is not possible. Excellent plans for reserves and wardens to accommodate the wintering populations of the highly endangered Siberian crane (*see also p.173*) in Iran and Afghanistan have obviously been shelved, but there's an ingenious solution to the problem. While we were at the crane breeding centre at the Oka Reserve in the USSR, the exciting news came through that some of their wing-tagged common cranes had been seen in Turkey. If the Turkish site is safe, the idea is to hatch the eggs of their captive Siberian cranes under wild common cranes as foster parents, who will then lead the young Siberians to a secure winter haven. The technique of designating another similar species as "tour operator" has worked with great success for the whooping crane of North America (apparently with no problems of correct mate recognition for the fostered birds) and is being tried with the Swedish population of the lesser white-fronted goose.

Protection of birds and habitat at the staging posts *en route* is also vital. One of the first acts of Lenin after the Russian Revolution was to ban hunting and create a reserve in the delta of the Volga River, where the slaughter of birds for the plume trade had severely reduced the breeding population of herons and ibises. Today, this reserve hosts thousands of breeders and millions of passers-by. The staunchest allies of waterfowl in North America are, not surprisingly, the hunters, who must buy "duck stamps" in order to participate in the hunting season. The entire revenue from the stamps is spent on improving and preserving waterfowl habitat at the staging posts.

The magnitude of the effort needed to protect migratory species, however, is far greater than the sum of these and other individual projects. Ultimately, only international and bilateral action plans agreed among governments will succeed. Many such agreements have been made, and now it is up to the signatory nations to implement them.

The wildlife trade

As migratory wild animals are threatened when they move naturally from country to country, so many more creatures, and plants, are threatened by "unnatural travel" - the wildlife trade. Whole organisms or their raw or reworked parts have long been exchanged in world markets; today, the horn of a rhinoceros is worth more than its weight in gold.

The sheer volume of trade is astounding. Some 45,000 elephants were killed for the world ivory trade in 1984; nearly half a million Venus flytraps

CASE STUDY
Stop the massacre

For many years now there has been a huge slaughter of birds as they migrate each spring from Africa into Europe. Hundreds of millions of birds are killed annually. Nets, traps, bird-lime and guns are used in a short-lived carnage that is a well-established part of rural life in many countries surrounding the Mediterranean. No bird is allowed to pass: falcons, egrets, doves and all kinds of songbirds fall victim. Depending on the region, they are caught or killed to protect crops, for keeping as cagebirds, for stuffing, for eating, or increasingly, simply for fun.

Hunting small birds has been a traditional activity that used not to cause too much harm to bird populations. Not only was it an important means of supplementing the diet and filling the pockets of poor people, but it also used to require considerable skill.

Now, however, the massacre has become a serious threat to the birds. Armed with increasingly sophisticated equipment, such as repeater shotguns, more hunters than ever are taking part. Even migrating seabirds now fall victim in Malta, where hunters go out in boats and set floating decoys on the water to lure birds to their death.

The birds are also suffering from other problems facing wildlife in general: destruction of food supplies and breeding grounds, pesticide poisoning, and so on. The drought in North Africa has also affected several species. The fact that the massacre takes place in spring makes the situation worse: it is against all management precepts to hunt animals at the start of their breeding season, rather than cropping them when the year's output of young have joined the population.

As well as arguments based on principles of ecology and management, the annual slaughter of migratory birds is criticized on the grounds that it is uncivilized. Catching birds by coating perches with bird-lime glue causes suffering, and chasing around the countryside in trucks cannot be considered traditional hunting. The practice of shooting spring migrants has also annoyed lovers of wildlife in those countries which form the destinations of the migrant birds. So the problem, and the complaint, is international.

In 1981, a Directive on Conservation of Wild Birds came into force in the EEC. As a result, protection is required for most wild birds, gamebirds are given protection in the breeding season, and

Live nightingale and male redstart, caught on a limestick in Cyprus. Bird-liming causes needless suffering to many birds each year.

member states are specifically required to ensure that migratory species are not attacked while returning to their nesting grounds.

However, the issuing of a directive and even the passing of international laws to implement it do not automatically mean safety for the migrants. The hunters not only outnumber local conservationists, but they are willing to resort to violence, as has been proved in Malta. If this was not enough, the hunters also have more political strength than the conservationists.

In 1984, the law that banned spring-shooting in Greece was repealed. The minister was quoted as explaining that spring-shooting was part of a regional cultural pattern and was confined to turtle doves - a gamebird in Greece. Conservationists monitoring the hunt have pointed out that groups of hunters coming from Italy are hardly part of Greek culture and that it was sometimes hard to find any turtle doves among the hunters' bags of golden orioles and cuckoos.

Trading in the wild

Whether transported alive, or exploited for ornament or aphrodisiacs, the animals and plants that suffer the wildlife trade generate billions of dollars annually. Though control is strengthening, many populations of species are seriously at risk.

Catskins, ivory, rhino horns, cacti and orchids are examples. And the rarer they become, the higher the price of an item, so making trade more profitable. A practical problem in trying to control trade in wildlife lies in its complexity. The map shows how parrots and ivory are exported from all over the tropics and, although they may be funnelled through restricted markets, they can be exported again. This makes it very difficult to find where the bulk of the trade is operating. The map also shows some black spots for import and export, and some examples of the types of plants and animals traded.

Trade in parrots

Showy talkative parrots make popular pets. Many thousands are exported to the West each year and some species are becoming rare. Until recently, a main route of import was through Amsterdam, although this flow was reduced considerably when the Netherlands joined CITES in 1984. Prior to this, in one 16-month period (May 1980 to August 1981), over 33,000 wild parrots were imported through Schiphol Airport. The main exporters are given below.

Latin America	SE Asia/Pacific	Africa
Total 15,200	Total 6468	Total 11,811
Peru 35%	India 52%	Tanzania 45%
Trinidad 16%	Singapore 33%	Zaire 17%
Brazil 12%		Senegal 11%
Uruguay 11%		Liberia 10%
Value $378,870	Value $187,534	Value $304,818

Walrus A demand for walrus ivory threatens this species.

The Netherland ratified CITES in 1984, effectively reducing the traffic in parrots through Amsterdam airport.

American ginseng Exported to the Far East for its alleged medicinal properties.

Mexico (cacti) E

Routes to Amsterdam of parrot trade (1980-81)

Senegal (cage birds) E

Hyacinth macaw Smuggled into Bolivia for export.

Bolivia (catskins) E

CITES

Although it is not possible for the world conservation community to control the cropping of species within a country, the trade across borders can be limited by international agreement. This is being achieved by the Convention on Trade in Endangered Species (CITES), which has been signed by over 90 countries since 1973. Signing the Treaty means that a government agrees to it in principle, but it has to be ratified to be brought into effect. However, as with all treaties, this does not necessarily mean that its terms will be enforced.

Countries signatory to CITES (acceded and ratified)

Countries signatory to CITES, but not yet ratified

Non-signatory countries

Black spots in trade

I Importers

E Exporters

The illicit trade in parrots, South America.

Trade in ivory

Most ivory comes from Africa and goes to the carving industries of Japan and Hong Kong. These two countries alone accounted for over 80% of the total ivory exports from Africa between 1976 and 1980. The table, right, indicates the proportion of imports into Japan and Hong Kong from their major suppliers. Following Sudan's ban on the export of raw ivory in December 1983, Japan simply increased its supply from other sources. Poaching and smuggling are very difficult to prevent when firearms are so common and the rewards are so high.

Country of origin	Importer			
	Hong Kong		Japan	
	83	84	83	84
CAR	33%	26%	33%	21%
Congo	—	16%	9%	16%
Sudan	48%	10%	24%	13%
South Africa	—	9%	—	—
Uganda	—	9%	—	21%
Zaire	—	19%	21%	11%
Total (tons)	558	249	475	474

A shipment of elephant tusks from Kenya. African elephant herds have been drastically reduced over the last few years by overhunting.

West Germany (falcons) I

Turkey (cyclamen bulbs) E

Whipsnake Indian whipsnake skins find their way to the USA, despite an export ban.

North Yemen (rhino horn) I

Pangolin Its skin is being traded illegally to supply the US boot industry.

Taiwan (giant clams) I

Philippines (sea shells) E

Ivory routes 1983-84

Clown fish Large numbers exported from the Philippines by the aquarium trade.

Nile crocodile Trade in wild populations now prohibited.

Indonesia (turtle shell) E

List of prohibited species

Under CITES, species requiring protection are placed on Appendix I or II. Those on Appendix I are threatened with extinction and trade is prohibited without an export permit. An export permit is also needed for species on Appendix II, which could be threatened with extinction in the future if trade is not regulated. The huge number of plants on Appendix II is due to the inclusion of 25,000 orchids and 1500 cacti. Because they are difficult to identify and threats to individual species are often not known, all species are listed.

	Appendix I	Appendix II
Mammals	179	303
Birds	133	618
Reptiles	52	340
Amphibians	4	7
Fish	7	15
Insects	0	49
Molluscs	26	5
Plants	87	c.27,000

(the insectivorous plants) were collected and sold by a single dealer in 1980; one million yacare caimans (alligator-like creatures) are taken every year for their skins in the Pantanal floodplain of South America; over seven million live birds, mostly wild-caught, were traded worldwide in 1975; and over 20 million wild butterflies are exported each year from Taiwan, to be pinned and spread for display on living-room walls. The cash involved is even more astonishing: an ocelot fur coat can fetch $40,000, a single orchid $5000, and nine birds of prey, recently smuggled into Saudi Arabia, sold for $200,000. In the USA in 1981 the trade in wildlife and its products was worth nearly a billion dollars!

While transformation of habitat is the primary cause of most species' decline and the effects on others of local and international exploitation are not known, there is abundant evidence that trade involving a number of species is the main reason for the catastrophic reductions in their populations: all of the rhinos for their horns, most of the wild cats for their pelts, many primates and leeches for medical research, orchids and bulbous plants for private collections, and parrots, songbirds, tortoises and even tarantulas for pet-lovers or menageries. Overall, the developing countries are the producers in the wildlife trade, and the developed countries the consumers; but if ever there was a case of killing the goose for the golden egg, uncontrolled trade is it.

Controlling the traders

Until recently, only a handful of countries had ever tried to supervise their internal and external wildlife trade seriously. But in 1973, owing to the patient and meticulous work of the IUCN over the preceding ten years, the Convention on International Trade in Endangered Species (CITES) was signed in Washington by 21 nations. Today there are 87 signatories. The purpose of the Convention is to monitor and regulate the trade in certain wild plants and animals and their products between countries. Species that are in danger of extinction in the wild (and those that look so much like them that customs officers might not be able to tell them apart) are strictly off-limits to commercial trade. Species (and their look-alikes) that could become endangered in the wild by uncontrolled trade are allowed to be commercially traded, but the flow is monitored carefully. If such species do become endangered, they are upgraded to the first category. (The Convention has no jurisdiction within countries, where overexploitation for internal trade can be just as detrimental or more to species populations.)

The spirit of the Convention is not to deny countries the foreign exchange that marketing their wildlife resources could bring, but to ensure that the market operates rationally and, therefore, sustainably. How well has it been able to guard the golden goose?

Discrepancies in export and import records - only one in 20 animal transactions and one in a hundred plant transactions match - show that there are serious problems. For example, in 1980 Switzerland reported importing 60 skins of grey monitor lizards from France, while France did not report exporting them to Switzerland. The illegal trade in wildlife is said to be more lucrative than drugs. Just as producers, pushers and users lie, steal and kill to market their goods, so do their counterparts in the wildlife business. And yet while ports of entry are superbly equipped for drug detection, and the penalties for pushing drugs are enormous, customs officers on the watch for illegal species trade often cannot distinguish one species from another, while fines for poaching are quite inadequate. Another dilemma is what to do with confiscated goods. Auctioning them off, with the proceeds going to the countries of origin, would only serve to keep the market going, and yet some of the developing countries have, understandably, asked for just that.

Whatever the problems, the Ark is in a better state, thanks to the Convention. Trade in endangered species is thought to be sporadic, and

Although the yacare caiman is legally protected, the value of one of the skins to a poacher is $3 (a princely sum to someone who earns only $70 a month in a legitimate job in the Pantanal), the "street value" is 20 times more, and that in the reptile-skin industry, 40 times more. Poachers and police have shoot-outs, and poachers fear for their lives if they inform on the middlemen. Customs officers in the USA cannot distinguish the yacare from the other, more abundant caiman species (which, inexplicably, is not on the protected list as a "look-alike") and the fine for poaching a yacare in Brazil is about the same as a speeding ticket.

CASE STUDY
Trade in rare plants

All cultivated plants are derived from wild ones. For years, travellers have delighted in bringing home seeds of new blooms for the garden. The house-plant trade, however, has an ugly side. Each year millions of wild plants are dug up, packaged and sold - even in supermarkets. Rare ones fetch enormous prices. Slow-growing plants, like cacti, and ones that propagate slowly, like cyclamens, are in demand because they are hard to grow. These same slow-growing, inefficient propagators are most at risk in the wild, and for the same reasons.

Over 80 countries have now signed the Convention on International Trade in Endangered Species (CITES). This shows goodwill, but has not solved the problem. The USA alone imports 10 million cacti a year, many "rustled" from the wild and sold at prices ranging from $25 to $1000. Cactus collecting is also making rustlers rich in Europe, Japan and the USSR. One-quarter of the cactus family is now in danger of extinction.

Orchids are another valuable group; many species have been exterminated by collecting, and many more are unlikely to last long. Even snowdrop bulbs are nearly all obtained from wild sources. Insectivorous plants are popular, too. One dealer has admitted to selling around 50,000 venus flytrap bulbs a month, collected from the wild in spite of being available from plant breeders.

Profits are a powerful incentive, and their loss would be a more effective deterrent than legislation. If customers did not pay premium prices for these illegal imports, wild plants might be left where they belong.

Rare Mexican cacti seized from a German smuggler at airport.

CASE STUDY
Ceremonial daggers kill rhinos

Daggers with rhino-horn handles are part of the daily dress in North Yemen.

Since 1970, the number of rhinoceroses in Africa has fallen from 45,000 to less than 6000. This carnage is entirely due to poaching. The rhinos are killed because a knob of hair on their nose is credited with mystical properties. Rhino horn is thus a valuable commodity, well worth the risk of being caught killing a protected animal.

One of the greatest threats to the African rhino is the North Yemeni ceremonial dagger. Still a common item of daily dress in parts of North Yemen, the dagger has a handle of cow, buffalo or rhino horn. Daggers with rhino horn handles are much more valuable than the rest, and mostly belong to rich men. In Sanaa, North Yemen, young men cash-rich with oil-field earnings, will pay up to $1000 for this status symbol.

About half of all poached rhino horn now goes to North Yemen. This represents a traffic of at least 1.25 tons per annum since 1980. Rhino horns weigh around 0.75-3.5 kilograms each, and are transported in 50-kilogram loads. In 1982, importing rhino horn into North Yemen became illegal. This has not had a very noticeable effect on the trade, although indirect evidence, such as the increasing cost of bribing customs officials, suggests that some pressure is being put on importers. It is doubtful whether the carvers of dagger handles, or even their wealthy customers, know much about rhinos. Import legislation is clearly not enough; it must go together with active enforcement and some propaganda. If the flow of rhino horn into North Yemen could be stemmed, the poachers' single biggest market would be lost and this would be a more effective deterrent than a handful of rangers doing their best to patrol vast areas of bush.

The rhinoceros has an even greater cultural significance in Nepal. Practically no part of a rhino is not used there. The most precious parts, the horn and hoof, belong to the king. In 1973, there were only about 200 rhinos left in Nepal. The Chitawan National Park was established in that year, and not a single rhino has been poached since 1976. In 1982, the rhino population had grown to 375. The value of rhinoceros products is very high in Nepal, but the penalty for illegal possession of such products is heavy. All rhino products in Nepal are obtained from the animals dying naturally.

These measures have clearly been very successful in safeguarding the Nepalese rhino, and it is tempting to suppose that a similar commitment, backed by similar resources, could achieve comparable results in Africa.

International protection for wildlife

Nature does not observe political boundaries, nor human rights of ownership and commerce. To protect the world's wildlife we must shape a global safety net of agreements that transcend national and sectoral interests and respect, instead, the boundaries and needs of the wild.

The world's wildlife and wild places are the responsibility of the world community, and many international treaties and laws now reflect this. However, not all nations yet accept their responsibility, and until they do, protection remains as weak as its weakest link. The international moratorium on whaling, for instance, is hardly effective so long as major whaling nations such as Japan still reject it.

The problem with an international treaty is that there is no way, other than public and diplomatic pressure, of getting the contracted parties to comply in practice. Persuading states to sign a treaty in the first place often requires that terms be sufficiently general not to give offence. And even then, there may be let-out clauses.

The earliest agreements were for protection of species, and often those of obvious commercial value. Bird protection, for instance, began in 1902 with the Convention for the Protection of Birds Useful to Agriculture, and whale protection with a "club" of whaling nations agreeing to protect their stocks. Protection agreements have since widened to cover protection of wild species and their habitats in their own right, but imprecise wording, and few signatories, still weaken many efforts.

In recent years, new and more powerful strategies have emerged, from the UNEP Regional Seas Programme to control of species trade through CITES and the Bonn Convention on migrants. These, and all protective agreements, urgently require more support, by every nation, if the safety net is not still to have many gaping holes.

Types of international agreement
The map shows present levels of support for four international conservation agreements.

The international Convention for the Protection of Birds, signed in 1950, typifies some older agreements – its impact weakened by too few members and imprecise terms.

The Bonn Convention on Migratory Species meets a prima facie need for international protection – migrants must be secure in all countries they visit or pass through. But it still lacks member nations crucial to complete route coverage.

RAMSAR or the Convention on Wetlands of International Importance has had some impact on conserving vital ecosystems, but still has too few members for full effect.

UNEP's Regional Seas Programme to clean up pollution and conserve marine habitats began in 1975 with the Mediterranean Action Plan. Exemplifying cooperation between neighbour states, it targets ten ocean regions.

Signatories to International
Convention for the Protection of
Birds 1950

Signatories to RAMSAR
Convention on Wetlands of
International Importance 1971

Signatories to both of the above
conventions

Signatories to Convention on the
Conservation of Migratory Species
of Wild Animals (CCMS) Bonn
1979

Signatories to all the above
conventions

 Coverage of UNEP Regional
Seas Programme

1 Mediterranean Region
2 Kuwait Action Plan Region
3 Caribbean Region
4 West and Central African Region
5 East African Region
6 East Asian Region
7 Red Sea and Gulf of Aden Region
8 Southwest Pacific Region
9 Southeast Pacific Region
10 Southwest Atlantic Region

The Juan Fernandez fur seal - a species not seen for almost a century - was rediscovered as a remnant population of 200 on an island off the coast of Chile. More detailed survey work (sorely in need of funding, however) may turn up further "missing" species; if they can be protected, the odds in the race to preserve genetic diversity may be shortened by a fraction.

A special case of the artificial maintenance of species for big business, with a concomitant decrease in genetic diversity, are the commercial seed banks. Large companies in the "gene-poor" developed countries have imported vast numbers of seeds from the "gene-rich" tropical countries, particularly of those species with potential as food crops. Although seeds are freely exchanged among some governmental research centres and botanic gardens, the commercial companies involved have secured control over the development and sale of strains by promoting legislation known as "Plant Breeders' Rights". Uniformity of plants is what the breeders want, of course, and they have banned sales of a number of older, and potentially very useful strains that don't meet certain commercial criteria. As well as putting a lid on genetic diversity, the companies sell their seeds back to the countries they came from at enormous profit!

the monitoring of trade in other species is considerably better than it was 15 years ago. And a number of countries are not only cracking down on poachers, but are offering training programmes to customs officers, increasing penalties for illegal trade and sending more thorough and current reports to the CITES headquarters in Switzerland.

Rational commercial management

One way of reducing the often uncontrolled and rapacious commercial exploitation of species in the wild is to establish a population, under more or less artificial conditions, from which individuals can be harvested without causing a decline in the numbers or quality of the source stock. In most cases this is easier said than done - it would be impossible to apply to marine mammals and migratory species, for example, and pilot experiments for providing sufficient primates for medical research this way have proven uneconomic. The relevance to species conservation of business ventures varies widely.

In some industries the lure of profits has promoted sophisticated research and development, leading to great commercial successes, like ranches for mink and fox and nurseries for ornamental plants. But the further such industries develop, the closer they come to domesticating their stocks, thus making them unrepresentative of their wild counterparts, which remain the only repositories of genetic diversity. Species conservation has been aided *only* if the pressure to harvest wild stocks has been reduced. If customers are satisfied with "farmed" products, all well and good, and even if "new blood" is occasionally required to maintain viability of stocks, it will do no harm to take it from a reasonably healthy wild population. Some would argue, however, that the very existence of the legitimate market for such products sustains the interest in a black market, whose "goods" are taken from wild species that can ill-afford the harvest. The quality of wild furs, for example, is considered superior to "ranched" fur, which explains the continuing decline of the wild cats.

By contrast, smaller-scale enterprises than the fur business seem to have more promise in terms of benefiting the species concerned, although it depends entirely on the species. In Papua New Guinea, forest butterflies are attracted to gardens by nectar-filled flowers, and there lay their eggs on the plants provided for their caterpillars' tastes. The caterpillars are collected and reared, and most of the adults are killed for the "living-room wall" trade, but enough are released to replenish the wild population.

Ranching of the big ungulates in Africa has been less successful than expected, however. One reason is that there is a problem with processing and marketing on a viable commercial scale, and another is that the attractive characteristics of the wild animals cannot be utilized under the currently practical management regimes. It has been suggested recently that a properly conducted harvest from the wild (cropping, rather than ranching), along with ensuring that the number of domestic animals is not too much for the environment to support, is the most efficient way to use the land and secure the continued survival of wildlife.

There are two big "ifs" here: sustainable cropping is possible if human greed can be controlled, and correct stocking rates are possible if the number of owners is not excessive. Putting voluntary limits on greed and having babies is, unfortunately, not typical of the human species.

Protecting critical populations in the wild

Many protected areas are designed to preserve the ecological integrity of a large region and, thereby, the genetic diversity of all its inhabitants. In other places, however, only relict populations of a few species survive (some recently "rediscovered"), reduced either by habitat contraction and degradation or direct overexploitation. If the factors which cause a decline can be identified and eliminated (and if the size of the remnant population

CASE STUDY
Protecting commercially valuable species

It is not necessary to kill in order to harvest. Yet human hit-and-run tactics have brought more than one animal to the brink of extinction. In China, the Himalayan musk deer is farmed so that its valuable musk can be taken regularly for use in perfume and medicine. Elsewhere in its range, it is seriously endangered as a result of wanton slaughter. Immature and female musk deer, which do not carry musk, are killed in great numbers, too, since hunters seem not to be able to distinguish them from the males that they seek. It is quite possible to take the animals' musk without killing them, as the Chinese have shown.

The Andean vicuna is valued for its soft, warm wool. Vicuna wool has been used since Inca times, when the wild herds were rounded up each year to be shorn. The Spanish Conquistadores, preferring quicker returns, simply shot and skinned them, and vicuna were almost exterminated.

In 1967, a reserve for vicuna was established in Peru. About 1500 animals were contained there, in an area of 6500 hectares, protected by a body of armed guards. By 1980 the area had increased to 520,000 hectares and the 48,000 vicuna there represented 80% of the world's entire population. The project was thus far very successful. When the vicuna reached this high population level, however, a controversial decision was made to cull some of the vicuna, which has since caused a temporary setback to the project's aims.

Administrative problems apart, the vicuna could soon be providing fleeces once more. There is no doubt that this creature, properly managed, could bring much-needed industry to the people of the high Andes.

Vicuna – valued for its fleece.

CASE STUDY
Crocodile farms on Papua New Guinea

A crocodile farm at Port Moresby, Papua New Guinea.

The swampy forests of Papua New Guinea were once swarming with crocodiles. Trade in crocodile skins has provided a good income for the country, and its government is working to ensure that this source of income will continue to grow and prosper.

In the mid-1960s, dwindling catches and smaller skins showed clearly that the crocodiles of Papua New Guinea could no longer sustain the unrestricted hunting which they had suffered for over 20 years. As well as introducing restrictions on hunting to conserve breeding crocodiles, the government at that time laid the foundations for a national crocodile farming industry. In spite of early teething problems, the scheme is now showing results.

The first farmed skins appeared on the market in 1979, when they accounted for less than 2% of total exports. By 1983, this proportion had increased to 10%, and it has continued to grow. Japan and France are the main importers; in 1983 they accounted for 99% of all the skins exported.

The system depends on inducing local hunters to collect small living crocodiles, which go to stock a variety of farms and ranches. These establishments, located near good food sources such as poultry farms and fish-processing plants, feed and rear the crocodiles to harvestable size. In practice, only the larger ranches, located near the best food supplies, rear crocodiles to full size. These ranches, together with some smaller specialist ones, also have plans for a breeding programme to back up the wild-caught operations.

Papua New Guinea is presently trading in wild skins and wild-caught ranch-reared skins. The ranch-reared skins will take on a larger share of the market each year while, at the same time, captive-bred skins will also become available. Achieving a balance between these two operations is widely regarded as a critical conservation issue. Captive breeding takes pressure off the wild, which is obviously very desirable. On the other hand, if captive breeding were ever to eliminate the need for a thriving wild population, then some wild habitats would lose their commercial value. Since the profit motive is so important, habitats where crocodiles are no longer needed would be at risk of being turned over to some other use, and all the other species that live there would also be threatened.

A combination of rearing and breeding, as is projected in Papua New Guinea, seems to be the best way to conserve the species as well as retaining thriving wild breeding stock. Expertise is increasing all the time, and the crocodile farms of Papua New Guinea will surely benefit many other commercially valuable species in the future by providing a successful model on which to base new schemes.

Mauritius kestrels (once the rarest birds in the world) live in marginal habitat. Their natural food is a bright green and red gecko, but where the native flora is choked out by exotics, the insect fauna on which the gecko feeds is much reduced, and so is the gecko. Supplementary feeding during the breeding season and careful management are helping to build up the population of Mauritius kestrels.

is not too low), there is a good chance that the species will recover - maybe never again as a fully fledged member of a wilderness, but alive and well none the less.

Bringing species back from the brink of extinction *in situ* is in some cases simple, but in most cases very complicated. If overhunting has been the problem, then an effective law prohibiting hunting will resolve the crisis, as shown by the comeback of the Russian saiga. Usually, a hunting ban is not enough, because other factors are operating to depress a population. Sometimes, the additional measure of preventing disturbance to its habitat is sufficient, even in a small area, as the Americans and the British, in designating "Critical Habitats" and "Sites of Special Scientific Interest" respectively, have demonstrated in their efforts to build up populations of some of their endangered species. More often, however, some form of benevolent interference is required.

Protecting endangered plant populations may involve putting a fence round a patch and periodically weeding out the exotic species. There are several of these managed enclosures now in Mauritius, whose unique plant communities have been driven into fragmented, remote areas by agriculture, and are still not safe from virulent introduced species such as wild guava and privet. I visited one of the earliest enclosure "experiments", and walking through the gate was like stepping into a botanist's version of Conan Doyle's *Lost World*, albeit only half a hectare in size! A parallel technique for boosting endangered plants and animals endemic to small islands is the eradication of the exotic creatures - the rats, cats, goats and rabbits - that have so devastated their homes. Some people would not call this "benevolent" interference, but it is the only hope for many unique insular species.

Promoting the best conditions for animals often means direct assistance. One technique, useful for animals whose natural roosting or nesting places have been disturbed or destroyed, is to provide artificial ones. Another short-term measure to build up the numbers of a critically low population is supplementary feeding, now being used with Mauritius kestrels (*see left*).

A longer-term approach is to transfer some of the individuals of the endangered population to another site - the principle of not keeping all your eggs in one basket. With plants it may be straightforward, especially for those species that can be propagated vegetatively, like the Bermuda sedge, a plant with graceful, arching leaves. A courageous botanist carefully disentangled a few individuals from the only clump left in Bermuda and planted them around the marsh in which they once lived; the marsh is now protected and the species is thriving.

Animal translocations are quite another matter, but there are some clever techniques, especially with birds. The procedure known as "double clutching" takes advantage of a female's tendency to lay more eggs if her first ones are removed. The first eggs can be placed under a non-breeding pair of birds in another area, or even under foster "parents" of a different species, as was successfully done with American whooping cranes and the Chatham Island robin of New Zealand. With mammals there's no such short-cut, although the new technique of implanting a foetus from an endangered species into a surrogate mother may one day be useful. A number of endangered species, notably among the African ungulates, have been helped out by the capture, transport and release of individuals into safer, more suitable habitats, where they've successfully reproduced.

Custodians of the future

The final option for protecting populations that are down to critically low numbers is to try it *ex situ*, which means "out of place", and for plants and animals this means away from the wild. Exercising this option has occasioned some of the most acrimonious debates in the history of the conservation movement, for there are people who would rather see an

CASE STUDY
Adder's tongue spearwort

More than 50 years ago, a botanist paid £53 for 290 square metres of marsh at Badgeworth. This little patch of Gloucestershire in the UK was one of only two known sites where a rare buttercup, called adder's tongue spearwort, grew. The nature reserve was carefully fenced with barbed wire and then left in peace for 28 years.

In all that time the adder's tongue spearwort hardly flowered. Only two of those years saw more than 100 plants flowering on the plot; five years saw no flowers at all, and two other years produced hundreds of flowers outside the reserve but none inside.

In 1962, a change of management brought a distinct improvement in the fortunes of this buttercup. From 19th-century field reports, it appeared that the plant had been seen growing on bare, recently disturbed soil. Here at Badgeworth it had not been disturbed for nearly 30 years. With care, a small plot was cleared and then trampled. Within two weeks, thousands of buttercups were growing there. Seeds which had laid dormant for years had at last been able to germinate.

Managing a reserve containing practically the whole of the world population of a rare species is a great responsibility. Researchers at Bristol University decided to store a supply of seeds in case of disaster and, in the course of investigating the best storage conditions, discovered that seeds survived best if they were kept in wet peat, left open to dry in summer and wetted again in the autumn. In fact, these were the exact conditions that existed on the reserve. It appears that the reason the buttercup managed to survive on the reserve was that it was a natural seed bank. It is now managed as such.

Adder's tongue spearwort.

CASE STUDY
The cahow - clinging on

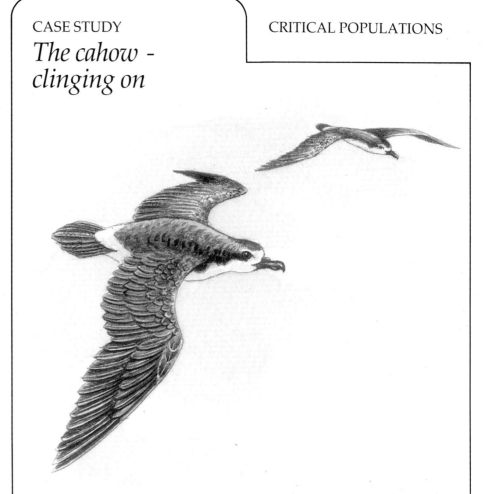

At the beginning of the 17th century the Bermuda dusk echoed to the shrieking of thousands of cahows. These petrels suffered from all the qualities that made the dodo extinct: they were plentiful and unafraid, tasty and easy to kill. Within 15 years they were thoroughly decimated by mariners. Then came the final blow. Famine on Bermuda sent 150 hungry settlers to Cooper's Island, one of the cahow's last outposts. A year later, when the Governor of Bermuda declared the cahow a protected species, it was too late. Not a cahow was to be seen anywhere.

Nearly 300 years later a petrel killed by a naturalist on Castle Island, near Cooper's Island, was identified as a cahow. Another dead specimen turned up in 1935, and a couple more a few years later.

Living, nesting cahows were found in 1951 - in fact a grand total of seven pairs was found on two islands. Four chicks hatched, and were promptly killed by rats. Active protection was now under way, and the rats were poisoned. Then another peril showed itself, in the shape of the white-tailed tropic-bird. Just when the cahow's egg is about to hatch, tropic-birds come in to nest in the same burrows and the first thing they do is dispose of the cahow's own effort. Intervention was again needed, but this time it was more difficult than poisoning rats. Many attempts were made to modify the entrance holes so that only cahows, and not tropic-birds, could enter. It took seven years to get this right. In the meantime eight more nest burrows had been found on another islet, and the total population in 1961 was estimated at 18 pairs.

In a few years, however, cahows were again in trouble and failing to rear young. This time the chicks were being poisoned by the pesticide DDT which had got into the cahows' marine food chain from continents thousands of miles away. The use of DDT declined, however, in the nick of time; in 1972, 27 breeding pairs raised 17 chicks.

The world cahow population is now over 100. In 300 years the cahow has failed to do any more than just hang on - but hang on it did. It is miraculous that the combined hazards of rats and tropic-birds did not finally finish it off before help arrived. It has now had more than a little help, and a great deal of devotion from at least one enthusiast, David Wingate, has enabled this remarkable species to make more progress in 30 years than it could manage alone in 300.

Indian elephant at London Zoo.

Botanical gardens and zoos undertake many conservation-related projects, from research on reproduction, nutrition and health of endangered species to studies of them in the wild. But of all aspects of the conservation movement, living collections are best placed to serve that of public education. Wildlife films are splendid, of course, but there's no substitute for seeing, hearing, smelling or touching the real thing, and if it makes people sad to see a zoo animal, even a happy, healthy one, then maybe they will work harder to protect the creature's wild home.

animal "wild and free" or dead, than surviving in captivity - and people who tend to forget that saving a species' habitat is the prerequisite for saving the species itself.

So far, aid to species survival by commercial breeding ventures has been dubious, and such enterprises should not be handling endangered species anyway. In the past, zoos and botanical gardens have done their fair share of pillaging the wild, but the motivations and methods of the more responsible ones have changed dramatically, and many are deeply committed to conservation. But can they make a difference?

The *ex situ* maintenance of organisms takes various forms. "Gene banks", set up mostly at specialist research centres, but also at a number of botanical gardens and even a few zoos, aim to keep in suspended animation the various tissues that contain genetic material - pollen, seeds, sperm, eggs, whole gonads, zygotes, embryos and even ordinary body tissues, like roots, blood and skin. Long-term storage is accomplished by drying, cooling or freezing, but regeneration is still at the science fiction stage (with the exception of some types of seeds, and even these must be periodically "grown out" and fresh seeds collected.) Storing tissues obviously takes up little space, but the techniques for maintaining whole, living organisms are much more advanced: plants and animals can live long and well in "protective custody" and produce large quantities of genetic material themselves - their offspring. Breeding is undertaken by specialist collections and public zoos and gardens, either in the country of origin of the species, where natural conditions of climate and nourishment can be provided and stress of transport is minimized, or far from home, where often the expertise and funds are more readily available.

All *ex situ* collections, from the hi-tech seed bank to the conservation-minded zoo, have two fundamental problems. The first involves genetic erosion in the populations of organisms they keep, and the second is simply one of space.

Plants that produce small, dry seeds are the species least likely to suffer loss of genetic variability *ex situ*. Such seeds can be banked by the tens of thousands, and if correctly collected, may fairly represent the "pool" of genes that characterize each species. Stored material, however, cannot adapt to a changing environment: a population with the same genetic features as, say, 20 years before when its seeds were banked, would be very vulnerable to the new kinds of pressures - more virulent pathogens or an altered microclimate, for example - likely to have arisen in the wild during its absence. The sooner that stored material can be re-stored to the wild, the better.

In breeding collections, populations can undergo the process of adaptation, but only in response to conditions of their artificial environments, which are very different from the pressures of their former wild environments. Furthermore, the numbers of plants or animals that are normally maintained are too small to be very fair representatives of their species' gene pools; and as the "founder" members of the populations die off over the years and their offspring breed among themselves, more genetic variation is lost.

Modern zoos and botanical gardens, however, are keenly aware of these limitations, and are developing strategies to overcome them. If *ex situ* populations are derived from a certain number of "founders", if pedigrees are meticulously kept and matings arranged with the care of royal marriages, and if stocks are managed on a worldwide, freely exchangeable basis, then there's no reason why, genetically, a captive population cannot be restored to the wild. But again, the sooner, the better, and some "re-education" may be necessary (*see p.146*).

The second problem shared by *ex situ* collections is, in the words of a well-known zoo director, that there are just not enough "staterooms" on the Ark in which to cosset all the species threatened with extinction today. To my mind, this is a more insuperable problem than genetic erosion, and underlines the fact that although the *ex situ* effort is a

CASE STUDY
The Durrells in Jersey

The author's personal account of the work of the Jersey Zoo.

Of all the roles that a modern zoo should play, the zoo that my husband, Gerry Durrell, set up in 1959, today fulfils every one, and has pioneered a number of them. We are now called the Wildlife Preservation Trust, and are supported by 15,000 members around the world. Headquarters are in Jersey, in the Channel Islands (UK), along with the zoo itself, and there are affiliates in the USA and Canada. We are only small: our entire annual budget is about one-fifth of the *advertising* budget of a major American zoo!

In Jersey, we maintain breeding colonies of threatened mammals, birds and reptiles, and have recently added a rather obscure toad and a little snail - although the cuddly species are good for "box-office", the less appealing ones also need help. We house animals from other collections, providing valuable space for extensions to their breeding programmes. Our animals are not bought and sold, but exchanged on breeding loans designed according to the mating strategies that will best preserve genetic diversity in the world captive populations.

Our staff members conduct research on husbandry, nutrition, reproductive behaviour and pathology on the animals in the Jersey collection and on their wild relatives, and present the results in our own and other reputable publications and at conferences. They also participate in or chair regional and international committees concerned with conservation. We operate local and international educational programmes for young people, and offer training courses in Jersey, leading to a university diploma, in the "art" of breeding endangered species to professionals from abroad, particularly from developing countries where there is currently such little expertise available. We provide technical and financial assistance to the pitifully underfunded animal collections within those countries to help them develop breeding, research and educational programmes similar to our own. We believe that, for the sake of survival of species in the long term, such programmes must take place in the species' country of origin.

We never forget, however, what Roger Payne, the well-known scientist concerned with research and conservation of whales, once said to Gerry: "I see

Top *Over 170 people from 36 countries have come to Jersey to learn the "art" of breeding rare animals and have returned home to jobs in conservation-related fields. Alex Forde from St Lucia worked with our colony of the St Lucia parrot, a bird seriously threatened by habitat destruction on its native Caribbean island.*

Right *The Mauritian pink pigeon, now down to 15 wild individuals, has bred well enough in Jersey and at the breeding facility on Mauritius to permit the trial release of birds into the "semi-wild" of the Mauritian National Botanical Garden. Methods developed in this project will be used when the time comes for a real release back to the wild.*

Above *The spacious enclosure at Jersey Zoo allows us to maintain a well-integrated group of lowland gorillas which participate in the coordinated breeding programme for all gorillas in the British Isles. Our silverback male, Jambo, has sired more healthy babies than any other gorilla in captivity.*

what you're wanting to do - to put them back *there* if there's a *there* to put them back to". We are involved in a number of projects that should culmninate in the repatriation of captive animals to the wild.

welcome and vital strategy for species survival, it must never replace the effort to save species in the wild - if there is a "wild" left in which to apply the effort. But because of human rapaciousness and stupidity, the only option for some species of plants and animals is captivity. The good custodians are striving to make the incarceration as comfortable and as temporary as possible.

Back to the wild

The primary purpose of taking animals and plants from the wild, however, is to put them back again, when it's safe. Zoos, gardens and specialist collections have only begun to operate as "half-way houses" like this within the last two decades, for the techniques and expertise are relatively new. The establishment of plants and animals in places where they are not native is often all too successful - they become pests and drive out the original flora and fauna - but the reintroduction of organisms to their former homes (assuming that the factors which caused their decline have been removed) depends on whether they themselves can fit back into an ecosystem that may have readjusted during their absence. For example, the projects to reintroduce the beaver to Britain and the lynx to Germany were short-lived, for it became clear that the beavers would cause insupportable damage to tree plantations, and the lynx were killed by hunters, afraid that they would be out-competed for game.

If the wild is "ready" for them, plants and animals can go back in a variety of ways, depending on the species, but there are several criteria that ought to be met by all repatriations, whether the intention is to reintroduce a species that has become extinct in the wild or to boost the numbers of a critically low population. First, the stock to be used should be as genetically similar to the wild (living or extinct) population as possible. For example, plans to help the Pyrenean goat by introducing a closely related subspecies were scrapped because of fears that it would interbreed with the few remaining "pure" goats. Second, for any species, but especially for those that have been away from the wild for more than a generation, the choice of stock should be made to avoid "favouritism". Otherwise, whatever natural genetic variation it possesses would be reduced (although conscious rejection of stock showing deleterious traits is necessary). Finally, the stock must be meticulously examined for parasites and diseases, especially if it is meant to become integrated into an existing population. Even eggs that will be fostered to wild parents (as for birds) or put back into suitable natural conditions for hatching (as for some amphibians and reptiles) should be screened.

Some plants do well from seed, as with the sowing of a piece of original North American prairie (*see p.57*). Others are best established in nurseries as cuttings or seedlings and then transferred, as in the project to re-create the rich laurel forests of Grand Canary Island being undertaken by the highly competent local botanical garden. Where and when sowing or planting take place must be designed to suit the species' ecological needs.

Putting animals back into the wild is probably trickier than it is for plants, and more so for birds and mammals than for the so-called "lower" animals (invertebrates, fish, amphibians and reptiles). Rearing procedures must prevent the animals from "imprinting" on their human caretakers, but at the same time teach them to find and like the kinds of food and shelter available in the wild. Release procedures must reduce the chance of the animals panicking and hurting themselves or disappearing over the horizon.

Repatriation has worked only if the formerly "captive" stock has produced viable offspring, and so follow-up monitoring is vital. Again, with plants, one can visit the plot and look for healthy seedlings nearby, but with animals it may mean dogging their secretive - but at long last, wild - footsteps for many years to come.

Now a symbol of resurgence and hope for all endangered species, the Néné or Hawaiian goose was reduced to a world population of less than 50 birds by 1950. Captive breeding at the Wildfowl Trust in Slimbridge, UK, raised the numbers, and the World Wildlife Fund flew successive groups of birds back to suitable islands of the Hawaiian group - first to captivity, then to freedom in the wild.

CASE STUDY
A "missing" tree is rediscovered

Easter Island is famous for its sculptures. Many of these are of wood, although there are no mature trees on Easter Island now. Its volcanic slopes were once covered with *Sophora toromiro*, a medium-sized acacia-like tree that is endemic to the island. This tree was ill-equipped to cope with debarking caused by introduced sheep and goats, however, and the last mature specimen died some time between 1955 and 1962. The island is now mainly covered by grassland, despite a tropical climate.

The *Plant Red Data Book*, published by the IUCN in 1978, described the toromiro tree as "probably extinct". This statement has brought in an interesting postbag. First came the news that Thor Heyerdahl had taken a seed pod from the last surviving tree in 1955 and given it to Professor Olof Selling in Stockholm; this had found its way to the botanical garden at Gothenburg, where several young toromiros are now growing. Then news came in of toromiros in New Zealand and Chile. Most surprising of all, however, was a report of young trees "planted secretly" in a garden on Easter Island itself. These young trees had been grown from seed obtained from the Chile source.

Were it not for botanical gardens, the last tree known from Easter Island would surely have become extinct. But now there is a very real possibility of returning it to the wild.

a. Leaf, natural size.
b. Eight seeds, natural size.
Sophora toromiro *grows up to 3m high, with pale green leaves covered in silky white hairs.*

CASE STUDY
The oryx comes home

One October day, in 1972, a party of hunters destroyed the last seven wild Arabian oryx in Oman. These also happened to be the last wild Arabian oryx in the world and, but for the foresight of the world's conservation organizations, that would have been the end of the story.

It had become apparent, in the early 1960s, that oryx numbers were falling fast. Traditional hunting groups had grown into large parties, travelling in upwards of 50 land rovers and desert vehicles, equipped with sophisticated weapons and even helicopters. The elegant desert antelope was a prime target, and clearly stood no chance at all of surviving this slaughter.

"Operation Oryx" was launched in 1962, with the aim of capturing some of the surviving oryx and keeping them safely in captivity. Three animals - two males and one female - were caught. These three, together with other captives from private collections in London, Saudi Arabia and Kuwait, went to the Phoenix Zoo, Arizona, where they were known as the "world herd" of oryx. Phoenix was chosen because of its desert climate; it was hoped that the oryx would breed there, and they did. By the time the last blow fell on the wild oryx, other breeding groups had also been established at Los Angeles and San Diego and, by 1978, there were over 120 captive oryx in the USA. About 100 more also lived in collections in the Arab world.

When the Sultan of Oman showed enthusiasm for restoring oryx to their native land, much had been learned

The Arabian oryx is a handsome, cream-coloured antelope with chocolate stockings and facial markings, and long, slender horns. It can live for years without drinking, obtaining its moisture from dew-fed vegetation, which it seeks out over long distances.

about breeding oryx in captivity. Nothing, however, was known about releasing captive-bred animals into the wild.

In March, 1980, five oryx were flown from San Diego Zoo to Yalooni in the Jiddat al Harasis desert region in Oman. A great deal of thought had been given to possible problems that zoo-bred animals might have when faced with a wide-open desert. When they arrived, the oryx were released into an enclosure one kilometre square where they could settle down together. Another group of five arrived nine months later, and were carefully and slowly introduced to the earlier group. By the end of 1981 the herd was well-established, and they were released on 31 January, 1982.

On 13 March, 1982, the first wild calf for 20 years was born in the desert of Oman. Its mother, who had refused to nurse her last baby, behaved perfectly and its zoo-born father stood guard over mother and calf as any wild oryx would.

Oryx from the world herd have also been sent to Jordan, where they have been breeding in captivity since 1979. A programme of gradual introduction to the wild has been started, as part of Jordan's effort to re-establish wildlife lost since World War II.

148   *Masai herding goats, Amboseli*

CHAPTER FOUR

The State of the Regions

Biogeographically speaking, most of the land mass of the planet is in the northern hemisphere, but to the south around the equatorial bulge, the lands and waters contain the greatest diversity in species and habitats. Further south, where the continents taper off, the plants and animals have evolved in long isolation from each other, and so there are greater numbers of endemic species. Anthropologically speaking, the countries of the North contain most of the money, technology and manufactured goods, and are known as the developed or industrialized countries, while the countries of the South (the developing nations) support enormous human populations and generally lack these manufactured items. Australia, New Zealand and South Africa are the exceptions to this rule.

The failure of humans to live in harmony with nature is acute in both divisions of the planet, but has manifested itself for different reasons in different ways. Alterations to ecosystems in the North are promoted by large- as well as small-scale schemes, whereas in the South, the ubiquitous, small-scale activities still have greater effect overall. In the North, people are often knowingly extremely wasteful of their natural resources. What is left of their wilderness is often cherished and well-protected, paid for by people and governments who can afford it. In the South, people are forced to be frugal, because there are so many of them, overusing some resources and underusing others.

Because of the imposed frugality, most people of the South cannot understand the concepts of nature conservation which motivate most people in the North, like "saving" rainforests, elephants and whales. If the subsistence farmer of the tropics needs another plot because the soil is exhausted in his, he goes to the adjacent forest, and besides, elephants trampled his crops this year. He has never even heard of a whale. Still, because the man is a farmer, he understands why the soil has lost its vitality, and can see the value of his traditional crop strains compared with the "miracle" crops. He also knows that he can rely on the forest for his medicines. He is essentially self-taught in the rudiments of ecology and genetics. Farmers of the North are not normally concerned by such matters, because they rely on sophisticated substitutes, often to the cost of the environment and themselves, but there always seem to be other substitutes to replace those that no longer work. Even less knowledgeable are the people who live in cities, both North and South, because they have lost contact with the ways of land, although they, too, suffer from abuses to nature.

To say that the developed countries are wealthier than the developing countries is to state the obvious, but to say no more is superficial. There is great wealth in some developing countries, but it is very irregularly distributed, even in those countries under socialist govern-

149

ments, and the offers of help from the developed countries sometimes hide a self-serving motive. Also superficial is the statement that the people of the developed and developing nations are of radically different origin and culture, and therefore have different attitudes towards the utilization of natural resources. In this post-colonial period of human history, the citizens of all countries are of all races, creeds and colours, and in most countries across the world anybody has a right to stand up and be heard.

All peoples must have, buried somewhere in their cultural past, traditions which once let them live in harmony with nature. These traditions, coupled with the sensible application of modern technology, could surely help diminish the dangers, common to us all, that stem from how we, as a species, are currently playing our role in the ecosphere. That it is possible is demonstrated by the fact that many countries have expressed great interest in the World Conservation Strategy and have committed themselves to developing National Conservation Strategies.

The following pages highlight the environmental problems that each of the major regions of the planet is experiencing most severely, and what the various countries are doing, or not doing, to solve them. So far, the most successful measures have been those that embody the principle of the World Conservation Strategy, whether or not the countries concerned have formally adopted the Strategy. The principle, which essentially concerns the safeguarding of nature, from pure air and water to the small creatures and plants in a remote mountain meadow, is in fact the vital key to human development towards a better life, and can only be achieved by reintegrating the needs of people with those of the natural world.

Europe

Europe was the first region to undergo major habitat alteration within historical times. The forests were replaced by people, crops and livestock at such a gradual rate, however, that new ecosystems could develop - artificial, but fully functional. The Mediterranean area is a skeleton of its former self, to paraphrase Plato, but the *maquis* supports a rich and unusual flora and fauna, as do the heathlands of Britain, most of which also owe their existence to human activities. Elsewhere, the face of Europe was eventually transformed into a chequerboard of pastures, farms and towns. Wildlife either adapted to the novel conditions or retreated to remote patches of wilderness. The only large mammals to become extinct as a result of the changes were the aurochs (a wild ox) and the forest tarpan (a wild horse). Many local extinctions occurred, however, not least because of overhunting (ibexes, mouflons and wild goats) and direct persecution (wolves, bears and lynxes).

As fragmented as the wild is today in Europe, there are still pressures to develop the small pieces that remain, even when such development is not obviously related to the actual needs of the human population. Why grub up the hedgerows of Britain to create more arable land when the country is staggering under a grain surplus? Still, a number of voices are being raised against environmentally unsound projects that are no longer viewed as supporting the long-term interests of the community as a whole. For example, the Wadden Sea, off the coasts of the Netherlands, Denmark and Germany, faces multiple threats from reclamation, gas exploration, dikes and pipelines, tourism, military exercises and harbour development. Yet in each of the countries concerned public support for *not* developing the Sea is incredibly strong, thanks to the tireless campaigns of their national conservation organizations. The complex of mudflats, marshes and shallow waters is now understood to be precious and important, as wintering grounds for more than five million birds and as nurseries to over half the fish in the North Sea.

150

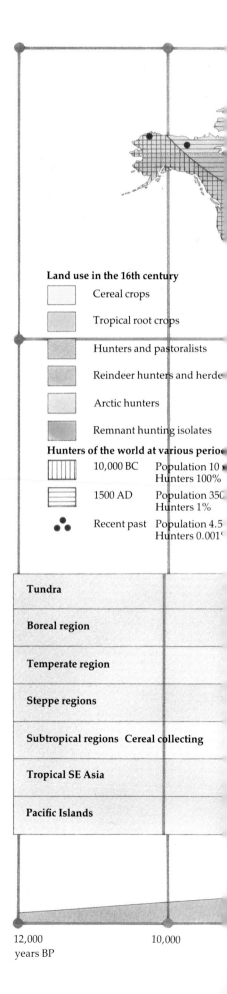

Land use in the 16th century

Cereal crops

Tropical root crops

Hunters and pastoralists

Reindeer hunters and herde

Arctic hunters

Remnant hunting isolates

Hunters of the world at various perio

	10,000 BC	Population 10 Hunters 100%
	1500 AD	Population 350 Hunters 1%
	Recent past	Population 4.5 Hunters 0.001

Tundra

Boreal region

Temperate region

Steppe regions

Subtropical regions Cereal collecting

Tropical SE Asia

Pacific Islands

12,000
years BP

10,000

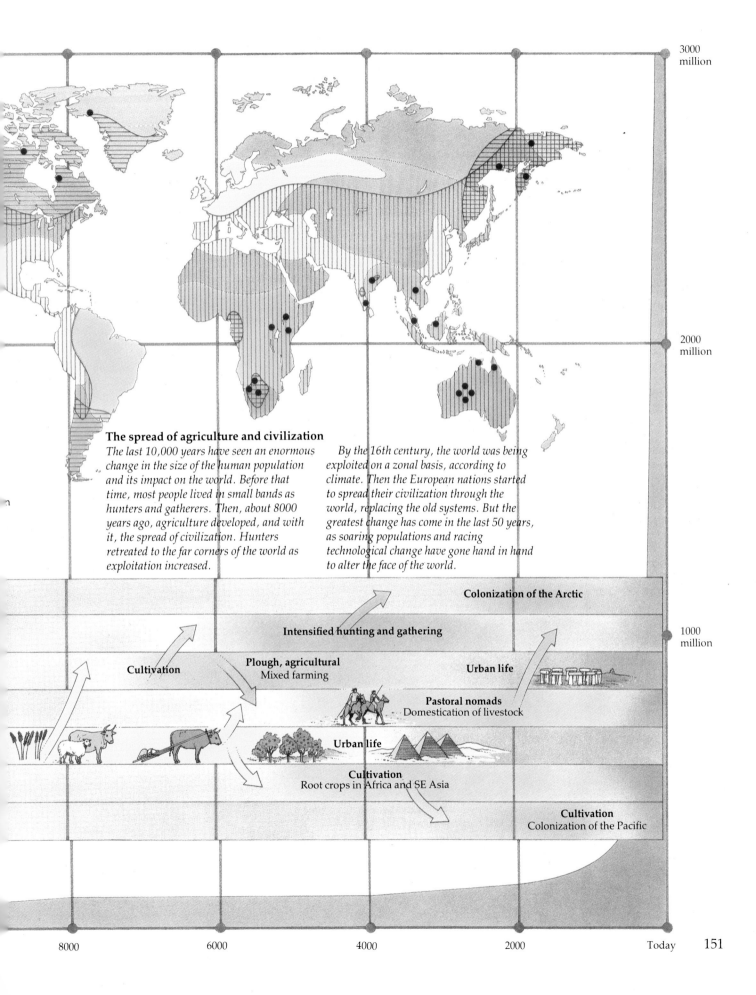

The spread of agriculture and civilization

The last 10,000 years have seen an enormous change in the size of the human population and its impact on the world. Before that time, most people lived in small bands as hunters and gatherers. Then, about 8000 years ago, agriculture developed, and with it, the spread of civilization. Hunters retreated to the far corners of the world as exploitation increased.

By the 16th century, the world was being exploited on a zonal basis, according to climate. Then the European nations started to spread their civilization through the world, replacing the old systems. But the greatest change has come in the last 50 years, as soaring populations and racing technological change have gone hand in hand to alter the face of the world.

Colonization of the Arctic

Intensified hunting and gathering

Cultivation

Plough, agricultural
Mixed farming

Urban life

Pastoral nomads
Domestication of livestock

Urban life

Cultivation
Root crops in Africa and SE Asia

Cultivation
Colonization of the Pacific

Europe

Largely composed of "advanced" nations, Europe has influenced the rest of the world for centuries with its culture and traditions. But its very affluence and industrial success now threatens its natural wealth.

Two wars have soaked up the energies of many of Europe's nations during this century, but 40 years of peace have now brought these same countries into an alliance of trading cooperation, with the formulation of a joint farming policy. The increased efficiency of farming, coupled with price-support schemes, have resulted in food overproduction. Meanwhile intensive farming and urbanization are eroding the countryside.

Pollution from industry has become an international problem during this century, notably the emissions produced by the UK, Belgium, Germany and Poland. Carried by the prevailing winds to the east and north, much of this pollution falls as acid rain in Scandinavia where it is causing damage to lakes and forests. Fortunately, there is now a growing environmental lobby striving to protect

Pollarded oaks in Spain
For centuries the natural evergreen oak forest of the Extremadura, Spain, was managed for its acorns which fed herds of pigs. In recent years, the area has been hit by swine fever and the farmers are switching to cereals. The oaks are managed by pollarding – lopping the branches – and although it is illegal to endanger the tree, they are often lopped so heavily that they die, or fires are "accidentally" lit near them. The result is that these trees, photographed three years ago, have now been replaced by cereal "prairie", and the cranes which migrate to Spain have lost their winter food supply.

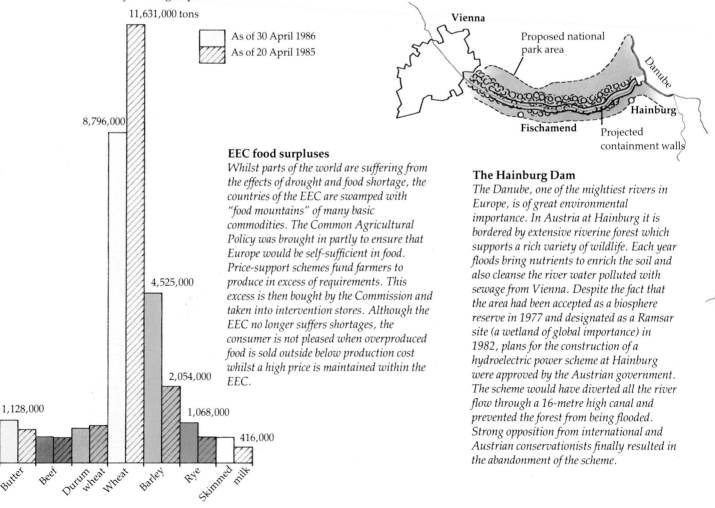

As of 30 April 1986
As of 20 April 1985

11,631,000 tons

8,796,000

4,525,000

2,054,000

1,128,000

1,068,000

416,000

Butter Beef Durum wheat Wheat Barley Rye Skimmed milk

EEC food surpluses
Whilst parts of the world are suffering from the effects of drought and food shortage, the countries of the EEC are swamped with "food mountains" of many basic commodities. The Common Agricultural Policy was brought in partly to ensure that Europe would be self-sufficient in food. Price-support schemes fund farmers to produce in excess of requirements. This excess is then bought by the Commission and taken into intervention stores. Although the EEC no longer suffers shortages, the consumer is not pleased when overproduced food is sold outside below production cost whilst a high price is maintained within the EEC.

Vienna

Proposed national park area

Danube

Hainburg

Fischamend Projected containment walls

The Hainburg Dam
The Danube, one of the mightiest rivers in Europe, is of great environmental importance. In Austria at Hainburg it is bordered by extensive riverine forest which supports a rich variety of wildlife. Each year floods bring nutrients to enrich the soil and also cleanse the river water polluted with sewage from Vienna. Despite the fact that the area had been accepted as a biosphere reserve in 1977 and designated as a Ramsar site (a wetland of global importance) in 1982, plans for the construction of a hydroelectric power scheme at Hainburg were approved by the Austrian government. The scheme would have diverted all the river flow through a 16-metre high canal and prevented the forest from being flooded. Strong opposition from international and Austrian conservationists finally resulted in the abandonment of the scheme.

ICELAND

NORWAY
4.7

SWEDEN

FINLAND

DENMARK

REPUBLIC
OF IRELAND

UNITED KINGDOM
4.7
5.0

NETHERLANDS

BELGIUM

LUXEMBOURG

WEST
GERMANY

EAST
GERMANY
4.5
4.4

POLAND

4.3

4.5

CZECHOSLOVAKIA
4.4

FRANCE

SWITZERLAND
4.5

AUSTRIA

HUNGARY

ROMANIA

YUGOSLAVIA

BULGARIA

PORTUGAL

SPAIN

ITALY

SARDINIA

BALEARIC ISLANDS

CORSICA

GREECE

SICILY

CRETE

⬤ National Parks

╱ pH levels of rain water

▨ Areas most susceptible to acid rain

Land cover

☐ Permanent ice and snow	
▨ Tundra and alpine	▨ Grassland, heath, marsh and steppe
▨ Desert	▨ Forest and woodland
▨ Semi-desert	▨ Cultivated land

The various schemes to dam and divert the flow of the Danube River in Austria, Hungary and Czechoslovakia have been the targets of organized protests involving all sectors of society (with the exception of industrialists, trade unionists and government officials). The primeval, riverine forests near Vienna are the largest of such ecosystems left in Europe and are home to an extraordinary variety of wildlife, from sea eagles to orchids. Even though Austria had signed the international and regional conventions for wetland and wildlife conservation (the Ramsar and Berne Conventions), it took a bloody battle between police and several thousand demonstrators before the government finally shelved the project. At about the same time, public opposition to the dams planned in Hungary began to be heard, and the government asked its partner, Czechoslovakia, to delay development. But the latest news is that the Hungarian project will go ahead (partially financed by Austria in return for electricity) and opposition be damned!

Conservation may have won a few battles in Europe recently, but it's certainly losing the war. Insidious, all-pervasive environmental problems, like acid rain and other forms of pollution, are the by-products of a whole way of living, and will not be quickly solved by demonstrators or governments. Meanwhile, persuading the peoples of developing countries to look after their environments and wildlife better than the Europeans do now and did when their own countries were undergoing development is rather like preaching "Do as I say, not as I do".

Africa

Europe gave birth to industry, but Africa gave birth to humanity. While little bands spread out to populate the world, those that stayed behind were probably involved in the faunal extinctions of the Pleistocene. The large animals that survived the spear and hand axe, however, evolved along with the Africans' cultures and traditions, and today represent the greatest part of the planet's contemporary megafauna. The only recent extinctions - two ungulates, the quagga and the blaubok - occurred at the hands of late settlers, the Europeans.

Europeans applied the philosophy and methods, wise and unwise, of land and wildlife management that they had developed in their home countries, and although it has become painfully obvious that even those suitable to European ecosystems have limited application in Africa, many post-colonial governments are still trying to impose them. The particular constraints of the African ecology and the human traditions which have evolved to cope with them are so seldom consulted by development planners, that it's not surprising that some of the worst environmental disasters to strike people, land and wildlife have happened in Africa.

The history of the fragmentation of the African wilds is very different from that of Europe. The colonialists set aside vast areas to protect the animals that were dying out because of their own excessive hunting. Early management practices were primitive, even to the point of shooting the big predators to "preserve" the ungulate herds. The Africans who lived nearby and had always relied on "bushmeat" to tide them over during lean years were now considered poachers. Meanwhile, away from the parks and reserves, the numbers of humans and domestic animals began to rise dramatically with improved medical and veterinary services, and more land was put to farms and pasture, by both Africans and Europeans.

As the population rose in Africa, the "good" land available to ordinary people became exhausted, and they were either pushed into the regions considered marginal for farming and raising livestock, or they tried to settle them deliberately, expecting certain techniques to render them productive in terms of crops and livestock. The good land kept by the wealthy was forced to the limits of productivity by expensive processes (irrigation) and products (fertilizers and pesticides) of dubious ecological longevity. The management of parks and reserves as whole ecosystems

CASE STUDY
Hands across the sea

Survival of the Mediterranean monk seal depends on special reserves being established in Greece and Turkey. Fewer than 500 seals are left, in groups scattered on Greek, Turkish, Yugoslavian and Tunisian coasts.

Three continents meet at the Mediterranean Sea, and 18 nations share its riches. Among those riches are a fauna of 7000 species and vitally important coastal tourist industries.

The maritime nations also use the sea as a dump. The sewage and effluent of 120 cities pour out into the Mediterranean. Although it covers an area of nearly three million square kilometres, it is almost entirely landlocked. Three times as much water is lost by evaporation than is received from rain and rivers, and this deficit is made up by a constant inflow from the Atlantic through the Strait of Gibraltar. Inflow is greater than outflow and, broadly speaking, pollutants dumped into the giant puddle that is the Mediterranean Sea will stay there and become more concentrated over the years.

The build-up of pollution has been going on for a long time, added to in recent years by 300,000 tons of oil per year flushed out of tankers into the sea. By 1972 the Mediterranean was considered to be one of the most badly polluted seas in the world, and it was clear that effective action had to be taken.

Whatever political differences may exist between Mediterranean countries, their physical dependence on the sea is common to all. In 1975, as part of UNEP's Regional Seas Programme, 17 of the 18 nations came together to work out an Action Plan. First on the list of protocols was the prevention of dumping from ships and aircraft; then came a plan for dealing with emergencies; a plan for land-originated pollution has also been drawn up and, finally, a scheme to protect specific areas of natural importance.

Since the Mediterranean Action Plan began in 1975, the level of pollution has not increased. Whether this success will now go on to achieve a real reduction in pollution depends on continued cooperation in the battle against the common enemy.

CASE STUDY
Acid rain - the silent scourge

Half of all the trees in West Germany are dead or dying. One in three trees in Switzerland is either sick or dead. Europe's forests, many of them only recently reprieved from the threat of the axe, are in the grip of a deadly epidemic. Apart from West Germany and Switzerland, trees in Czechoslovakia and Poland are badly affected, and those in France, Austria, Scandinavia and the UK are also giving serious cause for concern.

Coincidental with the spread of tree sickness, an increase in atmospheric pollution has also occurred, resulting in the phenomenon known as acid rain (*see also p.163*). It is estimated that 55 million tons of sulphur dioxide and 37 million tons of nitrogen oxides are emitted each year by Europe's heavy industry which react with moisture in the air to form sulphuric and nitric acids. This coincidence has been enough to stimulate attempts to cut industrial atmospheric pollution in many countries. In 1979, the "30% Club" was formed, with the aim of cutting sulphur dioxide emissions by 30% between 1980 and 1993. Eighteen countries have now signed this commitment, but the UK and USA are still conspicuously absent from the list.

Part of the difficulty lies in the circumstantial nature of the evidence linking tree deaths with acid rain. For a long time, it has been assumed that the increased acidity of the forest soil has been the main culprit. Acidified water leaches important minerals from the forest soil, and also liberates certain toxic ones, such as aluminium.

However, areas of extensive forest damage do not always correlate with intensity of acid input. Neither can the idea that air-borne pollutants directly harm the trees via their leaves be corroborated, as all the symptoms indicate that the sickness is within the whole tree, not just in its leaves.

One theory that is gaining credence implicates the air-borne oxides of nitrogen, which are also discharged from vehicle exhausts. Most woodland trees - conifers and deciduous trees alike - are heavily dependent on the fungi that live in the surface layers of their roots, in structures called mycorrhiza. The fungus obtains vitamins and carbohydrates from the tree, and the tree in turn gets water and usable minerals from the fungus. If the mycorrhiza are damaged by too much nitrogen in the air (in the form of nitrate and ammonium ions), then the tree's growth will be impaired and the roots will become prone to rot, especially in areas where the soil is already impoverished.

So far this seems to be the most plausible explanation. Although attempts to curb the release of nitrogen oxides from vehicles have met with strong opposition, it is believed by some that without some form of immediate action, all of Europe's trees could be doomed.

The Black Forest, West Germany. The trees of this magnificent forest are showing progressive thinning of their foliage and a reduction in the number of healthy branches. Their death is now inevitable.

THE STATE OF THE REGIONS
Africa

Africa, a land loved for its grandeur and natural wealth, is facing tragedy – famine and dwindling wildlife – with help arriving too little and too late.

With the exception of Egypt, the improvement in agriculture brought on by the "Green Revolution" has not been seen in Africa. Instead, lack of relevant research and poor advice on farming methods have led to impoverishment and erosion of soils and non-sustainable crop yields. The change from peasant subsistence farming to large-scale ranching and cash crops is also having dire effects on the environment. Several years of drought have worsened the situation, particularly in the Sahel, and desertification is causing many nations to depend on food aid.

The Aswan Dam disaster
Lake Nasser, created behind the Aswan High Dam, supplies 64% of Egypt's electricity and protects Egypt from drought. Constant irrigation has increased food production and helped Egypt's economy. However, it has not all been good news. Lowered fertility of soils necessitates increased use of fertilizers, and one-third of Egypt's arable land has problems of salinity and waterlogging. Silt is also clogging Lake Nasser. This, coupled with the seven-year African drought, has resulted in drastically reduced water levels. There is concern that Lake Nasser will soon be below operational levels.

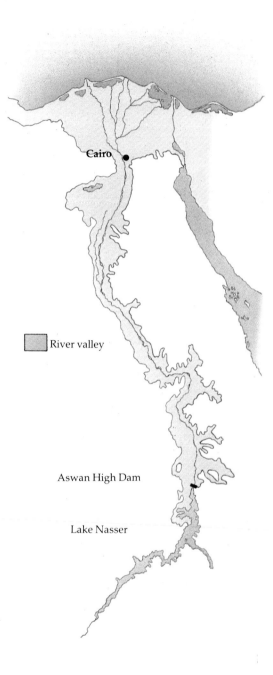

Cairo

River valley

Aswan High Dam

Lake Nasser

Destruction of the Tai Forest
Since the 1960s, the Ivory Coast has witnessed an enormous population growth. Large areas of virgin forest have been opened up, and widespread logging, poaching and gold prospecting now threatens the Tai Forest National Park, the last viable stand of West African tropical moist forest. Already 25% of the park has disappeared.

──── Fences

- - - Planned fences

✠ Massive die-offs 1 – 1961
                2 – 1964
                3 – 1970
                4 – 1979
                5 – 1983

○ Lake Xau dry since 1983

A Moremi Wildlife Reserve B Chobe National Park C Central Kalahari Game Reserve

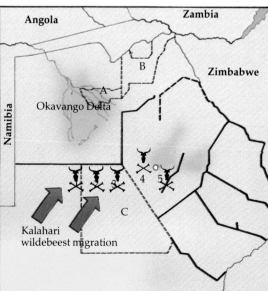

Angola

Zambia

Namibia

Okavango Delta

B

A

Zimbabwe

C

Kalahari wildebeest migration

South Africa

Beef barons in Botswana
Botswana is prospering on the results of a national policy to turn the country into one huge cattle farm. This includes the Kalahari Desert, one of the world's great wilderness areas. The numbers of beef cattle have doubled since the 1960s, and are still rising. To enable cattle stocks to be isolated at times of epidemics, hundreds of kilometres of fences have been erected. These are causing the deaths of thousands of wild animals, as they migrate in search of water.

Fears are now growing for the wildlife of the lush Okavango Delta. Soon the beef barons may decide to move in.

African countries experiencing famine since 1950

Estimated deaths		
1968-69	Nigeria	1,000,000
1973	Sahelian countries	100,000
1972-74	Ethiopia	200,000
1983	Ethiopia	30,000
1985	Ethiopia, Sudan	?

A famine-stricken continent

Increasing population and drought have led to appalling famine in much of the Sahel. Foreign aid has increased productivity of many cash crops, but with little benefit for the peasant farmer majority. Clustering of nomadic groups around newly drilled wells has led to severe overgrazing and accelerated depletion of already-scarce vegetation. The map, below, illustrates those areas that cannot support present populations, even if all cultivable land is used.

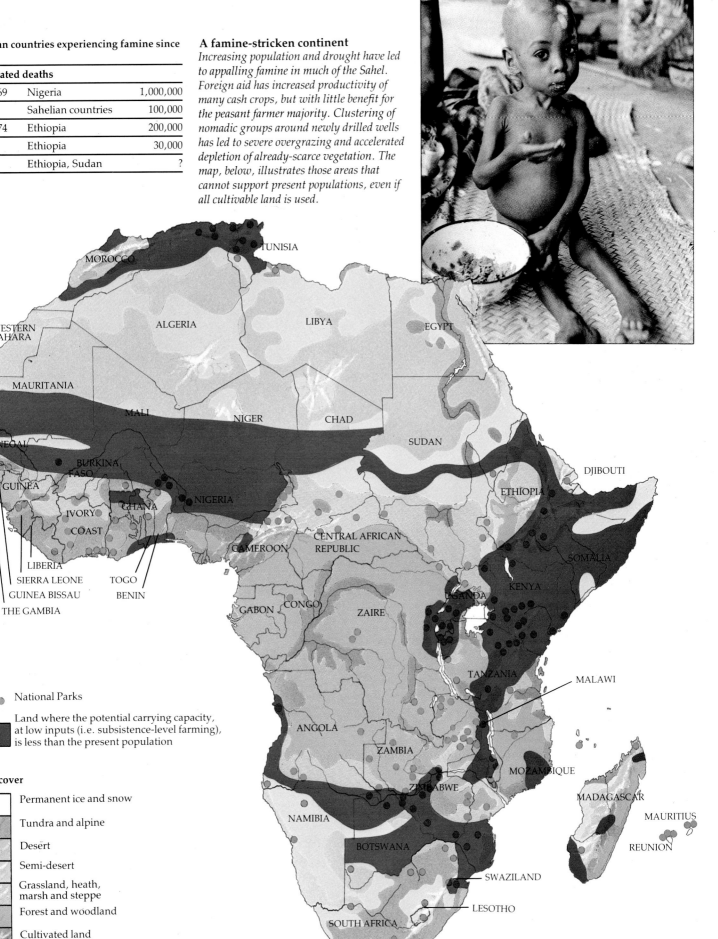

- ● National Parks

- ■ Land where the potential carrying capacity, at low inputs (i.e. subsistence-level farming), is less than the present population

Land cover

- Permanent ice and snow
- Tundra and alpine
- Desert
- Semi-desert
- Grassland, heath, marsh and steppe
- Forest and woodland
- Cultivated land

157

International concern over the plight of the mountain gorilla focused attention on its last stronghold, the Virunga Mountains of Rwanda, Zaire and Uganda. Thanks to the project initiated in 1978 by the Fauna and Flora Preservation Society on behalf of the gorilla, the Parc National des Volcans of Rwanda, which is home to over a third of the less than 400 gorillas left, is today a model of modern reserve management, integrating habitat and animal protection with the needs of the local people. The park has been declared a MAB reserve and encompasses a watershed forest vital to the well-being of humans, livestock and agriculture in the lowlands of Rwanda.

(including predatory animals) is being attempted now, but they are like oases in a bleak landscape. Nor are they really whole, for none but a few provide any niche for the people who evolved with them. Human pressure on their boundaries is severe and illegal encroachments are rife. Civil-war soldiers and big-time poachers, bred of the unrestful times in Africa, are finishing off what is left of the larger animals.

Although a handful of dedicated people in Africa are involved in sensible projects to rectify the situation, the overall picture looks grim. There are examples from every part of the continent that together would justify this statement, but perhaps the most telling is the story behind the dreadful famine of 1984 in the belt of countries that crosses Africa beneath the Sahara desert, from Mauritania in the west to Ethiopia in the east. Known as the Sahel, this land has long been known to be prone to drought. For centuries, the herdkeepers have imitated the behaviour of the wild animals, following the sporadic rains to sparsely distributed and ephemeral green pastures, and keeping their stock scattered in order to buffer any outbreaks of disease. People a little further south developed a complex system of cultivation and pasturage which allowed them to be more sedentary. When necessary, all people relied on the wild plants and bushmeat which naturally persisted in times of drought. Then, during the relatively wet period of the '50s, the herdkeepers moved further north, increasing their stock as they went, and the farmers to the south entered the former rangelands. Both peoples were pressed by their own and others' burgeoning populations and encouraged by their governments' vision of the technologies that would maintain them.

The rainfall began to taper off in the '60s, as everyone should have known it would. In the areas where grazing, cultivation and cutting trees for firewood had been intense, desertification set in. The technology offered by foreign aid agencies and eagerly accepted by the governments only made matters worse. The sinking of bore holes to make permanent wells in many places encouraged pastoralists to settle around them, and their numerous livestock ate up the forage and compacted the soil. Further breakdown of traditional patterns of land use resulted from the governments' desire to keep the pastoralists from moving across national borders with their herds and to have the farmers grow cash crops (again, with the "help" of technology), thereby altering their age-old system of cultivation and pasturage.

The current drought is part of a 25-year overall decline in rainfall in the region, and no doubt it is one of the severest in history. In the past, people also suffered immensely from drought, but the difference now is that the inherent resilience of the arid-land ecosystem has been lost, not by an "act of god" withholding the rains, but by the acts of people shunning or being directed to shun their rôles in the ecosystem.

The only solution is to let the land rest for awhile, but can the clock be turned back by people who have abandoned their traditional life styles? Will people cull their herds or do without cash for a while? Is there a way to marry tradition and new ideas in programmes based on sound ecology? The answer to the last question is yes, but the programmes have yet to be applied on a scale large enough to determine whether they will make a difference to the whole of the region. The "plan" offered by the United Nations between 1970 and 1980 should have been sufficiently broad, but it has been revealed that of the $10 billion spent, only one billion went to control desertification in the field, and some of these projects were for drilling water wells! (The rest was spent on programmes to "strengthen national capacities in science and technology" and to meet "production goals".) More successful have been the small field projects - the planting of native trees, the terracing of cultivated slopes, the use of simple, efficient cooking stoves - run directly by foreign governments and non-governmental organizations, like the IUCN, with the blessing of the national and, most importantly, the local authorities and the people themselves.

CASE STUDY

The dreaded tsetse fly - did it help protect African wildlife?

Blood-sucking tsetse flies inhabit 10 million square kilometres of tropical Africa, in a wide band across the continent that takes in 34 countries. They are associated with disease in humans (sleeping sickness) and animals (nagana), caused by a protozoan parasite, *Trypanosoma*, spread by their bite. Tsetse fly-infested regions were once treated as no-go areas, and simply avoided. With the advent of colonial rule, however, a long war with the fly and its protozoan guest began.

Many different lines of attack have been tried, and none has yet succeeded in eliminating the disease. The medical approach has concentrated on the disease itself, and the development of a vaccine that would help to eradicate the protozoa. This work still continues.

Empirical methods have concentrated on the parasite's hosts - the wildlife that acts as a reservoir of infection, and the tsetse fly itself. Following the observation that rinderpest, in wiping out 90% of the wild game of some regions, had also led to the elimination of tsetse in the same regions, widespread slaughter of wild game was begun in the 1920s. In the next 40 years, 1.3 million animals were killed in the campaign, in more than ten countries. It was not until the late 1950s, however, that the six species preferred by tsetse fly were identified, but by then the slaughter campaign was on the wane due to lack of success.

Another method that has been tried is clearance of bush, which removes the shade needed by the flies. Tens of thousands of square kilometres have been cleared, at great cost, and then had to be kept clear, at further cost. This method was fairly effective, but difficult and expensive, and was superseded by the use of insecticides.

Soon after the end of World War II, the insecticides developed in the war were being put to use in Zululand. Early experiments were successful and, to date, DDT, BHC (lindane) and dieldrin have been sprayed over 300,000 square kilometres of Africa.

Insecticides are very effective in controlling tsetse fly. As is now well known, however, they also destroy a lot more besides. Dieldrin in Zambia has been seen to kill 69 species of birds, reptiles, small mammals and fish. Many non-target insects are also killed, and some orchids have been eradicated due to poisoning of their pollinating insects.

DDT is known to be persistent, and the long-term effects of enthusiastic early use will probably continue for many years yet. Techniques and selected insecticides are improving, however, and eradication of tsetse flies is a distinct possibility.

Although tsetse control is becoming safer, the need for control is becoming more controversial. Before any control was attempted, the tsetse fly was an effective force for conservation in much of Africa. As long as tsetse control remained difficult and expensive, it was only undertaken in areas where the results - availability of land for settlement and use - were worth the effort. Now that vast areas can be sprayed from the air, tsetse-free areas are growing so fast that land already settled is in danger of being used less efficiently. There is a real possibility that the spread of livestock on to marginal land will become a threat to wildlife.

With the tsetse fly's declining hold on Africa, the future of wildlife in former tsetse country is in the hands of the planners and, ultimately, the politicians. There is a great opportunity here to develop a far-sighted land-use plan that could provide for rational economic development side by side with sustainable forest use such as rotational cropping, timber production and tourism. If this opportunity is missed, then the eradication of the tsetse fly may be Africa's misfortune.

Distribution of tsetse fly in Africa.

Both male and female tsetse flies feed on blood and therefore both are capable of transmitting disease. The abdomen of this particular tsetse fly is engorged with blood, having just fed.

At the other end of the spectrum in Africa are the wealthy cattle owners, who convert the meat to cash. The cattle boom in Botswana, courtesy of loans and markets provided by the World Bank and the EEC, turns over sales of $100 million a year by exporting beef to the West. Half of the three million plus head of cattle are owned by 5% of the citizens, black and white.

In places the numbers of cattle exceed the recommended stocking rate by ten times. They are driven deeper into the arid lands bordering the Kalahari Desert, artificially maintained by the digging of wells which is having the same effect on the vegetation as in the Sahel. The dread of foot-and-mouth disease has led to the erection of "veterinary fences", designed to separate the cattle-ranching areas from where the wild ungulates roam - the wildebeest, hartebeest, gemsbok and giraffe of the Kalahari. It is thought that close contact with these animals spreads the virus to the cattle, although some experts say that fences are absurd, because transmission is by birds or even dust particles. The fences have effectively disrupted the migrations of the wild herds to the northern rivers and lakes, the only sources of water during droughts. It is estimated that two million wild animals have died of thirst and starvation since the cattle boom started in Botswana. Incredibly, more fences are being planned, but there is not even a cattle tax to generate government revenues (and never likely to be one, as many of the biggest cattle owners are the politicians), and the human population of Botswana receives food aid from America!

Africa is a land of such contrasts. While the misery of some humans and animals has been alleviated by foreign money, methods and attitudes, how much more suffering is to come until people look again at how their own, very African, ecosystems function?

North America

North America is also a land of contradictions in how its people regard and treat its natural resources. There is the view that the bounty of nature is inexhaustible (an adaptive trait for pioneers), and the degree of wastage has been and is astonishing. At the same time, some of the strongest laws concerning the husbandry of resources have been developed and enforced in the USA and Canada.

The European settlers of North America set about clearing away the forests of the east for farming, and on reaching the fertile prairies in the middle of the continent, they killed off the vast herds of bison and pronghorn antelope without a thought to their future usefulness. Now over one-third of the area in the USA (excluding Alaska and Hawaii) is under some form of intensive land use - agriculture, grazing or urban development - and the remaining natural vegetation continues to lose ground. The profligate use of natural resources is reflected in the North American life style: the average calorie intake is almost 50% higher than that needed to stay healthy, and water consumption per capita in the USA is double that of Europe.

And yet, over a hundred years ago, the Americans established a national park, the first in the world, and the Canadians soon followed with parks designed to preserve the bison and the antelope. *Effectively* protected areas in North America cover a higher percentage of the land mass than in any other continent in the world. The public is now well-educated in environmental matters, and strong legislation to combat environmental problems, once they're publicly recognized, is often readily enacted. The astonishing erosion of three billion tons of topsoil a year from America's farmlands not only threatens the future of the nation's food-growing capacity, but pollution of the waters from soil run-off is estimated to cost over $2 billion a year in material damages. (Biological damages - the loss of wildlife - cannot be calculated, but may well outweigh the others.) However, sweeping new legislation should contain

CASE STUDY
The Yeheb nut could help in the Sahel

On the open bush savannah of Somalia, a valuable food plant may be facing extinction. Once so common that it made up fully half of all woody growth in the bush there, the yeheb has been much reduced by drought, war and goats, until it is now so rare as to be considered endangered.

Yeheb nuts - really the pod-fruits of this leguminous bush - have been a traditional food for generations of nomads in Somalia and the Ogaden. They are eaten fresh, boiled or roasted, and the plant also provides dyes as well as being useful for fuel and animal forage.

The yeheb bush is easy to grow: it roots deeply in sand and tolerates low rainfall and poor soils. Once established, it needs no tending, and would provide a valuable famine food for nomadic regions that do not support normal agriculture.

In its natural range in Somalia and Ethiopia, the wild yeheb is now limited to four small areas. It is, however, being grown in Kenya and Somalia. The plant has also been introduced into Sudan, North Yemen and South Yemen, and seeds have been sent to India.

Further development of the yeheb as a crop plant will include cultivating higher-yielding strains, improving propagation methods, and selecting strains for different soils and conditions. As well as being extremely important for the nomads who still occupy Somalia and Ethiopia, wild yeheb populations are vital to the breeding programme. They are the only source of the genetic variability on which the breeding programme is based, and any further development will depend on conservation of the wild populations of this plant.

The yeheb bush is a branching, evergreen shrub up to 2-3 m high. Its nutritionally rich nuts have a pleasant, sweetish flavour.

CASE STUDY
Lake Victoria and the Nile perch

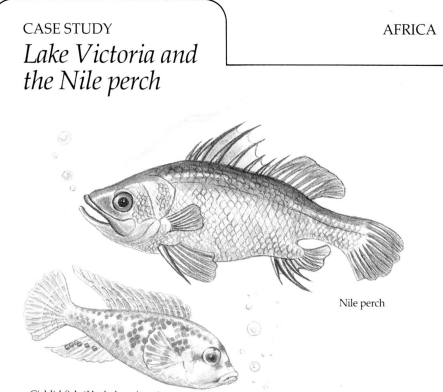

Nile perch

Cichlid fish (*Haplochromis* sp.)

An experiment in ecology in Lake Victoria, East Africa, proved the experts right but gave no cause for celebration. It has wrecked important fishing industries and annihilated some scientifically fascinating species.

Lake Victoria is a body of water the size of Switzerland, with shores in Kenya, Tanzania and Uganda. Its fisheries used to provide tilapia for Nairobi and supplied an abundance of small, easily preserved cichlids over a wide area.

In 1958, a large carnivorous fish, the Nile perch, was introduced into the Ugandan portion of the lake, in the mistaken belief that it would provide another useful catch. This action, taken despite contrary advice from ecologists, has devastated the local fishing. As the Nile perch spread from Uganda to Kenya and, finally, to Tanzania, nearly all the commercially valuable fish have vanished. Having eaten most of the cichlids, small perch are now eating prawns, whilst big ones are turning to cannibalism.

To make matters even worse, the local people do not like eating Nile perch. Because they are oily fish, they cannot be sun-dried but have to be smoked instead, which is leading to deforestation of some islands in the lake. Small fishermen are losing their traditional catches, but cannot compete with larger operators who have bigger boats and more expensive equipment to land Nile perch. The perch do not sell well locally, but are transported to more sophisticated markets, as far away as coastal resorts.

As well as nutritional and financial losses, the Nile perch has also been responsible for scientific losses. The hundreds of cichlid species in the lake are known to have evolved from a single species during the last million years or so, since the lake was formed. Many of these fish are now being gobbled into extinction before scientists have had a chance to study them.

A recent statement from the Food and Agricultural Organization concluded that "the introduction of Nile perch to utilise the ... cichlids of the lake may be regarded as successful in terms of its original objectives". The Nile perch has undoubtedly "utilised" the cichlids, but it wastes 78% of what it eats so, unless the "objective" was to reduce drastically the productivity of the lake at the same time as annihilating unique species, it can hardly be seen as a resounding success.

There is no way that this mistake can be reversed. Any introduction to a lake carries an element of risk, usually less easy to see than in this case, and the stakes are always too high to gamble with. The Nile perch will never be eradicated from Lake Victoria; whatever balance is ultimately achieved will be worse than it was before this outsider was carelessly let loose, and this lesson must be taken to heart by other nations considering "improving" their own fishing lakes.

North America

Regarded as the "Eldorado" to which millions of Europeans migrated for a better life, North America is a continent with a great wealth of resources and landscape - from the deserts, across the plains, the Great Lakes and the northern forests to the Arctic.

The new nations established with a free enterprise ethos are now amongst the most technically advanced on Earth, but their development has meant the heavy exploitation of land and mineral wealth and the decimation of the indigenous peoples. Intensive agriculture has led to water supply and pollution problems, and to serious soil erosion in the grain lands. Yet North American agriculture feeds the world. The now wealthy populations spend much energy and concern on aspects of conservation of the environment and wildlife and on exploring the "wilderness", including outer space. America has produced leaders and philosophers at the "cutting edge" of the conservation movement. Environmental movements are also concerned with pollution from pesticides, industry and household waste. (The USA produces vastly more rubbish per capita than any other country.)

The scandal of Negro Bill Canyon
Efforts to protect Negro Bill Canyon in Utah as a Wilderness Area have highlighted the conflict between the conservation lobby and those entrepreneurs who seek to use wild areas for anything from strip mining to motor racing.

This beautiful canyon, carved out over thousands of years by a tributary of the Colorado River, contains magnificent rock formations such as the Morning Glory Arch, one of the world's widest natural bridges. The walls of pink Navajo sandstone rise vertically, soaring above the cottonwoods and gambel oaks that grow below. The canyon is abundant with wildlife drawn by the year-round water course, which is in itself uncommon in this region.

In 1976, Congress directed the Bureau of Land Management to review its land holdings for a selection of areas to be designated in the National Wilderness Preservation Scheme, including Negro Bill Canyon. Whilst this was under review, in 1979, the local county commissioners twice attempted to bulldoze a road through the canyon despite the fact that a wilderness area must, by definition, be without signs of civilization including roads. The illicit removal of field reports, and the conflict of interests of administrative staff involved, resulted in the decision not to designate the canyon as a Wilderness Study Area. Appeals by the Utah branch of the Sierra Club succeeded in overturning this ruling, in the first successful appeal by conservationists. There have been many other examples of attempts to destroy areas before review, or of falsifying the evidence to be put to the BLM. But in this case, although still not finally decided, has pinpointed the problems encountered.

Soil erosion in the corn belt
Continued intensive agriculture in regions of light soils such as the Great Plains and corn belt of North America has caused problems of erosion. Top soils are removed by wind or heavy rainfall, and the structure of the soil is destroyed, thus reducing crop yields below economic levels. Agricultural debts are mounting to large figures in the United States. Government benefits to farmers, however, ensure that cultivation continues. Siltation of rivers can cause flooding and damage to river life, and also to marine ecosystems at the estuary. Run-off from agricultural land often contains pesticides and other agrochemicals that harm wildlife (nitrates, for example, which increase algal productivity in the river and can cause eutrophication (p.24), as well as possible health hazards to public water supplies.) With the memory of the dust-bowls of the '30s to spur them on, soil and agriculture scientists are testing less damaging cultivation techniques - "minimum till" and "trickle-drip irrigation" farming, plus biological pest control and soil management.

Tons of soil (in millions) eroded annually, as of 1977

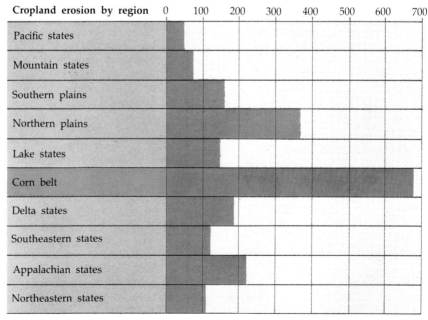

Cropland erosion by region	0	100	200	300	400	500	600	700
Pacific states								
Mountain states								
Southern plains								
Northern plains								
Lake states								
Corn belt								
Delta states								
Southeastern states								
Appalachian states								
Northeastern states								

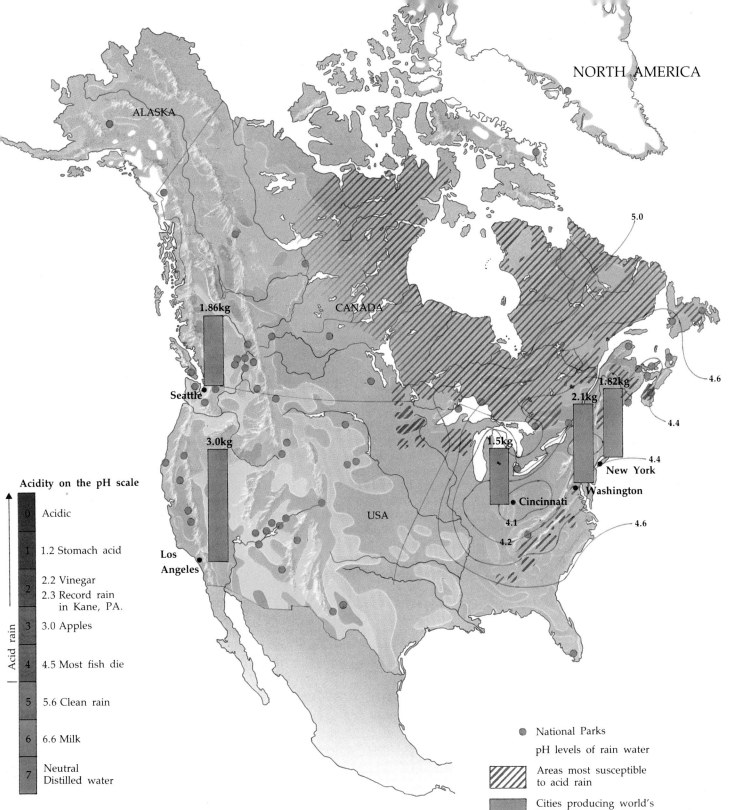

ALASKA

CANADA

1.86kg

5.0

4.6

Seattle

1.82kg

2.1kg

4.4

3.0kg

1.5kg

4.4

New York

Los
Angeles

USA

Cincinnati

Washington

4.1

4.4

4.2

4.6

Acidity on the pH scale

Acid rain

0	Acidic
1	1.2 Stomach acid
2	2.2 Vinegar
	2.3 Record rain in Kane, PA.
3	3.0 Apples
4	4.5 Most fish die
5	5.6 Clean rain
6	6.6 Milk
7	Neutral Distilled water

National Parks

pH levels of rain water

Areas most susceptible to acid rain

Cities producing world's highest levels of waste per capita

Land cover

Permanent ice and snow

Tundra and alpine

Desert

Semi-desert

Grassland, heath, marsh and steppe

Forest and woodland

Cultivated land

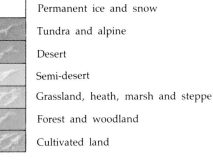

Acid rain and the 30% Club

Atmospheric environmental pollution has been a problem since the early 1900s. In the past, the solution has been simply to increase the height of the smoke stacks - so sending the pollutants high into the atmosphere to be carried hundreds of miles from the source. In the air, oxides of sulphur and nitrogen present in smoke combine with water to give sulphurous and nitric acids, which are then deposited as "acid rain". In northern latitudes, the base rock, the soil types and the plant cover of mosses and conifers are particularly susceptible to acid rain. Trees die, and lakes become so acid that fish can no longer survive. Airborne pollution from source areas such as the Ohio Valley, Pennsylvania and Sudbury, Ontario, are carried over Canada, and from the UK and Europe over Scandinavia, threatening northern forests over thousands of square kilometres. An agreement by countries to decrease sulphur dioxide emissions by 30% by 1990 was set up by the Economic Commission for Europe - the "30% Club". Twenty-one countries, including Canada and USSR, have joined. Notable exceptions are the USA and UK.

The only known population of black-footed ferrets in the world, located in Wyoming, is on the verge of extinction. Now down to less than ten animals in the wild, biologists believe that the numbers and range of these reclusive animals were cut back drastically in the first half of this century by the systematic extermination of prairie dogs, on which ferrets depend for food and burrows. The imminent extinction of America's most endangered mammal will be laid at the door of the state officials who dragged their heels in taking protective measures because they refused to take advice from "outsiders", i.e. biologists from other states.

the problem: "sodbuster" and "swampbuster" laws withhold subsidies to farmers who cultivate erosive soils or convert wetlands to crops, and the government hopes to acquire nearly 20 million hectares of eroded farmland for replanting with natural vegetation. On the other hand, some major environmental abuses, like the overuse of water in the west, have received little legislative attention.

The USA has provided a model for species conservation by its comprehensive Endangered Species Act of 1973, which outlaws disturbance to the habitats of the species listed, as well as hunting and trade. The Act has passed review with its "teeth" intact, most recently under an administration not noted for its understanding of conservation biology. It allowed a creature called the snail darter to hold up development of a huge dam in Tennessee, my home state, which is quite an achievement for a rare little fish, although it soon became clear that the dam project itself was "ill-conceived and uneconomic". But the contradictions inherent in North American environmental attitudes surfaced here, and, I'm ashamed to say, the dam was eventually built. A population of a few hundred snail darters was moved to another river, where it has at least maintained itself.

No clearer illustration of the contradictions can be found than the situation with the native peoples of North America, the descendants of settlers from Asia who preceded the Europeans by about 30,000 years. The Europeans nearly exterminated them in the push across the continent, but today their few voices are heeded, albeit hypocritically. The traditional rights of land usage of the Canadian Ojibwas, guaranteed by treaty, were threatened by a paper company whose pulp plant discharged mercury into the fishing river and whose logging schemes could have reduced the forest game. In spite of great public outrage, the government stopped neither the pollution nor the proposed logging. It made a partial grant towards converting the plant to non-mercury technology 13 years after the discharges began, and the paper company itself shelved the logging plans owing to financial difficulties. Meanwhile, other tribes have been exempted from the strict laws that protect marine mammals, so long as they hunt by traditional means. In fact, they are using modern and wasteful means. Contradiction in attitudes towards rational resource utilization, once primarily a European affliction, is clearly a contagious disease.

Latin America

The greatest environmental threat to Latin America is the destruction of the forests. In all developing regions forests are under severe pressure, but in Latin America there is one particular pressure of disturbing magnitude: cattle-ranching to make the so-called "hamburger connection" to North America. Whereas in other countries big-time cattle owners graze their herds on already open ranges, governments here virtually give away forested land to be cleared for the purpose, an offer the owners can't refuse. Heavy inroads have been made in the Central American forests and in Brazil, and Peru, Colombia and Bolivia are welcoming proposals from the cattle industry.

Forest destruction by loggers and clearfellers is as great in Latin America as it is anywhere else, and the landless people follow the timber roads to the interior. They cultivate the logged-over places and then work into virgin forests from the roads. The concentration of people is such that the land is left no time to rest and recover. Ironically, Brazil has had laws to protect its forests since 1605, and the first Forest Code was developed in 1939. It all reads beautifully on paper, and the provision that 50% of the land in Brazilian Amazonia must be left in "tree cover" sounds quite reasonable. But "tree cover" has been interpreted as including exotic timber plantations and orchards, and ongoing subdivisions of property into ever-smaller parcels make a joke of the 50% rule.

The Inuit and the bowhead whale

In 1947 the International Whaling Commission declared the bowhead whale a protected species. The only hunting permitted was a subsistence harvest conceded to the Alaskan Eskimos (now called Inuit) who depended on the bowhead for their living. Traditional hunting methods were not considered a significant threat to the bowhead's survival, since no more than 60 animals a year had ever been taken this way. Every part of the animal was used by the Inuit people, for food, tools, weapons, domestic utensils and even toys. Commercial whaling had accounted for over 19,000 bowheads between 1848 and 1915, when the commercial hunt collapsed.

In 1976, the number of bowheads was estimated at between 600 and 2000 whales. It seemed that the Inuit hunt, now equipped with more sophisticated equipment, would have to be stopped before all the whales disappeared. This controversial recommendation struck at the traditional rights and entire life style of the Inuit, and caused a great deal of resentment. Agreement was finally reached: the Inuit retained their right to hunt, but only with "aboriginal" equipment. Unfortunately, this exception did little to stimulate the cooperation of other local whaling communities.

From 1978, the Inuit whaling activities were closely monitored. It was found that the number of bowheads had been underestimated in the 1976 census, due to a lack of knowledge about the whales' habits. The number is now put at over 4400, and their reproductive rate is known to be higher than was previously supposed. Inuit catches since 1978 have averaged 20 a year, and the threat of extinction seems to have been lifted from the bowhead whale.

Bowhead whale being butchered by the Inuit in the Bering Sea off Alaska.

Water crisis in the southwestern states

Irrigation in the Imperial Valley, California. The state irrigates some 1.5 million ha of land to grow crops.

Texas may lose over a million hectares of farmland by the year 2000. The decline is already under way, with many farms in the southwestern states of America closing down each year. The cause of this recession is not reduced demand for their crops, but lack of water to grow them.

Water resources are not inexhaustible. They depend, ultimately, on rainfall, and the southwest does not have enough rain to support the level of agriculture that has developed there. The water used to irrigate farms has been borrowed from future rainfall, in a sense, by taking it out of groundwater reserves at a rate far beyond the rainfall's capacity to replenish them. Now these reserves are running dry.

Water consumption in the USA is higher than anywhere else in the world. In 1981, city dwellers who make up 90% of the population, used 160 gallons per head per day, three times as much as 30 years earlier. And yet a single 810-hectare irrigated farm in the southwest uses as much water in a day as a city of 50,000 people! California alone is losing 25 billion cubic metres of groundwater a year, and this is due to rise by 50% by the end of the century. Its rainless lands grow one-quarter of the USA's fresh fruit and vegetables, as well as cotton, sugar beet, cereals and soya for export.

The consequences of this loss of groundwater will be disastrous in every sense. As water becomes scarcer and more expensive, farmers will leave the land. The Dust Bowl experience of the 1930s, when unusual rains made the drylands usable for a few years before reverting to stubborn dryness, forced 500,000 people from the land. If the same number are driven away now, the land they leave behind could become another Dust Bowl, taking the remaining good land with it.

Drawing out groundwater leads to subsidence. The great Ogallala Aquifer extends under 430,000 square kilometres of Nebraska, Kansas, Colorado, Oklahoma, New Mexico and Texas. This huge natural reservoir has been the greening of the southwest, and it may well see its destruction. Falling at up to 1.5 metres per year, the water no longer supports the land above it.

The wilderness areas also depend on groundwater to sustain them between rains. One judge in the US has already ruled that, for the 24 wilderness areas in Colorado, their water resources must be protected. Other countries, too, have water problems. Mexico is suffering loss of water as well as pollution of some of its sources by agriculture in the USA.

A change of land use in the southwestern states is now inevitable. Whether it occurs voluntarily or through sheer lack of water in a decade or so is the only choice left.

Latin America

Political instability makes well-planned development difficult in Latin America. But even in those countries at peace over-exploitation and outside interference are common. The anchoveta industry of Peru even in its heyday was not providing for the local people. Across the Andes, destruction of the rainforests and grasslands is spearheaded by foreign capital, leaving the land-hungry poor to complete the ruination process by slash-and-burn farming.

Trans-Amazonian Highway
Begun in the 1970s, the Trans-Amazonian Highway has opened up large areas of the rainforest to exploitation. Clearance for timber, mineral extraction and agriculture can quickly result in degraded and eroded soils, yielding poor crops, and in further destruction by shifting cultivation. The natives suffer land loss, and many tribes have been decimated by introduced diseases.

The great continent of Latin America is, in terms of species, the treasure house of the world. But for its peoples, survival takes precedence.

MEXICO

BELIZE

GUATEMALA

HONDURAS

EL SALVADOR

NICARAGUA

COSTA RICA

PANAMA

Land where potential carrying capacity at low inputs (i.e. subsistence level farming) is less than present population

● National Parks

Land cover

Permanent ice and snow

Tundra and alpine

Desert

Semi-desert

Grassland, heath, marsh and steppe

Forest and woodland

Cultivated land

Nicaragua fighting for the forests
Nicaragua has the largest remaining tract of unspoilt tropical moist forest in Central America, covering 4 million hectares. But forest loss is now running at over 100,000 hectares per annum - due to the combined impact of increased shifting cultivation, cattle ranching for beef, and damage by counter-revolutionary efforts from neighbouring countries. Efforts are being made to conserve and replant Nicaragua's forests and to protect threatened species. Nicaragua has even appealed to the global community to declare part of the forest a World Heritage reserve, so making it free both of commercial destruction, and of war.

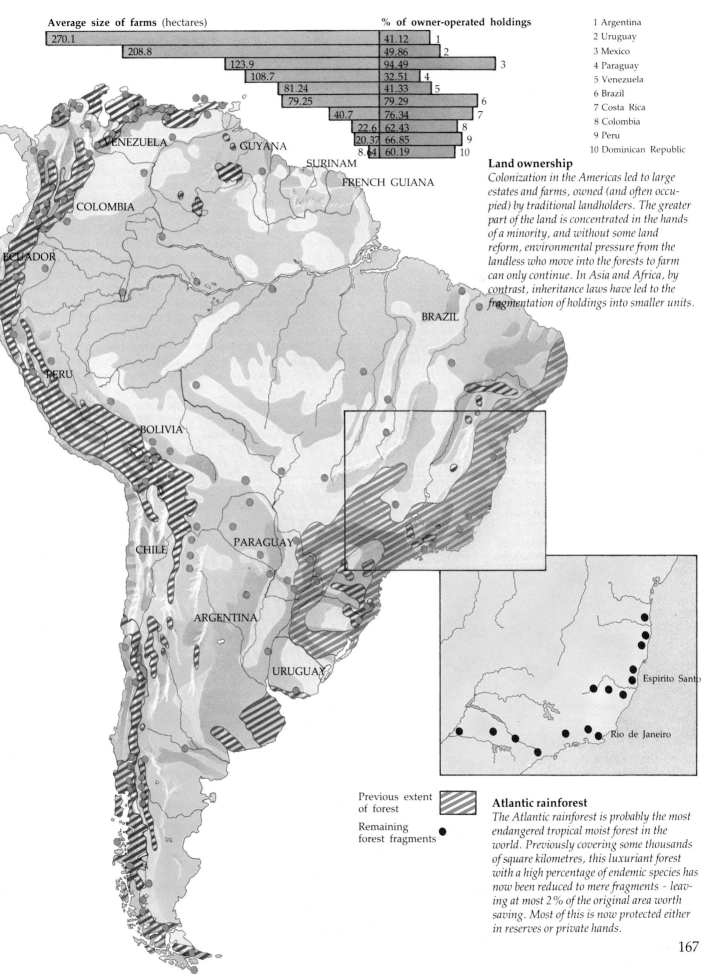

Average size of farms (hectares)

% of owner-operated holdings

270.1	41.12	1
208.8	49.86	2
123.9	94.49	3
108.7	32.51	4
81.24	41.33	5
79.25	79.29	6
40.7	76.34	7
22.6	62.43	8
20.37	66.85	9
8.64	60.19	10

1 Argentina
2 Uruguay
3 Mexico
4 Paraguay
5 Venezuela
6 Brazil
7 Costa Rica
8 Colombia
9 Peru
10 Dominican Republic

Land ownership

Colonization in the Americas led to large estates and farms, owned (and often occupied) by traditional landholders. The greater part of the land is concentrated in the hands of a minority, and without some land reform, environmental pressure from the landless who move into the forests to farm can only continue. In Asia and Africa, by contrast, inheritance laws have led to the fragmentation of holdings into smaller units.

Espirito Santo

Rio de Janeiro

Previous extent
of forest

Remaining
forest fragments

Atlantic rainforest

The Atlantic rainforest is probably the most endangered tropical moist forest in the world. Previously covering some thousands of square kilometres, this luxuriant forest with a high percentage of endemic species has now been reduced to mere fragments - leaving at most 2% of the original area worth saving. Most of this is now protected either in reserves or private hands.

167

At least there are still large forests in Amazonia, and many organizations within Latin America and abroad are working hard to save them (although the situation with Brazil's Atlantic rainforests is another matter – *see p.167*). Forestry departments throughout Latin America are engaged in research, training and planting programmes, and over a hundred institutions offer courses in forestry, some working in collaboration with their foreign counterparts. Chile has established enough pine plantations, leaving the native forests untouched, to become not only self-sufficient in her own industrial needs, but also an exporter of forest products. However, most of the training institutes are new, small and lacking in money, and Chile was lucky in having land suitable for the planting, processing and distribution of timber. The programmes are excellent, but seem embryonic compared with the growth of forest destruction.

Less public attention has been drawn to the plight of the other ecosystems. The natural grasslands and wooded savannahs are not as extensive as those of Africa, and are certainly not as well known, but the pampas of Argentina and Uruguay, the llanos of Colombia and the cerrado of Brazil all have, or have had, a spectacular wildlife. Much has disappeared from the pampas and llanos, but the Emas National Park in Brazil is the one park in which the cerrado is still well-represented (*see left*). Its tall termite mounds offer shelter and home to many birds and small creatures, just as trees do, and one of the inhabitants, a luminescent beetle larva, covers the mounds in the wet season, making the cerrado light up as if millions of stars had fallen.

It has been suggested that proper use of the Latin American open lands by the cattle ranchers would take some of the pressure off the forests. Meat production could be increased by ten times on today's pastures if improved breeds and better health care and management techniques were employed. Knowing the greed of the cattle industry, however, such a strategy should be contemplated only if more grassland areas are designated as parks and reserves and receive effective protection. Another universal conservation problem, but one especially pronounced in Latin America, is the illegal wildlife trade. Although all countries of South America participate in the CITES, there is a vigorous black market in live parrots and other birds, and the in skins of crocodilians, chinchilla, spotted cats and vicuna. In 1981, a kilo of vicuna wool smuggled into Europe was reported to fetch $600.

Giant anteater

The Emas National Park in the cerrado is the last haven for wildlife in all of the two million square kilometres once covered by cerrado but now planted in rice, soybeans and eucalyptus and grazed by cattle. Maned wolves, giant armadillos, giant otters, giant anteaters and marsh and pampas deer are just some of the endangered species still to be found within its borders. But the park is in danger of losing much of its value because boundaries were wrongly drawn and vital areas omitted. Uncontrolled fires are also a problem, killing giant anteaters and destroying gallery forest.

Northern Asia

The three nations of northern Asia, the USSR, China and Japan, share a similar attitude, although for different reasons, towards the use of natural resources. A phrase popular in the USSR not long ago sums it up: "the planned transformation of nature". As the haphazard activities of other countries have shown, transforming nature is ill-advised at best; the added arrogance of *planning* to do it can only lead to greater environmental problems. The effects of the steamroller tactics applied in northern Asia within the last few decades are all too apparent.

Soviets interfere with rivers on a massive scale. Numerous water reservoirs have been pinched off from the western and central rivers for municipal, industrial and agricultural purposes and to improve navigation and increase the production of electricity. These developments have radically altered the chemistry, temperature and flow of waters down their courses. Damage to fisheries costs a billion roubles per year, and most of the uses for which the reservoirs were created have been severely curtailed by eutrophication, siltation, salinization, chemical pollution and reduced water flow. But compromise is the name of the game in the USSR: the river waters brought millions of hectares of marginal lands into cultivation, staving off total economic disaster in the '70s, although much grain had to be imported and the detrimental long-term effects of using water in such lands were not addressed.

CASE STUDY
The hamburger connection

The wonderful forests of South and Central America are being sacrificed to the great American hamburger. Each year, 13,500 square kilometres of rainforest are burned to make way for cattle. The timber is not even used, just sprayed with herbicide and burned, together with everything in it. To date, cattle ranchers have destroyed timber worth $7.7 billion in Amazonia alone - two and a half times as much as commercial timber in the region has actually earned. For this destruction, the rancher gains a patch of land of such low fertility that it can support grazing for only ten years at most. Then more forest is burned, and the ranch moves on, leaving useless scrubland behind it. Even at this rate of travel, each head of cattle needs more than a hectare of grazing, and takes four years to reach a marketable size.

This wasteful exercise is aimed at an export trade worth $25 million a year to Brazil alone. From Central America, 133 million kilograms of beef are despatched to the USA every year, where most of it finds its way into the hamburger and frankfurter trade. One hamburger chain alone sells three billion hamburgers every year, using the equivalent of 300,000 head of cattle.

The environmental cost of this destruction is incalculable. The Atlantic forests of Brazil are now reduced to, at most, 2% of their former extent. As well as ranching, coffee, sugar cane, cocoa and eucalyptus have all taken their toll. Geographically separated from Amazonia, these forests contain a host of endemic species, including 13 endangered primates, like the woolly spider monkey and the golden lion tamarin.

In the central regions, ranches are using up natural prairie (the cerrado) as well as Amazonian forests. Even the reserves are damaged by the fires that spread from outside. One reserve, the Emas National Park in Brazil, had 90% of its area burned by six separate fires in 1980. Giant anteaters were burned to death, together with a great deal of the gallery forest. A decline in numbers of some of the little insect-eating warblers that overwinter in the gallery forest but which nest in the USA has already been noted. The hamburger may be gained at the expense of losing the bun, if the arable lands of the USA lose their insect-eaters.

The Amazonian forests cover a vast area, and contain about 10% of the world's known species of animals and plants. It is admittedly hard to imagine ranching consuming all of it. Nevertheless, Central American forests are in sight of the end; Nicaraguan and Costa Rican

Cattle ranching in cleared Amazon rainforest, Bolivia. Much of the beef is destined to make cheap hamburgers in the US.

forests will be gone by 1990, if the present rate of burning continues. The tragedy, for Brazil, is that the forest clearance is not even necessary. There are nearly 800,000 square kilometres of unused farmland in the south of the country, and it is even possible that a tenfold increase in productivity could be achieved on existing pastures by more efficient husbandry. Forest clearance is merely cheaper for the present, due to government policy and incentives.

The potential for constructive forest use in South America is very great. Brazil has established over four million hectares of eucalyptus and pine plantations, and could do a great deal more to meet the world's insatiable demand for timber and pulpwood. In Chile, plantation products earned $40 million in 1973, and financial incentives in the next ten years increased that market to $350 million per annum.

Even better is the Central American research on developing agroforestry - planting crops *with* trees rather than *instead of* trees. If this proves successful, agriculture might begin to coexist with plantations, reducing the demands on virgin forested land.

North Asia

North Asia is dominated by two great countries, the USSR and China, each with large expanses of unproductive land, and with rising populations.

China, with nearly four times the population of the USSR, and only half the land area, has concentrated its efforts on agriculture to feed its people, and latterly on population control. Chinese civilization stretches back at least 5000 years, and though much has changed, China is now recovering its contacts both with the past, and with the outside world.

The USSR has since 1917 maintained an emphasis on heavy industry, and a centralized government often unresponsive to environmental problems. The last 10 years, however, have seen conservation increasingly become state policy.

But modern Japan continues to over-exploit marine wildlife despite all pleas to desist.

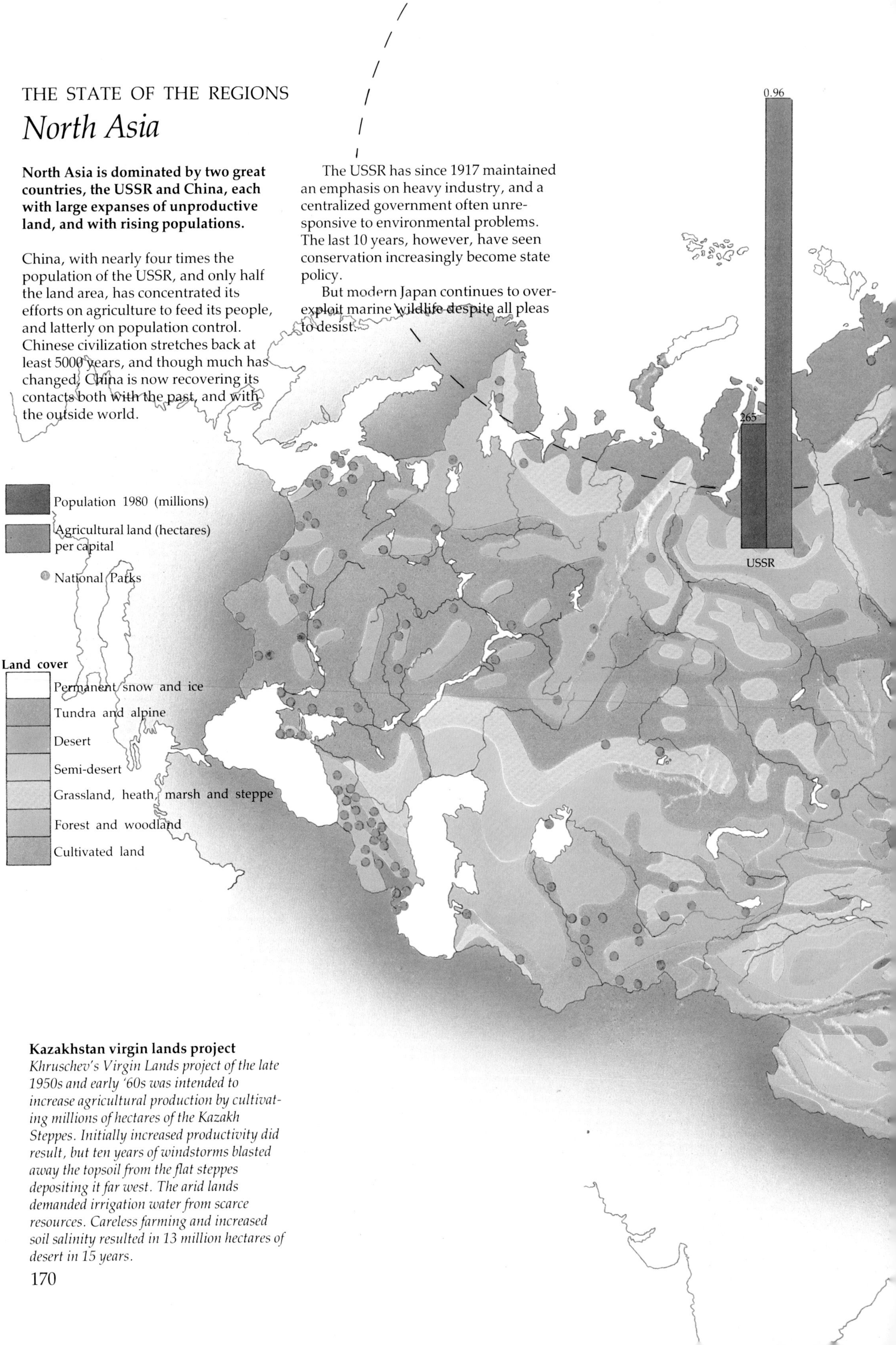

0.96

265

USSR

Population 1980 (millions)

Agricultural land (hectares) per capital

National Parks

Land cover

Permanent snow and ice

Tundra and alpine

Desert

Semi-desert

Grassland, heath, marsh and steppe

Forest and woodland

Cultivated land

Kazakhstan virgin lands project
Khruschev's Virgin Lands project of the late 1950s and early '60s was intended to increase agricultural production by cultivating millions of hectares of the Kazakh Steppes. Initially increased productivity did result, but ten years of windstorms blasted away the topsoil from the flat steppes depositing it far west. The arid lands demanded irrigation water from scarce resources. Careless farming and increased soil salinity resulted in 13 million hectares of desert in 15 years.

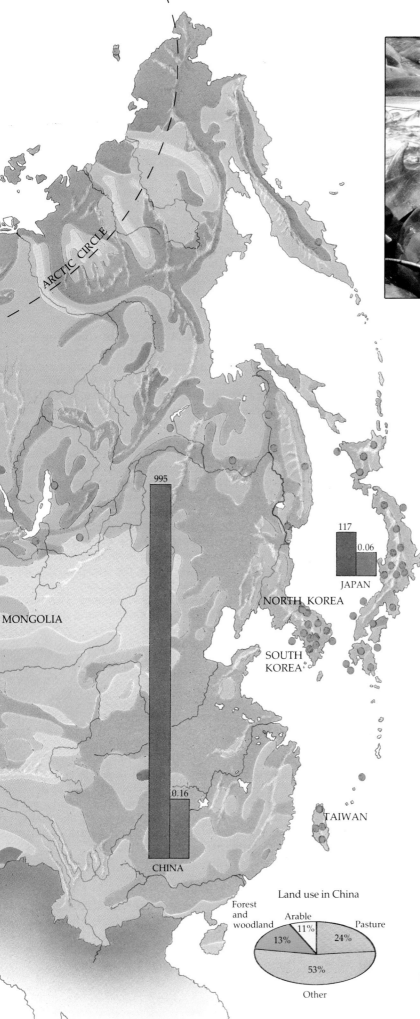

ARCTIC CIRCLE

MONGOLIA

995

117
0.06
JAPAN

NORTH KOREA

SOUTH KOREA

0.16

TAIWAN

CHINA

Land use in China

Forest and woodland
Arable
11%
Pasture
13%
24%
53%
Other

Dolphin fisheries in Japan

Whales are not the only marine mammals at risk from Japanese fishermen. Large numbers of dolphins of various species migrate in the seas around Japan and have long been caught for meat and oil. Many are captured in nets or harpooned but the majority are caught by driving methods. A whole school of dolphins are driven into a bay or on to a beach where they are slaughtered. As many as 5,000 are killed at one time by this method, making the estimated catch for Japan 25-30,000 per year.

Deforestation and afforestation in China

A broad sweep of the eastern half of China has a natural vegetation of forest land, ranging from evergreen coniferous forests in the north through deciduous and evergreen broadleaved forests to tropical rainforests in the extreme south. This rich vegetation has been lost over many centuries by clearances for timber and cultivation, until little remains of the original primary forests. Massive programmes of replanting have been undertaken, but not always with success.

171

The country still needs more grain, of course, and as the leaders have always thought big, the next idea was to reactivate the 19th-century plans for diverting water southwards from the rivers bound for the Arctic. Disruptions of regional ecosystems would undoubtedly be drastic, but if the polar ice cap began to melt (as it would with increasing salinity of the Arctic due to the loss of fresh water from the rivers), the effects on global climate could be disastrous. Predictions are shaky, but one of the more scientifically supportable is that precipitation in Middle Asia, which is the target of the irrigation schemes, would be reduced!

Most of the scientists we spoke to in our recent trip to the USSR expressed great reservations about river diversions, and the latest news is that the grandiose plan has been shelved in favour of improving rational use of existing resources. There are other indications of a shift in emphasis in environmental attitudes - less talk of transforming nature and more of working within its bounds. Perhaps at long last, the price of forced compromises has been seen to be too high.

The Soviets were not far behind the Americans in compiling lists of threatened species of plants and animals. Every republic has its own *Red Data Book* and its own laws protecting threatened populations, regardless of the status of the species elsewhere. Reserves are well buffered by surrounding zones of minimally utilized land, and there is virtually no poaching. The system of parks and reserves will be doubled by the end of the century to incorporate several representative areas of every type of ecosystem in the country.

If water resources are a major issue in the USSR, forests are the issue in China. The massive reafforestation programmes - supposedly 30 million hectares since 1949 - seem to have failed. According to eye-witness and uncensored accounts, only one-third of the plantings survived. The rest were destroyed by fire and illegal cutting or were simply official fabrications for fulfilling abstract targets. Meanwhile, destruction of nearly one-quarter of the native forests has occurred in this wood-hungry nation within the last 30 years, owing mostly to the lack of enforcement of existing laws, but not least to the policies of the state itself, setting outrageously unsustainable timber quotas and forcing people to clear the forests to grow grain, regardless of the suitability of the land. The outcome of this transformation of nature is painfully clear: advancing deserts from the north, the carrying away of 1.6 billion tons of soil each year by the Huang Ho (Yellow) River, the increasing frequency of droughts in Yunnan and record flooding of the Chang Jiang (Yangtze) River.

Chinese leaders are now fully aware of the magnitude of deforestation and its damaging effects. In an unprecedented scheme to make reaf-forestation work, villagers have recently been allowed to own woodlots, but the catch is that 80% of the trees must survive before ownership is granted. Meanwhile, however, other environmental monsters are being spawned in the central planning offices, like the huge hydroelectric dam on the Chang Jiang.

Japan is tiny but more economically powerful than the two giants of northern Asia and able to mobilize equally massive schemes of development in proportion to its size. It is crowded and polluted in parts, yet has retained two-thirds of its natural vegetation. Its "success", like that of so many industrialized countries, lies in exploitative forays into other countries, particularly its southern neighbours.

Southern Asia

Southern Asia is highly heterogeneous in terms of habitat and inhabitants. It ranges from the Levant (today erroneously called the Middle East) to Papua New Guinea, taking in the Indian sub-continent, the southerly lands of China, and to the southeast, the great Malayan peninsula and its associated islands. Here arose a great number of the crops used extensively today: wheat, rice, soybeans, sugarcane, tea, bananas and

The Chang Jiang Dam

Three Gorges on the Chang Jiang River - the proposed site for construction.

China is making plans for a massive dam across the Chang Jiang (Yangtze) River. The site chosen is in a region known as Three Gorges, a spectacularly beautiful 200-kilometre stretch of river passing through three mountain ranges, which has been an inspiration to generations of poets and painters.

Construction of the two-kilometre-wide dam will start in late 1986. It will begin generating in 1994 and reach its full capacity of 13,000 megawatts by 1999. Its 500-kilometre-long reservoir will totally flood ten cities, partially flood eight more, and drown 44,000 hectares of productive farmland.

American advisers have recommended that, in order to meet the ambitious schedule, construction should begin before design work is complete. As yet, many questions remain unanswered. Although it is intended to protect the area from floods as well as provide electricity, the extent of protection the dam will give has not been fully assessed, nor has the very real risk of landslides, which do occur in the region. Downriver, changes in flow will alter established patterns of erosion and deposition, and might be disastrous to fishing, shipping and the environment generally. The Aswan High Dam in Egypt (*see p.156*) has eroded the Nile Delta and brought salt water into irrigation systems, as well as preventing tons of alluvium from reaching the sea - an effect which has been blamed for a 90% decline in fish in the eastern Mediterranean.

China does need more power-generating capacity. The risks inherent in such a large-scale operation, however, would seem to be unnecessary in a land that has so many rivers. A number of smaller hydroelectric plants would provide the power without the environmental risks, and with far less serious consequences in case of break-down or sabotage.

The Siberian crane

Siberian cranes breed in the tundra of the USSR. From there, one group migrates to Iran for the winter, another group travels over Afghanistan to northern India, and a third group sets off to spend the winter in northeastern China. Once there were thousands of these stately white birds, Chinese symbols of long life and happiness. In 1980, only 33 set off on the long, dangerous journey to India and Iran.

The International Crane Foundation, based in Baraboo, Wisconsin, began work in 1977 to try to save these beautiful birds from extinction. With the cooperation of the Oka State Nature Reserve of the USSR, two crane eggs were transported from Siberia to Baraboo, where they hatched successfully. The next year, five more eggs were supplied, and now three pairs of Siberian cranes are living comfortably in the USA. Cranes lay two eggs, but raise only one chick, so taking an egg and incubating it under foster parents is one way of doubling the numbers.

Meanwhile, back in the wild, there was encouragement in the shape of 36 cranes in 1982, 37 in 1984, and 41 in 1985, spotted at Bharatpur, India, when they arrived for the winter. In 1978, 12 cranes were found on a duck-trapping complex in Iran; 16 were seen there in 1980, but none has been reported since this last sighting.

The Chinese cranes had been something of a mystery in 1977. About 200 of them were thought to exist, but their wintering grounds were not known. Then, in 1980, a population of over 800 was found at Lake Poyang, in the Chang Jiang (Yangtze) basin. Cranes had suffered badly in China, too. The Cultural Revolution had caused widespread slaughter of all species of birds, since Mao Tse-Tung had labelled them corn-eaters. Lake Poyang, which had not been surveyed since 1959, was in the process of being made into a reserve, and the Chinese were delighted to become part of the Siberian crane fan club.

Siberian cranes are not safe yet. Their wintering grounds depend on a fragile balance - *"water touching sky in summer, and all muddy bank with no end in winter and spring"*, in the words of a Chinese crane specialist. The Poyang Lake is threatened by the development of the Chang Jiang Dam, and wintering grounds in India and Iran are by no means secure.

In 1983 ornithologists from over 23 countries met in India to discuss the plight of the cranes. The governments of Afghanistan, India, Iran, Pakistan, China, the USA and the USSR are all working together to secure the survival of the lovely Siberian crane, their common link. It may yet live up to its symbolic role and enjoy long life and happiness.

These elegant Siberian cranes, seen here in Bharatpur, India, face a hazardous journey over Afghanistan and Pakistan when they return to their breeding grounds. Although these countries have agreed to protect the cranes from hunting, the hunters do not often abide by the law.

Southern Asia

Southern Asia was home to many early civilizations. Some were destroyed by invaders, but others failed because climate or ruination of the land destroyed their economic base - a warning to present day cultures.

Europe has always had its eyes on the fabulous Orient, as the source of many exotic commodities. Southern Asia is indeed rich in wildlife and species diversity, the original source of many of humanity's most valued domesticated species and crop plants. But its natural wealth is today under siege from hugely increased, and increasing, human numbers. This is the most populous region in the world, with one and a half thousand million inhabitants, around a third of the world's total. And despite the Green Revolution, hunger is endemic, along with poverty and massive environmental problems. Deforestation, and subsequent erosion and flooding, are the worst difficulties.

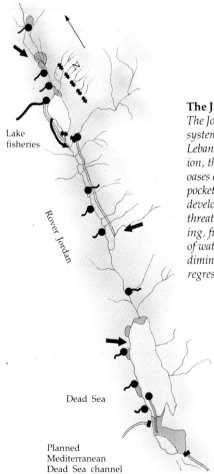

The Jordan River

The Jordan Rift valley is part of the great rift system extending from Mozambique to the Lebanon. It includes the Dead Sea Depression, the deepest in the Earth's crust. The oases of the Dead Sea are isolated tropical pockets, of great value for studying the development of species. However the area is threatened by farming, drainage, overgrazing, fuel gathering and tourism. Diversion of water has resulted in the lower Jordan flow diminishing by 60%, and the Dead Sea is regressing at 30-60 centimetres a year.

Nature reserves

➡ Urban sewage

Dried-out lake area

╫ Dam

Pumping stations and pipes

Proposed channel

Lake fisheries

Rover Jordan

Dead Sea

Planned Mediterranean Dead Sea channel

Planned Red Sea Dead Sea channel

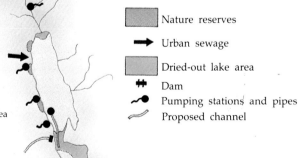

951 millions

685 millions

1980 2000

Indian population

In 1980 the Indian population stood at 685 million; it is expected to reach 951 million by the year 2000. (The average annual growth rate for the period 1980-85 was 1.9%.) In 1951, India was the first country in the world to adopt a national family planning programme. Birth rates have fallen, but there remain great problems. The majority of the population is rural, with higher infant mortality than average, and greater need for large families to work, cultivate the land, and fetch water and fuel.

The Sundarbans

One of the largest remaining areas of mangroves in the world, the Sundarbans cover 6000 square kilometres. The only remaining habitat of the Bengal tiger in Bangladesh, and home to the threatened leopard, mugger and estuarine crocodile, they also provide wood and fishing. The conflicting demands of wildlife and people must be resolved if this habitat is to survive.

Ecocide in Vietnam

Over 49 million kilograms of herbicides were sprayed on two million hectares of forest in South Vietnam from 1961 to 1971; and over three million kilograms of dimethylarsinic acid were sprayed on 300,000 hectares of growing crops.

South Vietnam had 5.5 million hectares of upland forest before the herbicides came. More than 1.75 million hectares of this land has been sprayed at least once. After a single herbicide dose, up to 30% of the trees are killed. After multiple spraying, all the timber trees may be killed. In these upland regions, trees regenerate badly, if at all. Mangroves also suffered; one-quarter of South Vietnam's 0.8 million hectares were sprayed, and all are dead.

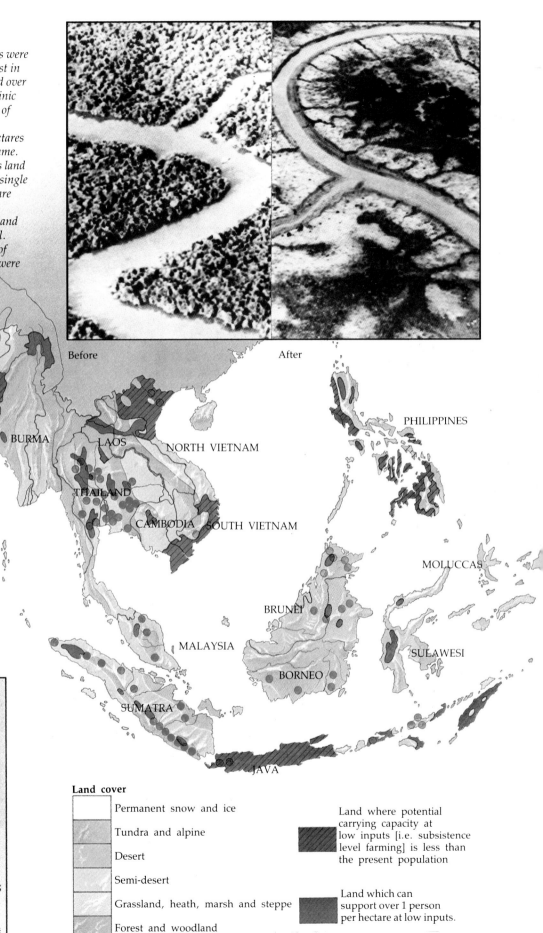

Before　　　　After

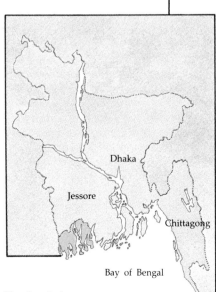

The Sundarbans

Land cover

- Permanent snow and ice
- Tundra and alpine
- Desert
- Semi-desert
- Grassland, heath, marsh and steppe
- Forest and woodland
- Cultivated land

Land where potential carrying capacity at low inputs [i.e. subsistence level farming] is less than the present population

Land which can support over 1 person per hectare at low inputs.

● National Parks

175

citrus trees. More of southern Asia than any other region has been designated as a top-priority area for the conservation of genetic resources of plants, both wild and traditionally cultivated strains. From Arabian deserts to Himalayan mountain forests to Bornean jungles live millions of people of diverse cultures and origins, many with ancient traditions of using nature wisely.

But from India eastward, the region holds fully half of the planet's human population - over two billion people - which in places is growing by more than 2.5% every year. Most of them live in rural areas, and the pressure on the soil, water and forests is enormous. In Java, where 100 hectares of fertile volcanic lowland soils support 600 people (one of the highest rural densities in the world), much of the island has been degraded by unsound agricultural practices. But, according to population projections, there will be on average less than a tenth of a hectare of land per person in Java in 15 years' time. As fine as the ancient traditions in southern Asia were, environmental degradation has gone so far and the population has risen so high that the people and their governments have either forgotten about the old, wise ways or find them too difficult to put into practice.

Nearly half of India is under cultivation, and over three-quarters of that faces serious environmental problems. Although various irrigation schemes have been responsible for increased grain production over the last 20 years (as in the USSR), the ruination of soils by salinization and waterlogging has happened or is about to happen on at least a quarter of the irrigated area. There has been a net loss in soil fertility in spite of the application of expensive chemical fertilizers. But erosion accounts for most of the threats. Halfway through this century, the desperate hunger for land, coupled with lack of financial and technical resources and the infrastructure to apply them, led to farming and pasturing practices in which soil conservation measures had no part. Now, all the houses built in India *every six months* use less soil for brick-making than is washed away into rivers, reservoirs and harbours. This amount is well over that lost annually in the USA, a country with an acknowledged erosion problem, but with a quarter as much again of farmland. The multiple damaging effects of siltation in India are costly and difficult to overcome.

As for deforestation in southern Asia, some blame a leftover colonial attitude that regarded trees merely as products to feed the growth of wood-based industries, and not as vital protectors of the soil, water and renewable forest products. In India, however, although the Forest Policy of 1952 stipulated that a third of the country should remain under forest cover, less than 11% is forested today. The records of the reafforestation schemes are highly suspect, like those of China, and some of the programmes involve the monoculturing of eucalyptus trees destined for the fibre market - hardly a stable forest ecosystem - by wealthy people on fertile lands. In Indonesia and the Philippines the practice of clearfelling for timber was much accelerated well into the post-colonial period.

Most encroachments into the wild places left to southern Asia, however, are being made by the "ordinary" people, pushed by their own extraordinary numbers. The luxuriant watershed forests of the highlands, stripped of their trees and other vegetation by too many wandering goats and cattle, too many little farms carved into steep hillsides and too many people searching for firewood, can no longer regulate the flow of water down the mountains, which results in flood, drought, erosion and siltation in the lowlands. The gravest watershed problems are in the Himalayas - it has been said that the 400 million people of the lowland plains of Pakistan, India and Bangladesh are "being held hostage" by the 46 million who live in the hills and mountains to the north, particularly in Nepal - but there are also serious problems in China, Indonesia, the Philippines and Thailand. With the loss of upland forests go their natural products, the traditional foods and medicines on which hill peoples rely, and the goodness of their soils that *can* support farming and grazing if

CASE STUDY
Transmigration in Indonesia

Indonesia, with roughly 150 million people, is the fifth most populated country in the world. And yet 65% of its population is crammed on to some 7% of its land area – principally the islands of Java, Bali and Madura. By contrast, large areas of its "Outer Islands", which include Sumatra, Kalimantan (part of Borneo), Sulawesi and Irian Java (part of New Guinea), are relatively sparsely inhabited. It was because of this imbalance that the Indonesian government launched its transmigration programme in 1978 in an attempt to relieve population pressure on Java. The project, partially financed by the World Bank, has cost $2 billion, and has been a resounding failure.

What the scheme failed to take into account were the reasons *why* so many people settled on Java in preference to the Outer Islands. Java, because of its exceptionally rich volcanic soils, permits an extremely intensive agriculture capable of sustaining some 2000 people per square kilometre in some rural areas, whereas the Outer Islands have thin, acidic soils, poorly suited to agriculture. Consequently, attempts to farm this infertile land have incurred significant environmental costs, including deforestation, soil degradation and malaria, while the yields have been disappointingly low. Not only this, but the transmigration programme has never succeeded in moving even 100,000 people per year, while the annual population growth on Java is more than two million. Clearly, transmigration is not the answer to Java's population problem.

However, the scheme, with all its faults, has actually served to highlight Indonesia's more successful family planning programme. Begun in 1969 and cleverly implemented at the local level by involving community leaders as the actual educators, field workers and distributors of contraceptives, the programme has achieved remarkable results. Population growth on Java dropped from 2.1% to 1.5%, which has meant half a million to a million fewer mouths to feed every year. Compared to resettlement, family planning has cost a fraction of the money, and has reduced population pressure much more effectively. And family planning leaves ecosystems, the guardians of soil, water, air and genetic resources, intact for future generations.

CASE STUDY
Nepalese watersheds: gone today, here tomorrow

The Himalayas - over 400 million people on the plains below are hostage to those using the hills above. Each figure represents one million people.

The Himalayas are a vast watershed for a large part of Asia. Forty-six million people live in the hills of India, Pakistan and Bangladesh, and their management of the land affects the lives of 400 million who live in the valleys below.

Barely 30 years ago, the Nepalese uplands were covered with forests. Now the forests are gone, cleared for farmland in the desperate race for food. Without its forest cover, however, the land cannot hold topsoil against the torrential rains. Soil washed from the hillsides silts up watercourses, ruining the fisheries and causing devastating floods on the plains below. As the soil is eroded, more forest is cleared for agriculture and firewood, and as the wood runs out, so goat dung is burned instead of fertilizing the land. Once begun, the stripping of the Nepalese uplands becomes an inexorable landslide, with every downpour taking its toll.

Unless a solution is found, it is likely that five million of the seven million people who live on Nepal's "Middle Mountains" will be driven from the hills by shortage of food. The government of Nepal, recognizing this problem a decade ago, set up a department of Soil Conservation and Watershed Management. A pilot scheme was begun on the steep slopes above the Phewa Tal, a lake whose potential fish and hydroelectric resources were being spoiled by silting. Incentives were offered for planting grasses and trees on eroded areas; terraces were repaired; and livestock was penned or tethered.

Restraining livestock enabled pastures to recover, and plantations of fuelwood trees became established on previously denuded slopes. Another consequence of controlling the animals was that there was fodder to spare; some could be sold, and the quality of livestock could be improved. Dung was easily collected from the animal pens, and more than twice the quantity as before went on to the crops. Increased fertility gave an extra crop of winter wheat, and in three years the average family income had quadrupled. To confirm the point, a spring that had been dry for seven years due to the denuded catchment began flowing three years after the livestock was tied up.

Since 1980, Nepal has received international aid to help with its efforts to reverse the watershed erosion. Ten projects have now been set up in over half of the hill districts of the country. One programme is directed towards restoring traditional systems of forest management. The use of dead wood for fuel and the felling of standing timber were once based on a code of conduct understood by all who lived in forest regions. Since 1957, when forests were nationalized, these codes have fallen into disuse. In 1978, nationalization was reversed, and ownership was transferred back to local communities, offering a good return for tending the forests.

A great deal of experience has now been gained in Nepal, and, although the damage may be great, it does seem that, with thought and care, repairs are possible.

done properly. The people are driving themselves down from the mountains.

Meanwhile, the wildlife of southern Asia, an extraordinary composite of northern Asian and African elements with a high number of endemic species, has all but disappeared in the settled regions, and is under threat even in the remotest. There is little conservation "ethic" on the whole in the Arab countries, and in Iran and Afghanistan, anything that moves is shot. In India it is thought that over 1500 plants are endangered, and about 130 vertebrates are under some form of legal protection. Tigers and elephants occasionally "fight back", inflicting damage to body and property, but the conflict is born of crowding them, and they are in serious decline, except where specific conservation efforts have been made. The more shy and retiring animals simply retreat to the places where they are least bothered by humans, but there are few such places left, and poaching is heavy. Traditional respect for living beings, once characteristic of this part of Asia, seems to have died.

The governments and people of southern Asia are certainly not unaware of their severe environmental problems, but the sheer magnitude of tackling them is daunting. As in Africa, solutions offered by high technology, applied on a sweeping scale, usually cause greater problems, not only environmental but also sociological, which in the long run increase the pressures on the environment. In India, for example, it is easier for farmers to obtain chemical fertilizers than to organize the return of dung and crop wastes to the soil. Although much of the organic materials must be burned for the cooking fires (because of deforestation and the failure of the afforestation programmes to supply fuel), a lot is wasted. In Nepal, it seems as if subsistence farmers have even been frightened into farming unstable hillsides by the possibility that unculti-vated land would be taken from them in grand reafforestation schemes.

As usual, the smaller-scale, village-level programmes have been the most successful. The Chipko Movement (*see p.207*) in India, seen in newspapers as made up of people who hug trees, favours the involve-ment of local communities with reafforestation efforts by the planting of the "5f" trees – those that provide fuel, fodder, fruit, fibre and fertilizer. In one poor village in India that had lost all its fields in a landslide, the building of three small reservoirs in "return" for preventing livestock from grazing in the watershed (but where the grasses could be cut) and working out an equitable system of water sharing has resulted in a ten-fold increase in grass production and the growing of two to three crops a year. Similar village programmes in Nepal are also promising.

If such local efforts can be increased, pressure on the remaining wild areas and threatened wildlife of Indomalaya could be reduced just long enough for the rapidly expanding system of protected areas to become truly effective. Although the amount of land under legal protection has quadrupled in the last 25 years (India alone added 33 national parks to its network of 19 between 1981 and 1984), it is very unevenly distributed around the region, and lack of supervision by trained staff in some areas means "paper" protection only. The "biosphere reserve" concept (*see p.84*) is strong in the planning offices of nearly every country, but will take time to be translated into reality.

Australia and Oceania

To the southeast of the most populated region of the world is one of the least populated - Australia, New Zealand and the far-flung islands of Oceania, scattered in their thousands over more than a million square kilometres of the Pacific. The native peoples are relative newcomers, arriving in the last tens of thousands of years or less, and, as with early colonizers everywhere, they had an impact on their environment. The Aborigines of Australia, Tasmania and other continental islands and the Maoris of New Zealand were responsible for creating open lands by

CASE STUDY
Project Tiger

Project Tiger is more than a campaign to save a wild animal. It is a campaign to save India. Tigers need forests, and so does India. The healthier the forest, the better for the tigers, and the better for humankind.

In 1970 a careful search for tigers showed that there were no more than 5000 in the whole of Asia. Forty years earlier, there had been 40,000 in India alone. Tigers had always been hunted enthusiastically, but the loss of 88% of India's forests had tipped the balance dramatically against them. The Caspian and Balinese tigers were extinct by 1970, only five Javan tigers were found, and a mere few hundred Siberian and Sumatran tigers remained.

The World Wildlife Fund launched Project Tiger in 1972, to try to save the Indo-Chinese tiger. An international appeal raised over a million dollars, and half of this was used by the Indian government to set up 11 tiger reserves. Fifteen reserves taking in a land area of 23,423 square kilometres - just over 2% of India's surviving forests - have now been dedicated to tigers. In a country as crowded as India, this could not be done without some cost to people, and 33 villages had to be moved out of the new

reserves. Such a drastic programme was only possible because of the personal interest of India's Prime Minister, Mrs Indira Ghandi, who for a time chaired the steering committee of Project Tiger.

There are now over 4000 tigers in India, compared with 1800 in 1977. World population is 7500, plus 1500 in zoos. Project Tiger has clearly been a success in so far as saving tigers from extinction is concerned. There are still tremendous problems, however, in conserving such an animal with so little of its natural habitat available. A tiger needs a large territory, and tigers naturally disperse over a wide area. When a reserve contains as many tigers as can coexist within its boundaries, the next generation of cubs will burst the bounds and spread through the surrounding countryside. Sugar-cane plantations are pleasant long-grass regions to tigers, and they frequently settle in such land, although they tend to avoid other agricultural territory. But the natural forests are no more extensive than they were 15 years ago, and tigers are increasingly coming into conflict with people. About 1800 tigers live in protected areas, but the rest are scattered wherever there is sufficient cover, water and game.

Tiger on a tree top in India.

Not being burdened with an instinct for gratitude, tigers are as fearsome now as ever they were. Hundreds of people have been killed by tigers since 1972, most of them accidentally as a result of startling a tiger or disturbing a female with cubs. A significant number, however, are falling victim to the 1% which prey on humans. Various techniques, such as aversion therapy via electrified fences and human dummies, are being tried out, and known killers are destroyed by game wardens.

On the reserves, environmental protection has brought about a great improvement. The variety of wildlife has increased, including endangered species such as swamp deer, elephant, rhino and wild buffalo. Water regimes have also improved with the recovery of ground-level vegetation; streams flow longer and suffer less silting during the monsoons.

India is still a crowded country, however, and conflict between human and tiger continues to symbolize the conflict between humankind and the wild. Not until this conflict is resolved will the tiger - and the human species - be truly safe.

Australia and Oceania

The lovely islands of the Pacific are undergoing the most rapid change of almost any region of the world.

Activities of countries such as the USA and Australia have long-term implications for the Pacific. Demand for timber has reduced much of the rainforests to fragments, and deforestation is fol-lowed by erosion. Industrial and mining pollution are serious problems, especially for mangroves and reefs. Many of the remote island groups are used as military bases or for testing nuclear weapons. The increasing population is putting the environment under pressure. This region has the highest species extinction per capita in the world.

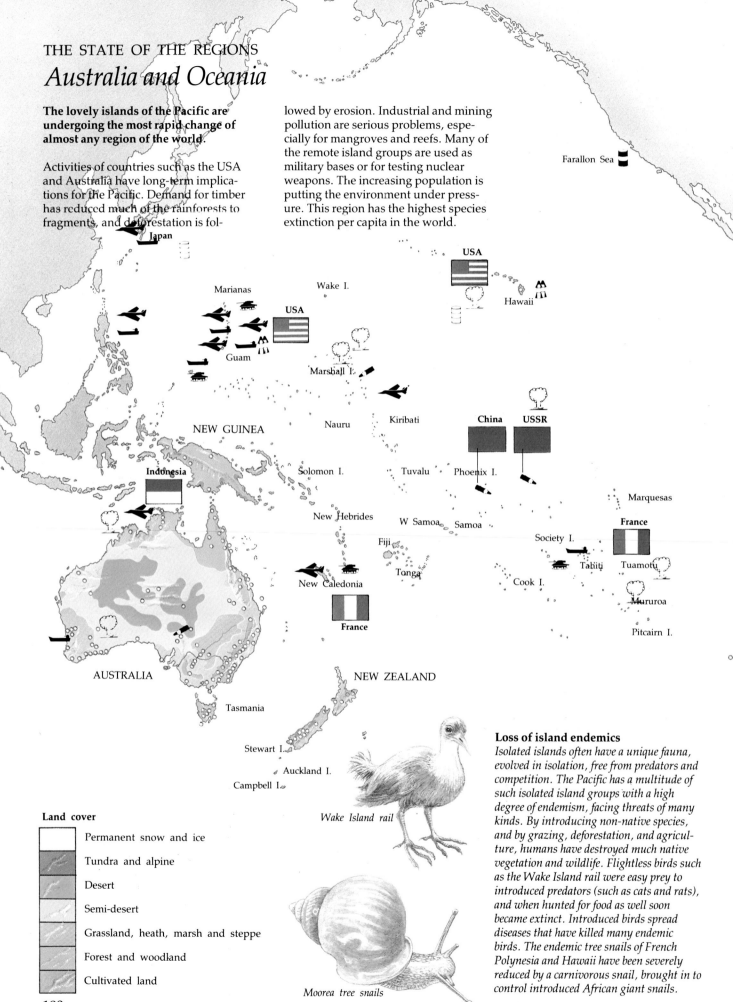

Wake Island rail

Moorea tree snails

Land cover

- Permanent snow and ice
- Tundra and alpine
- Desert
- Semi-desert
- Grassland, heath, marsh and steppe
- Forest and woodland
- Cultivated land

Loss of island endemics

Isolated islands often have a unique fauna, evolved in isolation, free from predators and competition. The Pacific has a multitude of such isolated island groups with a high degree of endemism, facing threats of many kinds. By introducing non-native species, and by grazing, deforestation, and agriculture, humans have destroyed much native vegetation and wildlife. Flightless birds such as the Wake Island rail were easy prey to introduced predators (such as cats and rats), and when hunted for food as well soon became extinct. Introduced birds spread diseases that have killed many endemic birds. The endemic tree snails of French Polynesia and Hawaii have been severely reduced by a carnivorous snail, brought in to control introduced African giant snails.

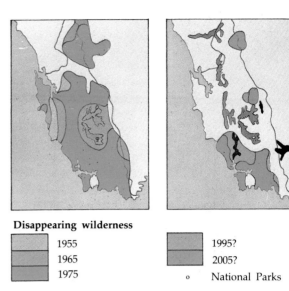

Existing water storage

Proposed water storage

King
diversion
scheme

Franklin
scheme

Albert
Rapids
scheme

Middle
Gordon
scheme

Disappearing wilderness

1955
1965
1975

1995?
2005?
o National Parks

Development schemes

Galapagos I.

Army base

Marine base

Air force base

Nuclear tests

Nuclear weapons storage

Missile test target

Dumping of nuclear waste

Tasmania, Franklin and Gordon River scheme

The plan to dam the Franklin and Gordon Rivers in Tasmania provoked the greatest furore yet on a conservation issue. The proposed new lakes would have flooded large areas of the newly declared World Heritage Site of southwest Tasmania - the last sizeable area of the wilderness that once covered Tasmania, and one of only three temperate rainforests left in the world. It is home to
many Tasmanian endemics and species that are no longer found on mainland Australia, and contains one-third of the total population of the majestic huon pine. Many huon pines are over 2000 years old. The fact that the dam scheme would contravene the spirit of the World Heritage Convention caused wide criticism. Protestors came from all over the world to prevent building of the dam. Many finished up in jail; but they succeeded in getting the decision reversed.

The backyard of the nuclear arms' race

The Pacific is the largest ocean, with many isolated island groups. Surrounded by some of the world's most powerful nations, it has been used by them for testing areas and dumping grounds for weapons of every type and power. Nuclear bomb testing has brought about forced relocation of peoples from their lands, plus radioactive contamination of human and wildlife populations over a wide area. Islanders from Bikini Atoll, where the USA carried out atmospheric atomic testing, have developed radiation-linked illnesses (but there are conflicting views on this, as certain areas of the Pacific have high levels of natural background radiation). Nuclear dumping is yet another hazard to the human population and to wildlife, and threatens the whole region. Many military bases have been set up by the world's major powers, on island groups throughout Oceania. While these may have strategic importance, their presence has led not only to the despoliation of the environment, but also to the destruction and Westernization of the cultures of the indigenous people.

Fraser Island

Fraser Island off the Queensland coast, the largest sand island in the world, has a unique ecosystem of huge sand dunes supporting tropical rainforest and "perched lakes". Mining for titanium, zirconium and uranium ores and sand threatened to destroy parts of this very sensitive environment. A Fraser Island Defence Organization (FIDO)
was set up, and in 1976, the Australian government banned any further mining in the island. Constantly challenged by the Queensland State Authorities, there is no guarantee that this ban will remain in force. Other islands, such as Moreton Island, also have mining possibilities, so any changes in the legislation will be keenly contested.

181

burning the native vegetation and for causing the extinctions of a number of large animal species; and the Polynesian settlers of Hawaii drastically altered most of the lowland forests, eliminating half the species of birds. The time over which most of these early changes occurred, however, was long enough for the people to develop within their own cultures certain practices, and sometimes attitudes, that ensured the rational use of the still extensive natural resources.

The coming of the Europeans put an end to most of these peoples and their way of life, and to much of the goodness of the land. Telescoped into the 200 years of their presence in the region is all that has happened and is happening to the natural resources of the planet at the hands of the modern person: the indiscriminate clearing of native vegetation in Australia and New Zealand for intensively managed farmland and pasture; the onslaught on the forests of Australia, Tasmania and New Guinea by the timber industry; and the needlessly cruel slaughter of kangaroos, often for spurious reasons. Meanwhile, the islands of Oceania are under pressure from burgeoning populations and the unplanned development of tourism. The elements of their native cultures, that allowed them in the pre-European era to sustain high human numbers in balance with available resources, are disappearing.

On the positive side, there are many strong environmental groups in the region to which the governments occasionally listen. They were instrumental in having the whole of the Great Barrier Reef declared as a park when exploration for oil on the reef was being planned. They stopped the building of a dam on Tasmania's Gordon River, which would have destroyed a wilderness already designated by the government as a World Heritage Site, aided, as with the controversy over the forests on the banks of the Danube, by the weight of international opinion.

The environmental transgression for which the Europeans here are notorious, however, is the introduction of non-native plants and animals to long-established and isolated ecosystems. Like opening Pandora's box, the accidental or deliberate release of literally thousands of species of foreign organisms, not just from Europe, but other regions as well, has turned the native flora and fauna topsy-turvy. Deliberate importations ranged from garden favourites and pets, to domestic stock and plants for crops and fodder, to animals for sport; accidental introductions included mice, rats and disease organisms. Early on, people did not understand the environmental implications for the native ecosystems, and there were even societies devoted to acclimatizing the foreign plants and animals. They were soon to find out, however, because the escapees began to take over, vigorously, voraciously or surreptitiously. Populations of gorse and red deer in New Zealand and prickly pear and rabbits in Australia exploded, and cats in New Zealand, ferrets in Australia and even insect-eating ants in Hawaii preyed on the native fauna. The "domino" effect of exotics is also seen in Hawaii. The reduction or extinction of the insects and other animals that pollinate some of the native plants and disperse their seeds have led to the plants' decline.

Humans play dominoes, too. The lodgepole pine, brought to New Zealand to stabilize slopes eroding under grazing pressure from introduced deer, has itself gone wild, taking over large tracts of native scrub. No less than half the species listed as rare and endangered in the *Red Data Book* of New Zealand were put there by the exotics.

Eradication of a few exotic species in confined areas, like the smaller islands, is possible, as has been brilliantly demonstrated by the New Zealand Wildlife Service. Keeping the numbers of a few others under control is also possible (although the objections made by the hunting and fishing lobbies of the region make it difficult). Very carefully considered biological control programmes also work. But in the places where too many of the original plants and animals - the spindles holding the threads of the ecosystems - have been shouldered out, the natural reality of these southern lands will remain a dream.

Hawaiian treecreeper

The endemic birds of Hawaii have suffered serious declines from avian malaria, because of a mosquito brought over in the last century and the arrival of its appropriate parasite a few years later with the importation of gamebirds for public recreation. Many honeycreeper species were particularly hard-hit by the disease.

CASE STUDY
Little agate snails of Hawaii

The islands of Hawaii are the most remote pieces of land in the world, more than 3500 kilometres across the Pacific Ocean from anywhere else. Nearly all of Hawaii's native plants and animals are unique to these islands.

Among these endemic creatures are the tree snails known as little agates (*Achatinella*). There are 41 named species, all presumably descended from a single ancestor that drifted there, perhaps on a stray log, many thousands of years ago. Now the little agates occupy a variety of trees and shrubs, and have evolved into a spectacular variety of different colours. Almost every single shell has a different pattern of colours, and this has been the start of their misfortunes.

Ever since the snails were reported by John Gulick to the Linnaean Society, collectors have been keen to collect *Achatinella*. Some collectors, in search of a full range of shell types, have amassed as many as 100,000 specimens, each one fractionally different from the next.

Collecting still goes on, but not on this scale - there are not nearly enough snails left, anyway. In 1970, 14 species were presumed extinct; 25 species were listed as endangered; and only two were common. By 1979, 22 species were extinct and the remaining 19 were all endangered. As well as the losses caused by collectors, *Achatinella* is threatened by habitat loss and a huge variety of introduced dangers.

Native plants have been replaced by imported ones, which *Achatinella* cannot eat. Introduced rats climb trees and eat snails. In 1936, somebody let giant African snails loose, and these voracious herbivores became a pest. An attempt was made to control them by introducing carnivorous snails - and they are feeding on *Achatinella*.

The plight of *Achatinella* is by no means unique. Introduced species have devastated many well-balanced ecosystems, especially on islands, and many species have been obliterated by thoughtless manipulations.

CASE STUDY
The kangaroo harvest in Australia

Kangaroos are the game animals of Australia. And as with game hunting all over the world, the killing of kangaroos for meat and skins is surrounded by controversy.

The sheer number of licensed kangaroo kills is greater than in any other wildlife cull in the world. This year (1986), about two and a half million animals will be killed legally. The number is decided each year on the basis of a headcount from the air in New South Wales, and on known kill rates in other states. There is heated disagreement over the accuracy of such estimates. Some conservationists believe that the present high quotas will lead to the extinction of red and grey kangaroos within 20 years. Other experts claim that kangaroos have an almost limitless capacity for recovery.

It does seem that kangaroos respond to reduced populations by increasing their rate of reproduction. A severe drought in 1982 halved the kangaroo population from 19 to 10 million, but in the four years since then it has risen to 15 or 16 million.

The question of ethics has nothing to do with whether kangaroos are endangered, however. Most of the objections to kangaroo-hunting are prompted by the vicious, mindless cruelty that finds an outlet in the guise of "hunting". Most professional shooters, working at night with powerful lights and accurate weapons, kill kangaroos quickly and humanely. In some cases, the kangaroos have been troublesome to a farmer, but the majority of shooters are simply killing their quota, hunting for a living. It is the others, groups of killers who go after kangaroos for "fun", whose actions cannot be justified on any grounds whatsoever. These parties are known to deliberately leave wounded animals in the hot sun for days before returning to kill and skin them; they kill animals by running them over, to save bullets; worst of all, some simply enjoy torturing the kangaroos. Some of the disgusting practices of these perverted hunters have been filmed, and this has caused an understandable outcry against the whole of the cull. Even the assurance that 99% of kangaroos are killed humanely means that over 300,000 must be killed inhumanely.

Controversy aside, however, there are a great many more large kangaroos in Australia now than there were when the first settlers came. Improvements in the interior, to make the land fit for sheep and cattle, have also helped the kangaroos. In most respects, kangaroos are better suited to survival in the arid lands of Australia than any of the introduced creatures. Given the water that is now available, it would make better sense to ranch kangaroos than to raise other, less efficient animals. Kangaroos and sheep eat the same amount of grass, but a kangaroo is 52% meat compared with 27% for a sheep. A market clearly exists for kangaroo products, or the cull would not be worth the hunters' expenses. Instead of the present controversial slaughter of wild kangaroos, kangaroo ranching would be an ecologically sound commercial proposition.

Victims of the kangaroo cull.

Tens of thousands pack Wembley Stadium at the Live Aid concert in London to raise runds for famine in Africa.

CHAPTER 5

Noah's Army

The grave implications of human damage to the self-sustaining mechanisms of the ecosphere are all too clear. But concerted action by some members of the offending species to halt the damage or reverse its effects has begun only recently, spearheaded by a diverse assortment of individuals and organizations broadly termed the environmental or conservation movement.

The members of this Noah's Army, whether they know it or not, are challenging people in many sectors of society to change a very fundamental belief - that there are always more natural resources to be had by pushing a little deeper into the wilderness or inventing any new way to get at them - and to alter their policies and life styles accordingly. The challenge is threatening, nonsensical or impossible to many people, and so the movement has been ignored or chided, accused of partisanship or fought against violently, and even within the ranks there have been opportunists, hypocrites and trouble-makers. But in spite of the problems, including the overriding one of lack of funds compared to all other human endeavours, the Army soldiers on, renewing morale and gaining strength with every little skirmish won. The most recent strategies are global on the one hand, with the emphasis on long-term results, and very localized on the other, with the emphasis on immediate results. The origins of both strategies are to be found in the history of the movement.

The earliest records of people consciously trying to protect the environment date back several thousand years, but the efforts were piecemeal, isolated and of interest to only a few. Nationwide "movements" involving a general populace began in the 19th century, in America with a public call for saving "wilderness", and in Britain with the craze for natural history studies and the subsequent animal and countryside protection societies. The first durable expression of the popular concern for the environment on a worldwide basis did not occur until the middle of this century. In a mood of post-war idealism and optimism, the International Union for the Protection of Nature was founded (later to change the second part of its name to read "Conservation of Nature and Natural Resources"), and about a decade afterwards, the World Wildlife Fund was created. In their early days, these two organizations worked mostly in the field of wildlife conservation and, therefore, attended to the remote places where wildlife lives.

The next popular environmental cause to be taken up had less to do with wildlife than with the very fabric of the ecosphere - the air, water and sources of food that were being contaminated by the outputs of our own "progressive" activities, like smog, pesticides, oil and radioactive materials. The 1960s saw a widespread re-examination of the values of progress, as young people in particular, but also many "establishment" scientists and writers, began to question the principles of consumerism

185

A timetable of conservation
1872 *Yellowstone designated first National Park*
1892 *Sierra Club formed with John Muir*
1893 *National Trust founded in Britain*
1909 *North American Conservation Congress*
1912 *British Society for the Promotion of Nature Reserves*
1922 *International Society for Bird Protection (now ICBP)*
1926 *Council for the Protection of Rural England (CPRE)*
1933 *Roosevelt's New Era until 1945*
1948 *International Union for the Protection of Nature (IUPN)*
1956 *IUPN becomes IUCN – the International Union for Conservation of Nature*
1959 *The Antarctic Treaty*
1961 *The World Wildlife Fund founded*
1962 *Rachel Carson's Silent Spring*
1965 *Concept of "Spaceship Earth"*
1967 The Population Bomb
1969 *Friends of the Earth founded Don't Make a Wave, later Greenpeace, founded*
1970 *Earth Day*
A Blueprint for Survival
1971 *International Convention on Wetlands*
1972 *International Convention on World's Cultural and Natural Heritage*
Stockholm UN Conference on the Human Environment Creation of UNEP
The Limits to Growth
1973 *International Convention on Trade in Endangered Species (CITES)*
1977 *UN Conference on Desertification*
1978 *The Antarctic Coalition begins*
1979 *International Convention on Conservation of Migratory Species*
1980 *The Brandt Commission*
Global 2000 Report
The World Conservation Strategy
1980s *National Conservation Strategies*
UN Charter for Nature
Man in the Biosphere (MAB) Programme
1985 *Band Aid rouses concern for Africa*
1986 *WWF Planetary Protection campaign Moratorium on commercial whaling World Bank Call for Action on Forests*

and unrestrained growth and to express alarm at the destruction of natural resources these entailed. The popular movement again sparked the formation of clubs and societies, now called "activist" or "pressure groups", and again the United States and Britain led the way. "Think-tanks" geared up and produced documents predicting doom and gloom if humanity carried on the way it had been doing. Governments finally had to listen.

The wave of governmental response included the creation of special agencies to deal with environmental matters, legislation to make the biggest of the polluting industries toe the line, intergovernmental conferences and agreements and, finally, organizations to oversee and try to lessen the detrimental effects of human impact on the environment. The activist groups, and those that preferred to keep a lower profile, gained in status and reputation and began to be consulted by governments, and, albeit reluctantly at first, by business and industry.

By now, towards the end of the '70s, the issues had multiplied. In addition to pollution and overexploitation of wildlife, topics of discussion included the limitations of conventional energy resources, habitat destruction, soil erosion, what to do about Antarctica (the last true wilderness on the planet) and, finally, the environmental catastrophes happening and likely to happen in the developing countries. Warnings about overpopulation are as old as Malthus, but never before had the effects been so starkly apparent in the poor countries of the South. The industrialized countries of the North suffer from pollution and loss of natural resources, but by technical means, including the exploitation of far-away resources, they have elevated their human carrying capacities. In the South the haphazard application of technology and lack of funds to clean up local disasters or buy resources from outside have brought the dangers of overpopulation into sharp focus. Once again, however, it seems to be up to the public in these countries to sound the alarm. While some of their governments walk arm in arm with the richer nations of whatever ideological persuasion, the people have increasingly been grouping themselves into non-governmental organizations, active or "quiet", to combat the ravages of mindless progress - pollution, deforestation and desertification.

In 1980 environmental concerns became truly global. The sorry State of the Ark was revealed by the findings of the Brandt Commission, set up to examine human development issues in the context of the relationships between the North and the South, and of the *Global 2000 Study*, a report to the American President on the planet's natural resources as projected for the year 2000. It was finally realized that rapid deterioration and loss of natural resources were outstripping human demand many times faster than most people had believed, and these included genetic resources - the wild plants and animals - so vital to human well-being in agriculture, medicine and industry. There were renewed fears for famine (which were subsequently borne out) and serious doubts about the stability of world climate in the face of deforestation and air pollution on a massive scale.

The World Conservation Strategy was launched, insistent that conservation of natural resources and the development of human welfare were inextricably linked. Noah's Army, its ranks swelled by many scientists and educators, some politicians and business executives and innumerable "ordinary" people, responded vigorously. Global environmental monitoring and data-base services were set up or strengthened, governments began to prepare their own National Conservation Strategies, schoolchildren planted trees, "green" political parties gained seats and large companies had to take better account of their environmental impact. And people, impatient for results, began to talk and act among themselves and with each other directly, within their own communities and between communities across national boundaries.

Noah's Army seems grand and strong, but in the following pages comes a realistic description of its battles in the context of the present State of the Ark. It's clear that there's no time for resting on laurels.

The rise of Noah's Army

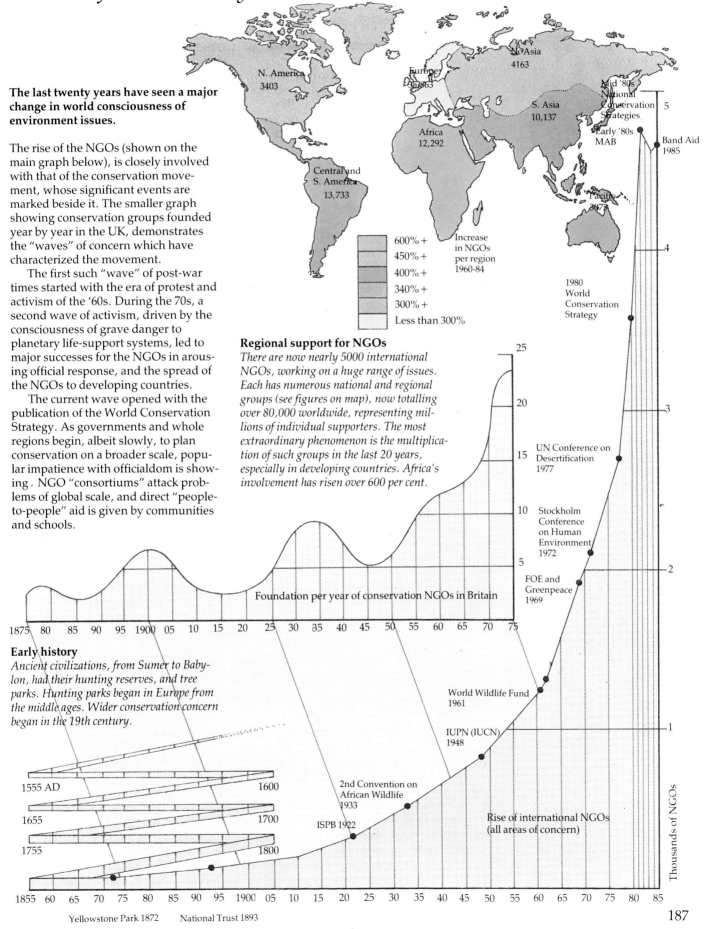

The last twenty years have seen a major change in world consciousness of environment issues.

The rise of the NGOs (shown on the main graph below), is closely involved with that of the conservation movement, whose significant events are marked beside it. The smaller graph showing conservation groups founded year by year in the UK, demonstrates the "waves" of concern which have characterized the movement.

The first such "wave" of post-war times started with the era of protest and activism of the '60s. During the 70s, a second wave of activism, driven by the consciousness of grave danger to planetary life-support systems, led to major successes for the NGOs in arousing official response, and the spread of the NGOs to developing countries.

The current wave opened with the publication of the World Conservation Strategy. As governments and whole regions begin, albeit slowly, to plan conservation on a broader scale, popular impatience with officialdom is showing. NGO "consortiums" attack problems of global scale, and direct "people-to-people" aid is given by communities and schools.

N. America 3403

Europe 3,863

N. Asia 4163

S. Asia 10,137

Africa 12,292

Central and S. America 13,733

Pacific 3073

Mid '80s National Conservation Strategies

Early '80s MAB

Band Aid 1985

600% +
450% +
400% +
340% +
300% +
Less than 300%

Increase in NGOs per region 1960-84

Regional support for NGOs
There are now nearly 5000 international NGOs, working on a huge range of issues. Each has numerous national and regional groups (see figures on map), now totalling over 80,000 worldwide, representing millions of individual supporters. The most extraordinary phenomenon is the multiplication of such groups in the last 20 years, especially in developing countries. Africa's involvement has risen over 600 per cent.

1980 World Conservation Strategy

UN Conference on Desertification 1977

Stockholm Conference on Human Environment 1972

FOE and Greenpeace 1969

Foundation per year of conservation NGOs in Britain

1875 80 85 90 95 1900 05 10 15 20 25 30 35 40 45 50 55 60 65 70 75

Early history
Ancient civilizations, from Sumer to Babylon, had their hunting reserves, and tree parks. Hunting parks began in Europe from the middle ages. Wider conservation concern began in the 19th century.

1555 AD — 1600
1655 — 1700
1755 — 1800

World Wildlife Fund 1961

IUPN (IUCN) 1948

2nd Convention on African Wildlife 1933

ISPB 1922

Rise of international NGOs (all areas of concern)

Thousands of NGOs

1855 60 65 70 75 80 85 90 95 1900 05 10 15 20 25 30 35 40 45 50 55 60 65 70 75 80 85

Yellowstone Park 1872   National Trust 1893

Selected as the symbol of the World Wildlife Fund in 1961, the Giant Panda continues to exert a strong popular fascination. This rare and delightful animal with its beautiful markings admirably exemplifies the value and beauty of all wildlife on the planet.

Only an estimated 1000 pandas remain in the mountainous Sichuan province, and these are faced with constant threats to their continued survival, especially from habitat destruction and the periodic mass flowering and die-off of the bamboo, their staple food.

A panda conservation programme, initiated by WWF, is now firmly established with the backing of the Chinese government.

The birth of IUCN and WWF

The International Union for the Conservation of Nature and Natural Resources (IUCN) was born in 1948, after the horrors of two world wars so painfully highlighted the need for a coordinated, constructive approach to safeguarding the world's natural resources. At the invitation of France and the fledgling UNESCO (the United Nations Educational, Scientific and Cultural Organization), representatives of 18 governments and 114 nature protection organizations, both national and international, met at Fontainebleau and signed a Constitution. Reading the Preamble to the Constitution today is very moving, for in it are the seeds of the World Conservation Strategy, formally proposed three decades later. The IUCN had much to do before the world was ready to consider seriously such a strategy, but the vision of the founders was truly remarkable.

The first task was to ensure the exchange of information and ideas held by the many organizations and individuals that had been working for so long in isolation from one another. To this end the IUCN created its Commissions, enlisting the voluntary help of professionals from all over the world, first in the fields of education, biology and park administration, and later including law and environmental planning. With the help of the Commissions, it began to organize international technical meetings on timely issues, widely circulating the proceedings and submitting them to government decision-makers, and to compile and publish informative lists of protected areas and of species of plants and animals whose numbers were declining (the *Red Data Books*). The IUCN carries on all these activities today, greatly aided by computerized centres that maintain data bases on environmental matters.

As well as being an authoritative, consultative body, the IUCN is a catalyst. One of its earliest projects dealt with the destruction of African wildlife, resulting in what is considered to be the turning point for conservation in Africa, for it inspired the leaders of the young countries to develop their own wildlife conservation programmes. Later projects led to the international conventions on wetlands protection (RAMSAR) and wildlife trade regulation (CITES), and, of course, to the World Conservation Strategy, and its growing implementation in the form of the National Conservation Strategies of individual countries.

As the work of IUCN gained momentum, it became clear that nature conservation was a very costly undertaking. Early in 1961 several eminent British conservationists and business executives, in consultation with the IUCN, conceived of the World Wildlife Fund. Its first public appeal, launched in Britain, had raised £40,000 by the end of the year. Altogether, WWF groups worldwide raised nearly $100 million by the time of its silver anniversary in 1986.

In their early days, IUCN and WWF had to adopt a "fire brigade" approach to conservation problems, not having the money nor the clout to mount a broader-based operation. Now, however, the conservation principles outlined in IUCN's constitution have become reality, and guide the thinking of both organizations, whether the issue is preserving a single species or all the world's wetlands, advising governments on wildlife legislation or halting desertification in Africa.

The rise of the NGOs

IUCN is unusual in the conservation movement in its "hybrid vigour": its voting members include state governments (56 as of mid-1984), unilateral and multilateral government agencies (123) and non-governmental organizations, commonly referred to as NGOs (316). The NGO with which it collaborates most closely is, of course, the WWF, but there are many others, some of which pre-dated the IUCN by a number of years.

One of the earliest was the Sierra Club, founded in 1892 in America by the Scottish-born naturalist, John Muir, who said that its goals were based

WWF and
IUCN members
and projects 1984

☐ Countries with IUCN
groups or affiliates

▨ IUCN member states

▨ WWF national organizations

▨ Countries with organizations
linked with WWF

☐ Each square represents
one or more projects in
a particular country

WWF and IUCN projects

In 1984, IUCN managed nearly 500 individual field projects around the world, for and with WWF and other groups. The projects were hugely diverse, both in scale, and in aims. They ranged from protecting turtle beaches in French Guinea to setting up rainforest reserves in Cameroon, from anti-poaching operations in Uganda to the much published Project Tiger of India. Less publicized are the many projects at community level, for education, for help with sustainable agriculture and soil management, or for combination of water provision with watershed afforestation. Less publicized too is the work of IUCN and WWF in advising governments, agencies, and NGOs, even commerce, on conservation aspects of their enterprises.

Over the years, WWF and IUCN have planned and promoted a series of international conservation campaigns - the wetlands campaign being one of the most recent. Their scope has steadily broadened, from species protection, to habitat concern, to management of the world environment. In 1986, to celebrate their silver anniversary, WWF launched a new slogan reflecting their global concern - "Planetary Protection".

IUCN and WWF around the world

Nearly all countries in the world now have national branch of WWF, and/or an IUCN branch or State membership, or affiliated groups. WWF national organisations (the NOs) have considerable autonomy. While contributing to the global fundraising of WWF, and participating in international campaigns, they also work on education and public awareness at home. Many support study and protection of indigenous species, whether the Muriqui monkey of Brazil, or the bandicoot of Australia, or the hare of West Germany (below) whose meadowland lifestyle is changed and challenged by modern agriculture, as are the meadows themselves.

The bandicoot's story

The little eastern barred bandicoot, a marsupial of Australia's savannah plains, has become something of a wildlife celebrity. Driven back by habitat loss and new predators - including domestic cats - the remaining populations are making their last stand around the city of Hamilton. There one group, housed precariously in a city dump, drew the attention of a local researcher, and eventually the sympathy and support of press and media. A campaign to protect the bandicoot, supported by WWF Australia, is both involving the community, and making this small endangered marsupial a symbol of Australia's threatened indigenous wildlife.

The remarkable Green Belt movement in Kenya exemplifies the new style of NGOs of Africa and the developing world. Led mainly by women, it emphasizes local efforts to manage local resources, and is concerned with the preservation of topsoil and stabilization of climate as well as the sustainable use of tree products. Foresters teach the people how to find the seeds of native trees, bed them in the village nursery and then transplant and take care of them properly. Finally, local people are paid a small amount for each surviving tree. The project began with very little money, but is now supported by the United Nations and, not surprisingly, the US National Council of Negro Women. So far sixty village nurseries have produced two million trees.

not on "blind opposition to progress, but opposition to blind progress". Another, but with more of an international scope at the time was the Society for the Preservation of the Wild Fauna of the Empire, established in Britain in 1903, and now the excellent and active Fauna and Flora Preservation Society (FFPS). Yet another was the International Council for Bird Preservation (ICPB), set up in 1922.

These early NGOs were mostly concerned with "preservation" of the species and habitats they saw doomed by human activity. The era of fire-brigade tactics continued through the 1950s, but the following decade saw the rise of campaigning on broader ecospheric issues, like air and water pollution, intensified by a series of environmental disasters, from Minamata disease (mercury poisoning) in Japan to oil spills from the tanker, the *Torrey Canyon*, and the blow-out off Santa Barbara, California. In the first pictures coming back from the Apollo spacecraft, the earth was perceived as a lonely, delicate orb, entirely reliant on the systems of the biosphere that the actions of humanity were busily destroying. The avidly read books of the '60s, *Silent Spring* and *The Population Bomb*, continued the theme of doom.

The swell of popular concern culminated with Earth Day in the spring of 1970 when thousands of people gathered in thousands of places across the United States to make their point. The small pressure groups, like Friends of the Earth and the one eventually known as Greenpeace, came of age as influential, international, NGOs and many of the older organizations, like the Sierra Club, began to take an active interest in campaigning. Others, like the FFPS and the ICBP, preferred to work behind the scenes, but were no less energetic. Their field projects were better grounded now on broad ecological principles rather than purely protectionist attitudes, and they emphasized the need for the education and training of the human component of the ecosystems where their "target" species or habitats resided.

A variety of low-profile organizations were strengthened in the course of the '70s, some beavering away at local projects, like family-planning centres, others at analysis of the state of the environment. The latter, the think-tanks, have made their mark on the world's policy makers by bringing them together with scientists and conservationists to confront the issues in a realistic manner. Examples are the London-based International Institute for Environment and Development and its work in marine affairs and the Washington-based World Resources Institute that has proposed an action plan for the management of tropical forests.

The enthusiasm and impatience expressed by people from the developed countries on Earth Day matured into a collection of NGOs that governments and intergovernmental bodies could not ignore. They provided a global, long-term perspective on environmental issues, sadly lacking among governments until then. What's more, as "grass roots" and "field" organizations, they took the issues abroad, offering a focus on the very real, but neglected environmental problems in the developing countries, and providing a solid base from which the citizens of those countries could act.

The strengthening of support for the few existing NGOs in developing countries and the proliferation of new ones in the '70s is astounding, from the local wildlife societies of Africa, once seen as cliques of expatriots, but now playing a vital role in wildlife education and in anti-poaching programmes, to groups that campaign against industrial pollution in the crowded cities from Brazil to the Philippines. There are over 5000 NGOs in tropical countries concerned with forestry, many of them directly involved in projects to protect forests or to replant degraded areas.

The NGOs of developing countries are not as well organized nor as wealthy as their counterparts in other countries, but their governments, who once viewed them with suspicion or as the whims of foreign meddlers, are coming to realize their potential as a work force to carry out some desperately needed environmental salvage.

CASE STUDY
World Wildlife Fund in Brazil

The muriqui, or woolly spider monkey, is one of the world's most endangered primates, found only in the Atlantic Forest region of Brazil. The dramatic decline in its numbers and the rapid destruction of its habitat have become both a focus for concern and a symbol for the conservation movement as a whole in Brazil.

Largest of the New World species, weighing up to 18 kilograms and 1-1½ metres in length, the muriqui never leaves the forest and rarely descends to the ground. Extremely agile, with long hook-like hands and a large prehensile tail strong enough to support its entire weight, it subsists entirely on a diet of leaves, fruit and flowers. It lives in groups of 20-30 individuals, with the females producing a single offspring every 2-3 years.

The muriqui's forest habitat, a unique ecosystem quite distinct from Amazonia, used to stretch more or less continuously from the north to the south of the country. Now only 2% of this original forest remains.

A hundred years ago there were an estimated 400,000 muriqui living in this vast region. Recent surveys, begun by WWF US, have so far located only 300 remaining, in ten widely separated forest patches. WWF is now working hard to ensure the survival of these remnant populations by improving protection in existing parks and reserves, by supporting ecological studies and by the establishment of a captive breeding programme. These efforts, combined with a public education campaign in Brazil, have already succeeded in greatly increasing awareness of the plight of the muriqui and its forest habitat both locally and around the world.

CASE STUDY
Save Taman Negara!

Above left *Stalactites in a limestone cave in the Taman Negara.* Above *Giant tree buttresses in the ancient forest.*

Sahabat Alam of Malaysia (SAM) is Friends of the Earth's most dynamic sister group in southeast Asia. Founded in 1977, it has already established an impressive track record as the region's leading proponent of the idea that development cannot be achieved at the expense of the environment.

Amongst the numerous issues it has tackled are lead in petrol, pollution from unregulated industrial discharges, occupational safety, poor sanitation, oil spills, deforestation, overfishing, water shortages, pesticide dumping and wildlife protection. Its publications to date include an annual *State of the Malaysian Environment* report, a monthly newspaper and a report entitled "Pesticide Problems in a Developing Country: A Case Study of Malaysia".

It is also concerned with spreading awareness of environmental problems in other parts of the world and, to this end, is associated with the Asian Environment Society, the Pesticide Action Network, the Antarctic and Southern Ocean Coalition and the Campaign for a Nuclear-free Pacific.

One of Sahabat Alam's most decisive victories to date was to force the cancellation of a government plan to build a hydroelectric dam across the Sungei Tembeling River, which would have flooded part of the protected Taman Negara. This ancient forest is a wilderness area of great environmental importance covering a total area of 4343 square kilometres. Established as a national park in 1939, it was explicitly set up "...in perpetuity, for the propagation, protection and preservation of the indigenous flora and fauna."

It contains not only several species of the dipterocarp family - amongst the tallest trees in the world, highly prized for their timber - but also numerous fruit and palm species of commercial value, oaks and laurels, the silver-trunked tualang and the rare mengkundor trees. It is a botanist's paradise, for nowhere else in peninsular Malaysia can one find such a great diversity of habitats and plant communities.

Equally rich in wildlife, the forest contains 250 species of birds, seladang (wild ox), leopards and tigers, sun bears, barking deer, wild pigs, several species of primates and the rare Sumatran rhinos.

The environmentalists pointed out that the proposed dam project would not only destroy this rich and valuable rainforest but would also wipe out archaeological sites in the area and lead to the displacement of some 3-5000 native people, whose historic culture would be disrupted.

Sahabat Alam mounted a vigorous national campaign beginning on June 21st, 1983 and within seven months had collected 45,000 signatures on their petitions. Thousands of other protest postcards were sent directly to the Prime Minister and the issue was taken up widely in the press. Under this pressure, the scheme was dropped.

By saving Taman Negara, Sahabat Alam gained valuable credibility both for themselves and for the principles and effectiveness of non-governmental action on behalf of the environment.

Education in conservation

The International Centre for Conservation Education (ICCE), which officially opened on June 5th, 1984 (World Environment Day), stems from a 1975 WWF project aimed at promoting conservation in developing countries. An independent centre with charitable status, operating from a period residence in the heart of the Cotswolds, UK, it has been directly involved over the last ten years with educational projects in more than 50 countries.

Discussions with the UN and other international conservation and development agencies had emphasized the need for simple and effective means of communicating environmental conservation on all levels, from rural populations and schoolchildren to government officials and decision-makers.

In its early days, the Centre carried out a good deal of research into the most appropriate educational materials. Audio-visual (AV) programmes proved to be most useful and 85 of these have been produced to date. Compared with film or video, they are based on very low-cost technology and can be rapidly reproduced and distributed.

ICCE realized that, for these materials to have maximum effect, they must reach out beyond the main centres of population into the rural communities. So in 1976 two prototype Mobile Education Units were sent into Gambia and Senegal in West Africa, where they toured schools, colleges and villages giving displays, talks and AV presentations. In Gambia the Unit was just one part of a "model" national conservation education programme

A mobile education unit in service in Ruanda, set up for a slide show and discussion on local environment problems.

involving conservation educators using material developed especially for Gambian audiences.

In 1979 alone 25,000 people were exposed to the programme and the response was so enthusiastic that the idea has since been taken up by the wildlife club movements in Cameroon and Uganda, by the Chongololo clubs of Zambia and the Wildlife Departments of Sri Lanka and Ethiopia.

The mobile units themselves carry a portable generator, 16-mm film projector, slide-tape unit, public address system and display screens. Back at home base, the ICCE has become increasingly involved in the production of simple, low-cost educational materials such as posters and booklets. They also provide comprehensive back-up support to information centres and conservationists working in remote areas.

All equipment offered has been "field tested" and there is a fast photographic, printing and spare parts service, made available through ICCE's trading company Conservation Education Services (CES), all of whose income is used to support the operation of the Centre.

ICCE also provides an international training course for people of developing countries working in environmental education. This includes seminars on the global environment as well as practical training in the use and maintenance of communications equipment.

Population Concern

In 1984 the Conference on International Population held in Mexico City, which played host to representatives from 150 countries, recognized that population pressure was the main threat to the natural environment.

Current predictions show that each year for the next 30-40 years, the world will have to find room for an additional 85 million people. In theory the world can produce enough for everyone; in practice, food resources are not evenly distributed and, by the year 2000, 36 countries will still be unable to feed their populations from their own lands.

Population Concern has been working for the last ten years to raise awareness of these issues at both local and governmental levels. It has raised over $1.5 million for family planning, education and health care programmes and is currently active in more than 20 countries.

Amongst these is Bangladesh, one of the poorest and most densely populated countries in the world. Its population of 98.6 million is set to double in 22 years' time at the current rate of growth. Almost half the population has no access to clean, safe water; one in seven babies dies in its first year; and the average life expectancy is only 46 years. Against this background Population Concern is working to provide practical help and information on family planning, immunization and sanitation.

The actress, Susan Hampshire, with mothers and children at Population Concern's family centre in Bangladesh.

Greenpeace - the Warriors of the Rainbow

1975-7 Greenpeace confronts Soviet whaling ships. In one incident, their eco-navy drives a zodiac up the slipway of the 600-foot factory ship, Dalniy Vostok, and demands an end to whaling.

1970 The ships Greenpeace I and Greenpeace II voyage to protest against the nuclear test site at Amchitka, Alaska. Within a year, the site is closed and is made a bird sanctuary.

1976-82 Greenpeace members and volunteers confront seal hunters, drawing worldwide attention to the annual bludgeoning of over 200,000 baby harp seals for their fur.

1978 Rainbow Warrior halts slaughter of grey seals in Orkneys. 1982 members drift at personal risk in front of huge toxic waste ship to stop dumping in North Sea.

1978 Greenpeace stops killing of 6000 dolphins in Japan by publicizing high mercury levels which make then unfit to eat. 1981 Greenpeace volunteer jailed for freeing 150 dolphins.

1978 The Rainbow Warrior launches massive campaign against Icelandic and Spanish whalers and protests Atlantic nuclear waste dumping. In 1980 is seized by Spanish government, escaping custody 5 months later.

1979-82 Greenpeace vessels try to stop dumping of radio-active wastes in mid-Atlantic. In 1983, the Sirius is bombarded with tear gas and stun grenades in Cherbourg, while protesting further dumping.

1981 Greenpeace campaigner chains herself to Japanese whaling harpoon, forcing ship to return to port, so that sperm whales are saved.

1972-4 Greenpeace III is rammed by French military vessel at Mururoa Atoll atmospheric nuclear test zone. In 1981-2, Greenpeace III returns to protest underground testing of neutron bomb.

1983 Large fine levied against Greenpeace after members boarded and occupied a Peruvian whaling ship.

1977 Two Greenpeace members narrowly escape an explosive harpoon as they protect a fleeing sperm whale.

1985 RAINBOW WARRIOR BOMBED AND SUNK IN AUCKLAND HARBOUR. Fernando Pereira was killed.

1978 A Greenpeace crew travels to Chile and Peru to film pirate whaling operations.

Saving the whales

Saving the dolphins

Nuclear and toxin-free environment

Saving the seals

"When the Earth is sick and the animals have disappeared, there will come a tribe of peoples from all creeds, colours and cultures who believe in deeds not words and who will restore the Earth to its former beauty. This tribe will be called the 'Warriors of the Rainbow'."

This ancient Red Indian legend was taken to heart by the first group of Greenpeace protestors who set out, in 1971, to prevent a US nuclear test in the Aleutian Islands off Alaska by sailing into the test zone.

It set the style for an organization whose non-violent, direct action protests have captured the headline news and the imagination of millions around the world. Now established in more than 15 countries with a fleet of boats of their own, Greenpeace is constantly in the public eye as it strives to preserve the natural environment and raise public awareness through carefully planned campaigns.

The organization has its roots in protest against nuclear weapons, the most immediate threat to life on Earth. After the Aleutians testing programme was stopped as a result of its efforts - the area is now a bird sanctuary - the action moved to the South Pacific where Greenpeace staged a determined campaign to

try and stop the French from testing their nuclear weapons in the atmosphere above the Mururoa Atoll.

In this it was again successful but underground tests continued. Greenpeace's insistent campaign led to the French secret service blowing up its boat, the *Rainbow Warrior*, on July 10th 1985, an incident which caused the death of one crew member and provoked world-wide protests. Membership in many countries trebled as a result.

The anti-whaling and-sealing campaigns, which began in the mid-1970s, were a natural progression for such a marine-based protest group. By positioning themselves between the whales and the harpooners, Greenpeace members dramatized the confrontation for TV audiences and drew public attention to the activities of the whaling nations.

Similarly when Greenpeace took to the Newfoundland icefields, blocking the path of sealing vessels and spraying seal pups with harmless dyes that rendered their pelts unusable by the fur trade, the public responded with financial support and massive consumer boycotts of seal products and furs.

Chemical and radioactive waste dumping were two other activities that Greenpeace targeted in the early 1980s as direct threats to the marine environment.

In 25 years, Greenpeace has established groups in more than 15 countries and conducted a series of attention-raising, carefully staged maritime "confrontations" all around the world's oceans, on issues from nuclear testing to saving the world's remaining whales.

Again their members put themselves at considerable personal risk by steering their inflatable boats directly under the tipping platforms of the waste ships or chaining themselves to the cranes.

Most recently Greenpeace members have scaled factory chimneys in protest against acid rain, sailed to Antarctica to declare the frozen continent a world park and hiked into the Nevada test zone to draw attention to American nuclear testing there.

Such eye-catching action is only possible through careful planning, and is only successful when combined with the kind of solid scientific reports and political lobbying that has given Greenpeace an outstanding reputation within the scientific and conservation community.

By allying the Quaker idea of "bearing witness" with a deep ecological awareness and an understanding of the modern media, Greenpeace tries to ensure that the natural environment will not be destroyed without a struggle.

193

The Musk ox died out in Northern Asia about 3,000 years ago. But the recent recreation of two viable herds of muskoxen in the USSR, now numbering more than 100 animals, is a good example of what inter-governmental co-operation in conservation can achieve.

The formation of both herds, located in the eastern Taimyr Peninsula and on Wrangel Island, began with the introduction of fifty animals from the wild herds of Canada and Alaska in 1974. The muskoxen were kept in enclosures to begin with to establish stable herd relations, but now roam free.

By filling an empty ecological niche in this way, Russian scientists hope to exploit vast areas of meagre arctic "pastures" and consolidate the survival of muskoxen for the future.

Governments take action

The role of governments in the management of the planet's natural resources has ranged from raping them to cherishing them, from total ignorance to a dawning understanding. Unfortunately, the latter roles have developed very late in the day, spurred only by public pressure.

Early exceptions occurred in the United States at the time of President Theodore Roosevelt (in office from 1901-1909) who agreed with a number of foresters and hydrologists to some far-sighted plans of rational resource management, in which this meaning of the word "conservation" is thought to have been publicized for the first time. Roosevelt even tried to organize a world conservation congress along these lines in Europe, but was out of office before it could happen. Meanwhile, a few "international" conventions on the protection of wildlife were signed among the European countries - on migratory birds useful to agriculture and African game animals threatened by overhunting. Most governmental departments concerned with natural resources within a country were buried in higher-level branches whose brief was to develop the resources commercially, which in those days meant little thought for sustainable use.

Whatever the motivations behind it, the public outpouring of concern, sentiment, distress or anger over the state of the environment in the '60s moved the heavy machinery of officialdom. The United Nations convened a Conference on the Human Environment in Stockholm in 1972, which gave wide publicity to the concept that human beings were an integral part of the ecosphere and that conservation and development had to go hand in hand. The United Nations Environment Programme, UNEP, was formed at the Stockholm conference and given the job of co-ordinating environmental work among the other UN bodies and promoting international projects. Although it has been the "poor sister" in the UN, hampered by lack of money and influence, UNEP has accomplished a lot. It set up the Regional Seas Programme to monitor, control and research marine and coastal pollution. It operates environmental monitoring services, in co-operation with the IUCN centre in Cambridge, England, and advises various aid agencies on the environmental implications of projects they fund in the developing countries.

Agreements among nations also flourished in the '70s -- conventions on wetlands and the wildlife trade, on marine pollution and migratory species, and on sites important to the world's natural heritage. Regional co-operation, too, has increased, from protection of the polar bear against hunting by the five northernmost nations to the establishment of transnational parks and reserves in North America, Central America and Africa. Many more projects are being planned, from efforts to save the rare kouprey, by Vietnam, Laos and Kampuchea, to a self-imposed quota system on elephant ivory exports by about 30 African countries. Notice, however, that most of these agreements are apolitical and non-controversial. Negotiations where the economic stakes are higher are often in a terrible tangle, as with the International Whaling Commission, the International Tropical Timber Agreement and the Convention on Long-Range Transboundary Air Pollution (which deals with "acid rain").

Also in the '70s, many high-level branches were created within governments, among both developed and developing countries, to deal specifically with environmental issues. These are stronger and better funded in the developed countries; but there are problems, differing only in degree, common to all: failure to carry out research or publish the findings, weakness when compared to the financial and industrial sectors or to the vested interests of senior officials in conflicting enterprises. Still, these branches of government have achieved major successes in the management of wildlife and habitat, in promotion and enforcement of environmental legislation, and in assessing the potential environmental impact of various development schemes. They are

CASE STUDY
Government wildlife services

Government action through revitalized wildlife services is a little-known but important aspect of conservation in the mid 1980s.

In New Zealand, the Wildlife Branch, originally established in 1945, has gained an international reputation for developing techniques that have saved some of the world's rarest birds from extinction. Saving the takahe, 70% of whose chicks were dying in the first month of life, required rangers to control predators, incubate eggs and hand-rear chicks. Cross-fostering was used in the case of the Chatham Island black robin. Eggs were transferred to the nests of another species, persuading the robin to breed two or three times in a season. Other rare species have been relocated in offshore islands that have been cleared of predators.

The US Fish and Wildlife Service has been grabbing headlines for different reasons. From the mid-1970s onwards it was clear that poaching of rare species involved organized crime, and a special operations branch to do undercover work was established.

In 1981 the Service broke open a multimillion dollar trade in live, exotic reptiles - a classic "sting" operation which led to charges against more than a hundred people who had been dealing in such endangered species as San Francisco garter snakes, Jamaican boas and Indian pythons.

An even bigger case was the three-year undercover investigation code-named "Operation Falcon" which uncovered a worldwide smuggling ring handling birds of prey for use by falconers or for breeding purposes. Whether the operation has closed down the black market in these birds remains to be seen.

The threatened peregrine falcon.

CASE STUDY
Zambia's National Conservation Strategy

Above *Elephants gathering at a water hole. The ivory trade is one target of the Zambian Conservation Strategy.*

In 1984 Zambia became the first African country to produce a National Conservation Strategy, an initiative inspired by President Kaunda. The document was produced by a multi-disciplinary Task Force, chaired by the National Council for Scientific Research, organized by the Ministry of Lands and National Resources, assisted by IUCN and funded by the Dutch and Swedish governments.

The Strategy's key components are: a philosophy for sustainable development, examining the efficiency of agricultural production; a natural resources development plan, allowing a diverse base for economic growth while ensuring conservation of all resources; and a schedule for the first 12 months of activity.

Zambia's needs for such a strategic plan are cogently argued. The country's reliance on copper constitutes one of the highest levels of dependence of any country on any one commodity. This alone has become a severe restraint on development.

Recognizing this fact, the government has implemented policies to change the country's development base from mining to agriculture, which has two important consequences: first, virgin lands would have to be opened up and production on current farming land intensified; second, this would put a strain on the natural resources on which agriculture depends and ways would have to be found to ensure renewability.

Zambia is fortunate that, at present, its conservation problems remain manageable. Nevertheless the Strategy outlines many areas for concern requiring appropriate action. Heading the list is deforestation, caused by land clearance, overcutting of fuelwood, overgrazing and burning, leading to a whole cycle of environmental problems. Forest management, extensive tree-planting and agroforestry practices are recommended solutions.

Soil erosion is becoming widespread due to overgrazing, badly constructed roads and poor farm practices. Soil conservation techniques are to be widely employed with full community participation. Pollution is also serious in certain localities, from pesticides, mines and factories. Control systems are to be implemented.

Wildlife is one of Zambia's key resources, now threatened by poaching and the destruction of habitat. The Strategy urges a concerted effort to control the ivory trade in particular. It also examines the rôle of sustainable development in key areas of human activity: industry and mining, population, water, tourism and energy. It discusses how the Strategy might be financed, planned and organized, and how the Zambian people can be actively involved.

The underlying theme of the Strategy, which emphasizes the wise management of natural resources, is to "make the most of what we have". By adopting a common-sense, multi-disciplinary approach to the future, Zambia has established a model which it is hoped other countries will emulate.

usually responsible, too, for the preparation of National Conservation Strategies for governments that have accepted the principles of the World Conservation Strategy. As of mid-1986, 40 nations (29 developing countries and 11 developed countries) are working on Strategies. Most are still in the preparatory phase, but the question remains: who is going to pay? If there's a will, the developed countries have enough finance and trained staff to implement their own Strategies, but the developing countries will have to rely heavily on international aid.

Where the money comes from

Most aid for development (in the broadest sense, encompassing food, health, education, energy and industry) conventionally comes from governments and non-private banks. Among governments are the agencies of single nations, like the United States Agency for International Development (USAID), or of groups of nations, and the UN agencies, like the Development Programme (UNDP), whose outright grants are made up of contributions from UN member countries. The banks are, of course, lenders, and are very much tied to government regulations and self-interested policies. Most work within regions - the Americas, Africa and Asia - but the World Bank is everywhere, and its loans in 1984 totalled $16 billion, about three-quarters of all multilateral, non-private bank loans, and much more than the total from UN agencies.

The NGOs raise funds directly from the public. Altogether the sums they channel to developing countries must be enormous, but the individual grants are miniscule in comparison to the funds available from governments and banks, and co-ordination of effort may be lacking.

The question is: how much of the aid, voluntary or official, coming from wealthy countries is spent on the rehabilitation or sustainable development of natural resources in the poor countries?

Until the '70s governments and banks paid scant attention to the potential environmental effects of dam-building, road and factory construction or irrigation and other agricultural improvements, much less to pressing environmental needs, like bolstering good forest and soil cover and populations of wild plants and animals. Even as late as 1977, UNDP felt that a representative from UNEP need not be a member of the inter-agency task force that was to coordinate UNDP projects - the rep would simply be invited to attend "when necessary"!

One of the many outcomes of the Stockholm Conference was to inject an environmental conscience into at least some of the aid agencies, notably the World Bank and USAID. These bodies prepare environmental impact assessments for all their projects, USAID being particularly conscientious. The approach is not altruistic, for in the long run, prevention of a disaster is less costly than curing it. More and more projects dealing directly with environmental problems are being funded. Both World Bank and USAID have good tropical forestry programmes, and the Bank has also recently been concerned with the protection of tribal peoples, and the correct use of pesticides. In 1980 the Bank persuaded eleven major aid agencies, including the UNDP, to sign a Declaration on the Environment by which they all agreed to undertake policies and practices with careful environmental regard. They also accepted that adherence to the Declaration must be monitored.

Unfortunately, only a small fraction (though a growing one) of the funds from these bodies is devoted to projects directly concerned with the conservation of natural resources (see right). Many of their other projects are environmentally unsound, in spite of all the assessments and the Declaration. The World Bank is involved in destructive cattle-ranching schemes in Central America and southern Africa, in the ill-fated Indonesian transmigration programme *(see p.177)*, and in projects damaging to mangrove habitat in Mexico. Furthermore, the banks, including the private ones, impose crippling interest rates on their loans.

Money – where it comes from

Conservation is grossly underfunded. A few days of the arms race would pay for the total $8 billion now called for to save tropical forests (below).

This sum is, in fact, ten times what the World Bank spent on all environmental work in 1984, ironically, Band Aid in 1985 raised funds equal to one ninth of this and more than ten times the money available to IUCN for managing nearly 500 projects in 1984.

It is hard to estimate government contributions to environment protection - figures often include agricultural and other development schemes which may be irrelevant, or counter productive.

NGOs make a huge, largely unmeasured contribution, and one which doesn't rely on money alone. Much of their effort rests on small investments to sustain larger voluntary effort, with results greater than their cash cost suggests. Most of their funds come from membership or public donation.

The total in each column is represented by the inset proportion in the column to its left

World military spending 1984
US$ 75 billion

Total World Bank lending in 1984
US$ 16 billion

World Bank environmental spending 1984 (including agriculture)
US$ 800 million

Band Aid sums raised for Africa 1985
US$ 90 million

IUCN conservation projects 1984
US$ 8.5 million

WWF support for IUCN 1984 US$ approx. 2 million

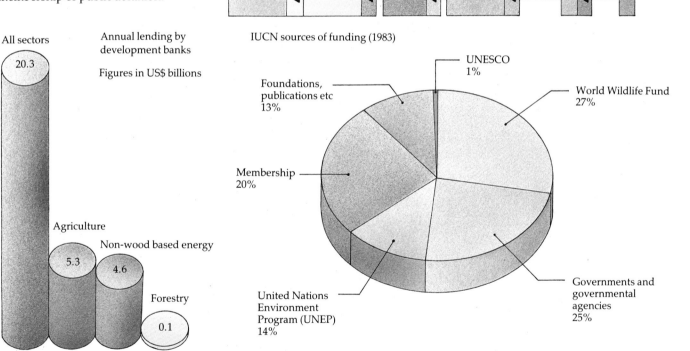

Annual lending by development banks

Figures in US$ billions

All sectors
20.3

Agriculture
5.3

Non-wood based energy
4.6

Forestry
0.1

IUCN sources of funding (1983)

UNESCO 1%

Foundations, publications etc 13%

World Wildlife Fund 27%

Membership 20%

Governments and governmental agencies 25%

United Nations Environment Program (UNEP) 14%

Money for the forests

Three very different organizations, the World Bank, UNEP, and a Washington-based NGO called the World Resources Institute, have outlined a programme for controlling deforestation in the tropics which would require initially 8 billion dollars - a staggering sum in context of normal forestry funding levels. As the diagram above shows, forestry is the cinderella of development. Of the total $20 billion lent by development banks, only a hundred thousand dollars went to forests. The new proposal takes the form of a "call for action" to funding sources, and lays the groundwork for longer-term investments too, required to reverse the effects of destruction.

IUCN and conservation funding

IUCN has a unique place in conservation. Half NGO, half official body, it draws funding from governments, UNEP, WWF donations, and its own publications and services. It also manages projects costing millions of dollars. Through the World Conservation Strategy, IUCN wields a great influence on the course of conservation worldwide.

The position of the borrowers is also largely negative. Governments of developing countries that have requested foreign aid have themselves shied away from strong environmental policies, afraid that the extra costs of safe-guarding natural resources during development would cause the investors to lose interest in the projects. Meeting the urgent needs of the people is, of course, necessary, but it is also more politically popular than ensuring their long term welfare. The failure of the costly UN Plan of Action to halt desertification in Africa, for example, falls partially on the shoulders of the African governments, who gave low priority to the execution of the actual field projects that would have had long-lasting results.

Commerce in conservation

As with governments and big banks, the attitudes of the business world shifted in the '70s towards environmental concerns. Most large companies now have explicit environmental policies, and some have even taken a leadership role, with self-imposed standards of using natural resources more rigorous than called for by governments.

The majority of effort lies in the realm of control of air and water pollution. As early as 1963 the European oil refiners formed a study group, which is still going strong, to advise on pollution and how to mimimize it, and less than ten years later, the world's major oil companies voluntarily introduced compensation schemes for pollution damage. In 1974, as a result of the Stockholm Conference, an international association representing all parts of the petroleum industry was created to work with UNEP and to answer for the industry's impact on the environment. Among the leading lights in the association are Shell, and British Petroleum *(see right)*. Shell pioneered a procedure, now used by all large oil companies, to retain oil residues on board tankers, thereby reducing pollution from cleaning operations. It develops and applies technology for water and air purification and waste recycling, not just for plants in Europe and North America, but in the developing countries as well.

The chemical companies, too, have formed associations within Europe and the United States to advise on the environmental impact of their products and practices and to make recommendations. Some large companies in other fields are their own "watchdogs" - Rio Tinto Zinc sponsored detailed ecological studies in Papua New Guinea (presumably adjusting its mining operation accordingly); IBM in Britain has an admirable sustainable development policy, directed toward economizing on energy and and preventing noise and pollution by its plants.

Perhaps these companies have found a conscience, although there are plenty of NGOs around to help them remember their environmental responsibilities. But they have also found that quite often "pollution prevention pays" (a motto of the 3M Company), for by purifying and recycling wastes, their consumption of water, energy and raw materials is reduced and, in the long run, they will save money.

This encouraging "spot-check" for good behaviour among the large companies belies the problems, a number of which could be easily rectified. Environmental policies set by head-office do not always filter down to the project or plant managers in the field nor to the people whose lives are directly affected by the operations. Education programmes are needed, which should instruct in environmental and social matters. Many companies still send their obsolete technology and products to the developing countries, where local companies are not loathe to use them. When trouble occurs, all too often parent companies are quick to disclaim any responsibility. But ignorance is no excuse in any country - information on advanced clean technology and products, and on environmental guidelines, standards and data bases, is readily obtainable by all businesses and governments from the International Chamber of Commerce and UNEP.

Various commercial companies now do direct conservation work. Shell is aiding reafforestation in Haiti, British-American Tobacco supports tree-planting in Kenya. In Sao Paulo, Brazil, the Energy Company is helping restock rivers and forests damaged by its own activities; in Belize, Tate and Lyle helps local farmers turn citrus crop wastes to animal feed. But most companies steer well clear of touchy issues. Fur began to fly, for example, when the Mattel toy company announced in 1985 that it would be donating one dollar from the sale of each of their "Snuggles the Seal" dolls to the Humane Society of the United States (HSUS) for their anti-sealing campaign.

The Wildlife Legislative Fund of America (WLFA) and the newspaper Fur Age Weekly *mounted a national counter campaign calling for a deluge of protest mail to be sent to Mattel from sportsmen and the fur trade. The pressure led to Mattel withdrawing its support for HSUS, but the hunting and fur lobbies' glee was short-lived. Less than one month later another toy company, LJN Toys Ltd of New York, announced they would be carrying the Snuggles dolls under a similar arrangement with HSUS.*

CASE STUDY
Earthlife: a new style of conservation

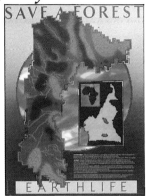

Earthlife characterizes a new style and approach to environmentalism which aims to find ways of generating economic activity from the world's natural resources without destroying them. What this means in reality is a partnership between venture capital and conservation, a style of sustainable development likely to be widely imitated as the finite limits of our planet become more obvious to the world's industries.

Headed by a charitable foundation, Earthlife has two wholly owned subsidiary companies, Bioresources and Rural Investment Overseas (RIO). The foundation itself deals with research, information and educational activities. Bioresources concentrates on developing practical and lasting alternatives to the destruction of the forests by identifying and exploiting new tree and plant products valuable for food and medicines. RIO seeks to assist social and economic advance in developing countries by promoting more effective agricultural investment.

Earthlife's main demonstration project for all these ideas is the campaign to save Korup in Cameroon, one of the richest rainforests in Africa. Korup itself will be totally protected, apart from limited tourism, but the surrounding marginal forest areas will be surveyed for new industrial and pharmaceutical products. Also on the margins, an agricultural "buffer zone" is to be created in which high-yielding agricultural techniques will be tested.

Earthlife believes such a package of measures is essential for real and lasting conservation. If successful, two other national parks in Cameroon will go ahead which, taken together, will total in area a tenth of all the properly protected rainforests in the world.

CASE STUDY
BP at Wytch Farm

British Petroleum's Group Environmental Services division, staffed by an interdisciplinary group of scientists and engineers, specialises in all aspects of assessment and management of environmental impact in terrestrial, marine, freshwater and atmospheric systems.

By integrating environmental consideration at the earliest phases of project development, they aim to avoid expensive delays, ensure a continuing license to operate and minimise exposure to liability claims for environmental impairment.

Their work begins with the preparation of a comprehensive Environmental Impact Assessment (EIA).

If development goes ahead, the Group is then involved in a monitoring operation for the life of the project and will try to ensure that, when work is completed, the site is returned to as near its natural state as possible.

BP are particularly concerned about oil and chemical spillages, which can be very damaging to their public image and have developed a wide range of equipment and techniques to deal with such eventualities.

The Group runs training courses for BP managers, monitors worldwide developoment of environmental legislation, represents BP in such groups as the UN Environmental Programme and liaises with wildlife, conservation and landscape protection organisations.

All of their expertise has been called on for BP's proposed development of the Wytch Farm oilfield in Dorset, Britain's largest onshore oil reserve. Wells were first drilled there in 1973 but production was stable at a modest 5,500 barrels a day. However, further drilling revealed the existence of a much larger accumulation of recoverable reserves, equivalent to those of a medium-sized North Sea field.

BP estimated that to recover this would require the sinking of 50 new wells on three sites, raising production levels to 60,000 barrels a day.
One of the proposed sites will be on Studland Peninsula which contains a national nature reserve and a unique combination of marine, freshwater and land habitats - the only place in Britain where all six British native reptiles are to be found.

Two other sites will be on tiny Furzey island in Poole Harbour, which lies next to Brownsea Island, one of the National Trust's most zealously guarded sanctuaries.

The measures they propose include: acoustically clad and screened equipment to limit the noise; extensive landscaping and screening, taking full advantage of the local topography and vegetation; routing pipelines around sensitive areas; designing and colouring buildings and equipment to blend in with the landscape.

The surface of drilling sites will be sealed and surrounded with limed ditches to prevent any possibility of contaminating local ground-water. In some areas, construction times will be limited to the summer months to avoid disturbing the large number of wildfowl that overwinter in the area.

The whole development is due to begin in 1987. Only time will tell how successful such measures will be.

The "nodding donkey" oil pumps at Wytch Farm, well screened from public view.

Keeping track of the current status of endangered wildlife and environments is the vital task of the IUCN Conservation Monitoring Centre. Established in January 1983, with headquarters at Cambridge, England, and a facility at Kew Gardens, its unique information services aim to place the correct facts in the right hands at the right time.

Its four major units, linked by a sophisticated computer system, continuously collect, analyse, interpret and disseminate data on threatened animal and plant species, the wildlife trade and protected areas. This information is made available to all parts of the global conservation network in the form of special reports and the renowned series of IUCN Red Data Books, which have now become standard reference works in the conservation world.

There are other, more fundamental problems in the business world. The "good housekeeping" (a motto of Shell) policies are mostly in-house. Companies do not seem to realize that "ecosphere" is derived from a Greek word meaning "house" and that the additive effects of their practices reach far beyond the door of any one company, good or bad. During the transfer to clean technology, the costs are usually passed on to the consumer; the companies say that people expecting to use natural resources, like clean air and water, must pay for them. At the same time they themselves are robbing other natural resources, like the agrochemical industries in the seed business *(see p.140)*. The bosses of businesses everywhere, public or private, do not seem to know when and why to leave the environment alone; to put it another way, they feel it is not in their interest to say no to people's rising demands for goods and services.

Scientists and educators

Two fields of human endeavour that play a more direct role than most on behalf of the ecosphere are science and education. The scientists find out how the ecosphere works, whether we're overplaying our hand and how we can save the game, and the educators try to make everyone else understand as quickly as possible.

The picture of scientists locked in laboratories or chasing butterflies in a meadow no longer tells their whole story, for most of them have something to say on environmental matters, and many are actively engaged in solving the problems. The ecologists are foremost; but ecology is a very broad word, drawing on the expertise of people in many fields, from geomorphology (the study of the changing face of the planet due to physical forces like gravity, water and wind), to the physics and chemistry of air, water and soil; from biochemistry, biogeography, and plant and animal physiology and behaviour to social anthropology and economics. (Economics is simply the study of how members of *Homo sapiens* barter outputs for inputs among themselves. Other living beings do it too, as when a plant trades nectar for pollen with an insect.) The study of how numbers of organisms are affected by their surroundings - the physical and living environment, including members of their own species - is called population ecology, and it grades into genetics when numbers are so low that there are not enough "good" genes to allow a population to maintain itself naturally.

There is "pure" scientific research and "applied" research. Pure research means that it doesn't serve an immediate or known human use. I've heard it said among eminent conservationists that since plenty is known about ecological problems, we should turn all our energies to solving them, and forget pure research. It's true that there's more than enough to do in conservation, but there is still so much to be learned, from why whole forests are dying Europe to why a single species, like the Large Blue butterfly of Britain, cannot thrive. Inventories of plants and animals and studies of the processes of the particular ecosystems they inhabit must precede applied research on how to manage an area as a nature reserve or exploit its resources sustainably.

Another aspect of pure science that merges into applied science is simply the monitoring of the environmental situation. Keeping a check on natural conditions, like how much carbon dioxide is in the atmosphere or what species of fish or algae live in a river, lets us know there may be something amiss if they alter, and tracking the changes in pollution levels or vegetation cover has obvious application in susbsequent management strategies. Monitoring takes place from space, the air and the ground. The American satellites, including LANDSAT, and now the French SPOT, "read" the heat reflected from the earth, which varies according to amount and type of vegetation, and the information is used to make vegetation maps. Surveys from airplanes provide a double check on vegetation and land use patterns (and are also used for counting large animals, wild and

CASE STUDY
Scientists volunteer help for Madagascar

Many scientists in nature conservation donate their expertise voluntarily, to specialist advisory groups or at a local biogeographic level. A few years ago the author hosted a meeting in Jersey of scientists concerned with conservation in Madagascar, that amazing island where nearly all plants and animals are endemic, but where so many are threatened with extinction. Representatives of the Malagasy government also participated in the meeting and requested that an International Advisory Group of Scientists (IAGS) be established to screen proposals for field research by foreigners in Madagascar to ensure that the needs of conservation would be met.

"I was elected Chairman of IAGS" says the author. "It consists of seven volunteer scientists from France, Britain, Germany and the United States, representing the fields of botany, ornithology and mammalogy. Since IAGS began working, we have formally screened nearly 30 proposals, ranging from faunal and floral surveys to lemur behaviour. If they pass the strict review by ourselves and our specialist consultants, the proposals are recommended to the Malagasy authorities. The authorities, including their own scientific teams from the University of Madagascar, then discuss the proposals and accept or reject them. This whole procedure, although lengthy, is the best possible assurance that field research by foreigners will be of high quality, and that conservation efforts will be made at every level, from government projects to local education."

The author at the Jersey conference with Malagasy government scientists and conservation colleagues.

CASE STUDY
Field science helps save the cranes

Common cranes observed in the oak woods of western Spain, their winter feeding grounds, during the GRUS survey work.

The common crane (*Grus grus grus*) has lived throughout Europe for thousands of years but, as with so many other species, human society is now having a dramatic influence on its way of life. Although not considered to be endangered, almost all its breeding sites south of Scandinavia have been destroyed and it was clear to conservationists that its wintering habitats were under threat.

In order to preserve these it was first necessary to build up a clearer picture of the cranes' movements and life style. The migratory flyways from its Scandinavian breeding grounds were more or less known and it was estimated that at least 10,000 cranes wintered in western Spain (Extremadura) and possibly in Morocco as well. Further information was lacking.

The task of discovering the cranes' overwintering habits was taken on by the Spanish Coordinating Federation for the Protection of Birds (CODA), an umbrella organization founded in 1978, which then had about 20 regional and local member societies.

"Project Grus", financed by a series of European countries through ICBP's Migratory Birds Committee and coordinated by Dr M. Fernandez-Cruz of the Spanish Ornithological Society, began with the arrival of the first cranes in autumn 1979 and continued until the last bird had left Spain, the operation being repeated the following season to double-check results.

This impressive scientific survey, which involved the mobilization of hundreds of field ornithologists and game wardens, revealed that 18-20,000 cranes spent the winter months in Spain. Their wintering sites and flyways, their daily habits and space requirements were recorded - all of which made the problems clear.

In western Spain the countryside's main feature for centuries has been the oak woods whose acorns have provided the cranes' basic winter food. These woods are being cleared at an appalling rate, forcing the cranes to congregate in growing numbers on fewer sites. This, in turn, has resulted in crop damage with thousands of birds feeding on the farmers' fields.

When CODA began "Project Grus" their aim was to get the scientific knowledge necessary to find practical solutions to the problems. Already plans have been laid in western Spain to establish protected areas for the birds.

In October 1985 the first meeting of a European Crane Working Group was held in Hungary where it was agreed that a European crane survey should be carried out in 1988/89.

Much remains to be learned. It is still not clear how many of the cranes cross over to Morocco each winter or if there are big fluctuations in the crane populations arriving in Spain for the winter. But the important principle of the need for scientific cooperation between countries and non-governmental organizations has been clearly established, a cooperation that is vital if the crane is to be saved.

domestic), and earth-bound scientists collect "ground-truth". The results flow into monitoring centres around the world, such as those set up by UNEP and IUCN, and are used for devising strategies for the management of natural resources.

In industry, agriculture and forestry, scientists are engaged in developing technologies that will impinge, one way or another, on the natural world. As governments and businesses gain environmental awareness, they should be asking the scientists they employ to come up with methods, machines and materials that have as little harmful impact on the environment as possible. Scientists are often the targets of claims that their results are designed to please their employers in government or commerce. Worse still, some scientists are actively "muzzled" by their employers and not permitted to publicize their findings. The way to get round both of these all-too-human problems is to insist on independent scientific checks of any study of an environmental situation.

There is great urgency today for environmental education in every sector of society, from children in school to adults in offices or cropfields, from technicians to planners to politicians. With education comes understanding of the life-support systems of the planet and, one hopes, the desire and the ability to maintain them properly. But the educators have an enormous task ahead of them.

More people need to be trained as professional conservation scientists, and before graduate training commences, the candidates must go to university. The Soviet Union and India have established ecology-based curricula at their instititions of higher learning (and in their schools), but financial cutbacks and outright lack of funds for universities in other countries are crippling the scientific battalion of Noah's Army. The training of technicians to assist research and carry out management strategies in the field is also sorely needed. Most important of all is the training of the immediate users of natural resources - the farmers, herders, fishers and woodcutters - in adapting new methods and materials to their particular environments and societies, or in reviving appropriate old ones. Programmes sponsored by governments, especially with the help of development aid agencies, are generally good in this respect, though there need to be more of them. Businesses and development banks are beginning to ensure that on-the-job instruction and field demonstrations are regularly offered along with their operations. Nearly all of the IUCN/WWF conservation projects provide for technical training and local education.

The public-at-large, that amorphous entity so difficult to define, is the primary target for educators. The most receptive to the new ways of thinking about the ecosphere are, of course, the young people, and many good projects have been undertaken to reach them, both in developed and developing countries. There are the various nature organizations devoted to the young, from the Audubon Society's Expedition Institute that offers academic degrees earned in America's "wilderness classrooms" to the Chongololo and Conservation Clubs of Zambia, the Wildlife Clubs of Kenya, and the Millions of Trees Clubs of India. In Britain, television companies and businesses, like Channel 4 and Kodak, sponsor conservation activity competitions for young people. Many of the metropolitan zoos and botanical gardens in the developed countries (and a few in developing countries, like the Madras Snake Park in India) provide excellent educational experiences for their young visitors, and some offer group activities.

In countries where populations are mostly rural, teachers have the problem of simply gathering together enough students to do their jobs properly, unless a good rural school system is in place. Mobile education units *(see p.192)*, carrying books and films (and generators) are very popular among children and adults, but hardly adequate alone. "Distance" education, using correspondence courses, radio, and satellite-beamed television, is working well in some countries, but still

CASE STUDY
Tanzania's Wildlife College

One of the most remarkable institutions for education in natural resource man agement was established in 1963 in Mweka, Tanzania - the College of African Wildlife Management. This college was the first in Africa to provide professional training in this important field.

Previously, most personnel of African game departments had no formal training and most senior park managers were expatriate wildlife biologists. In the 22 years of its existence, Mweka College has trained more than a thousand game assistants and wardens from 16 countries. Virtually all protected areas in eastern Africa - now covering more than 12 million hectares - are staffed by Mweka graduates.

It was in 1961 that President Julius Nyere, in his Arusha Manifesto speech, proclaimed his government's full support for the conservation of wildlife and wildlife management training.

Located in northern Tanzania, Mweka College is a large, well equipped complex with 14 instructors and 60 support staff. It provides easy access to a range of parks and reserves which incorporate a variety of ecosystems, from alpine moorlands to marine habitats. Thirty per cent of the students' time is spent in field training, the rest in classroom studies. The main subject areas are:
● Natural sciences: zoology, botany, ecology, earth sciences, geography.
● Wildlife management: inventory, utilization, range, research, vehicle maintenance, ballistics.
● Estate management and conservation education: park management, administration, construction, law, first aid, survival techniques.

Mweka's success has provided a model for programmes in other countries, such as the Garoua College in Cameroon and the Naivasha Institute in Kenya. Its annual intake of 80 students come from all parts of Africa and work throughout the continent when they leave. Many now hold leadership positions in wildlife departments, and international organizations.

Its key rôle in changing attitudes was recognized by the World Wildlife Fund which awarded the College its International Award for Conservation Merit in 1981. Despite this success, however, Mweka is troubled by financial insecurity and rapidly rising costs and is faced with having to lower its enrolment figures in the future.

CASE STUDY
Field education in St Helena

The little island of St Helena, a British dependency in the mid South Atlantic, is making a headstart on rehabilitating its devastated natural vegetation in a unique collaboration between conservation scientists, local people and schools and the St Helena government. At the prompting of IUCN and FFPS, a survey by horticulturalists from the Royal Botanic Gardens at Kew, England, turned up isolated populations of many of the island's endemic plants, thought extinct, and a programme was planned to breed and reintroduce these species to restore the island's natural habitat.

At Kew, scientists are pioneering the propagation techniques needed, concentrating especially on the endemic shrubby species best suited to saline and semi-arid soils, such as the St Helena gumwood, scrub wood and tea plant.

On St Helena, WWF has helped fund a nursery to grow the seedlings, and local people are being trained in horticultural skills. Grant aid from Britain's Overseas Development Administration (ODA) is sustaining the rescue programme. An area of the High Peaks is being cleared of exotic weeds and replanted with endemics such as the St Helena redwood, the she cabbage, and the St Helena olive. The St Helena ebony, believed to be extinct for 100 years but rediscovered by a Kew botanist in 1980, has been re-established, too.

The rare island flora of St Helena is brought back to life by reintroduction of young nursery-grown indigenous trees.

Planting of endemics is now part of St Helena's official forestry policy. Forestry officers have been to Kew for study, and it is planned to offer St Helena school leavers short courses at Kew in horticultural practice. From primary to technical level, schools now teach the ecology of the island. The education and forestry departments are working together, providing nature rambles, talks, slide shows, and active projects.

Students learn to propagate the endangered species, grow them in the nursery, and travel in parties to plant them out in forest reserve sites. In a small arboretum, planted in the past with introduced pine and eucalyptus, students are now clearing areas for native species. A guided forest trail is planned, illustrating the impact of exotics on native species, and eventually, endemics once found in association will be planted together in the arboretum to recreate the original ecology.

Symbolizing the regeneration of St Helena's wilderness and the islanders' commitment to it, the new central school now planned on the island will be landscaped with endemic species, as both a lesson, and a memorial, to the work of local citizens and schools.

203

When Greenpeace prompted a US consumer boycott of Norwegian fish imports into the US, in protest against Norway's opposition to a whaling moratorium, it cost the Norwegian fishing industry several million dollars in lost contracts before they agreed to cease handling whale meat.

Consumer boycotting also worked in the push to get Nestlé to change its infant-food marketing practices in developing countries.

But boycotting one company may open the door for another less reputable one. Boycotts only work if they can generate publicity on a large scale and if they're specific enough to be effective.

suffers from lack of distribution of centrally produced materials designed for the particular needs of an isolated community and from lack of the stimulation provided by a good "old-fashioned" teacher.

Environmental education must reach young and old alike, but while young people are eager for it, the older ones are less so, or simply haven't got the time. A man in India said that he didn't feel like watching agricultural programmes on satellite TV after working in the fields all day; women in Africa do most of the farming and then come back to babies and household chores in the evening. It is often said that educating the young is most important, for they will become the next users of the planet's resources. The problem is that present usage is so wrong, the planet can't wait for the children to grow up.

The political will for change

One of the main reasons for urgency in adult environmental education is that well-informed constituencies should put well-informed people into public office to represent them. By their day-to-day decisions and stands on issues, politicians have tremendous control over how the environment is used. Unfortunately, most politicians in office or aspiring to office are abysmally ignorant when it comes to understanding how the ecosphere works. One prominent American political figure will forever be remembered among conservationists for his statement that trees cause pollution because of their oxygen emissions!

The activism of the '60s and '70s, however, made well-established political parties consider environmental issues more seriously. It spawned a new breed of politican, and full-fledged environmental parties in Europe. The "Greens", as the new parties are loosely termed, now hold seats in the local governments of many countries, in the national legislative bodies of several and in the European Parliament, indicating a widespread concern for the environment among the general populace. That concern is very real, but the immediate strength of the Greens is probably not. Superficially, their problem is that they have aligned themselves with other political groups that are considered by the established and powerful parties (and their supporters) to be antithetical to European values. More fundamentally, they ask for a radical change in the ways of thinking and behaving of most people in the world that is not likely to be soon forthcoming. They question people's pride and fear - those of the "tribe" that insist on the strength of spear, cannon or nuclear missile taking precedence above all else, and those of the male that have long shifted the double burden of work and child-rearing onto females in most societies. They also question people's pocket-books - whereas all other political leaders or parties, regardless of ideology or nationality (or of paying lip service to environmental issues), call for economic growth for our species, and as rapidly as possible. Yet most thinking people know that this can only mean a headlong plunge into disaster, because of the limits to natural resources.

Some of the most effective political groups achieve their aims by lobbying established political institutions - an activity which is even more successful when supported by public protest, especially of the kind that embarasses governments. There are, of course, all too many countries where little politicking is permitted. But most governments in power are alike when it comes to protecting natural resources; they can't afford to upset powerful interests, so it's business as usual - which normally entails continued nonsustainable use of natural resources. There seems to be no such thing as enlightened rule for the environment, or for living resources, in the world of power politics.

The Greens carry on in Europe, despite their near impossible task. Their main success is at community level; but their very existence implies hope - there is genuine concern among many people for the State of the Ark, and they may, one day, form the political majority.

CASE STUDY
The American art of lobbying

Lobbying is the art of forcing a specific change in attitude, legislation or government policy. This can be done on the streets and through the media in campaigns aimed at creating the climate where a decision-maker has no choice but to make the decision you're lobbying for.

Or it can be done through the courts and no-one does it better than the Natural Resources Defense Council (NRDC), widely considered the most effective lobbying and litigating group on US environmental issues.

Its two main lawyers, David Hawkins and Richard Ayres, have for 15 years been dogging Congress, the Environmental Protection Agency and the courts to tighten control on acid rain, increasingly a major problem in the northern United States and Canada, and on other forms of industrial pollution. In the process they have gained a formidable reputation for shaping environmental law and driving public policy, combining in-depth legal knowledge with political and media skills to great effect.

Launched in 1970 by the Ford Foundation, the NRDC combined the talents of graduates fresh out of Yale Law School with establishment New York lawyers, who shared the ambition to set up a public-interest environmental law firm. It has grown from a handful of attorneys with a $100,000 grant to a diverse national group with a $6 million budget and 55,000 active supporting members.

NRDC believe that it's not enough for Congress to pass a law – the law has to be enforced but it won't be enforced unless there are a lot of people who are demanding it.

Though their subject is new, NRDC's campaigning style and the use of the courts and the constitution to effect change are *not* new to the United States, of course, but part of the political heritage. The work of Ralph Nader, especially in fighting the huge American motor corporations to achieve safety for car drivers, followed a similar pattern. Nader's style of aggressive citizen activism led to the coining of the term "Naderism" - used to descibe active consumer rights campaigning through the courts and media.

CASE STUDY
The European Greens

In an era when established political parties seem incapable of explaining or tackling the interlocking set of problems facing the world, it is clear to many that a new form of politics is required if we are to survive this century intact.

Green politics, with its systemic view and its emphasis on ecology, social responsibility, grassroots democracy, women's views and non-violence, offers just such a new form, and one which is becoming increasingly attractive to voters in many Western democracies.

Green politics is now active in West Germany, Belgium, Ireland, Sweden, Austria, France, Luxembourg, Switzerland, Holland and the UK. Prototype Green parties also exist in many other countries in different forms and there is increasing international cooperation between all parts of this rapidly expanding network.

Most successful of them all is *Die Grünen* in West Germany, which developed out of a small group of liberal and conservative ecologists, the Action Committee of Independent Germans, and Green Action Future, founded by a former Christian Democrat politician named Herbert Gruhl.

These two joined forces to form a Green association to run candidates for election to the European Parliament in June 1979. It was Gruhl who created the now famous slogan: *"We are neither left nor right; we are in front."* Their new-style politics quickly attracted the support of various other citizens' groups and by January 1980 they held their first constitutional convention.

If they were considered outsiders to begin with, opinions soon altered when, on the 6th March 1983, the Green Party captured 5.6% of the votes and got 27 MPs into the Bundestag. The success of the German Greens echoed through European politics, and was given strong popular appeal by the charismatic figure of Petra Kelly.

Since that initial breakthrough, which established the credibility of Green politics worldwide, their progress has been marred by internal divisions caused by the differing styles and attitudes contained within the Party. These range from the fundamentalists, who believe that involvement with conventional politics will inevitably lead to a dilution of the Green message, to more pragmatic views from candidates who wish to form alliances with existing parties in order to wield greater power. It remains to be seen how such problems will be resolved.

In Britain, which does not have a system of proportional representation, the Green Party has yet to secure a seat in Parliament. However, Green political ideas have now been taken up by the three major parties. The strong pressure of environmental groups and the work of such organizations as the Green Alliance, a cross-party ecological initiative, have changed the nature of the political debate and forced new issues into the agenda. In the USA, ecopolitics operate more strongly at the state level and through powerful lobbying in the courts.

So it appears that, whatever the structure of the existing political landscape, the ideas contained within Green politics will find expression. New ideas take time to establish but it is safe to predict that the Green view will be a force for the future.

Petra Kelly, charismatic leader of the German Greens, speaking at the Nuremburg Trubunal in 1983.

205

The principle of getting ordinary people from the local community, particularly children, involved as "guardians" of wildlife and the natural environment is becoming increasingly established around the world.

In England, members of the Oxfordshire and Kent naturalists' trusts maintain an annual 16-week 24-hour guard over the rare monkey orchid, illustrated above, of which only thirteen plants survive.

Also in Britain, amateur coast-watchers are being employed by the Nature Conservancy Council to help them monitor the impact of pollution and activities like bait digging.

In Gibralter, a four-week, round-the-clock watch by children of St Christopher's School meant that one of the Rock's four known nesting pairs of peregrine falcons bred successfully, without their chicks being stolen by collectors, for the first time in ten years.

In Michigan, USA, the public and the Michigan Humane Society have been fighting the gun lobby in their efforts to keep the State a refuge for the mourning dove, a harmless bird that is legally hunted in 35 other US states. Michigan's National Resources Commission created an open season for hunters on the bird, but public pressure led to an injunction on the hunt.

The Indian Society of Naturalists (INSONA) have been appointing local children as "Guardians of the Trees", urging them to bring cases of threatened trees to the society's attention.

The future of the Arabian oryx, which was extinct in the wild in the 1970s, has been entrusted to the Harasis, a desert people of Oman. The animals are being reintroduced into the remote, stony plateau of the Jiddat where they once roamed free, homeland of the Harasis who have sworn to protect them, and are managing the new herd.

206

The power of the community

Real "grassroots" movements are born in communities and therefore have a social significance and durability within a community greater than any plan imposed from on high. Environmental planners and managers should take advantage of such community energy, for without it any project designed to encourage the rational use of natural resources will meet with difficulties.

Traditional types of community resource management usually operate on a sustainable basis, because they developed in the days when human populations were lower. Communities are often pleased to resurrect the traditions, and with appropriate modern modifications, the systems become sustainable once again and service higher numbers of people. The mixed cropping of corn and rice in Indonesia, for example, is more productive than monoculture when used with nitrogen fertilizers. Other social traditions, from shifting agriculture to the possession of an automobile by every member of the family, are clearly not workable under the extra burden of population, and so alternatives must be found - but only the community itself knows what options will work for it.

One sector of the community that has been neglected in practically every society in the discussions of alternative management schemes nonetheless contains well over half the population - the women and the small children dependent on them. The failure in India of a biogas plant, which converted cow dung into enough cooking fuel for every house in the village, happened because of the men's greater interest in other forms of energy that would power farm equipment. Without consulting the women, the men simply stopped bringing in cow dung for the plant. They ate just as well though, because the women went back to the drudgery of collecting firewood and wastes to burn in the stoves. Discussion of community matters between men and women is still frowned upon in many cultures, although some women have begun to assert themselves. In a Himalayan village they refused to let the men sell a public forest for a seed potato farm. Had the sale gone through, the women - young, pregnant and old - would have had to walk over ten hours a day on three days out of four to fetch fuel and fodder. (As it is, they walk seven hours.) Unfortunately, the sons and husbands were not gracious losers in this argument, and community harmony was certainly compromised. In other cases, however, the outcome of women taking the lead in matters of natural resource management has been to the benefit of all the local people, as the Chipko movement in India has shown. Women have also been the keys to success in projects to promote fuel-efficient stoves in Honduras, to implement soil conservation measures in Lesotho, and to plant trees in China, El Salvador, Honduras and Kenya.

The Green Belt movement in Kenya *(see p.190)* is a remarkable example of women's leadership in local efforts to manage local resources. It also illustrates another important aspect of community efforts - that planning and help from higher levels of governments or NGOs are vital to success, so long as they're not viewed as interference. If people voluntarily curtail their overuse of a resource, like forest trees or wild animals, they must be offered support in developing alternative strategies, and compensated for their loss until these bear fruit - but always by methods in keeping with sustainable resource utilization. This approach is paramount in the modern concept of managing protected areas, especially the biosphere reserves *(see p.80)*, but should be applied in any community development programme.

Grassroots community efforts have another spin-off in addition to the actual practice of good conservation where it's most needed. People are stimulated to participate in public affairs, which in turn will make the politicians, educators, scientists, businesses, aid agencies, banks, and governments and NGOs more aware of and more responsive to the needs of the local community.

CASE STUDY
Community in action: the Chipko Movement

The historical roots of the Chipko Movement are to be found in the Bishnois or "Twentyniners" of Rajasthan in India, a Hindu sect for whom protection of trees and wild animals is a religious duty.

The sect was founded in the late 15th century by Jambeshwar the son of a village headman, who had a vision of man bringing disaster on himself by destroying nature. Renouncing his inheritance, he set out to teach people to care for their health and environment; enshrining his beliefs in 29 principles for living.

Still flourishing in modern India, the Bishnois' history includes an infamous incident when, in 1730, the Maharajah of Jodphur sent his axemen to cut down the few trees left in the area but the Bishnois forbade it. Enraged, the Maharajah's minister ordered the work to proceed, even after women rushed in, hugging the trees to protect them. Legend has it that 363 Bishnois women died on that day.

In the early 1960s, communities in the Himalayan ranges of northern India were faced with disaster. Twenty years of intensive and indiscriminate logging in the region combined with the demands of the growing population for firewood and land to cultivate had resulted in severe deforestation and torrential floods and landslides were commonplace. The able-bodied men were deserting the villages for the plains in search of work whilst the women were forced to travel further afield every day in search of firewood and water.

Chipko Andolan, the conservation movement of the Himalayas, was born in April 1973 when Chandi Prasad Bhatt, a community leader, urged the people of Gopeshwar to "hold fast", or "chipko", to the trees in their forest, which had been allocated to a sports company to make tennis racquets for export.

When the contractors arrived the village women flung their arms round the trees to prevent them being felled. Their successful action on that day rapidly inspired the spread of the movement among the hill women of other towns and districts in the north Indian states. The late Prime Minister Indira Ghandi subsequently gave the Chipko movement her blessing and advocated that all Indian states should take conservation measures to protect the nation's forests.

Sunderlal Bahaguna has said: "In one of our religious books it is written that a tree is like ten sons because it gives ten valuable things: oxygen, water, energy, food, clothes, timber, medicinal herbs, fodder, flowers and shade."

The state of Uttar Pradesh has now banned commercial felling in the hills.

Sunderlal Bahaguna on a visit to Geneva to receive a WWF award

Women of the Chipko movement protecting trees in northern India.

St Francis in meditation, painting by Francisco de Zurbaran

In September 1986, Assisi, Italy, home of St Francis, the patron saint of ecology, became the symbolic centre of ethical concern for our living planet. A major initiative by the World Wildlife Fund to celebrate its 25th Anniversary Year led to the events at Assisi - pilgrims from all the faiths and all the countries of the world gathered there for a conference on conservation and a multi-faith religious and cultural festival. Assisi was an invitation. An invitation to people to answer the challenge issued the World Conservation Strategy - that the world needs a new ethic of conservation and concern. An invitation to come as themselves - as Buddhists, Christians, Muslims, Jew or Hindus; as priests, imams or shamans; as storytellers, dancers, singers; as conservationists, philosophers, scientists, teachers, economists, or farmers - and to show that no one ideology has an exclusive claim to teach us how to save the earth.

Conservation today and tomorrow

The general awareness that our species is only one of the working components of the ecosphere, each of which buoys up the other, came about in the '60s and matured in the '70s. Now, more than halfway through the next decade, how is what we've learned being applied?

Grassroots community projects are springing up everywhere, but more importantly, they're being aided by other communities. The genuine empathy on the part of richer people for poorer people, among whom the need for rational conservation of resources is so clearly critical, is expressed by the growing number of communities in the North that "twin" themselves with those in the South. The idea was conceived by a town in Nova Scotia that provided direct aid to a village in the Ogaden Desert in Africa, and has been taken up by a number of cities in Canada and the United States, and now in Europe too. A London borough, Kensington and Chelsea, is linked to a group of villages in the Sudan, and finances tree-planting and education projects there.

More and more large companies are devoting efforts to research and development of technology that *prevents* environmental damage. Having had to take remedial measures (reluctantly in many cases, forced by public pressure and governments), they have found that prevention is less costly than cure. Even Shell, one of the culprits in the seeds scandal *(see page 140)*, describes in its company brochure the virtues of "integrated pest management", which involves the biological control of crop pests in conjunction with cautious and minimal use of chemical pesticides. It remains to be seen whether Shell is paying lip service to the concept, but as it has been announced, Shell's shareholders should insist that the company put its money where its mouth is.

The general environmental awareness of the '80s has produced some strange bedfellows. Commercial companies and nonpartisan, conservation-oriented think-tanks have begun to talk seriously to one another, and indeed, rely on one another. In Britain, the Centre for Economic and Environmental Development, born out of the British National Conservation Strategy, bridges the gap by co-ordinating technical expertise to advise business and industry on environmental matters, and meets part of its expenses by donations from them. Development banks and aid agencies have also teamed up with independent think-tanks. One of the most exciting projects has been undertaken by the World Bank, UNEP and an organization called World Resources Insititue (WRI) that operates out of Washington. A "task force", led by WRI personnel, researched and produced the document *Tropical Forests: A Call for Action*, which outlines in great detail an $8 billion programme for 1987-1991 to combat tropical deforestation. Whether the banks the governments and the private sector will come up with the money remains to be seen.

The other strange bedfellows involved in joint conservation in the '80s are perhaps not so strange - the NGOs directly concerned with wildlife and the environment. Although each has its particular style and strategy, some very different from others, they have shown that they can work together in effective collaboration. The Antarctic and Southern Ocean Coalition (see right) is a group of about 150 such organizations from 30 countries, including the World Wildlife Fund, Greenpeace, the Audubon Society, the Sierra Club and Friends of the Earth, all striving for the protection of the southern polar realm in perpetuity.

The present decade is a time of massive public response to environmental issues. People do take action now, whether it's about populations of species (ourselves included, witness Band Aid), whole species, habitats, whole ecosystems or the water we drink and air we breathe. And, finally, some people are even ready to listen again to the teachings of the great religions, so long forgotten, that wisely describe our true position and responsibility in the ecosphere. Whatever deities there are should find the World Conservation Strategy delightful reading.

CASE STUDY
Acting together: the Antarctic Coalition

The vast ice continent of Antarctica, the last great wilderness on Earth is a unique wildlife habitat, the feeding ground for millions of whales, seals, penguins and birds, and plays a key role in regulating our climate and the ocean ecosystem.

Since 1959, Antarctica and the waters south of 60° South Latitude have been under the general administration of the Antarctic Treaty Consultative Parties (ATCPs). The Treaty recognizes 'that it is in the interest of all mankind that Antarctica shall continue forever to be used exclusively for peaceful purposes and shall not become the scene or object of international discord'. It prohibits any 'measures of a military nature' or nuclear development, formally encouraging in their stead international cooperation in scientific investigation.

The original twelve signatories (Argentina, Australia, Belgium, Chile, France, Japan, New Zealand, Norway, South Africa, USSR, UK, USA) have been joined by seven other nations in recent years (Brazil, Chile, China, India, Poland, West Germany, Uruguay).

Seven ATCPs have laid claim to sovereignty over portions of the continent. Under Article IV of the Treaty, these territorial claims have been held in abeyance, with claimants and non-claimants "agreeing to disagree" over this contentious issue.

The ATCPs did successfully negotiate agreements on seals and other marine living resources. The original twelve ATCPs have unanimously accepted the Agreed Measures for the Conservation of Antarctic Fauna and Flora, and issued guidelines on expeditions, research bases, waste, protection of species and tourism.

However the newer Treaty members have not yet implemented these measures, which, in practice, are voluntary. The Treaty system lacks any centralized environmental review body or agreed regulatory authority.

Recently, the activities of this "club" of nations has begun to attract increasing concern from the international community, principally because the Treaty contains no provisions to govern exploitation of any resources in the Antarctic and, under its terms, cannot be modified in any way until 1991.

Concern has heightened particularly because of discussions amongst the ATCPs over exploitation of oil and mineral resources to be found in the Antarctic.

The result of this concern was the strengthening of the Antarctic and Southern Ocean Coalition (ASOC), an extraordinary global consortium, first formed in 1978, which now includes 150 major conservation and environmental organizations from WWF to Greenpeace, in 30 countries. Although excluded from any formal participation, this powerful group of world NGOs closely monitors all developments concerning Antarctic resource exploitation, and advises the powers – that – be on recommendations for new, environmentally sound terms for the Treaty when it is renewed in 1991.

ASOC believes Antarctica should be maintained as a "World Park", a demilitarized zone which would function as both an international science laboratory and a wildlife sanctuary, and proposes the establishment of an Antarctic Environmental Protection Agency to ensure these aims are met. It argues that Antarctica may be the best monitoring zone for global pollution, and is also concerned about the growing and uncontrolled exploitation of krill, the key component of the Antarctic ecosystem. Vast "swarms" of krill provide the main diet for the already endangered blue whales. ASOC recommends the establishment of sanctuaries in which krill fishing is banned.

These environmental and conservation organizations are also urging that governments agree to a long-term moratorium on all mineral exploitation in the region. As they point out, a battle over "strategic minerals" could endanger the continent's demilitarized status.

Below Antarctica, *the world's last wilderness. Adelie penguins abound on islands within the Antarctic circle.*

Individuals

Noah's Army
Ultimately, all the work of conservation rests on individuals, on people who care, from trained scientists and politicians to ordinary citizens. And these personal initiatives, small or large, happening all over the world, add up to a powerful force for change. Noah's Army is led, not by generals, but by the foot soldiers in the field.

RICHARD HILL
Richard Hill is best known as the founder of Birdland, the bird sanctuary at Bourton-on-the-Water, in the Cotswolds. But he also owns two penguin islands in the Falklands and has a special concern for these unusual birds. In 1985 ten King penguins were sent to him after being rescued from Taiwanese fishermen.

PHIL AGLAND
He was 27 when he set out for the Cameroon with borrowed money and camera equipment to make a documentary about Korup, Africa's richest surviving rain forest. He was to spend two and a half of the next five years making his film, which won the award for scientific achievement at the first international wildlife film festival. Korup then became the centre of Earthlife's campaign to protect and manage rainforests *(see p.199)*.

GERTRUDE BLOM
Gertrude Blom is a Swiss-born photographer and explorer, anthropologist and ecologist, who for more than forty years has been fighting to save the last great stretch of tropical rain forest in Central America.

Arriving in Mexico in 1940 from Europe, she became a member of the first government expedition into the Chiapas forest to make contact with the Lacandon Maya Indians, a group that hadn't yet been involved with missionaries.

She is still fighting for the forest and its peoples in her eighties. When she first went there the Lacandon covered 13,300 square kilometres and housed 2000 people; now only 6000 square kilometres remain and the population is 200,000.

Bob Geldof (with arm raised), and other stars, at the Live Aid concert.

DICK PITMAN
Conservationist Dick Pitman is a freelance writer and photographer who has conceived and spearheaded the campaign to save Zimbabwe's black rhinos, the last 2000 of which are threatened by poachers. Pitman, who spent considerable time in the wild as a game ranger, is also chairman of the Zambezi Society, which successfully campaigned to preserve the rhino's habitat.

The rhino campaign has raised more than $100,000 to date to equip an anti-poaching force in the Zambezi Valley, its efforts being linked to those of the Department of National Parks and Wildlife. A national rhino conservation strategy is in preparation.

SUE AND LES STOCKER
Britain's first hedgehog hospital has been established as part of the Wildlife Hospital run by Sue and Les Stocker at their home outside Aylesbury. A registered charity, it provides a complete health service for wild animals, including surgery and convalescent care. Patients have included snakes, bats, owls, minks and badgers.

BOB GELDOF
He has been described as a cross between Mother Teresa and James Dean. Born in Dublin, his unsettled childhood and turbulent schooldays made him an opinionated loner. His band, the Boomtown Rats, scored two Number One records before going out of style. He survived to achieve worldwide fame with Band Aid *(see p.196)*.

JOHN KIMMEY
The Talavaya Centre in Santa Fe, New Mexico, is the brainchild of John Kimmey, a former teacher and anthropologist. Established initially to preserve and perpetuate ancient seed strains such as Hopi blue corn and amaranth - a grain the Aztecs knew - it now also seeks to preserve both the foods and culture of the Pueblo and native Hispanic farmers who originally raised the plants.

The Centre, awarded a UN Medal for Environmental Leadership in June 1985, operates a sizeable farm garden and sells bushel baskets packed with 55 lbs of Southwest Indian crop seeds which aid groups can send to African farmers.

DIAN FOSSEY
One of the world's foremost primatologists, American naturalist Dian Fossey was brutally murdered on December 27th, 1985 by an unknown assailant who broke into her cottage.

For almost eighteen years she had made her home in the Virunga National Park in Rwanda, where she studied, befriended and protected a dwindling group of highly endangered mountain gorillas.

Originally an occupational therapist from Louisville, she was inspired by Dr Louis Leakey to begin her primate studies. In her early years at the Karisoke Research Centre that she established in Rwanda, she fought a constant battle to drive Watutsi cattle from the national park and stop farmers from degrading the forest.

Top *Jeremy Mallinson of Jersey*   Above *Alison Richard with lemurs*

But it was the poachers who became her main obsession even before they killed her favourite gorilla Digit on December 31st, 1977. A motherless three year old, Digit was the first of the gorillas to trust her and for 13 years they lived side by side. A fund she established in his memory continues to finance anti-poaching patrols.

She was buried, as she wished it, in a cemetery she built for gorillas killed by poachers. The gorillas that remain owe their survival to her efforts. Her work and her life and death will not be forgotten.

ALISON RICHARD

The author first met Alison Richard in the early '70s in a forest in Madagascar, where she was promptly given a lesson in how to cook properly on a camp stove. A professor at Yale University, Alison studies the population ecology of the rare lemurs of Madagascar, particularly in the arid south. She and her colleagues in America and Madagascar work closely with the *firaisana* (local community) to protect a remnant of forest where the lemurs live. The people have built a barrier of cactus around it, and funds from the project, partially supported by the WWF, have paid for an underground water reservoir for the village.

JEREMY MALLINSON

Jeremy Mallinson has led the international effort to recover live contraband more precious than gold. The Golden-headed lion tamarin is one of the rarest monkeys in Brazil and hotly traded on the world black market. Jeremy and his team are persuading the holders of "illegal" tamarins to restore ownership to Brazil and to place the animals in proper facilities in Brazil and elsewhere. The tamarins will be managed internationally as an integrated breeding group to ensure the survival of the species until adequate protection in the wild is achieved. Jeremy is the Zoological Director of the Jersey Wildlife Preservation Trust.

THE McKEEVERS

Larry and Kay McKeever are the founders of the Owl Rehabilitation Research Foundation (ORRF), based in Ontario, Canada, where every year more than one hundred owls from across Canada and the USA are treated. Of these birds some fifty per cent are rehabilitated for release back into the wild.

Their pioneering work has been in using damaged wild owls for captive breeding. Seven native Canadian species have bred annually at the centre since 1975 and the McKeevers have shown that it is possible later to release captive offspring into the wild successfully .

JOHN HORSMAN

A British farmer, John Horsman is successfully reaping a commercial harvest while employing policies which many said would not work. John runs his 350 acres with two staff, devoting about six per cent of his land to conservation. He set about tree-planting as soon as he took over the farm, preserves his old high hedgerows, re-thatches his own old barns, and has reclaimed and preserved 11 ponds on his land. Wildlife is flourishing, and the farm is doing well, too. In 1986, John Horsman won the top Country Life award as the farmer who has done most in all the UK to encourage wildlife conservation on his land, and yet farm commercially.

Conclusion

To halt and reverse the deterioration of the ecosphere, to let Gaia refresh and renew herself, to stop the rot that is weakening the Ark and help repair the timbers - this is the single most urgent task challenging our species in today's uneasy, but on the whole still peaceful world. Should we soon suffer global war, I am convinced that the root cause will be environmental, and not religious, cultural, or even social, although the immense pressure of human numbers and their immense demands on natural resources will most likely spark it off. If global war comes, the result will not be as it was for the last two: much suffering and destruction, but afterward a new age of technological advance and a mood of optimism. No. It will bring devastation, regression and despair, maybe forever, or at least for a very long time. And the unsolved issues of human development and the conservation of natural resources which caused it will be regarded in what's left of human memory as no more than a feather carried away on the wind.

Let's assume that global war does not overtake the planet, and that we pay serious attention to the idea that, for the sake of the future, conservation and development should go hand in hand. The diverse troops of Noah's Army have come up with many different ways of proceeding.

There are "stop-gap" measures, aimed at saving human populations, natural habitats or whole species of plants and animals imminently threatened with death, devastation or extinction. In theory, these measures are straightforward, for it takes only money and good will to implement them. In practice, they are very complicated, usually because not enough money can be raised before it's too late, and in the case of preservation of habitat, the good will of the "saviours" often clashes with the strong will of other people using or intending to use the region. Some users can be overruled by their governments, whereas others must be compensated for their losses, and again it boils down to a question of money. Of course, there are some great success stories, in which lack of money or clash of will were overcome. Huge sums, for instance, have been raised by rock concerts, whose organizers ensure that the money actually gets to the starving people for whom it's intended. Extensive networks of national parks or reserves have been established in tropical countries whose forests are being lost at an alarming rate, as in Central America. Big, expensive rescue operations have been undertaken by governments and conservation groups to save particular animal species, from tigers and pandas to condors and mountain gorillas. But what are the prospects for the long-term success of these stop-gap measures in the face of the growing human population and its growing demands for natural resources?

Another option favoured by some very powerful battalions of Noah's Army is the massive application of modern technology as the long-term solution to environmental problems. The proponents of technology are absolutely right that it can solve some of the problems, for we have gone so far down the road of applying it wrongly that the planet needs extra help in cleaning up the messes. But the question is: what sort of technology? This option has a great deal of funds at its disposal, in contrast to the previously mentioned ones, especially if the schemes are large and grandiose. People like to spend money on such things as new dams, irrigation works, agricultural chemicals, human settlements, and laboratories because someone - a company, a bank, a government - usually gets a kick-back, not necessarily money, but something just as important, like political good will. Therefore, the backers and partners are in such a rush that the planners can't see the wood for the trees.

They take little account of the eventual consequences of how the technology is applied. Why, for example, are big dams proposed when little dams would serve the need for electricity and do less damage to the environment? What's worse, however, is that sometimes the planners of such schemes do take account of the consequences - there's no excuse not to now, for the response of the environment to most such activities is well known - but the lure of short-term gain often tips the balance towards "development" that will result in long-term loss.

These negative aspects of mega-technology do not mean that all today's supporters of technological schemes are afflicted with short-sightedness or greed. The new movement toward "appropriate" technology, adapted to the community or environment it must serve, is having some success. A lot of research has gone into developing clean and efficient ways to use resources, from the recycling of noxious wastes by industry to fuel-saving cooking stoves. There are innovative ideas too for more sustainable patterns of resource use, requiring little in the way of material technology. The product of good scientific observation and experimentation, these include rotational pasturage for wildlife and livestock, new designs of fish nets to exclude or release large animals, and restrictions on exploration of the tundra to winter when traffic can use snow-packed roads rather than damage the fragile vegetation of summer.

Whereas money can provide for stop-gap measures and sensible technological and other initiatives, it cannot take care of the rest of the solutions proposed by Noah's Army. A return to some of the older traditions of sustainable resource use, suitably modified to work in modern times, may require at first an input of money, to compensate people for losses incurred by, for example, planting something other than cash crops or reducing the amount of pesiticides they use. But the support of communities for new ideas, or the decision by others to go back permanently to "traditional" and less wasteful lifestyles (even if it simply entails having one automobile in the family or not using so many electric lights) are things that money can't buy.

The argument for returning to traditions is unhelpful, however, in situations where they worked well only in the context of low human populations. The practices of shifting cultivation and subsistence livestock herding are today devastating tropical ecosystems, but the people are behaving no differently from their forebears. It's just that there are nearly a billion and a half more people in the tropics now than in 1950.

The other strategies put forward to ensure that human development and conservation of natural resources proceed together are very grand and global.

One of these strategies is that people adopt an *eco*-political in place of the current *geo*-political worldview. Conventional politics assumes that sovereign nation-states are the supreme and autonomous units that define and direct global affairs. But so many of the affairs now that spark international disputes are those that cannot be contained within national boundaries, no matter how hard we try, whether it's refugees fleeing from their ravaged soils or one nation's pollutants, deliberate or accidental, poisoning another's fish stocks, forests or people. Conventional politicians and respected statesmen must begin to realize that human well-being is reliant on the condition, not of nations, but of the ecosphere. Long-lasting friendly relationships will best emerge out of cooperation over the management of ecosystems, even if they're labelled on the map as "belonging" mostly to this country or that.

Another of the strategies calls for a change in the world economic order. It involves a carefully worked out transition from a growth economy, in which everyone strives to get richer, to a steady-state economy in which everyone gets only as rich as sustainable use of resources allows. But because some people live at and below subsistence level now, a halt to material growth would condemn them to misery forever, and so a redistribution of wealth would be required. It needn't take the form of a bloody revolution. It would take the good will of people in the rich nations to retreat from *over*-development and help the people of poor nations to advance from *under*-development. Paul Ehrlich, the eminent American ecologist, points out that this doesn't mean that rich people would have to live in caves and cook over buffalo chips. In 1980 he calculated that if each person in the United States decided to cut energy consumption by half, the level of energy use in the States would be the equivalent of that in France. My husband and I have a little house in France - I can say with authority that one lives very comfortably in that wonderful country.

We conservationists have sometimes been warned off by the economists, told not to meddle with things we don't understand. But it can be said of the conventional economists (and the politicians they advise) that *they* meddle with things they don't understand - the workings of the ecosphere and the role that every species, including our own, must play in recycling its set of finite resources.

Finally, there is the "strategy" that appeals to the human spirit - our species' deep feeling for nature and the living beings that share the planet with us, as once encouraged by the great religions. Real love and respect for nature - for Gaia, or Mother Earth, or whatever name anyone gives to her spiritual form - can only lead to greater understanding of her, and indeed of ourselves, for we are just as much a part of her as every sparrow, every tree and every waterfall. Gandhi is supposed to have said that some people are so poor that God can only appear to them in the form of bread. If we can understand that bread comes from grain, which comes from plants, which come from soil, water, air, light and people's energies in the fields, then what so desperately needs to be done to save the world and all living things will follow quite naturally.

All these actions or proposals - those that money can buy, like the various rescue operations for humans, habitats and whole species of plants and animals, and those it can't, like the decision to use the best of the old traditions and the switch from conventional politics, economics and religion to a more ecological worldview - could combine to save the world. But virtually none of them have any long-term value unless every person on the planet is committed to seeing them through. They can be organized and helped along by the various sectors of society, like government, business, science and education, that operate at a higher level than the individual. But they will *never work* if they're *imposed* on people from on high.

This is the lesson I've learned from writing this book, and why the book ended with a chapter called "Noah's Army". It is individual effort that stimulates another person to make an effort, and another and another, until finally the sectors of society to which they belong also make the effort. This lesson is also a lesson from biology, not surprisingly. Evolution is the change over generations in features that characterize a species - as when the ancestors of giraffes grew longer necks or the ancestors of penguins grew smaller wings - and it operates at the level of the individual. Individuals respond to their environment by living or dying. Those that live pass on the features that allow them to cope with their environment to their offspring, who then, if they live, pass them on to the next generation. So the features spread through succeeding generations to become characteristic of the species. The changes needed in the human way of thinking and behaving towards Gaia, if we are to be sure that our children and grandchildren will indeed live on and inherit her promise of happiness, will be brought about only if each and everyone of us decides to make them.

Think globally, act locally - a guide for individual action

Any guidelines for individual thought and behaviour toward Gaia are likely to be incomplete, because people's situations are so very different from one another. On finishing this book, however, I've come up with the following ones that seem to me to be generally applicable and not too presumptuous, given the gravity of what we've done and are doing to our Ark.

● **Have children at "replacement rate".**
This means having only two surviving children for every couple. If you've not had children yet, seriously consider having only one, or none. If you've had your children, and more than two, tell them you'd be delighted with no more than four healthy grandchildren.

● **Learn about the environment.**
If you're going to school or college, include one or more of the environmental sciences in your studies, preferably ecology. If you've finished school, you could go back and take an ecology course. If you've never been to school, nor have the opportunity to go now, ask others who've been what ecology is all about or watch environmental programmes on TV. Even if you live in a little village far away from a city, it is possible to get films and teachers to come to the village by asking your community leaders to contact someone in central government.

● **Read the World Conservation Strategy.**
(Or have it read aloud to you.) It is available from IUCN (1196 Gland, Switzerland) in English, French, Spanish and other languages, for about $5. If you cannot afford it, ask your library or local government office to obtain it. Then find out about your own country's National Conservation Strategy. If one has not been prepared, ask your government why.

● **Think about the consequences of your profession, and of your lifestyle.**
If they are damaging to the environment, directly or indirectly, adjust your behaviour accordingly. Try to persuade friends and work colleagues to do the same. If you or they don't know how, or can't, ask for information and help to make the adjustments. If you are in a position of influence at work, use it to help the environment.

● **Respect the resources of the planet.**
Try to keep your "consumption" of new goods within reasonable levels, and not to waste or overconsume water, energy, or food (especially meat). Be an alert consumer, too - read up on endangered species or cruel farming practices, and avoid buying their products. And support local efforts at conserving resources, such as bottle banks, or collection of waste paper, for recycling.

● **Join a local environmental organization.**
Join an organization that promotes rational use of the environment near to you, or appreciation of nature. But first read its publicity brochures and examine its accounts (or ask someone you trust to tell you these things) to make sure that you wholeheartedly believe in what the organization is doing and know that it is spending money wisely. Support your chosen organisation in the best way you can, offering your money or your services.

● **Join a national and an international environmental organization.**
Organizations which are concerned with wider issues, or with help to communities and environments overseas, need your support. Again choose them carefully, but then give your best effort.

● **Use your vote well.**
Enquire about the environmental policies of political parties, as well as those of individual candidates for local government or people running for election to central government, or even people standing for office on committees or other groups you are involved in. Then use your vote well, and press your elected representative to lobby on environmental issues.

● **Care for animals and plants.**
Be sensitive to the needs of animals and plants around you. Don't trample on, or uproot wild plants. Protect trees if you have them on your land. Be kind to animals, and respect them. If it is necessary to kill an animal, do it without causing it to suffer.

● **Defend your own ecosystem.**
Be sensitive to the needs of the ecosystem you live in, and if you see it threatened with degradation that could cause even a minor malfunction, help raise a strong public outcry. If your ecosystem has been damaged, participate in a public programme - or start one yourself - to rehabilitate it.

If every person in the world planted and nurtured one tree, Gaia would be eternally grateful.

Sources

Map References
The base maps are mostly drawn to a homolographic equal area projection adapted from Gall's. Species and habitat data from IUCN/CMC unless otherwise specified.

CHAPTER 1
Pages 20-21   The ark in motion
Ehrlich, P.R. and A.H., and J.P. Holdren *Ecoscience* W.H. Freeman 1977. Strahler, A.N. and A.H., *Introduction to Environmental Sciences* Hamilton 1974. Cox, Healey and Moore *Biogeography* 1973. Simmons, I.G. *Biogeography: Natural and Cultural*, 1979. Meggars, B.J., Ayensu, E.S. and Duckworth, W.D. eds. *Tropical Forest Ecosystems in Africa and S. Africa* 1973 Smithsonian Inst. Press. *African Journal of Ecology* 19, 1-6, 1981. *Scientific American* Sept. 1970. *The Times Atlas of the World*, Times Books, London. "El Nino's ill wind" *National Geographic* Vol. 165, 1984

Pages 24-5   Life support systems
Ecoscience (ibid). Krebs, C.J. *Ecology* 1978. *Biogeography* (ibid).

Pages 28-9   No room for our friends
McEvedy *Atlas of World Population History*, Times Books, London. *Ecoscience* (ibid). UN population trends. Myers, N. *The Gaia Atlas of Planet Management*, Pan Books, 1985. *Global 2000* A Report to the President 1980.

Pages 32-3   Damaging the ark
World Conservation Strategy IUCN, UNEP, WWF, Geneva 1980. UN desertification figures.

CHAPTER 2
Pages 40-41   Life communities
"A Classification of the Biogeographical Provinces of the World by Miklos D. F. Udvardy", *IUCN Occasional Paper* No. 18, Switzerland, 1975. Atjay, G. L., P. Ketner and P. Duvigneaud, *The Global Carbon Cycle*, John Wiley, New York, 1979.

Pages 46-7   Forests under threat
Udvardy (ibid). Forest Resources Assessment Project, FAO, 1981. *Paradise Lost?* Earthlife in association with *The Observer*, 1986 *GEMS Pack Information Series 3*. Williams, D.L. and Miller, D., NASA, 1979, *Monitoring Forest Canopy Alteration with Landsat*.

Pages 54-5   Open lands
Erosion hotspots from information supplied by Hall, D.O., and N. Myers in *The Gaia Atlas of Planet Management* (ibid).

Pages 62-3   Wetlands, lakes and rivers
The Times Atlas (ibid). IUCN data. *Ecoscience* (ibid).

Pages 70-1   The ocean wilderness
Map projection after Athelstan Spilhaus. *Ecoscience* (ibid). *The Times Atlas of the Oceans*, Times Books. IUCN data and occasional papers.

Pages 76-7   Islands - evolution in isolation

The Times Atlas (ibid). Endemic plant taxa and threats from IUCN/CMC Threatened Plants Unit.

Pages 80-1   Protecting our heritage
Batisse, M. *The Biosphere Reserve: Tool for Environmental Conservation and Management* Foundation for Environmental Conservation, Switzerland, 1982. "Threatened protected areas of the world", *IUCN Bulletin*, Vol 15, No 7-9. *IUCN Bulletin*, Vol. 15, No 7-9. IUCN data base. UNESCO.

CHAPTER 3
Pages 90-1   The plant kingdom
IUCN Conservation Monitoring Centre and Threatened Plants Unit. WWF Plants Campaign Fact Sheet. Trautmann, Dr. W. "Threatened Vascular Plants" in *European Nature Conservation - 20 years on*, 1984.

Pages 94-5   Plant diversity
IUCN Conservation Monitoring Centre and Threatened Plants Unit. World Bank Data.

Pages 98-9   The animal kingdom
IUCN database. *The Gaia Atlas of Planet Management* (ibid). Richlefs, R.E. *The Economy of Nature*. British Museum estimates.

Pages 102-3   Invertebrates - the teeming millions
The IUCN Invertebrate Red Data Book, IUCN, Gland (1983). *A Field Guide in Color to Insects* by Jiri Zahradnik, Octopus, 1977. IUCN database. Myers *et al The Gaia Atlas* (ibid). *Global 2000 - A report to the President*, 1980.

Pages 108-9   Vertebrates - threatened on all fronts
The IUCN *Red Data Books* (Mammals, Amphibia, Reptilia) and IUCN database. ICPB. Simmons *Biogeography* (ibid).

Pages 114-15   The plant eaters
"The Status of Rhinos in Africa" by David Western and Lucy Vigne. *SWARA* March/April 1985. "A Time for Decision" Elephants and Rhinos in Africa IUCN 1982. Black rhino range in *Oryx*, Vol. 19, No. 4, p.216.

Pages 118-19   Invertivores
IUCN data base. Stebbings, Dr. R. E., Institute of Terrestrial Ecology. *Red Data Books*.

Pages 122-3   The meat eaters
"The Peregrine Falcon," RSPB Information Sheet. Woodwell, G.M., Wurster, C.F., and Isaacson, P.A. (1967). "DDT residues in an east coast estuary; a case of biological concentration of a persistent insecticide." *Science* 156 821-824, IUCN *Red Data Books*.

Pages 126-7   Creatures of the Sea
The Times Atlas of the Oceans, Times Books, London. International Whaling Commission papers. *Ecoscience* (ibid). *Red Data Books*.

Pages 130-131   Animals on the move
The Mystery of Migration edited by Robin Baker, Macdonald, London (1980). "Ascension Island Green Turtles", Archie Carr. *Copeia*, 1975, No.3. "Conserving the

Monarch Butterfly", Rodolfo Ogarrio, *Focus/WWF US*, May/June 1984. *Bird Migration*, Chris Mead *Country Life. The Evolutionary Ecology of Animal Migration*, R.R. Baker, Hodder & Stoughton, 1978. *The Migrations of Birds*, Jean Dorst, Heinemann, 1962. "Flying Visitors" - a map prepared by ICBP, UNEP and COMMPACT.

Pages 134-5   Trading in the wild
"Recent developments in the raw ivory trade of Hong Kong and Japan", J.R. Caldwell, *WWF Traffic Bulletin*, June 1984, Vol. VI, No.2. Caldwell, J.R. and Jonathan Barzdo, "The World Trade in Raw Ivory", 1983 and 1984, a report prepared for the CITES Secretariat (IUCN), March 1985. Van den Berg, M., van der Plas-Haarsma, M. and Wijker, N., "An analysis of Psittachines Imported at Schiphol Airport during 1980 and 1981", *WWF Traffic Bulletin*, May 1983, Vol V, No. 1. *Focus* WWF-US Vol. 5, No. 5, Sept 1983.

Pages 138-9   International protection
RAMSAR Convention publications. UNEP Regional Seas Programme report. ICBP.

CHAPTER 4
Land cover data from *The Times Atlas of the World*, Times Books, London 1983. National Parks data from IUCN and government sources.

Pages 151   The spread of agriculture and civilization
Lee and De Vore *Man the Hunter* (1968) Aldine Press. *The Times Atlas of World History*, Times Books, London. McEvedy C. and R. Jones, *Atlas of World Population History* Allen Lane 1978.

Pages 152-3   Europe
Norwegian Institute for Water Research data in *Time* 8.11.1982. EEC data. WWF study papers. *New Scientist* 10 May 1984.

Pages 156-7   Africa
Harrison, P., "Land and people, the growing pressure", Earthwatch paper 13, 1983. "The changing forest - the Tai project" UNESCO Courier, 1981. "Wildlife driven to the wall in the Kalahari" *Sunday Times* June 1985.

Pages 162-3   North America
National Atmospheric Deposition Program data in *Time* 8.11.1982. US Dept. of Agriculture data in *Wildlife Digest* 9.1985. UN center for Housing, Building and Planning (Waste). Sierra Club papers.

Pages 166-7   Latin America
Harrison P. "Land and people, the growing pressure" Earthwatch paper 13 1983. "Brazil - Atlantic Forests" IUCN/WWF paper. *Oryx* Vol. 18 No. 1. "Nicaragua" IUCN Tropical Forest Campaign fact sheet. *Guardian* article 23.10. 1985 World Bank data in Kurian, G. T. *The New Book of World Rankings*.

Pages 170-1   North Asia
China Vol 5 No. 1 1980 World Bank. FAO. IUCN data.

Pages 174-5   Southern Asia
Harrison, P. "Land and people, the growing pressure" Earthwatch paper 13, 1983. *Environmental Conservation 12 (3) 1985. Tropical Forests: A Call for Action* (ibid).

Pages 180-1   Australia and Oceania
Ambio 11.5.1982. *Wildlife* December 1982. "Fraser Island: an environmental milestone", *New Scientist* 26.5.1977. ICBP, *Asian Pacific Environment* Vol.3 No.3 1985

CHAPTER 5
Page 187   The rise of Noah's army
The Yearbook of International Organizations 1985/6. McCormick, J. *User's Guide to the Environment* Kagan & Page 1985. Lowe, P. and J. Goyder, *Environmental Groups in Politics* George Allen and Unwin, London.

Page 189 WWF/IUCN projects
IUCN Annual Report 1983/4; WWF Australia papers and reports; WWF NO newsletters.

Pages 197   Money - where it comes from
Partnership for Conservation, IUCN 1985. *Tropical Forests; a Call for Action* 1985, World Resources Institute, Washington. World Bank data.

General Text References

Ehrlich, P.R., A.H. Ehrlich and J.P. Holdren. 1977, *Ecoscience,* W. H. Freeman. *Gaia Atlas of Planet Management,* 1985, Gen. Ed. N. Myers, Pan Books. *The Global 2000 Report to the President,* 1982, Penguin. *World Conservation Strategy,* 1980, IUCN, UNEP, WWF. Smith, R.L., 1980, *Ecology and Field Biology,* Harper and Row. Ehrlich, P.R. and A.H. Ehrlich, 1981, *Extinction,* Random House.

General Chapter References

CHAPTER I
Lovelock, J., 1979, *Gaia, A new look at life on Earth,* O.U.P.

CHAPTER II
Moore, D.M. (ed.), 1982, *Green Planet,* C.U.P. Strahler, A.N. and A.H. Strahler, 1974, *Introduction to Environmental Science,* UNEP, 1982. *GEMS* report.

CHAPTER III
Grzimek's Animal Life Encyclopaedia, 1972, Gen. Ed. B. Grzimek, Van Nostrand Reinhold Co. *Red Data Books,* IUCN, ICBP (birds). *IUCN Bull.,* 1985, 16 (1-3). *IUCN Bull.* 1984. 15 (7-9)

CHAPTER V
McCormick, J., 1985, in *User's Guide to the Environment,* Earthscan.

Specific Text References

INTRODUCTION
Collar, N, 1986, *Oryx* 20 (1). Hanks, J., 1984, *The Environmentalist 4* Suppl. No. 7. "Population Misconceptions", 1984, Population Concern, London. Beskes, F., 1985, *Env. Conserv.* 12 (3). *The Bible.*

CHAPTER I
Page 19 "Biosphere" in *Encyclopaedia Britannica*
Page 24 Cheke, A.S., 1984, in *Biogeography and Ecology of the Seychelle Islands. New Scientist* 25 August 1983.
Page 28 Gould, M.S. and I.R. Swingland, 1980, *Biol. Conserv.* Diamond, J.M., 1986, *Nature* 320:112.
Page 32 Whittaker, R.H., 1975, *Communities and Ecosystems.* Christian, J.J., 1983, *Natural History,* Oct King, E., 1980, *Uniterra,* Nov/ Dec.
Page34 World Bank, 1985, *Rapid Growth and Human Carrying Capacity.* Fisher, J., N. Simon and J. Vincent, 1969, *Wildlife in Danger,* Viking.
Page 36 "An Introduction to the World Conservation Strategy", 1984, IUCN and UNEP.

CHAPTER II
Page 39 McNeely, J.A., 1984, in *Conservation, Science & Society,* UNESCO. Kusten, B., 1971, *The Age of Mammals,* Weidenfeld and Nicholson. Simmons, I.G., 1979, *Biogeography.* Miller, 1980, Phd Thesis, Stirling University. Cracraft, J., 1980(?) *Nat. Hist.*
Page 44 Shard, M., 1980, *The Theft of the Countryside,* Temple Smith.
Page 48 Middleton, J. and G. Merriam, 1985, *Biol. Conserv.* 33: 133-145. Chapman and Feldhammer, 1982, *Wild Mammals of North America.* Voronitsyn, S. 1982, *Radio Liberty Research 198-.*
Page 50-52 Whitaker, R.H., 1976, *Communities and Ecosystems. GEMS Information Series* No.3., Nairobi, April 1982. Guppy, N., 1984, *Foreign Affairs* 62 (4): 928-965. Earthlife in assoc. with *The Observer,* 1986, *Paradise Lost?.* Berkmuller, K., 1984., IUCN. *IUCN Bull.,* 1980, 11 (5). Westoby, J., 1983., *IUCN Bull. 14* (10-12). Poore, D., 1978, UCN General Assembly Paper. Caufield, C., 1983, *New Scientist* 1 Sept. Jacobs, M., 1980, *BioIndonesia* No.7. Whitmore, T.C., 1980, in *Conservation Biology,* Sinauer. Lanly, J.P., 1982, *Tropical Forest Resources,* FAO, Rome. Stiles, F. G., 1985, ICBP Tech. Publ. No. 4. *Tropical Forests: A Call to Action,* 1985, World Resources Institute, Washington.
Page 56 *Ecology of North America.* Chapman and Feldhammer, *op cit.* Mondor, C. and S. Kun, 1984, in *National Parks, Conservation and Development,* Smithsonian Press. *Environmental Research Perspectives in South Africa,* 1984, S.A. Nat. Sci. Progr. Report. Kortlandt, A., in *The Tropical Rain-Forest: The Leeds Symposium:* 205-226
Page 58 World Bank, 1985, *Rapid Growth and Human Carrying Capacity.* Newby, J., 1982, *WWF Monthly Report,* June, Project 1624.
Page 60 Dunbar, M.J., Chernov, Y.I., 1985, *The Living Tundra.* C.U.P. Burton, R. briefing notes.
Pages 66-8 *IUCN Bull.,* 1985, Oct.-Dec. Lovejoy, T.E., 1985, in *Amazonia,* Pergamom Press. 328-338. IUCN 1984 Wetlands Pack I. SSC Newsletter, 1984, No.3. Kusler, J.A., 1983, *Our National Wetland Heritage,* Environment Law Institute. WWF pamphlet, "Wetlands". Botts, L., 1982, *Parks 6* (4). Barnes, E.A., *Estuarine Ecology,* Inst. of Biol.

series. Dahl, L., 1975, in publication of Nat. Parks Authority, New Zealand.
Page 72 Wells, S., 1985, *Oryx 19* (3). Salm, R.V. and J.R. Clark., 1984, in *Marine and Coastal Protected Areas,* IUCN.
Page 74 Mitchell, B. and J. Tinker., 1980, *Antarctica and its Resources,* Earthscan. Salm, R.V. and J.R. Clark., 1984, in *Marine and Coastal Protected Areas,* IUCN. Wilson, R., 1986, *WWF News 39.*
Page 78 Fisher, J., N. Simon and J. Vincent., 1969, *Wildlife in Danger,* The Viking Press. Burns, C.W., 1984, in *National Parks, Conservation and Development,* Smithsonian Press. Long, J.L., 1981, *Introduced Birds of the World,* Universe Books. Loope, L.L., and C.P. Stone, 1983, in *First International Biosphere Reserve Congress,* Minsk. Salm, R.V. and J.R. Clark., 1984, in *Marine and Coastal Protected Areas,* IUCN.
Page 82 Miller, K.R., Biosphere Reserves in concept and practice". Diamond, J.M., 1975, *Biol. Conserv.* 7: 129-146. Willis, E.O., 1974, *Ecological Monographs* 44: 153-169. Burton, R., 1982, *Wildlife,* March 11. Myers, N., 1979, *New Scientist* 23 August. Lusigi, W. and J. Robertson, 1981, *UNESCO Courier,* April. Nair, N.C., 1978, *Journal of the Kerala Natural History Society* 2: 17-21.
Page 84 Garratt, K., 1984., in *National Parks, Conservation and Development,* Smithsonian Press. Lucas, P.H.C., 1984, in *National Parks, Conservation and Development,* Smithsonian Press. Batisse, M., 1982, *Env. Conserv. 9.* (2). *Tropical Forests; A Call to Action,* 1985, World Resources Institute, Washington. Bull, G.A., 1982, In *Towards the Biosphere Reserve,* Proc. of Int. Symp. U.S. Department of the Interior.
Page 86 Eltringham, S.K., 1984, *Wildlife Resources and Economic Development,* John Wiley and Sons. *Parks 1* (2): 1-4. Sayer, J.A., 1981, *Parks 5* (4): 13-15. Stockly, M., 1984, *Nexus 6* (3): 1-7. Budowski, G., *Parks.* Thresher, P., 1981, *World Animal Review 40.* Abrahams, E.A., 1983, *Parks 7* (4): 12-13. Suvanakorn, P. and R.J. Dobias, 1985, in *Conserving Asia's Natural Heritage,* IUCN. *MAB 34:,* 1975 (Original meeting on integrated ecological research and training needs in southern Asian mountain systems.) Jefferies, B.E., 1984, in *National Parks, Conservation and Development,* Smithsonian Press.

CHAPTER III
Page 89 Kuengler, E.J., 1961, *Limnol. Oceanogr.* 6: 400-415 (cited in *South,* 1980. Lucas, G.L., 1984, in *National Parks, Conservation and Development,* Smithsonian Press. Nault, L.R. and W.R. Findley, 1982, *Desert Plants 3* (4).
Page 94-6 Chhabra, R., H.S. Baddesha and D.L.N. Rao, 1985, *Ambio 14* (16). Plants Campaign Fact Sheets, WWF/IUCN. WWF *Wetlands Pack 2.* Threatened Plants Unit, *Plant Pack 2.* Moore, D.M. (ed.), 1982, *Green Planet,* C.U.P. Prescott-Allen, R., 1984, *WWF Monthly Report,* March.
Pages 102 and 104 Collins, N.M., 1980, *Tropical Ecology and Development,* 113-121. Salm, R.V., G. Usher and I.S. Suwelo, 1984, *WWF Monthly Report* Project 3108. Speight, M.C.D., 1985, *Naturopa 49.* Edwards, J., 1982, *Financial Times* 25 September. *Wildlife,*

SOURCES

1983 September. Deakin, R., 1981, *Wildlife 23* (5). Tepedino, V.J., 1979, *Great Basin Naturalist Memoirs*, No.3. Brigham Young University. Bourne, R., 1975, *Defenders of Wildlife*. Munro, J.L., 1982, Paper presented at 35th meeting, Gulf and Caribbean Fisheries Institute, Nassau. Usher, G., R.V. Salm, I.S. Suwelo, 1984, *WWF Monthly Report* Project 1819.

Pages 108 and 110 Opler, P.A., 1977, *The Science Teacher* 44, (1). Oliver, W.L.R., 1985, Memorandum to Conservation Committee, Wildlife Preservation Trust. Fisher, J., N. Simon and J. Vincent, 1969, *Wildlife in Danger*, Viking.

Page 114 Sokolov, V.E. and B.D. Abaturov, 1984, *Acta Zool. Fennica 172*: 247-249. Kotlandt, A., in *The Tropical Rain-Forest: the Leeds Symposium*: 205-226. Eltringham, S.K., 1984, *Wildlife Resources and Economic Development*, John Wiley and Sons.

Page 118 Rose, C., 1985, *WWF News 38*. Wachtel, P.S., 1985, *International Wildlife* May/June. Connell, G.W. and J.A. Friend, 1985, *Landscape 1* (2) 21-26. Newman, J.R., E. Novakova and J.T. McClave, 1985, *Biol. Conserv. 31*: 229-248.

Page 122 Ehrenfield, D.W., 1970, *Biological Conservation*, Holt, Rinehart and Winston. Eltringham, *op cit*.

Page 128 Holt, S., 1985, *WWF News No.38*. Holt, S., 1983, *Oryx XVII*.

Page 132 *IUCN Bull.* 1984, 15 (1-3). Caldecott, J. and S. Caldecott, 1985, *New Scientist* 15 August. Archibald, G., 1981, *Natural History 90* (3). Burton, R., (unpubl. manuscript). Animal Research and Conservation Centre, 1982. Thiollay, J.M., 1985, in *Migratory Birds: Problems and Prospects in Africa*, ICBP.

Page 136 Inskipp, T. and S. Wells, 1979, *International Trade in Wildlife*, Earthscan. Lyster, S., 1985, *International Wildlife Law*. Hyman, R., 1985, *International Wildlife* (Jan/Feb). Sand, P.H., 1980, *Naturopa*. Joyce, C., 1985, *New Scientist* Dec. Barzdo, J., *IUCN Bull. 14* (10-12). Caldwell, J.R., and J. Barzdo, 1985, Report prepared for the CITES Secretariat on Ivory Trade.

Page 140 Griggs, T., 1983, *Garden* (Jan/Feb). *The Guardian*, 1986, 14 Feb. Allain. A., 1982, *Development Forum*, Jan/Feb. Eltringham *op cit*.

Page 142 Strahm, W., 1985, *WWF Monthly Report*, June, Project 3149. T.P.C. Newsletter, 1980, No.5.

Page 144 *Botanic Gardens and the World Conservation Strategy*, 1985, International Conference organised by IUCN. Thompson, P.A., "Preservation of Plant Resources and Gene Banks within Botanic Gardens". Veprintsev, B.N. and N. Rott, 1979, *Nature 280*.

Page 146 Background and position paper on "Introductions, reintroductions and restocking" 1983 IUCN. "Reintroduction of Species", 1985, Memo from the Directorate of Environment and Local Authorities for Council of Europe. *Botanic Gardens and the World Conservation Strategy*, 1985, Excursion Guide.

CHAPTER IV

Page 154 Jackson, P., 1985, *IUCN Bull. 16* (7-9). *WWF News*, 1984, Jan/Feb. Grout-

Smith, T., 1986, *BBC Wildlife*, Feb. Mitchell, D., 1985, *Env. Conserv. 12* (1). Caufield, C., 1984, *New Scientist* 10 May. *World Bird Watch*, 1985, (1). Mallinson, J., 1978, *The Shadow of Extinction*, Macmillan.

Pages 158 and 160 *Desertification in the Sahel: Diagnosis and Proposals for IUCN's Response*, March 1985, Conservation for Development Centre. Glantz, M.H. and R.W. Katz, 1985, *Ambio 14* (6). Krebs, J.R. and M.J. Coe., 1985, *The Sunday Times*, 23 June. Coe, M.J., 1980, in *Conservation Biology*, Sinauer.

Page 164 Suffling, R. and G Michalenko, 1980, *Biol. Conserv.* 17. *Outdoor News Bulletin*, 1985, Wildlife Management Institute, Washington, 29 Nov. Mosher, L., 1985, *Ambio 14* (6). Klopatek, J,M., R.G. Olson, C.J. Emerson and J.L. Jones, 1979, *Env. Conserv.* 6. Mondor, C. and S. Kun, 1984, in *National Parks, Conservation and Development*, The Smithsonian Press. Strickland, D., 1981, *Natural History*, February. Weinberg, D., 1986, *Natural History*, February. Opie, J., 1983, in *Yearbook of Science and the Future*, Encyclopaedia Britannica.

Page 168 Burton, J., 1986, *Oryx 20* (1). Rankin, J.M., 1985, in *Amazonia*, Pergamon. Costa, J.P. de O., 1983, *The Environmentalist 3* (5). Camara, Adm. I. de G. and R.A., Mittermeier, 1984, in *National Parks, Conservation and Development*, Smithsonian Press. Tropical Forest Campaign fact sheet, WWF/IUCN. *Tropical Forests: A Call for Action*, 1985, The World Resources Institute, Washington. Redford, K.H., 1985, *Oryx 19* (4). Erise, F., "Brazil's Finest National Park". *TRAFFIC Bull.* 4 (3).

Page 172 *The Times*, 1986, 5 March. Tolmazin, D., 1979, *New Scientist*, 6 Dec. Gribbin, J., 1979, *New Scientist* 6 Dec. Elias, T.S., 1983, *Science 219*. Voronitsyn, S., 1982, *Radio Liberty Research* No. 198. *Tropical Forests: A Call for Action*, 1985, (ibid). Smill, V., 1983, *Ambio 12* (5). Caufield, C., 1985, *New Scientist* 5 Dec. Becker, J., 1985, *New Scientist* 24 Oct. Pryde, P., 1972, *Conservation in the Soviet Union*, C.U.P.

Pages 176 and 178 Ehrenfeld, D.W., 1970, *Biological Conservation*, Holt, Rinehart & Winston. Nar, N.C., 1979, *J. Kerala Natural History Society 2*. Panwar, H.S., 1985, in *Conserving Asia's Natural Heritage*, IUCN. Shiva. V., J. Bandyopadhyay and N.D. Jayal, 1985, *Ambio 14* (6). "The State of India's Environment: A Citizen's Report." 1982. Centre for Science and Environment, New Delhi. World Bank, 1985, *Rapid Population Growth and Human Carrying Capacity*. Singh, S., 1985, in *Conserving Asia's Natural Heritage*, IUCN. *Tropical Forests: A Call for Action* (ibid). Ives, J.D., 1984, *IUCN Bull. Suppl.* Feb. "Species Conservation Priorities in the Tropical Forests of South East Asia", 1982, *Occasional Papers of the IUCN/SSC* No.1.

Page 182 Loope, L.L. and C.P. Stone, 1984, in *Conservation, Science and Society*, UNESCO/UNEP. Douglas, A.M., 1980, *Our Dying Fauna*, Creative Research. Burns, C.W., 1984, in *National Parks, Conservation and Development*, Smithsonian Press. Ovington, J.D., 1983, *IUCN Bull.* 14 (7-9). Ford, J., 1986, *New Scientist*, 9 Jan. Chapman, M.D., 1985, *Env. Conserv.* 12 (3). *IUCN Bull.* 15 (1-3).

CHAPTER V

Pages 185-6 McCormick, J., 1985, in *User's Guide to the Environment*, Kagan Page. Lowe, P. and J. Goyder, 1983, *Environmental Groups in Politics*, George Allen and Unwin.

Page 188 "Partnership for Conservation", 1985, IUCN Pamphlet. Stonehouse, B., *Saving the Animals*, The World Wildlife Fund Book of Conservation.

Page 190 *Ecoforum*, 1984, 9(4). Barnes, J., 1984, in *International Organizations in Marine Affairs*, Butterworth. *Tropical Forests; A call for action*, 1985, (ibid).

Page 194 *Africa Now*, 1985, Jan. 'Earthscan feature', 1986, 28 Feb.

Page 196 Myers, N., *The Sinking Ark, IUCN Bull.*,1985, 16 (10-12). *The World Bank 1985*, Annual Report. 1983/4 IUCN Report. Stein, R. and B. Johnson, 1979, *Banking and the Biosphere*, Lexington Books. *Ecoforum*, 1985, 10 (6).

Page 198 Royston, M.G., 1984, World Resources Institute Conference on the role of multinational corporations in environmental management of developing countries. Earthlife in Association with *The Observer*, 1986, *Paradise Lost?* "Compensation for Oil Spills at Sea", 1979, Shell Briefing Service. Johnson, B., 1986, CEED discussion paper No.3. *WWF News*, 1986, 39. "IPIECA 10th Anniversary 1974/1984", 1984, International Petroleum Industry Environmental Conservation Association, London. Joyce, C., 1985, *New Scientist*, 25 July. Shell World, 1984, August/Sept. *Quality*, 1983, 44, Bulletin of Shell. "The Agrochemicals Business", 1983, 3, Shell Briefing Service. "Good Housekeeping", 1985, in *Shell World*, Feb./Mar. "Protecting the Environment: B.P.'s Approach", 1983, B.P. Briefing Paper, Apr.

Page 200 Brown. P., "Red Light for the Greens". Collins, N.M. and J.A. Thomas, "Why This Decline?". *GRID 1985*, A GEMS publication, UNEP.

Page 202 *Tropical Forests; a Call for Action*, 1985, (ibid). "Millions of Trees" in *Ecoforum*. *WWF News*, 1984, Jan./Feb. WWF News, WWF Canada,"Indian Wildlife Action Plan". Rumble, G., in *Development Forum*. Agarwal, A., 1976, in *New Scientist*, 24 Jan. Seshadri, D., in *Oryx 18* (2). Brochure from National Audubon Society Expedition Institute.

Page 204 Schwarz, W., *The Guardian*, "Margin of Error". Chessyre, R., 1986, *The Observer*, 27 April. Clarke, R., 1983, *Undercurrents 59*, April/May.

Page 206 *Tropical Forests: A Call for Action*, 1985, ibid. Agarwal, A. and A. Anand, 1982, *New Scientist*, 4. Nov.

Page 208 CEED Publicity Pamphlet. "Kensington and Chelsea plan on Sudan Forest", 1986, local press. *Tropical Forests; a Call for Action*, 1985, (ibid). Letter from the Director of "The Antarctica Project" to Ken Laidlaw, dated 19 Feb. 1986.

CONCLUSIONS

Wilson, T.W.. Breaking Points of a Misplanned Planet, original MS supplied to Gaia.

Picture sources

Page 2 S. Dalton, NHPA. **6 to 7** Tony Morrison. **7** inset F. Jackson, WWF. **11** top L and R, P. Morris, Ardea. **11** bottom Francois Gohier, Ardea. **14** Jean Paul Ferrero, Ardea. **15** A. Bannister, NHPA. **18** Adrian Warren, Ardea. **23** Aspect. **27** Robert Harding. **30** Laurie Sparham, Network. **31** M. Rock, Hutchison Library. **32** top Tony Morrison. **32** bottom Barry Lewis, Network **33** top Paul Goriup, ICCE. **33** bottom J.L. Mason. **35** top L Eric Lindgren, Ardea. **35** bottom R Robert Harding. **37** P. Wilson, Hutchison Library. **38** N.A. Callow, NHPA. **43** Michael Leach, NHPA. **45** top W. Jesco Von Puttkamer, Hutchison. **45** bottom L Jean-Paul Ferrero, Ardea. **45** bottom R E.A. Janes, NHPA. **49** Hellio and Van Ingen, NHPA. **50** Tony Morrison. **53** Institute of Terrestrial Ecology. **57** top R A. Jennings, Hutchison. **57** bottom L Francois Gohier, Ardea. **59** top R P. Morris, Ardea. **59** bottom L. Greenhill. **61** top R Kenneth W. Fink, Ardea. **61** bottom L S. Krasermann, NHPA. **62** Victor Englebert, Susan Griggs. **63** J.P. Ferrero, Ardea. **64** Ake Lindau, Ardea. **65** top L Lee Durrell. **65** bottom R Virginia Winther. **67** E.R. Watts, Robert Harding. **69** Patrick Fagot, NHPA. **70** top Francois Gohier, Ardea. **70** bottom F. Jackson/WWF. **73** top R Sue Wells, ICCE. **73** bottom L Brian Hawkes, NHPA. **79** Paul Goriup, ICCE. **81** N. Owen, Hutchison. **83** top R R. Bierregaard. **83** bottom L R. Hancock. **85** Hutchison. **87** David Doubilet, Oxford Scientific Films. **88** S. Robinson, NHPA. **93** WWF International. **96** S. Krasemann, Bruce Coleman. **97** Ivan Polunin, NHPA. **101** Jan Taylor, Bruce Coleman. **105** John Mason, Ardea. **111** Gerald Cubitt, Bruce Coleman. **113** top L Hutchison. **113** bottom R J.L.G. Grande, Bruce Coleman. **114** Ardea. **117** Dennis Green, Bruce Coleman. **121** Bomford and Borkowski. **125** L F. Jackson, WWF. **125** R Bill Wood, NHPA. **128** Popperphoto. **129** top L Timothy O'Keefe, Bruce Coleman Ltd. **129** bottom R S. Krasemann, NHPA. **130** George D. Lepp. **133** Ardea. **134** Jany Sauvanet, NHPA. **135** Mark Boulton, Bruce Coleman. **137** top R Charles W. Friend, Susan Griggs. **137** bottom L W.Barthlott, WWF. **141** top R John Mason, Ardea. **141** bottom L Francois Gohier, Ardea. **143** Frank Lane. **144** Bruce Coleman Ltd. **145** top, centre and bottom P. Coffey, Jersey Zoo. **147** M. Boulton, ICCE. **148** Y. Arthus Bertrand. Ardea. **152** Liz and Tony Bomford. **155** Robert Harding. **156** Bernard Regent, Hutchison. **157** Jenny Mathews, Format. **159** Stephen Dalton, NHPA. **162** Cal Briggs Office, ADM Services. **165** top R Sally and Richard Greenhilll. **165** bottom L Steve McCutcheo, Frank Lane. **166** top Michael Freeman, Bruce Coleman. **166** bottom Jenny Mathews, Format. **169** Tony Morrison, South American Pictures. **171** top Hardy Jones, Earthviews. **171** bottom C. Weaver, Ardea. **173** top L Hutchison. **173** bottom R Mandal Ranjit, Frank Lane. **175** Popperphoto. **179** Mandal Ranjit, Frank Lane. **181** G.E. Schmida, NHPA. **183** top L M. Hadfield. **183** bottom R Douglas Boglin, NHPA. **184** Rex Features. **186** Francois Gohier, Ardea. **190** Pauline Cohen. **191** L and R Friends of the Earth, Malaysia. **192** top L Mark Boulton. **192** bottom R Population Concern. **195** Lee Durrell. **196** Rex Features. **199** top L Earthlife. **199** bottom R British Petroleum. **200** Lissie Wright. **201** top R I.V. Boroviczeny. **201** bottom L Lee Durrell. **203** Simon Goodenough, Kew. **205** Petra Kelly, Rex Features. **207** topWWF/Michele Depraz. **207** bottom BBC. **208** National Gallery. **209** James Snyder. **210** Rex Features. **211** top Robert Ratner. **211** bottom Lee Durrell.

Index

INDEX

Acknowledgements

Author's acknowledgements
Preparing a book such as this one is clearly a co-operative effort, and so I give my grateful thanks to my team-mates, particularly to Robert Burton, who obtained the research material and provided excellent briefing notes, to Chris Madsen and John May, who wrote the case studies, and to the people at Gaia with whom I worked most closely – Michele Staple, my patient and meticulous editor, Patrick Nugent and Bridget Morley, who created the design, and Joss Pearson, who is the brilliant inspiration behind us all. The amount of time I was able to spend writing was greatly increased by help on the home front, and I thank John Hartley and Joan Porter especially, but also Simon Hicks and Mrs Boizard for the variety of chores they did whilst I was locked in my attic study. Last, but certainly not least, I thank Gerry for doing all the cooking (while at the same time recovering from a hip operation and writing yet another book of his own) and for not getting too jealous of a friendly Apple Macintosh.

Gaia acknowledgements
In preparing State of the Ark, Gaia have drawn on help and friendly assistance from a great range of sources, and wish to thank them all for their patience in answering queries and supplying data and articles. First and foremost, thanks go to Lee, a marvellous author to work with, and to Robert for their mountains of work under pressure of time; also to Lissie Wright, Martin Jenkins, Jo Taylor, Sue Wells, Tim Reed, and all the staff at CMC; to Hugh Synge for his plant data, Keith Eltringham for reading the text, and to staff at WWF UK and International, at IUCN, and at the International Council for Bird Preservation, especially Tim Dee. Special thanks in particular go to Jonathon Kingdon for his painting and his good humour in meeting our needs; to Michele (who worked right up to the arrival of her first child) and Patrick and Bridget for bringing the book to life; and to Ken Laidlaw, John May, Chris Madsen, Terry Gross, Leslie Gilbert, Maureen Rusted, Alastair Banbury, Steve Parker, Susan McKeever, Imogen Bright, David Pearson and other helpers for all their work. Gaia would also like to thank the following people and organizations: Brian Bell (New Zealand Wildlife Service), Russ Mittermeier (WWF US), Quentin Bloxam, John Hartley and Phillip Coffey (Jersey Wildlife Preservation Trust), David Cumming (National Parks and Wildlife Management, Zimbabwe), staff at FOE and Greenpeace and UNEP, WWF Australia, India, Germany and Holland, CODA (Spain), SAM (Malaysia), Utah State Historical Society, Mark Boulton of ICCE, The Ecology Centre (London), OXFAM, all the various picture libraries and their staff, and especially – for miracles under deadlines – John Brewer, Allen Woodcock and Barry and all the staff at Marlin Graphics, Michael Burman and Bob at F.E. Burman, Anne Rennie and Lucy Boase at Mondadori, London, On Yer Bike and Red Star at Liverpool Street.
    And, of course, Gerald Durrell.